A Study of Hinduism

A Study of Hinduism

by
DHARMDEO N. SINGH

VIKAS PUBLISHING HOUSE PVT LTD

VIKAS PUBLISHING HOUSE PVT LTD

576, Masjid Road, Jangpura, **New Delhi**-110 014
Phones: 4314605, 4315313 • Fax: 91-11-4310879
Email: vikas@gobookshopping.com
Internet: www.gobookshopping.com

First Floor, N.S. Bhawan, 4th Cross, 4th Main,
Gandhi Nagar, **Bangalore**-560 009 • Phone : 2204639

F-20, Nand Dham Industrial Estate, Marol,
Andheri (East), **Mumbai**-400 059 • Phone : 8502333, 8502324

Distributors:

UBS PUBLISHERS' DISTRIBUTORS LTD

5, Ansari Road, **New Delhi**-110 002
Ph. 3273601, 3266646 • Fax : 3276593, 3274261
E-mail: ubspddel@del3.vsnl.net.in • Internet: www.gobookshopping.com
• 10, First Main Road, Gandhi Nagar, **Bangalore**-560 009 • Ph. 2263904
• 6, Sivaganga Road, Nungambakkam, **Chennai**-600 034 • Ph. 8276355
• 8/1-B, Chowringhee Lane, **Calcutta**-700 016 • Ph. 2441821, 2442910
• 5-A, Rajendra Nagar, **Patna**- 800 016 • Ph. 672856, 656169
• 80, Noronha Road, Cantonment, **Kanpur**-208 004 • Ph. 369124, 362665

Distributors for Western India:

PREFACE BOOKS

Shivali Apartments, Plot no. 1, 25/4 Chintamani Co-operative
Housing Society, Karve Nagar, **Pune**-411 052 • Ph. 346203

Printed at Ramprintograph, Delhi-110 020

Contents

Preface

Hinduism and its different aspects have fascinated of a good many Westerners in recent years, but few of them actually know what it stands for, including some of those who profess to practice, teach, or write about it. Almost all scriptures of Hinduism are written in a way of which one can take practically direct meaning of it and another can take underlying meanings. I have lived in USA and UK for more than 36 years and have seen waves of Indians have immigrated in bulk to the West since nineteen sixties. The second generation is growing up in an environment where they are asking about their religion, temples, and their roots. Almost all large cities in USA have now at least one Hindu Temple. In the temples, they worship a deity or idol, about which they know little except that it is their gods and they are supposed to worship it. Different temples have different idols as the main deity in the sanctum along with a number of other idols. It is rather confusing for the young minds when they do not know what these deities represent and why their figures are similar and differ from the human face and/or structure. They always ask about the way we worship and why we worship them.

The idea behind this book is not to give a very comprehensive spiritual view but to arouse interest of the reader to know further on the subject. However, the book is intended to play not of a mere appetizer but also to provide some spiritual food and nutrition to persons with scientific bent of mind. It also hoped that while some articles will remove some doubts about, and create some faith in Hinduism and some others would stimulate new thinking because the concepts given therein are different from the concepts widely accepted today. I hope that new concept provided in some of the chapters would receive unbiased consideration by the reader rather than be pushed aside because of its new approach or new scientific ideas. I do not claim any extraordinary knowledge of spirituality. My genuine interest in knowing and imparting the Truth in a spirituo-scientific perspective to the new generation of children growing in foreign countries where they know or hear more about other religions and wonder about their own Hindu way of living and practice *dharma* (religion).

I sincerely thank my spouse, Reva, for inspiration and understanding the time I spent away from her. My grand sons and grand daughter have really inspired me to write this book to answer their genuine questions and inquisitiveness about our own religion that they used to ask me. I really thank them. Discussing my ideas with my numerous friends and colleagues have given me strength and courage to venture to take up this project. I really appreciate them for their time and valuable suggestions.

Nashville, TN. USA   **Dharmdeo N. Singh**
June 1998

Part I

Chapter 1

Religion and Dharma

The word religion is derived from the Latin word *religare*, which means 'to bind'. Religion may be said to bind us by rules, laws or injunctions so that we may not degenerate, and be in misery—bodily, mentally or spiritually. Religion is the art of living through right action. The purpose of religion is to make you a good human being, a good citizen, a happy and contented person. Religion, at least its ethical portion, helps to build character and prevent individual and national disintegration. This will ensure ethical living and character-building, remembering all the time that education without character, science without humanity and commerce without morality is useless and dangerous.

Metaphysics, the science of religion, is also called philosophy. It searches beyond science and seeks to probe into the ultimate origin of the Universe and what makes it function. Physical science says that the world is made of matter. Metaphysic wants to know where that matter came from and what makes it function. When we say a man is dead, we are describing a body devoid of life and function. What was it then which, before death, lent it life and made it function?

Science is not anti-religion. Both are engaged in the finding unity, the one from which every thing comes. As soon as science reaches that perfect unity, it would cease to progress, because it would reach the goal. Thus chemistry wants to discover that one element out of which all others could be made. Scientists have now proved that even matter is nothing but energy. An atom, the smallest unit of matter, consists of neutrons, protons, and electrons, all of which are in a continuous state of violent vibration. Enormous volume of energy is released in the case of atomic fission. The energy produced as a result of fission provides an added proof that matter, consisting of the entire world and beings, is all energy and the manifestations of the God who is all energy; that is to say matter and energy are the same. The physical body performs its function as long as the soul resides in it; the body would perish without the soul. Physics would stop when it would be able to discover one energy of which all the others are but manifestations. Similarly, the science of religion seeks to reach that perfect unity of matter and energy which is life's origin, an ultimate goal, that pure soul of which all souls are but delusive manifestations. This is the goal of all science. Macrocosm is all of the universe, that which includes all the planets, the sun, the moon, the stars, the world and the intervening space. Human being, the microcosm, is all the world in miniature.

We are living in an age of science. A modern mind is not easily prepared to accept God is truth and the world is illusion (*Brahman satyam, jagat mithya*) unless it is proved beyond doubt by scientifically approved methods. The truth is realized by the direct intuitive perception of the *rishis* and preserved in the Vedas displaying uncanny anticipation of several fundamental postulates of modern scientific discoveries. Science provides the resources of means of livings, whereas religion teaches the art of living and a wise man uses these resources. Science and religion thus serve different needs of humans and, as such, they are complimentary, not contradictory. Humans needs both science and religion, and they need each other. Religion can be approached through faith and belief only. Both science and religion are engaged in finding happiness for the human being. Science is finding happiness of the outer body while religion's endeavour is to find permanent inner happiness of the mind, intellect and soul.

Scientists have probed the mystries of physical sciences and made wonderful inventions, whereas the scientists of religion have made deep study of metaphysics—the first principles of nature—the science of being. They have analysed life and life's phenomena, and probed into the secrets of nature. Religion is the science of self-perfection, whereas science has limited scope; both, however, are engaged in finding the ultimate origin of things. Physicists probe the workings of atoms and elements, but from where do these elements come? Chemists seek to discover one element from which all other elements can be made. Someone has rightly said, 'where science ends religion begins.' The goal of science and religion is to achieve the unit of origin. Physicists are trying to discover the energy of which all the others are but manifestations. The religious scientist seeks to reach that perfect unity that is the origin of all matter and energy, the ultimate goal and of that pure soul of which all souls are but delusive manifestations.

Einstein, the great physicist, said: "Everything is determined, the beginning as well as the end, by forces over which we have no control." And further he said, "It is religion that gives me strength to remain true to purpose despite countless failures."

A philosopher was crossing a river and enjoying the beauty of nature. He asked the boatman: 'Do you know philosophy?' On being told 'No', the philosopher remarked: 'Half of your life is wasted and gone'. Shortly after the storm, lightening and thunder, there was a danger of the boat capsizing, and the boatman asked: "Do you know swimming?" On being replied to in the negative the boat worker said: Then your whole life is gone. The lesson learned here is that science and religion must go hand-in-hand; one cannot do without the other.

Max Planck, the great mathematician and the discoverer of the Quantum Theory, was led to conclude that consciousness is fundamental. Matter is a derivative of consciousness. We cannot get behind consciousness. Everything we talk about, everything we regard as existing, postulates consciousness.

Eddington, a great physicist and philosopher also endorses'...this when he says amongst the new properties with which we propose to dower the atom we shall probably have to include a rudiment form of consciousness....'The mind of God in particular is to be regarded as infinitely extended throughout space and time....The idea of a universal mind or logos would, I think, be a plausible inference from the present state of scientific theory.

The philosopher Joad says: "It is interesting to notice how closely the metaphysical speculations, which are based upon modern science, agree." Einstein and Planck uphold the traditional distinction between appearance and reality. Known reality, they suggest, is mere phenomenon or appearance; but behind the phenomenal manifestation there must be an ultimate force; beneath the outer phenomenon, there must be an inner reality. And essence, force and inner reality are not to be known by an intellectual faculty, since our reasons and senses know, are always the spatially and temporally limited phenomenon to which our minds have contributed. Nevertheless, since they are in some sense known, they must be known by a process of revelation to an intuitive faculty of direct insight. So revealed, reality is seen to be spiritual and even personal. Thus, with regard to the most fundamental issues of metaphysics, the speculations of modern physicists seem to bear out and to support what is, perhaps, the main traditional mystic view".

Thus great scientists and philosophers of this century have arrived at almost similar conclusions by a scientific analysis. Since every object in the universe is the sum of its qualities and the qualities exist only in the mind, the whole objective universe of matter and energy does not exist except as a construction of consciousness, an edifice of the conventional symbols shaped by the senses of person.

To corroborate the modern views, in the *Kathâ Upanishad* (I:3.12), the seers had already established the same conclusions by intuitive perception. "He is the secret Self in all existence and does not manifest Himself to the vision; yet He is seen by the seers of the subtle by a subtle and perfect understanding."

Spirituality is essentially the science of consciousness. The expanded awareness acquired by consciousness of the individual resulting in direct perception of human experience and knowledge, and of their value in relation to our lives come directly from personal conduct and spiritual effort. For the acquisition of such insight and vision, it requires not only prolonged and concentrated intellectual effort but also a victory over our base instincts of lust, greed and selfishness, i.e. the practice of right conduct. Most of us question the usefulness of the value and necessity of such efforts.

Hence, the crisis of character brought forth by our unwillingness to make such an effort is manifestly seen in our individual lives which shows serious deterioration in the mental and physical health of most of us. It will not be an exaggeration to say that 80 per cent of the civilized world's population suffers form some kind of mental illness. The reasons for this state of affairs are obviously the unbridled pursuit of sensuous pleasures by all available means. Today we find discord at every level—family, community, national, international—as a result of the blatant disregard of the essential human ethical and moral norms.

The only way to rectify this disastrous situation is to re-establish firmly all positive ethical values, then try to convince the science-minded intelligentia of the truths of the human spirit and its meaning and purpose if humanity is to be saved from moral degradation. Science alone could annihilate the human species, as weapons of mass destruction have been produced in the latter half of the twentieth century with the sole intent of destroying God's most precious creation.

Hindu scriptures are full of evidences of the existence of the *âtman* or soul. One can experience the soul with the perception by the senses. In our sleep we see, hear, afraid and run. This act of seeing without eyes, hearing without ears and running without legs is accomplished by none other than the soul. Another example, when man dies, his eyes, ears, legs and other organs are still present but he cannot see, hear, run or do other vital functions without the soul. Yogis or ascetics can take the soul elsewhere from the body.

Animal life has four principle characteristics—eating, sleeping, defending and mating. These characteristics are common to both animals and human beings, but intellect or reasoning power and religion is the special concern of human beings. Human life is no better than animals' life without religion. In human society, there is some form of religion directed at self-realization and one's eternal relationship to God. For most people religion is performed for the sake of economic development, and economic development is required for sense-gratification. Fious activities and religious functions are performed with an aim to acquire some material gain. In modern human civilization, the economic desires of the people appear to be fulfilled in another way, no one is interested in religion now. In this materialistic world, there is a keen competition between men, communities and even nations in an attempt to gratify the senses, but real religious persons or devotees of God are above all this. Devotees do not compete for material gain, rather they work for liberation from the material bondages. They are on the path back to God where everything is eternal, full and blissful. Such transcendentalists are non-envious and pure at heart. Half of the troubles of religion are due to misconceptions about God. It is for this reason that the seers of India made belief in God secondary and right conduct the primary factor in man's spiritual evolution.

There are three fundamental urges in man: (1) survival, (2) knoweldge, (3) happiness, the very attributes of *âtman*—*sat-chit*-ânanda. This is the Hindu concept of God. *Sat* stands for perfection, real, everlasting; *Chit* for consciousness, knowledge; *ânanda* for happiness. For a pragmatic consideration only, we emphasize the blissful aspect of God and our motives for bliss, leaving out the aspects of *sat* and *chit*, i.e. conscious existence. God comes within the calm experience of man. It is in bliss-consciousness that we realize Him. There can be no other direct proof of His existence. It is in Him as bliss that our spiritual hopes and aspirations find fulfillment—our devotion and love find an object.

Evidently God cannot be better conceived than as bliss, if we try to bring Him within the range of every one's experience. No longer will God be a supposition then to be theorized over. We can make the religion universally necessary if we conceive God as bliss. Human being wishes to attain bliss. If he wishes to achieve the bliss in the proper way, he is going to be religious through approaching and feeling God, who is described as very close to his heart as bliss.

As the true image of sun cannot be perceived in the surface of moving water, so the true reflection of the blissful nature of the God cannot be understood owing to the waves of disquietude with the changing states of body and mind. As the disturbed waters distort the true image of the sun, so does the disturbed state of the mind distort the true, ever—bliss nature of the inner self.

DHARMA

The religious ethics found in the Vedas is called *dharma*. The meaning of *dharma* is "that which holds" the people of this world and the whole creation. *Dharma* found in the Veda means the path of righteousness, a disciplined path, methodical living, living one's life according to the codes of law prescribed by our ancestors in the Vedas and Upanishads. According to Bhagavat Purana (I:17:24), *dharmic* (righteousness) living has four aspects: "austerity (*tap*), purity (*shauch*), compassion (*dayâ*) and truthfulness (*satya*); and unrighteous (*non-dharmic or adharmic*) life has broken the first three of the qualities with pride (*smaya*), contact (*sang*), and intoxication (*madya*)." The best meaning of the term *dharma* is the "law of being" without which the things cannot exist, as light and heat in the sun without which the sun is no sun. Similarly, the essential factor in human being is life—the *âtman* without which he cannot exist. Therefore, the *dharma* of human being is *âtman*. Hence, any good *âtmic* quality is called *dharma*. *Dharma*, therefore, implies duty, a course of conduct. Anything that helps human being to reach God is *dharma*, and anything that hinders human being from reaching God is *adharma*. Hinduism describes *dharma* as the natural universal laws whose observance enables human to save himself degradation and suffering. If we follow *dharma*, it will make us contended and happy. *Dharma* is the moral law combined with spiritual discipline that guides one's life. Hindus consider dharma the very foundation of life. Atharva Veda describes dharma in a symbolic way: *Prithivim dharmanâ dhritam*, i.e. "This world is upheld by *dharma*." The essence of *dharma* lies in possessing a certain ability or skill, a certain power and spiritual strength. *Dharma* is the single most important factor that distinguishes a human from an animal. *Dharmena hinah pashubhih samânah*, i.e. "Without *dharma* one is nothing but an animal." Vedic *dharma* is always fruitful because its basis is unique combination of *brahmateja* (spiritual brilliance) and *kshâtraviraya* (physical prowess). Author of Ramcharitramânas, Tulsidas defines the root of *dharma* as compassion. This word was taken by Lord Buddha to write his immortal book of great wisdom, *Dhammapada* (Dharmapada).

Upanishad says, "*Satyam vada, dharmam chara*": Truth is to be spoken, walk the path of righteousness. There is a saying in Sanskrit, *Dharmo rakshati rakshitaha*, i.e. *dharma* protects those who follow the path of righteousness. It means that those who do not follow this path, will ruin themselves.

The social scientists of ancient India, the *rishis*, have classified all the human aspirations under four broad categories that cover all the requirements of human being, physical and spiritual. (1) Practice of *dharma* gives an experience of peace, joy, strength and tranquillity within ones-self and life becomes thoroughly disciplined; (2) *Kâma* is the fulfillment of legitimate desires that are necessary for a dignified and honest living for one's own well-being and that of others; (3) *Artha* is the earning of wealth in honest ways for economic security and fulfillment of *kâma* (desire); and (4) *Moksha* is the liberation from the cycle of rebirth of the soul and return to the eternal soul of the divine. Of these four values, the majority of human beings pursue only *artha* and *kâma*, money-making and enjoyment. The more sensitive and psychologically developed human beings pursue *dharma*, while very few are conscious of the *moksha*—ideal spiritual aspiration.

Dharma is the law of existence and, therefore, covers both religion and ethics. It is the entire way of life of a Hindu. By observing the rules of *dharma*, we can guide our life in perfect harmony and save ourselves from misery and bondage. These laws are given in greater detail in *Prithvi Sukta* of the Athurva Veda and *Manusmriti*, the code of conduct by the great *rishi* and law-giver Manu, and the other similar *smritis*. One brief statement of *Prithvi Sukta* propounds *dharma* as: 'The great truth and the powerful *rita* and the initiation into knowledge of the Vedas sustain this universe.' The laws that sustain the entire cosmos are called *dharma*. *Manusmriti* prescribes ten essentials rules for the observance of *dharma*: "patience (*dhriti*),forgiveness (*kshama*), piety or self control (*dama*), honesty (*asteya*), sanctity (*shauch*), control of senses (*indraiya-nigrah*), descrimination or reason (*dhi*), knowledge or learning (*vidya*), truthfulness (*satya*) and absence of anger (*akrodha*). These ten are the marks of *dharma*) (*Manusmriti*, VI. 92). Manu also further writes, "Non-violence, truth, non-coveting, purity of body and mind, controls of senses are the essence of dharma" (*Manusmriti*, X. 63).

It is clear from the above description that *dharmic* laws govern not only the individual, but all in society. The purpose of the *dharma* is not only to attain a union of each self (soul) with the Supreme Reality, it also suggests a code of conduct that is intended to secure both worldly joys (*abhyudayam*) and supreme happiness (*nisriyasa*). Rishi Kânda has defined *dharma* in *Vaisesika* as follows: "That alone is *dharma* that confers worldly joys and leads to supreme happiness" (*Vaisesika* II). Hinduism is the religion that suggests methods for the attainment of the highest ideal, i.e. eternal bliss here and now, on this very planet, not somewhere else in Heaven.

Religion resides not just in books and temples, but in the minds and hearts of human beings. A book is mere paper and ink when there is no mind of a human to read and understand it. A temple is mere brick and mortar when there is no heart of a man to worship and meditate.

The personal, domestic and social life of the Hindu is largely governed by the rules of what he regards as his religion, so is that of the Muslim, Jewism and Confucian. This is the case with the followers of the other religions and forms of the Vedic religions, known as the Zoroastrian, the Buddhist, the Jaina, the Sikh; though perhaps the element of the ritual is less prominent and that of the ethics is more. Loatism is mostly a profound philosophy, the same in essence as *vedanta-yoga* and *tasawuf*; its practical side is Confucianism. Shintoism nobly regards the human being as naturally virtuous, and teaches mostly rituals.

All religions endeavour to fulfill the ideal duty according to the conditions by which they take their birth and grow. But unfortunately, by and by, the custodians of each and every religion begin to do the ordering too much, become over-conservative, rigid, narrow, domineering greedy and despotic, and lose touch with the changing times. Then politics and science begin to do the ordering, and gravitate to perhaps worse extremes.

The founders of the great religions have all taught mankind the tenets of religion, and many were philosophers. Ancient and modern, western and eastern philosophers have perceived that this unknown and unknowable is our very self (*âtman*), the all-pervading, universal supreme principle of the consciousness of life. All scientists, philosophers and religious persons agree that the world is not a soul less mechanism, and this world is not the work of blind chance. There is a mind behind the veil of matter, give it what names we will J.T. Sunder's article, Is Modern Science Outgrowing God? in The Modern Review, Calcutta), July 1936. Albert Einstein, who postulated the Theory of Relativity said, "I believe in God.... who reveals Himself in the orderly harmony of the universe. I believe that Intelligence is manifested throughout all Nature. "He further said: "Science without religion is lame; religion without science is blind."

Religion is as necessary as science, so long as human beings suffer from the fear of pain and death, and in so long as the will of the human heart demands, the solace that only religion can give. People feel this need acutely, intensely and perpetually. That is why religion survives. Those who cannot envisage the past and present, and those who cannot comprehend the meaning of such actions have no craving for religion, and as such exist within the mind-realm of animals. Those who have thought very deeply and have examined the *before* and the *after* have seen all there is to see; they have indeed found eternal *now* and the infinite *here*, the ever-present and the omnipresent, between the *before* and the *after*; they have found the secret of their own infinite self—they also no longer care about religion. They have achieved the purpose of religion.

References

1. Pahlajani, T.B., *What is Religion?* Bombay: Bharatiya Vidya Bhavan, 1985.

Chapter 2

Hinduism

Hinduism is the original religion of the Indians. It is the oldest of all living religions of the world. The name *Hindu* was first used by the medieval Muslim invaders to describe the dwellers of the *Sindhu* river valley. The religious practice of this culture we now know as *Hinduism* and is also known by the synonyms, *Sanatana dharma* and *Vedic dharma*. Sanatana *dharma* means 'Eternal Law' and Vedic *dharma* refers to the 'Religion of Ritualistic Practices' as granted by the *Vedas*. Hindu scripture is the oldest in the world and is the mother of most world religions.

Lord Buddha was born a Hindu and made some changes in the Hindu religion. He founded what is now known as Buddhism. Lord Mahavira also made some amendments in Hindu religion, and Jainism in its present form was born. It is believed that Lord Jesus, too, had lived among the sages of India for the quest of spiritual knowledge. He lead a highly religious life in Kashmir and Banares. (Kersten, Holgear). A careful study of Christianity and Hinduism will show that they are not very different from each other in essence (See Chapter 17).

In the past, from time to time India was invaded by outsiders, such as the Hunas who had no religion, the Turks and Iranians with Islamic faith and the British with Christian faith. Yet, unbelievably, Hindu religion stood firm and strong—so much so that today it is stronger than ever. The secret of the survival of the Hindu religion lies in its tolerance—tolerance of outsiders and their beliefs. It is often said that Hinduism is not just a religion but a way of life and social practice. Hinduism does not condemn other religions and beliefs. Hinduism also does not force anyone to accept its teachings. It allows everyone to think and reason for himself. Hindus do not believe in a 'judgement day' and in the ideas of 'Heaven' or 'Hell'. They believe that the *âtman* (soul) by its good or bad *karma* (deeds) gets reborn again and again to purify itself and ultimately achieves *moksha*, which is the union with the Universal Soul or God. Indeed, Hinduism does not condemn even those who do not believe in God. It teaches to worship God in the manner that best suits the person. It is rightly said, "All paths lead to the same God, just as cows of different colours all give us the same white milk"

(Upanishads). "Truth is one; wise men call it by different names." (Rig Veda I. 164.46).

However, Hinduism is a complex and rich religion. No founders' initiative, no dogma, no reforms have imposed restrictions of its domain; on the contrary, the contributions of centuries have been superimposed without ever wearing out the previous layers of development.

In the view of Hinduism, an eternal life belongs to the path of spiritual progress, the quest of liberation, the tendency to renunciation, and finally the intensive concentration on problems. Other cultures have more often reserved this type of life for theologians or philosophers. Hinduism, which is highly popular in its practices and external manifestations, is essentially also a religion of the learned: it cannot be understood if *Vedanta* and the *Samkhya* have not been fully comprehended, or if there is no idea of the immense network of symbolism that underlines and links together all Indian thoughts.

Hinduism is a continuation of the Vedas. Not only did the Vedas offer in an embryonic development but most of the characteristics of Hinduism developed with the passage of time. The oldest Veda, *Rig Veda* was composed with a view toward ritualistic sacrifice. Sacrifice was at the centre of vedic religion: A succession of oblations and prayers, fixed according to strict liturgy, in which the culmination was reached when the offering was placed in the fire, sometimes with vegetables, animals or plants. There were no prayers dissociated from the cult, and there were neither temples nor idols; but there existed a body of paid priests who performed the ceremonial sacrifices. A patron and his wife could also participate. The scenario varied greatly from a simple daily oblation in the fire (*agnihotra*) to horse sacrifice (*Ashvamedha*) to celebrate the king's victories, or was anointed at the time of his coronation (*râjasuya*). Moral obligation demands the exercise of good acts, of giving (give to receive).

Towards the end of the Vedic period, i.e. towards the 5th or 6th century BC, there appeared a new text, the *Upanishads* or Equivalences. Without abandoning ancient modes of thought, these texts reveal some sort of gnosticism which attempts to explain by way of parables that the *âtman* or individual soul is identical with *Brahman* or the Universal Soul. Thou art that, that is to say, Thou, the individual, art identical with the ultimate principle of things. This is the supreme truth that leads to liberation. Thenceforth, the world of the gods, the external apparatus of the cult, which had already been strongly reduced in the *Brahmans*, tended to disintegrate.

After the *Upanishads*, Hinduism became popular and flourished. Suddenly we encounter a religion open to all tendencies. While certain *Upanishads* show a discrete beginning of Hinduism, the massive following of the religion was the result of the great epic, the *Mahâbhârata*, and its contents. It is a sort of unbalanced Iliad; warlike narrations are mingled with mythological scenes and moral discourses. Its culmination point is the Celestial song, *Bhagavad Gitâ*, which is a sermon addressed to Arjuna by Sri *Krishna*.

The epics find their natural continuation in the *Purânas* or 'Antiquities', which are large compilations dealing with religious practices, mythology and cosmogony. The *Purânas* are a major source of semi-popular Hinduism. They also provide a wide diversity of approach toward the Divine, unknown in ancient periods. The cult of the idol gained momentum during this period with the development of monumental iconography. The idol of the god is accompanied by a particular attribute which can become autonomous. For example, in the *Shaivite* context, this attribute is often a *linga*, a phallic emblem, which is of distant non-Aryan origin.

At a later time, sectarian theism developed in Hinduism, such theism as Vaishnavism of the worshipers of Vishnu, the Shaivism of the worshipers of Shiva, and the Shâktism of the worshipers of Shakti or power, a name exclusively given to the consort of Shiva. A fourth sect, called Smârtas, who do not belong to the above three sects nor follow their sectarian scriptures (*agamas*), but worship all gods without any exclusive preference according to the ancient traditions (*smritis*) come into being. Overwhelming majority of Hindus are non-sectarian. The common people are taught that the worship of a specific or a personal god is only halfway in man's journey to the Ultimate Reality. There are five elements which contribute to the unity of Hinduism: (1) common scriptures, (2) common deities, (3) common ideals, (4) common beliefs, and (5) common practice.

(1) Scriptures

The most important common scriptures are the Vedas, the epics (the Ramayana and Mahâbhârata), and the Bhâgavata Purâna; the Bhâgavata Purâna may not be held sacred by some Shaivaite sects. There are four Vedas, *Rigveda*, Sâmaveda, Yajurveda: and Athurveda. Each of the Vedas consists of four parts: *mantras*, which are the basic verses, *brâhmanas*, the explanations of those verses or hymns and of the related rituals, the *aranyakas*, meditations as their meanings, and *Upanishads*, mystical utterances revealing profound spiritual truths. As the Upanishads come at the end of the Veda, the teaching based on them is called *vedanta*, for *anta* in Sanskrit means the end. The teachings of the *Upanishads* were essentially summarized in Bhagavad Gitâ, which forms a part of the *Mahâbharata*.

(2) Deities

The common deities are derived from the Vedas and epics. Though the Vedas address many gods, the Vedic seers in the search of truth discovered that there is one *Supreme Spirit* . The gods worshiped by men are only partial manifestations of the *Supreme Spirit*. It is quoted in a vedic passage, "Reality is one; sages speak of it in different ways." It means that every god whom men worship is the embodiment of a limited ideal, of which he is the symbol in one aspect of the Absolute. The common people generally wanted some concrete embodiments of the Divine, while the learned, who knew better, were tolerant of, and even encouraged, all popular forms of worship. They established three important functions of the Supreme, i.e. Creation, Protection and Destruction, as three gods—*Brahmâ, Vishnu* and *Shiva,* known as the *Triad* or *Trinity,* analogous to Father, Son and Holy Ghost of Christianity. The power that was associated with each of these great gods was also later personified and represented as his consort. The consort of Brahmâ was called *Sarasvati* (the goddess of speech, learning and wisdom), that of Vishnu was called *Lakshmi* (the goddess of wealth and prosperity), and that of Shiva was called *Shakti* (the goddess of power and destruction). The imagination of the people did not stop there. They have provided the great gods with their own appropriate homes such Saket for Ram, Dwarikâ for *Krishna,* Kailash for Shiva, or *Loak,* their own attendants, their own vehicles, and even their own progeny.

(3) Ideal

The common ideal virtues of Hindus that help to facilitate a good life are purity, self-control, detachment, truth and nonviolence. Purity means both ceremonial and moral purity. Hindu scriptures direct human beings to have purity of mind and spirit. Similarly, self-control implies both physical and mental control. Hinduism takes into account all the factors of human personality—body, mind, soul and spirit—and prescribes a graded discipline for all. The higher phase of self-control is detachment from life. For example, domestic affections, family ties, love for home and friends are all good in themselves, but as long as we are passionately attached to these earthly things, we are only on the lower ranks of the spiritual ladder. Love, affection and friendship are indeed divine qualities, and the more we cherish them, the nearer we are to the Supreme Spirit. But the way to cherish them is not to be blindly attached to them. Truth for Hinduism is far more than mere truthfulness; it means the eternal reality. Mahâtama Gandhi described Hinduism as a quest for truth through non-violence (*ahimsâ*). Truth is always associated with non-violence and together they are considered to be the highest virtue. Perhaps the greatest exponent of nonviolence in modern times was Mahâtmâ Gandhi. He pleaded that the non-violence must be practiced not only by individuals but also by communities and nations, and in all spheres of life.

(4) Beliefs

Some fundamental beliefs of all schools of religious thoughts in Hinduism are related to: (a) the evolution of the world; (b) the organization of society; (c) the progress of an individual; (d) the four-fold end of human life; and (e) the law of *karma* and rebirth.

(a) **Evolution of the World:** According to one of the *Upanishads*, it came about through successive stages beginning with matter and going on through life, consciousness, and intelligence to spiritual bliss or perfection. At one end of the cosmic scale there is pure matter in which spirit lies dormant, and at the other end is pure spirit in which matter lies dormant. Between these two extremes, there are various orders of dual beings composed partly of matter and partly of spirit. Spirit becomes richer as it ascends the scale, and matter become poorer. The spirit appears as life in vegetables, as consciousness in animals, as intelligence in humans, and as bliss in the Supreme Spirit. So there is a gradual ascent from matter to life, from life to consciousness, from consciousness to reason, and from reason to spiritual perfection. A good human is nearer to the Supreme Spirit than a bad human, and a saint is also nearer to the Supreme than a sinner. He is nearer the Supreme Being who has such spiritual qualities as, goodness, justice, mercy, love and kindness. He is nearer to the animal if he has more such qualities as cruelty, selfishness, greed and lust. Thus, the universe is a vast amphitheater in which there is a colossal struggle going on between spirit and matter, giving rise to various orders of beings, ranging from the lifeless stone to the omniscient Supreme Spirit.

The law of spiritual progression is an unerring standard for us. It decrees the spiritual values such as truth, beauty, love and righteousness are very important; next come intellectual values, such as clarity, cogency, subtlety and skill; then come biological values such as health, strength and vitality; the last, at the lowest level, come such material values as riches, possessions and pleasures.

The Hindu sages judged the greatness of nations not by the empires they possessed, nor by the wealth they accumulated, nor by the scientific progress they achieved, but by the degree of righteousness and justice they had. Their teaching is that man's true progress is to be judged by moral and spiritual standards, and not by material and scientific standards. This teaching has also been in our own lifetime underlined and emphasized by Mahâtmâ Gandhi.

(b) **Organization of Society:** Belief of the Hindu for the organization of the society grows from the first principle of spiritual progression. In accordance with this principle, Hindu law givers tried to construct an ideal society in which men should be ranked not according to their physical and numerical strength or wealth or power that they possess, but according to their spiritual progress and culture. In view of the Hindu, number, strength, wealth and power should be subordinated to learning, virtue, and character.

There came into existence in the early pre-historic times the four classes: *Brâhmans* (teaching class), *Kshatriyas* (military class), *Vaishyas* (mercantile and agricultural class) and *Sudras* (the labourer class). The earliest reference to the four castes is found in the *Rigveda*, where they are represented as forming parts of the body of the creator. Not only were the four castes conceived as the creation of God but they were also said to conform to the cosmic law of spiritual progression, the most spiritual class occupying the top and the least spiritual the bottom. Each class should perform its own duties and all should cooperate with one another in working for the common welfare. The class system was also based on the nature of human being. The special feature of the Hindu religion is the division of society into four classes or *varnas*. These classes are universal and present in all capitalistic and communistic societies. All human beings have to pass through these classes according to the theory of evolution. Division was mainly based on the temperament of each individual or the predominance of any one of the three *gunas* (*sâttvik, râjasik* and *tâmasik*). According to our scriptures human nature has three fundamental qualities, purity (*sâttvik*), energy (*râjasik*) and inertia (*tâmasik*). It was supposed that those in whom purity predominated formed the first caste, those in whom energy predominated formed the second caste, those in whom inertia predominated in varying degrees formed the third and fourth classes. The good actions of a man in this life are for his promotion to a higher class in the next life. The system thus had its own merits and demerits. It provided the division of labour, it cut short competition, and gave full weight to the principle of heredity. It gave no scope for individual genius, it made too much of the accident of birth, and it killed all initiative. The caste system, with its rigid walls of separation, is bound to pass away because it has become completely out of place today.

"The *Brahman* is His mouth; the Rajaya (*Kshatriya*) His arms; His thighs are *Vaisya*; the *Sudra* is born from His feet" (Rig Veda X-XV-12). This indicates that just as in human body, the different organs perform different functions so also in human society different people perform different functions according to their temperament. The above Rig Veda's *mantra* explains that the intellectuals with preponderance of *sâttvic* qualities are called Brâhmanas. They lead the people in the right direction, both in matters mundane and spiritual. Therefore, they are represented as the mouth of Brahman or Supreme Lord. The people who acquired the spirit of sacrifice and valour, and protect the people, are known as Kshatriya, who also have preponderance of *râjasic* qualities. The Kshatriyas are represented by two arms of Brahman. One who provides society with its necessities and the production of its wealth is known as Vaisyas. The Vaisyas are represented by the thighs of Brahman. The Sudras are the working or serving class, with a preponderance of *tâmasic* qualities, who are represented by the feet of Brahman.

In *Gita*, Lord *Krishna* says, "The four castes were created by me on the basis of man's qualities (*gunas*) and characteristics and acts (*karma*)" (*Gita* IV.13). He further said, "Oh Parantap (Arjun), *Brâhmans, Kshtriyas, Vaisyas* and *Sudras* are divided on the basis of their *gunas* (qualities) and past *karmas*" (*Gita* XVIII.4). Lord *Krishna* told Arjuna, "The duties of *Brâhmanas, Kshatriyas* and *Vaisyas*, as also of *Sudra* are distributed according to the *gunas* (qualities) born of their own nature" (*Gita* XVIII: 41). He further said, " serenity, self-control, austrity, purity, forgiveness, and also uprightness, knowledge (wisdom), realization and belief in God, these are the duties of a *Brāhmana*, born of his nature" (*Gita* XVIII: 43). "Heroism, vigour, firmness, resourcefulness, not fleeing from battle, generosity and lordliness are the duties of a *Kshatriya* (a member of the warrior class) born of his nature" (*Gita* XVIII: 43). "Agriculture, cattle-rearing and trade are the duties of a *Vaisya* born of his own nature; and actions consisting of service is the duty of the *Sudra* bornof his own nature" (*Gita* XVIII: 44). Sacred law proclaimed by Manu compiled in the law-book known as *Manusmriti* where following duties of four castes or classes were prescribed : "In order to protect this universe He, the most resplendent one, assigned separate (duties and) occupations to different persons" (*Manusmrti* I:87). "To Brāhmanas he assigned teaching and studing (the Veda), sacrificing for their own benefit and for others, giving and accepting (of alms)" (*Manusmrti* I:88). "The Kshatriya he commanded to protect the people, to bestow gifts, to offer sacrifices, to study (the Veda), and to abstain from attaching himself to sensual pleasures" (*Manusmrti* I:89). "The Vaisya to tend cattle, to bestow gifts, to offer sacrifices, to study (the Veda), to trade, to lend money, and to cultivate land" (*Manusmrti* I:90). "One occupation only the lord prescribed to the Sudra, to serve meekly even these (other) three castes" (*Manusmrti* I:91).

These four classes are now known as castes which are natural division of the society for maintaining cohesive and balanced order. Now the people consider it as their birth right to belong to a particular caste for their personal gain rather than the duties it imposes. The Brahmanas and the Kshatriyas claimed their privileges with ardour and shrank from the heavy burden of duty that accompany and adorn them. Even in *Manusmriti* it was made clear that those who do not perform their duties according to their state in life cannot belong to that *varna* or class. "Just as a wooden toy elephant cannot be a real elephant, and a stuffed deer cannot be a real deer, so, without studying scriptures and the Vedas and the development of intellect, a Brâhmana by birth cannot be considered a Brâhmana. The only common thing amongst the three examples in their name" (*Manusmriti* II.157). "Advija (Brâhmana) who undertakes work other than the study of scriptures and learning, or who practices vocations not corresponding to his state in life, becomes a Sudra in his won life-time" (*Manusmriti* II.158). *Manusmriti* further emphasizes, "A Sudra can become a Brâhmana by his own act (*karma*) and the development of his *âtma*, and a Brâhmana can become a sudra by his own karmas. The same rule applies to those born Kshatriya or Vaisya" (*Manusmriti* II.168). Bhagavatam also accepts the division of Hindu society into the four *varnas* according to the present (*karma*) act and not just as a result of birth. This is clearly stated as follows: "The special characteristics that identify a particular caste, should these marks be found in people of other *varnas*, they must be considered to belong to that *varna* with which his characteristics identify him, not to the *varna* of his birth" (*Vishnu Bhagavatam* VII—IX. 35).

Both in ancient and recent times innumerable examples are given of the people born in a lower caste or of unknown ancestry were treated as *brahmarishis* and *maharishis*. Vyasa, who has compiled all Vedas and has written Mahabharat, including Gitâ, and Bhagavatam, was born to a fisher-woman. Visvâmitra, a *Kshatriya* by birth was accepted as a *brahmarishi;* Rishi Javalâ of unknown ancestry was accepted as a great *rishi;* Rishi Matanga belonged to sudra caste was honored as *brahmarishi;* Rishi Gargya, a kshatriya was accepted as a *brahmarishi;* Maharishi Mudgil; a Kshatriya was pronounced a Brahmana by Rishi Bhrigu. Maharishi Vâlmiki, the author of the Ramayana, though a hunter, is acknowledged a great *rishi*. Maharishi Sutya was born of Brahâmin mother and Kshatriya father. Candra Gupta Maurya, born Sudra, became a mighty emperor after dethroning the last king of the Nanda dynasty. Even in medieval and modern times, a number of non-Brahmins became preceptor of *dharma*. Maharishi Aurobindo, Swami Vivekananda, Mahatma Gandhi, though not born Brahmins, are all held in the highest esteem as preceptors of the Hindu religion.

(c) **Progression of the Individual:** The progression of individual is also built upon the same concept of spiritual progression. The Hindu sages divided the ideal life of an individual into four successive stages, called *âsramas:* the *(brahmacharyâ or kshâtra)* student, the *(garehastya)* householder, the *(vanaprastya)* recluse who withdraws from the world, and the *(sannyâs)* religious mendicant, who renounces the world. Stages indicate the path of progress for the ideally ordered life of an individual. When the active life is over, and after all the duties that fall to his lot are discharged, the householder should retire to a quite place in the country to meditate and study spiritualism. Then the recluse becomes a *sannyasi*, who has renounced all earthly possessions and ties. In this final stage, one need not observe any distinctions of caste, or do any rites and ceremonies.

(d) **Four-fold End of Human Life:** The goal of life for a man is fourfold: *dharma* (religiosity), *artha* (economic development), *kâma* (sense gratification) and *moksha* (liberation). While *artha and kâma* pertain to material pursuits, *moksha* is the ultimate aim of liberation from rebirths, which is the goal of human life. The *dharma* forms the bedrock of the other three values, since whatever might be the goal in mind—material or spiritual—it has to conform to *dharma*, which is the theme of both epics, the Râmayana and the Mahâbhârata. The study of these epics provides insight into the nuances of *dharma*. The very conception of the scheme of *purusharthas*, goals show that life can become meaningful only when all these values are pursued. It was through adopting *dharma* that the heroes of the epics had attained immortal fame. If one's life is wedded to *dharma* then all the other ends in life are relaized on their own without any effort; whereas, when the material ends of *kâma* and *artha* are pursued to the neglect of *dharma*, life can only end in misery.

Dharma means righteousness, morality or virtuous conduct as applied to the world; *ârtha* means worldly prosperity; *kâma* means enjoyment and *moksha* means liberation or release from the cycle of birth and death as the highest of human goals or values. Thus the ultimate aims of man's life is *moksha*. It means becoming a perfect spirit like the Supreme Spirit. *Dharma* and *moksha* are generally described as spiritual. Hindu philosophy is concerned only with the latter, but this does not mean that it discards the other three. *Dharma* and *moksha* are two facets of the same thing; *dharma* in the sense of 'right action' was the corollary and the prelude to participation with the infinite. *Artha* and *kâma* can only be used for help or are instrumental in achieving *dharma* or *moksha*, although their final aim is how to achieve liberation or *moksha*. The first three of these values apply especially to the first two stages of a man's life, but partly also to the third stage. *Moksha* applies especially to the fourth stage and, in a lesser degree, to the third. The effort to achieve *moksha*, especially in the fourth stage of life, is aided by ethical discipline practiced in the first three stages and carried over to the fourth. Ethical discipline includes, first, conformity to conventions of caste; second, adherence to ideals of non-injury and non-violence; and third, the practice of telling the truth. Non-injury and non-violence, though especially stressed by Jainism, are virtues in all the philosophies of India. Truth is stressed in the best known Indian epic—*Mahabharata*—and elsewhere.

The achievement of *moksha* not only results in immediate bliss *per se*, it also sustains the bliss by ending the dreaded cycle of births and deaths. The cycle of births and deaths, that is, the pre-existence in another human or animal body of every man now living, and his fate of rebirth in another form after the death of his present body, is generally taken for granted in Indian philosophy. It is a further assumption that if *moksha*, liberation, is sustained rather than merely achieved for a brief time, then the cycle is broken.

(e) The Law of *Karma*: This is a unique characteristic of the religious thought of India. Just as the law of cause and effect works in the physical world, the law of *karma* works in the moral world. When we put our fingers into a fire, they are burned. Similarly, whenever a man steals, his moral nature is injured. On the other hand, whenever a man helps someone, his moral nature is improved. The law of *karma* has an extension beyond the present life. We carry with us our own past. The mental and moral tendencies that the soul acquires in a particular life as a result of its motives and actions work themselves out in suitable surroundings in the next life. The state of human life depends upon the good or evil one has done in the preceding lives. Thus our characters and destinies shape themselves from life to life, and do not depend on the arbitrary decrees of God. According to Hindu belief, God is not a judge sitting in heaven meting out our punishment. Instead, our own accumulated balance of work in accordance with law of *karma* performed by our self determines its course for the next life. The individual self tries in every life to achieve purity till it mingles with the Universe Self.

Suffering is fundamental in life. In large parts, we suffer due to our own fault. Here are two Indian interpretations of the tenet, the orthodoxtenet and the liberal. According to orthodox, our suffering in this life is due to our misdeeds committed in an earlier life or in earlier lives. This is the theory of *karma*, the burden of the moral consequences of our former conduct. It entails the concept of *samsara*, the cycle of births and deaths. According to the liberal interpretation, our suffering is due to our failure to take advantage of the way to eliminate suffering. Thus, both orthodox and liberal Hindus hold that suffering is due, at least in large part, to man's own faults.

The Indian recognizes not only the pervasiveness of suffering, but also the availability of a way to a more abundant, blissful life, a life in which pain can be contained. The way to eliminate suffering is to eliminate attachment. We suffer because we badly want, and cannot always have, comfort for ourselves and pleasure for those we love. We are attached to comforts and pleasures. We are attached to family and friends. We are attached to life. Nevertheless, all these objects of attachment are subject to the dissolution, and that is why we suffer. No attachment no suffering, says the Hindu.

(5) Practices

Under these we may include not only certain rituals common to large sections of Hindus, but also individually every religious Hindu has his own chosen deity or *ishta-devatâ*, on whose form, features and qualities he concentrates his mind and whose image he worships. At the same time he is taught to recognize that the deity is only a means to the realization of the Supreme Spirit. It is to be achieved by the gradual transformation of the worshiper into the form of the deity who is worshiped. The first step is when the mind is made to dwell on some concrete form of the deity and thus to overcome its inherent tendency to distraction. In the final stage of religious life, there is no need for any ritual. A *Sanyasi* performs no rites nor any of the ceremonies. Internal worship consists of prayer and meditation. The meditation is often strengthened by *japa*, *mudrâ*, and *nyâsa*. *Japa* is the repetition of a group of mystic syllables, *mantra*. The *mantras* are composed of syllables ranging from one to hundred. Here we find a tribute to word as form for many of the syllables, while others consist of a simple mention of the divine name such as 'Rama! Rama'!. This type of prayer is an aid to mental concentration and is thought to bring about the desired effect of protection, fulfillment of promise or expiratory virtue. *Mudrâ* is a gesture of the hands and fingers calculated to visualize and emphasize the intention of the mind, and *nyâsa* consists of placing the hands of the worshiper on different parts of his body—the forehead, arms, and chest—in token of identification of himself with the deity or the deities he worships. Other elements of personal worship are the study of the scriptures, and above all, meditation. Strengthened by *yoga* exercises, meditation can lead to such a paroxysm of tension that the executant can accomplish the ultimate aim proposed in all Indian religious thought; a state of union with the Absolute *Brahman*. Agricultural, collective and commemorative rites are many. Still more numerous are the 'vows' (*vrata*) which have restrictions or types of activities to which an individual submits himself freely at a fixed time in order to attain a certain religious merit or to obtain a definite objective which he desires.

Yoga is the process of mental discipline that is common to all Hindu sects. The word *yoga* means union. It is in this sense that the word is often used in the *Bhagavad Gitâ*, which indicates three paths leading to the goal of union with God; *karma yoga* or union through disinterested service, *bhakatiyoga* or union through self-forgetting love and devotion, and *jñânayoga* or union through transcendent divine knowledge. Like Mahatma Gandhi, a man may choose to lead an active life in the world and make every one of his actions an offering unto God, or like Ramakrishna, one may devote his whole life to the loving worship of God, or like Sankara, one may seek to realize God through philosophical inquiry. In addition to these three, Patanjali, author of the *Yoga Sutras*, defines *yoga* as the method of restraining the functions of the mind. *Upanishads* and *Bhagavad Gitâ* accept yoga as legitimate means of concentrating one's mind on the Supreme Being. Patanjali's *yoga*, is also called as *raja yoga*, which culminates in rapt contemplation of the Reality, a state of mind called *samâdhi*.

The Indian philosophy is based on peace of mind, acceptance of yourself as you are without addiction or attachment to illusions, recognition of yourself as a worthy human being without attachment to fetishes or guilt complexes. The way to eliminate attachment is to wake up from our slumber of largely unconscious habit action (unawareness or ignorance of self) and to become self-aware. In *Mundaka Upanishads*, (III.1-3, 5, 8), a bird on a branch is described as watching another bird on a nearby branch. As the second bird moves, the first bird watches him move. As the second bird eats, the first bird watches him eat. As the second bird turns his head, the first bird watches him turn his head. Be the first bird yourself. As you stand, watch yourself stand. As you eat, watch yourself eat. As you turn your head, watch yourself turn head. As you do anything, at any time, watch yourself doing or feeling, acting or being acted on, observe yourself being in a state, condition, or situation. But there are degrees of intensity of self-awareness. Constant practice of the exercise of self-awareness, over a period of a week, a month, a year, or many years, deepens the degree of self-awareness that one achieves. At first, a man achieves a superficial level. Then one plunges more deeply. In a high degree of intensity of self-awareness, man transcends—in knowledge and perhaps in actuality—the opposites of self and not-self. This means that one senses oneself as united with the not-self. That is, one either is united with the not-self and one knows this, or at least one clearly seems to be united with the not-self, and the seeming is so vivid that nothing else that seems at all seems more vividly. In other words, one feels then that if one ever knew anything to be true or real, then one knows this union to be true or real. Achievement of this state of conscious immersion in and identification with 'the allness' results in unspeakable bliss, and is called *nirvâna*. The achievement of it is *moksha* (liberation). Its psychological aspect is called *samadhi* (a mystic trance characterized by a sense of union with 'the all'). It is evident by a feeling of the *buddhi* (enlightenment). *Samadhi* is thought of as a temporary state; *moksha* or *nirvana* is an enduring state. The achievement of *moksha* not only results in immediate bliss, per se "I" also sustains the bliss by ending the dreaded cycle of birth and death. The cycle of birth and death, that is the pre-existence in another human or animal body of every man now living, and his fate rebirth in another form after the death of his present body, is generally taken for granted in the Indian philosophy. It is further assumed that if *moksha*, liberation, is sustained rather than merely achieved for a brief time, then the cycle is broken. Every man should seek *'moksha'* at the appropriate stage of his life, namely, the fourth stage.

Bibliography

Brown, K., *The Essential Teachings of Hinduism*, Rider Book Publisher, London, 1988.

Chaudhuri, Nirad C., *Hinduism*, New York, Oxford Univ. Press,1979.

Kersten, Holgear, *Jesus lived In India: His Unknown Life Before and After Crucifixion*, Element Book Ltd., Longmead, Shaftesburg, Dorset, SP78PL, England.

Morgan, K.W. (ed), *The Religion of Hindus*, New York, Ronald Press Company, 1953.

Organ, T.W., *Hinduism: Its Historical Development*, New York: Barron's Educational Series, Inc., 1974.

Radhakrishnan, S., *The Hindu View of Life*, London, Oxford University Press, 1966.

Renon, Louis, *Hinduism*, George Braziller, New York, 1962.

Sarma, D.S., *Essence of Hinduism*, Bombay, Bharatiya Vidya Bhavan.

Swami Shivananda, *All About Hinduism*, The Divine Life Society, Shivananda Nagar, U.P.

Zachner, R.C., *Hinduism*, New York, Oxford University Press, 1979.

Chapter 3

Hindu Scriptures

By any conservative estimates, the Vedas are more than 3000 years old and many people recite them daily in India. Throughout these millenia, the Vedas have been passed orally from generation to generation. They have been preserved through memorization so meticulously that when modern scholars began investigating the Vedas in the last century, it was found that the same *Rigveda* was recited without variants in all different parts of India, from north to south, and from east to west. This, despite the fundamental differences in native language from one region to another. Why is it that such elaborate care was given to the acurate transmission of the Vedas, something unprecedented anywhere else in the world ? It is because the Vedas are believed by Indian tradition to be an actual part of the eternal song of nature, which was seen and heard by ancient seers, and thus to embody the cosmic order, the laws of nature. Sound is believed to be what manifested the world and what now sustains it. Through the power of sound, the recitation of the Vedas is thought to perpetuate the cosmic order. Any mistake in their recitation could lead to serious consequences to the world, and this is why they were memorized so carefully. So for many Indians, the Vedas are sounds, *mantras*, whose effectiveness is not dependent on meaning. Modern scholars, on the other hand, have disregarded the sound aspect and have focussed on the meaning, interpreted from their point of view. The Vedas are here seen to have been handed down to us in order to produce a more enlightened age. As such, they contain wisdom of benefit to humanity today, provided that we can access it. Madhusudan Ojha (1866—1939), Raj Pandit of Jaipur, wrote over one hundred books in Sanskrit, attempting to restore this lost understanding of the language of symbolism, showing that the vedic texts are filled with doctrines pertaining to a universally applicable natural law. So, in agreement with tradition, the Vedas embody the cosmic order (*rta*); not only does the recitation of the Vedas sustain the cosmic order, but the understanding of Vedas explains the laws of that cosmic order. Vedas were translated into European languages only in the last century. Modern thinkers who read these ancient books are humbled by the realization that the wisdom they proudly claim as the triumph of twentieth century Western progress is, indeed, very ancient.

The Vedas claim a relation with the modern world. Present day people want a practical message from these divine revelations. Life with all its variety is dwelt upon in them, though the ideas are not congently prsented in a single place. The main message of the Vedas is that God is not separate from the world. The theoretical aspect of the Vedas deals with the idea of God, soul and world, and how they are interlinked. The form the philosophic portion while the practical side takes shape as rituals. One can find throughout the Vedas an understanding of the human problems and a sympathetic approach to them. The God of the Vedas is beyond our words, yet He is made intelligible to the human mind.

There are four Vedas: *Rig Veda,* which is mainly composed of songs of praise; *Yajurveda,* which deals with sacrificial formulas; *Sâma Veda* which refers to melodies; and *Athurva Veda,* which has a large number of magic formulas. Although the four Vedas may appear different in certain observances or percepts, in the mode of recitation, etc., all of them have a common goal, viz., to ensure the well-being of the universe and to help every one towards spiritual progress. A distinguishing feature of the Vedas, is that no Veda says 'this is the only way'. All of them say that any good path followed with faith and loyalty, and any god or *devatâ* worshipped in whatever way, will lead one to the true goal. Further, there is no other book of religion in this world which advocated the pursuit of diverse paths. Every religion says that its doctrine alone will lead to heaven. The Vedas alone have such a breadth of vision as to say that the same truth can be realized in many ways by those pursuing diverse routes. This is the greatness of the Vedas.

Apart from their religious, social and humanistic aspects, these ancient statements also portray the political systems prevelent in those time. Many sages were connected with kingdoms and hence we find reflections of their political thought in their hymns. The Vedas clearly indicate that the power in a person who controls a territory is derived only from the people. According to these devine dictates, debates and discussions were vital to understand truth.

Traditionally *Rig, Yajur,* and *Sâman* are known as *Trayi,* the Triple Vidya or the three-fold knowledge, because they deal with *jnana* (knowledge), *bhakati* (devotion), and *karma* (action) are in prose, verses and songs. *Rigveda* underlines the path of *jnana* or knowledge, the Yajurveda that of *karma* or action, Sâmveda that of bhakati or devotion and *Athurvaveda* represents a synthesis of the three. *Yajur* and *Sâm Vedas* repeat *Rigveda* to a great extent, but *Athurvaveda* is a collection of original hymns and borrows little from the *Rigveda.* These four together form the foundations of Indian religions, philosophical and cultural systems. All other scriptures or *shâstras* are derived and based upon the fundamental knowledge of Vedas. Each Vedic texts contains following four sections: (i) Samhitas, (ii) Brâhmans, (iii) Aranyakas and (iv) Upanishads, together they comprise the *sruti*, that which was heard by the ancient *rishis*. These four types of vedic text are said to correspond to the four stages, or *asramas*, into which life was traditionally divided. The first or student stage is when the *samhitas* are memorized for recitation; the second or householder stage is when the *yagnas* or sacrifices are performed according to the instructions of the *brahmanas*; the third or forest dweller stage is when the inner significance of the *yajnas* is contemplated according to the instructions of the *aranyakas*; the fourth or renunciate stage is when only the wisdom leading to liberation is sought according to the instructions of the *Upanisads*.

(i) *Samhita* contains basic texts of the Vedas comprising collection of hymns, prayers, benedictions, sacrificial formulas and litanies. The utterances of hymns are called *mantrâs*. Verses which have been revealed to intense thought and intuition have the power of saving the soul of the one who cherishes them. *Samhitas* dated as late as 1000 BC were followed by the Brahmanas.

(ii) *Brâhmanas* or prose treatises explain how to perform the *yajnas* or sacrifices, which are enjoined in the *samhitas*. They also disscuss the significance of sacrificial rites and ceremonies. *Brahmanas*, dated around 800 BC, give practical advice on sacrificial and other rites and general rules of conduct. *Brâhmanas* lists what the Vedic *karmas* (rituals) are (rituals) to be performed and explains how they should be performed. When the *mantras* contained in a *Veda Samhita* are converted into action, called *yajna*, the *brâhmanas* serve the purpose of a guide book or handy manual explaining how each word should be understood, or what construction should be placed on each word used; in other words, the proper use of the mantra.

Brâhmana advocated that a person should leave the town or village and seek the solitude of the forest. *Yajna* and other rituals are prescribed only for those who live in homes and lead the life of house-holders. But it has to be understood that Vedic rituals are intended to confer not only material benefits, but also mental purity by constant discipline. Having obtained mental purity (*chiththa shuddhi*), one must seek the solitude of forests for further concentration and meditation. Chanting of Vedas, performance of *yajnas* and rules of discipline are all meant as preliminaries for the ultimate meditation on the true nature of the self and true nature of reality.

(iii) *Aranyakas*, or forest treatises, give symbolic interpretations of *yajnas* which are partly included in the Brahmanas and partly reckoned as independent. *Aranyakas* means 'forest-dwellers' and are the first of the great teachings arising from the practice of renouncing the world to take up study and meditation in the forests. *Aranyakas* are the immediate predecessors of the *Upanishads*. Western scholars estimated the date the *Aranyakas* and *Upanishads* at between 700 and 300 BC.

The *Aaranyaka* portion of the Vedas are meant to explain the inner meaning, the doctrine or philosophy contained in the *Samhitas* as *mantras* and in the

Brâhmanas as *karmas*. According to *Aarnyakas*, it is important to understand the reasons why *yajnas* are required to be performed. *Aaranyakas* are the result of the meditation of sages who sought the solitude of the forests.

(iv) *Upanishads*, deal with the wisdom (*jnana*) leading to liberation (*moksa*), and thus have formed the basis of an independent system, or *darsana*, called *Vedanta*, the 'end of knowledge (*veda* = knowledge; *ânta* = end). The ultimate goal or aim of the Vedas is contained in the *Upanishads*. Thus, the *Upanishads* are the 'end' of the Vedas both in the sense of textual presentation and realization of the end-product. The supreme purpose of the Vedas and Vedanta is to thus make a man into a liberated soul. They are revealed by the great sages of ancient times who acquired this knowledge through realization of God within themselves. *Vedânta* is both religion and philosophy. As religion, it discovers the truths of the inner world, and fosters the same discovery by others; and as philosophy, it synthesizes the science of the inner world with the other sciences of the outer world, to present a unified vision of total reality, and to impart to human life and character depth of faith and vision, along with breadth of outlook and sympathy.

Religion, according to *Vedânta*, is super sensual knowledge; it is not supernatural, but only supersensual. *Vedânta* does not speak of any supernatural revelation. What lies within the sphere of the senses is not the concern of religion; nor has it the competence for it, says *Vedânta*, which will always hold in this field in preference to the verdict of religion.

If *Samhita* is likened to a tree, the *Brâhmanas* are its flowers and the *Aaranyakas* are its fruit, in an unripened state, the *Upanishads* are the ripe fruits. The direct method of realizing through the path of knowledge (*jnâna mârga*) the nonduality (*abhedha*) of the Supreme Being and the soul are explained in the *Upanishads*.

VEDAS

I. The *Rigveda* is entirely in verses and a major portion of it is for use in sacrifices, which comprises 10,589 hymns or *mantras* divided into ten books or *mandalas*. The 10 *mandalas* or books are further subdivided into *anuvakas* (lessons) and *suktas*. Thus *Rigveda* is a great book of knowledge and revelation comprising 10 books, 85 *anuvakas*, 1080 *suktas* and 10589 *mantras* or hymns. Their primary concern is peace, prosperity and liberation to a better world. This also represents the earliest phase in the evolution of religious consciousness where we have not so much the commandments of priests as the outpourings of poetic minds who were struck by the immensity of the universe and the inexhaustible mystery of life. *Rigveda* used two different concepts, generation and birth, and something artificially produced to account for creation. Heaven and earth are the parents of the gods; or the creator of the world is a smith or a carpenter. *Rigveda* is familiar with the four-fold distinction of (i) the Absolute, the One, beyond all dualities and distinctions, (ii) the self-conscious subject confronting the object, (iii) the world-soul, and (iv) the world. The *Upanishads* or the *Vedanta* contain the secret doctrines and much of the ancient Indian thoughts and wisdom.

Rigveda is wholly in the form of hymns in praise of gods (*devatas*). Since in the beginning and end it talks of *agni* or fire, some think that the purpose of the Veda is fire-worship. It would be more correct if *agni* or fire is taken to mean the light of the soul's consciousness (*âtma chaitanyam*)—the glow of the soul's awakening. *Mantras* are the forms in sound (*sabda roopa*) of the devas (gods). In *yajna* (sacrificial rituals), the chant of a *mantra* pertaining to a particular *deva* (god) calls forth that *deva*. Direct offering or oblation to them is not proper. Only oblation made in *agni* (fire), along with the chant of the prescribed *mantras*, will make them assume the form in which they become acceptable to *devas*. The *devas* do not have physical bodies like ours. The sacrificial fire converts the oblation to a subtle state before carrying it to the Devas. This transformation is also due to the power of the *mantra*.

Rigveda contains hymn in praise of all gods or *devatas*. Wise men honour it, for it describes the ways of social living better than others. For example, the marriage rites have been created on the pattern of the marriage of Soorya's daughter, which it details. Dramatic situations like the dialogue between Purooravas and Urvasi also find a place in *Rigveda*.

II. The *Yajurveda* is concerned with vedic sacrifices, many of which are no longer offered in their original form. The sacrificial ritual is chiefly in two recessions, the white or *Shukla Yajurveda* since it is a collection of pure *mantrâs*, and the dark or *Krishna Yajurveda* because this collection includes sacrificial formulas such as those found in the later *Brâhmanas*; it consists of both prose and verse to be chanted during a sacrifice. Sacrificial rites involve two priests, one to perform the physical actions and the other to chant the sacred hymns.

The word '*yajus*' is derived from the root '*yaj*', which means worship. The word *yajna* (sacrificial worship) is also derived from it. True to its name, the chief purpose of *Yajurveda* is to give the *mantras* in *Rigveda* appearing in the form of hymns a practical shape in the form of *yajna* or worship. It also describes in prose the procedural details for the performance of different *yajnas*. The *Taittareeya Upanishad* and the *Brhadaranyaka Upanishad*, are of the *Yajurveda*, pertaining to the *Krishna* and *Sukla Yajurveda* respectively.

III. The *Sâmaveda* is a musical rendering of the *Rigveda*. Out of 1549 *mantrâs* in the *Sâmaveda*, only 75 are original, the rest are from the *Rigveda*. With certain repetitions, the number is 1810. A mysticism of *Sâmaveda* singing is developed more fully in the *Upanishads*, and all later musical practices are based on the belief that the art of music is an aid to meditative practices and salvation. As for the understanding of divinity, the *Sâmaveda* states that Nature is the gods, rather than something that is ruled by the gods. There is a latent Divinity in everything.

Sâma means to bring *shânti* or peace to the minds. In other words, to make the mind find happiness in peace. Of the four methods of tackling an enemy, viz.

sāma, dāna, bheda and *danda*, the first is *sāma* or conquering the enemy by love and conciliatory words.

IV. The *Athurvaveda* consists of hymns for procuring expiation for sins and for appeasing the gods, imperfections and rites for harming enemies, hymns for securing welfare in agriculture, trade and other activities, and for creating love, concord and understanding between husband and wife, father and son, teacher and students. The compilation of the *Athurvaveda* is dated after the other three Vedas. *Athurvaveda* literally means 'fire-priest knowledge' and it is in this Veda that we find the practical arts and sciences. It is full of charms and medicinal secrets while also taking in the wider context, praising and explaining the nature of life and time.

Athurva means a *purohit* or priest. The *mantras* in the *Atharvaveda* were brought to light by the *rishi* called Atharvan. This veda contains many types of *mantras* designed to ward off evil and hardship and to destroy enemies. Amongst the ten major *Upanishads*, three, viz., *Prasna, Mundaka* and *Māndukya*, are part of this Veda.

UPANISHADS

The four Vedas have a total 1180 Upanisads, one from each Sākha, *Rigveda* 21, *Yajurveda* 109, *Sāmaveda* 1000 and *Athurveda* 50. Most of these have been lost with the lapse of time and only 108 now exist. Of these, the principal *Upanishads* are ten: *Isa, Kena, Katha, Prashna, Mundaka, Mandukya, Taitiriya, Aitareya, Chandogya, and Brhadaranyaka*. Shankara, the great Vedantic philosopher, wrote commentaries on eleven of the *Upanishads*, the afore-mentioned ten and the eleventh being *Svetasvatara*. He also referred to the *Kausitaki* and *Mahânarâyana*. These, together with the *Maitri*, constitute the fourteen principal *Upanishads*. Among the ten principal *Upanishads*, the *Isa, Kena, Katha, Prasna* and *Mundaka* may be regarded as more introductory or preparatory in nature in the understanding of the great truths of the universe. But it is the *Bradaranyaka, Chandogya, Aitareya, Taittiriya* and *Mandukya*, that rise above the level of ordinary instruction and stand as most exalted specimens of direct encounter with Reality. The *Brihadaranya* is like an omnibus, where anything can be found anywhere. The *Chandogya* is of more a realistic form. The *Aitareya* is the story of creation, cosmology. The *Taittiriya* is many-sided, but its main issues are psychological, explaining the composition of the indivdual, thus forming, together with the *Aitareya*, a practical text on the story of creation. The *Mandukya Upanishad* is very brief and seems to sum up the intentions of all the *Upanishads* in just twelve *mantras*. The *Upanishads* can be divided into seven broad divisions: (i) 10 major *Upanishads*; (ii) 25 *Sāmanya vedânta*; (iii) 14 *Sāiva*; (iv) 8 *Sâkta*; (v) 14 *Vaisnava*; (vi) 20 *yoga*; and (vii) 17 *Sannyâsa* or a total of 108. Sri Upanisad Brahman Yogin is the only one who is believed to have offered his commentary on all the 108

Upanishads. Some of the *Yoga Upanishads* have found a single version (Appendix 1).

The dates of the *Upanishads* are difficult to determine. The ancient prose *Upanishads*, *Aitareya*, *Kausitaki*, *Chandogya*, *Kena*, *Taittriya*, and *Brhadaranyaka*, as well as the *Isa*, and *Katha*, date back to 800 and 700 BC.

The word *Upanishad* is derived from *upa* = near, *ni* = down, and *sad* = to sit. Groups of pupils sat near the teacher to learn from him the truth by which ignorance is destroyed. The student-teacher dialogue is the modus operandi of the *Upanishads* and it is this dialogue which has passed on Vedic knowledge for thousands of years.In ancient times masters and sages sat together in congregation and discussed the problem of life, of here and hereafter. The questions such as: What is life? What is this world, and what is our duty? What are we expected to do and in what way are we to behave, and so on. Is there a life beyond, or is this life everything? Is this earth the evaluating principle of all, or is there something beyond? *Upanishad* texts are records of experiences and explanations of masters who set themselves in tune with ultimate Truth. It is not a lecture that is delivered, but a wisdom that is communicating to the soul by the soul. It is a conversation between soul and soul, and not merely a discourse given by a professor to the student.

We do not know the names of the authors of the *Upanishads*. Some of the chief doctrines of the *Upanishads* are associated with the names of renowned sages such as Aruni, Yajnavalkya, Balaki, Svetaketu, and Sandilya. They were perhaps the early exponents of the doctrines attributed to them. The great analogy for which the *Upanishads* are renowned is that of the waker-dreamer-deepsleeper. This beginningless, endless Universe is the dream of Brahman. We are the dreaming figures in that world which is constantly in the process of being dreamt up. It is uncreated and created at every moment in the same sense that the dream world is uncreated and created by the dreamer at every moment until he or she wakes—at which point the dream world dissolves.

1. Isa *Upanishad*

This *Upanisad* derives its name from the opening words of the first *mantra* 'Isa'. This, the smallest of the *Upanishads*, consisting of only 18 short verses, speaks of many important topics, including the claims of the path of knowledge and the path of action, the paradoxical nature of the *âtman*, the nature of the unattached sage. This teaches us that by offering the fruit of all actions (*nishkâma karma*) to Him, is a means to attain God. Further, it is stated that when one understands that everything is of the same spirit, then he realizes that the world is an illusion and grief vanishes, and joy and happiness come into his life. The main point is that God pervades in everything and that all living things are but one and divine. It is by renunciation and absence of possessiveness that the soul is saved.

2. Kena *Upanishad*

The *Kena Upanishad* is also known as the *Talavakâr Upanisad*. As the name 'Kena' indicates, this *Upanishad* asks, 'By whom ?'—that is, who is the real power behind the functions of the universe, external in nature and internal in man. In reply the *Upanishad* gives an account of a single unitary reality, the *âtman*, as the inspirer of the functions of both man and the universe, of sense-functions in man and functions of the elements in the external world. While knowledge of the unqualified Absolute alone can result in emancipation, knowledge of the Absolute as God prepares the way for such knowledge.

"It is the life-spirit '*âtman*' by whose power the ear hears, the eyes see, and life itself functions. But this self is different from what is known and beyond what is unknown—'That which makes the tongue speak, but needs no tongue to explain'; that which makes the mind think, but needs no mind to think;' 'That which makes the eyes see, but needs no eye to see;' 'that which makes the ears hear, but needs no ear to hear;' 'that which makes life live, but needs no life to live;' that alone is spirit.The eyes cannot reach it, neither can speech, nor the other sense-organs do that either. Similarly, what the mind does not comprehend, sight fails to see, hearing fails to grasp, and the life-force itself does not enliven, but what cognizes the mind, perceives sight and hearing, and directs life, that alone is *Brahman*, and not what people here in the world say or worship. And such wise men who perceive or experience this truth attain immortality."

The *Upanishad* is famous also for its saying, "It is not understood by those who (say they) understand It. It is understood by those who (say they) understand It not." The wise realized *Brahman* in all beings. The Self within and the *Brahman* outside are one and the same. Self realization, this *Upanishad* says, can be had in this very life and also gives the warning that the opportunity of being born as a human being should not be missed but utilized in obtaining this end. "The living man who finds Spirit, finds Truth. But if he fails, he sinks among fouler shapes. The man who can see the same Spirit in every creature, clings neither to this nor that, attains immortal life." "Spirit is known throgh revelation. It leads to freedom. It leads to power. Revelation is the conquest of death."

3. Katha *Upanishad*

The *Katha* get its name from a school of the *Black Yajurveda*. It is perhaps the most philosophical of the *Upanishads*. Among its important features are: the dialogue between Nachiketas and Yama (the god of the world of departed spirits) on the question of what happens to the soul after death. Passion, anger, hate and fear belong to the mind and do not belong to *âtman*. Hunger, thirst and such other wants pertain to the body and not to the *âtman*. We should thus learn to practice to identify all objects and substances, which are other than *âtman*. If we constantly practice this way of thinking, the deep rooted feeling that 'I' comprises only the *âtman* and the body and mind fading and will eventually vanish. Thus I can be the pure *âtman* without getting involved with the many impurities which assails the body and mind. We should regard our body clothed in flesh as a sheath situated close to the *âtman*. We should train the mind to view the body as an external object, and as 'not I' or 'not mine'. Then, it would not be necessary to think in terms of getting liberation after death. *Moksha* means liberation of *âtman* from all attachment. A liberated *âtman* finds happiness within himself. Thus he gets free from mortality and becomes immortal. What causes misery to us is the body and through it the mind. The absence of misery and being always blissful is what is called 'heaven'—*moksha*—in all religions. All faiths, other than the *advaita* doctrine, say that to enjoy eternal bliss, one has to go to another world (heaven). Adi Sankara has prover that whilst living in this world itself by totally giving up bodily (including mind) attachment, one can enjoy greater bliss than what is available in heaven or *moksha* (*Brahama Sutra Bhâsha* 1.1.4). *Bhagavad Gita* also says that the two main enemies who stand in the way of our reaching this blissful state are desire and passion/anger.

The story of the conversation between the Yama, the God of death, and Nachiketas was as follows: Yama offered three boons to Nachiketa. As the first, Nachiketa asked that his father's anger should calm down and that when he is sent back to him, his father should welcome him. These were assured by Yama. As the second boon, he requested to be taught the fire sacrifice which leads one to Heaven. This was taught with all the attendant rites and ceremonies. As the third wish, he wanted to be taught as to what happen to one (*âtman*) when one dies. Man must find his soul first and when he realizes that the Eternal Spirit in him is divine, he is on his way to immortality. To attain this, one has to concentrate on the divinity of the soul and its freedom. It is *Om* which is Brahman and is supreme and he who knows it achieves everything. He who does not realize this and sees the universe with all objects in it as different and not as the one reality, is born, dies and is reborn. For those who have realized the truth, there is no death, they get *moksha*. The famous saying of this *Upanishad* is that the knowledge of the supreme is not gained by argument but by the teaching of one who possesses intuition.

4. Prashna *Upanishad*

As the name indicates (*Prashna* means a question), this work has its origin in the questions (six in all) which philosophers ask the sage Pippalada. His answers evolve at the end quite a systematic philosophy on creation, human personality, and the metaphysical principle in man. Six pupils approached sage Pappalada and questioned him. How did creation begin? Who are gods or *devas*? How does life get connected to the body? What is the truth about the states of awakening, sleep and dreaming? What is the benefit of worshipping *Omkara*? What is the relationship between the *purush* and *jeeva*? All the questions are convincingly answered and the pupils satisfied.

5. Mundaka *Upanishad*

Mundaka means shaven-head—tonsure. This *Upanishad* is to be followed by persons like *sanyâsis* with mature minds and a disposition free from attachment. Verses of *Mundaka Upanishad* are the core of the *Bhagavad Gita*. This is the most poetical of the *Upanishads*. The philosophy expressed is mostly eclectic, and generally speaking, the subject-matter is that which is common to all the *Upanishads*. Worthy of special mention, however, is the theory of a higher (*para*) and a lower (*apara*) kinds of knowledge. The former is that by which the unchangeable self is realized. The highest wisdom is to know Brahman and be one with Brahman, i.e., the unchangeable Self. The lower is that which relates to all other subjects. Here a distinction between wisdom and knowledge is made out. Wisdom relates to Brahman and remains highest kind forever as compared to knowledge of matter, work and their interactions. For those who prefer the *jnâna mârga*, i.e. the way of knowledge for attaining *moksha* or liberation of birth and death, is held out as the best means. *Moksha* is realization of oneness with *Brahman*, as when the flowing rivers from whatever source they arise, lose their names and forms, when they enter the ocean.

'Truth alone triumphs' (*satyamevajayate*), a motto of India, is a *mantra* from this *Upanishad*.

6. Mândukya *Upanishad*

Named after the sage—teacher Mandukya, this *Upanishad* has given to Indian thought the famous theory of the four states of consciousness, namely, waking, dreaming, dreamless sleep, and the fourth state *turiya*, which alone is real. The fourth aspect, which is neither subjective nor objective experience is said to be one of 'pure unitary conscience'. Reality is considered as mere consciousness. When one becomes aware of this, awareness of the world is lost and a blissful sense of peace or transcendental stage is attained. Here these states are explained in their relationship to the mystic syllable, *Om*. Both psychologically and metaphysically, this doctrine has had a great influence on Indian thought. *Manduka* means a frog. One reason appears to be that the frog does not have to climb each stair. It can jump from the first to the fourth stair or state.

7. Taittriya *Upanishad*

The distinctive feature of this *Upanishad* is its description of the ethical teaching of the times as brought out in the form of a discourse between the teacher and his pupils—sometimes called a 'convocation address'. Out of ignorance or *avidya*, one identifies himself with the five sheaths encasing the soul leading up to the ultimate bliss of *Brahman*. The five sheaths or covering are the material, breadth, mind, intellect and bliss. The individual soul is only the universal soul shackled by the gross body. Thus '*Pramâtman*' becomes '*Jivâtman*'.

The personal 'I' when it gets merged into the Eternal Self, then those who perceive this can say '*Aham Brahmâsmi*' i.e. I am Brahman. The *Upanishad* is so named because it is a part of the *Taittriya Aranyaka*.

The *mantras* used in a most of the rituals (*Karmânushtâna*) are taken from this. Percepts such as 'Tell the truth, follow the righteousness' (*satyam vada, dharmam chara*) appears only in this. Mother, father and teacher should be treated like divinities (*mâtri devo bhava, pitri devo bhava, aacârya devo bhava*)—these *mantras* are found only in this *Upanishad*. It also contains the famous verse, "May we both (teacher and disciple) be protected; may we both obtain sustenance; let both of us at the same time apply (our) energies (for acquirement of knowledge); may our reading be illustrious; may there be no hatred (amongst us). Peace, peace, peace."

8. Aitareya *Upanishad*

As the name suggests, this *Upanishad* is only a part of the large *Aitareya Aranyaka*. This also deals with how a *jeeva* (soul) enters the mother's womb from the father, then is born in the world, takes birth again and again in various worlds according to sin (*pâpa*) and merit (*punya*), and how liberation from birth and life is possible only through realizing the nature of *âtma*. The idea of life after death is brought out more clearly than in other places in upanishadic literature, but the *Upanishad* is most famous for its doctrine of the *âtman* as intellect. There is an imploring to Brahman to remove the veil of ignorance so that the reality may be seen and enable the seeker to understand the spirit of the scriptures.

9. Chandogya *Upanishad*

This is one of the oldest and best known of the *Upanishads*. Many important teachings are contained in it, but perhaps the most popular passage in the whole work is the story of Satyakama Jabala and his truthful mother, in which it is demonstrated that the status of the *brahmin* is determined by the character rather than by birth. The central teaching of the *Upanishad*, associated with the philosopher Aruni, is the basic doctrine of the identity of the *Atman*, the physical principle within , and the *Brahman*, the universal principle of nature. In this *Upanishad* is also found a delineation of the significance of the mystic syllable *Om*, as well as some of the famous theories of creation, such as the Cosmic-Egg theory. Uddalaka asked his son, Svetaketu, who returned home after twelve years of study, "Did you ask to be imparted that knowledge by which the unheard is heard, the unthought thought and the unknown known?" Having not had it he asked his father what that knowledge was. Uddalaka then tells him, "At the beginning there was Existence alone, i.e. only *One*, without any other. This *One* thought and projected itself as many. Thus the universe was projected and then came all beings, in all of which was that *One*. That *One* is truth and self and added '*Tat tvam asi*', i.e. That Art Thou". Further Uddalaka taught Svetaketu that Brahman is the subtle essence of everything and that He is the Self. It is just like salt dissolved in water remains unseen but imparts its saltishness to the water. People walk over a hidden treasure many times, not being able to discover it. Similarly, all being in Brahman every moment and yet do not find Him.

The name of the *Upanishad* is derived from '*chandoga*', the name of certain priests specialized in the Sâma Veda.

10. Brhadaranyaka Upanishad

This *Upanishad* is the longest—the name means 'great forest-book'—the most famous, and one of the oldest of all the *Upanishads*. In it is found, among many other valuable passages, the famous discourse between the great philosopher Yajnavalkya—perhaps the greatest of the Upanishadic sages—and his wife Maitreyi. It is in this discourse that we find one of the best expressions of the transcendental *âtman* as universal and undifferentiated consciousness better portrayed. Maitreyi said: "My Lord, if this whole earth full of wealth, belonged to me, tell me, should I be immortal by it or not? "No," replied Yâgnavalkya: "Like the life of rich people will be thy life. But there is no hope of immortality by wealth" (*Brhadaranyaka Upanishad* II.IV.2). Mâitreyi asked: "Tell me that, indeed Sir, of what you know of the way to immortality." Then he said: "Verily, O Matreyi, everything is not dear that you may love everything; but that you may love the Self, therefore everything is dear." "It is the Self that should be seen, heard of, reflected on, and meditated upon. Verily, by the seeing, by the hearing of, by the thinking of, and by the understanding of the Self only all this is known" (*Brhadaranyaka Upanishad* II.IV.3-5).

It is in this *Upanishad* that the *âtman* is described negatively as '*neti, neti*' ('not this, not this')—meaning that it cannot be described as this or that (4.2.22). It is not like anything known to us. According to the *Neti* doctrine, first the world, body and mind have to be rejected and the *âtman* will be realized as transcending classification or description through words. After such realization, the feeling will be that of eternal bliss and all creatures are also made of the same bliss or the juice of happiness or *ânanda*.

Important passages in this *Upanishad* are developed to define *Brahman*, and to the consideration of the various theories of the nature of the absolute or ultimate. When Brahman is realized, it establishes the identity between *self* and *brahman*. The self is in the soul as oil is in the seasamum seed and when by truthfulness and meditation self is realized and identity of the self and *Brahman* established, then one has attained blissfulness. For such there is no birth, death and birth again and such person gets *moksha*.

11. Svetâsvatâra Upanishad

This is one of the recent *Upanishads*. Summary of the main *upanishadic* doctrines is found in this and the idea of devotion to a personal God is also developed. In it some of the ideas of *samkhya* (dualistic system) and *yoga* philosophies (*advaita* or non-dualism) find clear expression. The *Upanishad* does not expound any single doctrine or philosophy in particular, but it gives an eloquent exposition of the best thought of the times. The emphasis, however, is in the direction of theism rather on the Absolutism stressed in most of the *Upanishads*. Here there is self-inquiry by the pupils and the saint Svetâsvatâra gives his findings. The sages say that the power of self-consciousness in all living beings is due to *Brahman* (God) being present there. When *Brahman* is realized or attained, it establishes the identity between self and *Brahman*. The self is in the soul as oil is in the seasamum seed. When self is realized by meditation and identify the self and *Brahman established* then one has attained blissfulness. For such there is no more birth, death and birth again as such become immortal.

This *Upanishad* gets its name from the name or title of the sage who is said to have taught it to his disciples.

12. Kausitaki Upanisad

Sage Kausitaki is the philosopher of this *Upanishad*, which excels in the delineation of *prâna* (the breathing spirit) as the prime mover of the universe. *Prâna* is ultimately identified as the higher subjective reality as well.

Sage Kausitaki said: 'The *prana* is the Brahman unto whom the other sense organs carry their offerings, i.e. the knowledge and the various experiences relating to the world of names and forms.' Then Painga joined to say, 'The *prana* is the Brahman, and it prevails over the mind as the overlord.' When the vocal-organ speaks, the *prana* speaks in unison. Similarly, when the eyes see, the ear hears, the mind ideates, that is, when each one of these organs functions jointly with the vital energy inherent therein, then all of them together function likewise in unison, each inhibiting for the time being its own characteristic function. Thus, it establishes its identity with the *prana* at the time of cognition. When any one of the organ loses its vitality (whether of perception, or of action), then that alone ceases without detriment to the function of the others. But on death, and with the departure of the *prana*, the functions of all the others too cease.

13. Maitrey Upanisad

Here, the inspiring sage is Maitri, from whom the work gets its name. This *Upanishad* is important for its very clear account of the two forms of the *âtman*, the nominal and the phenomenal, or the *âtman* and the *bhutâtman* (literally, the changing self, or the 'elemental self'). The latter reaps the fruits of good and bad actions while the former abides 'in its own greatness'.

Once Lord Siva said to the sage Maitreya: 'The body is said to be a temple. The *âtman* is the Siva alone. So, one should worship him with complete identity as 'He' and 'I' are one (*jiva-brahma aaikya bhava*). True knowledge consists of seeing non-difference in one and all. Meditation means in the removal of the impurities in the mind.

Then Maitrey disclosed his own experienc and exclaimed: 'The quiescent state is the supreme state of the self in the real sense of it, i.e. 'I am Brahman, I am all the worlds, pure supreme, true knowledge, consciousness and the impartial one. I am devoid of duality, beyond speech and beyond even the mind and the rest. I am the holy Pranava (OM). I am he, the pure Brahman.

14. Mahanarayan Upanisad:

This *Upanisad* is in the form of a discourse between the guru and his disciple on Mahanarayan as the all-pervading self.

Of his own, once Lord Narayan desired, 'Let me create.' From him came into being chief vital principle (*prana*) here as *hiranyagarbha*. Then the cosmic intellect, the mind as *mahat-tattva* (one of the eternal verities), then all the organs of perception and action, also ether, air, fire, water and earth (as subtle elements that prop the universe), then the five gross quintuplicated elements and the real came to be. From him came into being also Brahma, Visnu, Rudra and all others, including the Vedic *mantra* (Gayatri). And all these derive their strength and seek their repose in him alone. This is the essence of the *Rigveda*.

Apart from Narayan, there is not even a speck. He is the spotless, smearless, the indescribable, pure, radiant, etc. He who knows thus becomes Vishnu himself. This is the essence of the *Yajurveda*.

Smriti

Samhitâ, Brâhmana, and *Upanishad* writings are known as the *sruti* (that which was heard). The portion of Vedas are called *srutis*, orally communicated by God, and heard, but not composed or written by *rishis*. It means that knowledge of the Vedas was received by *rishis* in a state of super-normal consciousness. All authoritative writings outside the Vedas are referred to as *Smriti* (that which is remembered). *Smriti* is written by man. These *Smritis* are generally listed under five headings: *vedângas*, or the limbs of the Vedas; *dharma sâstras*, which includes codes of laws, commentaries and digests and manuals; *nibandhas*, rituals and domestic rites; *purânas*; and the *epics*. Associated with these are the *agamas* or sectarian scriptures, and the *darsanas* or six schools of philosophy.

Agamas give all the rules of worship of the 'formed deities' or *Saguna Brahman* for the benefit of the masses, explaining the principles and rules of a particular aspect of the *Nirguna Brahman* who takes the form of *Saguna*. While most vedic rituals were in Sanskrit, understood only by the educated, *Agamas* reached the illiterate and the devout masses as simple stories and rituals for an image that the masses could see and visualize the Ultimate Reality in its various aspects and forms. They explain the external worship of God which gives us *jnana* or knowledge, *yoga* or concentration.

Saiva Agama glorifies *Saguna Brahman* as Siva which has given rise to the Saivism aspect of Hindu thoughts and philosophy.

Saaktha Agama glorifies God as *Shakti* or Supreme Mother of universe. *Shakti* is the creative power of Siva.

Vaishnava Agama glorifies God as Vishnu. Its teaching leans toward *Vishshta-advaitan*

Thus the *Agama* were written for the three main forms of Deities, Siva, Vishnu and Sakthi. Three *Agamas* consider that their form of God as the Ultimate Creator and Protector of all universe and all lives therein. The fourth division is the ritualistic *Smartha Sampradaya*, the followers of the *Smrithi*, who accept the *Agamas* and temple worship.

Vedangas

Vedângâs, as the word indicates, are the limbs of the Vedas and are meant to be of help in studying them in the correct and proper pronunciation of the various *mantrâs*. *Vedangâs* are also known as *Sâstras*. *Vedangâs* have the 64 sciences that deal with phonetics, grammar, etymology, prosody, astronomy and ritual codes which serve as handbooks for sacrifices. The five *upavedas* are supplementary Vedas, taking up where Athruvaveda left off to deal with the various aspects of the material world. *Ayurveda* deals with the science of medicine, both preventive and curative, embracing anatomy, physiology, hygiene and surgery. *Dhanurveda* deals with military sciences such as archery and charioteering. *Gandharvaveda* deals with the performance arts of music and dance. *Sthaptyaveda* takes in mathematics as well as its practical applications in the visual arts and sciences: engineering and architecture, sculpture and painting.

Dharma Sastras

The oldest known form of this most widely accepted of all Hindu philosophies is the *Brahma sutra* of *Badarayana* which contains 555 aphorism (*sutra*). The first *sutra* announces the purpose of all—now, then, a desire to know Brahman (*Athato Brahman jigyasa*). *Dharma Sâstras* are concerned with conduct, the way of righteousness, dealing with personal hygiene, manners and polite behaviour, morality, administration of the state and justice, seeking of spiritual salvation and the duties which must be performed in carrying out domestic rituals and sacraments. The Laws of Manu (*Manusmriti*) are supposed to be remained as the ultimate authority on moral law through the subsequent centuries.

Nibandhas

Later there grew digests and manuals, called *Nibandhas*, which were the codification of Vedic laws, and decisions of all aspects of conduct, including such topics as gifts, pilgrimages, vows, worship, auspicious features of the human body and descriptions of articles of utility. They also deal with all the rituals to be performed from the time of conception until the death of the individual.

Puranas

The *Purânas* and *Itihâsas* have been composed by *mahârishis* so that recalling the Almighty's glorious deeds could benefit future generations. *Purânas* are the detailed descriptions of old stories. The meaning of *purân* is *pura api navam*— thought old, yet it is new. The epic (*ithihasa*) narrates the events that actually took place. *Purâna* deals with the essential features of creation, secondary creation, continued creation out of the primitive matter, the pedigree or period of Manus, the dynasties of the ancient kings and their histories. There are eighteen principal *Purânas* (*Mahâpuranas*) and eighteen auxiliary *Purânas* (*upapurânas*). The principal *Purânas* are divided into three groups which are ostensibly devoted to either Brahma, Shiva or Vishnu, who emerged as the three different manifestations of the same Absolute Reality. They are given to us as historical narratives and stories, written for the benefit of the common people and suitable for all mankind from the inquisitive child to illiterate devotees to intellectual scholars. The *Purânas* developed as a reinforcement and amplification of the Vedic teachings, dealing with the stories of creation, periodic dissolution and recreation of the world, giving the histories and genealogies of the gods, sages, and forefathers, and recording the history of the dynasties which rules on the earth. The most popular of the *Purânas* is the *Bhâgavata* which glorifies Vishnu and deals with the ten great reincarnations of Vishnu. Similarly *Suta Samhita* is devoted to Shiva. Of all these, the most popular ones are *Shiva Purana, Skanda Purana, Srimad Bhagavatha Purana* and *Vishnu Purana*. The popular portion of *Markandaya Purana* is the 'Chandi' or 'Devi Mahatmiyam'. It is usually read during the ten days if Dusserrah or Navaratri *puja*. It has worship of God as the Divine Mother as its theme.

Epics

The two great epics of Hindu culture are the *Râmâyana* and the *Mahâbhârata*, whose significance and prominence cannot be under-estimated. It would be virtually impossible to find any Hindu in India or in South-East Asian Hindu country who was old enough to speak but could not give an elaborate account of these two epics. These epics and their divine protagonists, Rama and *Krishna*, both the incarnations of the god Vishnu, have left no corner of Hindu life uninfluenced. The epics incorporate the *Purânic* accounts of creation, cosmography, *dharma*, and stories of heroes, sages and gods. They are also the mines of wise sayings which guide the masses in all walks of life's activities.

1. Ramayana

Râmayana was written in Sanskrit by the sage Sri Valmiki; it relates to the story of Sri Rama and his three brothers who are the sons of king Dasaratha. Ramayana contains 7 cantos, divided into 500 chapters, and contains 24,000 verses (the *utara kanda* included). While scholars will often say that Vâlmiki based his tale on folk traditions that came many millennia before his appearance—and while there may be some truth to this—it is his version of the *Râmâyana* that most people consider the earliest and most authentic. Perhaps the earliest rendition of the Râma story, barring the Vâlmiki text itself, is found in the *Mahâbhârata*. Variations on the Râma story can also be found in many of the major *purânas*, and through these the tale has filtered through to South India, where an eleventh century sage named Kampan rewrote the *Râmâyana* in Tamil known as the *Irâmâvatâram*. Kampan's retelling of the epic was followed by Budharâja's Telugu version (the *Ranganâtharâmâyana)* in the thirteenth century, and by Krttivâsa's Begali version in the fourteenth. With the medieval *bhakti* renaissance in the sixteenth century came many new *Râmâyanas*, most notably the Sanskrit *Adhyâtma Râmâyana* (the "esoteric Tâmâyana), probably composed somewhere in South India, and also the *Anadarâmâyana* and the *Bhusundirâmâyana*, the latter work models itself so closely on the *Bhâgavata Purâna* that it has often been called *Râma-bhâgavata*. But the most famous vernacular version, also from the sixteenth century, is Tulasidâsa's Hindi *Râmcaritmânas*. The *Râmâyana* is not only known and loved in India, but throughout South and Southeast Asia and, indeed, in much of the rest of the world as well. Whether it is called the *Ramakien* in Thailand or the *Serat Rama* in Indonesia, the *Yama Pwe* in Burma or the *Maharadia Lawana* in the Philippines, Vâlmik's *Râmâyana* (or the *Râmacharitmânas)* in India or ISKCON's *Illustrated Ramâyana* in America—whether it is conveyed through music and mime, poetry, popular folk tales, dramatic performances, video, comic nooks, epic narrations, or what have you—the stories and personalities associated with the *lila* of Râma have captured the hearts of over one billion people, while literally hundreds of thusands of others, through devotional movements and secular learning institutions are aware of the *avatâra* of Vishnu.

The epic teaches us by personal example how man should conduct himself in conformity to *dharma.* It has not lost its appeal, from the time of its composition by Sage Valmiki because the truths and the morals the epic relates have eternal value. Every aspect of life in perfection is shown with Sri Rama and others as ordinary human beings. Rama's character is depicted as an ideal son, king, brother, husband and a friend. The brothers show examples of affection and mutual service. Sita is shown as the ideal wife and woman. Sri Hanuman stands as an example of an ideal and unique *karma yogi* and devotee (*bhaktya*).

Tulasidasa narrated the Rama story in Hindi. His version has become so common that for many it is the Ramayana. His *Râmacharitramânasa*, 'Lake of the Deeds of Rama', was begun in 1574 at Ayodhya and finished after some considerable period at Varanasi. Tulasidasa repeatedly states that his doctrine derives from the *Vedas* and *Puranas* and often refers to Valmiki as the prime source for the Rama story. He borrowed extensively from the *Adhyatma Ramayana*. Tulasidasa synthesizes the two extremes represented by Valmiki and the *Adhyatma Ramayana*. Valmiki's stress upon *dharma* (the thesis) and the Adhyatma's stress upon *nirguna Rama* (the antithesis) are integrated in Tulasidasa's stress upon *bhakti* or devotion (the synthesis).

Valmiki had depicted Rama as a great man, Tulasidasa established him as God for protection, an *avatara* or incarnation of Vishnu. The *Puranas* had described Rama as God. Tulasidasa humanized him, made him a living and lively character and an object of popular appeal, love and respect. Thus Tulasidasa has shown us that God has descended to level of man, and man has ascended to the status of God in Rama.

As early as *Dwapar*, Arayana had been practicing Vedic rituals and worshipping Vishnu. In the Northern part of India, people were mostly *Vaishnavaites* and Southern people were *Shaivaites*, worshipping Shiva. Frequently, the *Shaivaites* were destroying sages and ascetics of *Vaishnavaites* faith in performing *Homam yagya* and sometimes the sages were killed or captured as slaves. Remarkably enough, Tulasidasa kept his epics, *Ramacharitramanasa* free from any intolerance or trace of conflict between different ideologies. He seeks to reconcile in his poetry the worship of Rama with the worship of Shiva. This perhaps saved North India from the fury of the clash between the *Shaivaites* and *Vaishnavaites*. In search of Sita in Lanka, Hanuman sees signs of *vaishnava* worship and is thus led to Vibhushana, with whom he has an edifying conversation. Also in the Lankakanda, Rama erected a Shiva linga at the causeway *(Svatabâna)*. Tulasidasa was essentially a *bhakta* or devotee but also acknowledged the claims of the rival paths of *karma* and *jnana*. He also brought about a harmonious adjustment between asceticism and domestic life. One way his poetry was an expression of his own devotional thoughts and feelings, yet in another it is a guide to good life for people who have not renounced the world.

Man's real enrichment depends on the internal, not external. Externally he may be crude, ugly or primitive, yet it is possible for him to be morally great and in all surrender to God. Some such lesson seems to be conveyed to us through characters like Guharaj, Hanuman, Jatayu and Jambavan in the Ramayana. Externally, they were sub-human or primitive, nevertheless these characters were depicted as advanced ethical beings capable of loyalty and friendship and heroic self-sacrifice. They are specially noted for their appreciation of the spiritual excellence shining through the characters of the hero and the heroine.

On contrary, man may externally develop a highly scientific civilization, acquire immense wealth and power, erect palaces, drive chariots and forge deadly weapons of war, and yet he may be morally and spiritually a very primitive being, given greed, violence and sensuality. The *râkshasas* and their king Râvana are example of this kind of morally low beings or devils.The splendour, the wealth and the technical efficiency of Lanka was described. Lanka symbolised isolation and the sea surrounding it stood for the ocean of *samsâra* or

Lord Ganesha

Sri Durga Maa

Sri Vidhya Saraswati

Sri Vishnu

Jai Shiv Shambu

Shiva Ling

Lord Nataraja

mayâ, encircling the soul. For a comparison, Ayodhya and its king and people were great both morally and materially. Ayodhya means a land of eternal peace.

Râvana was a grandson of the sage Pulastya and had an inheritance of learning and culture to his credit. Some people think that title of *dasa-sisa,* or 'ten-headed one', was a tribute to his intelligence. But Pandit Ramchandra Dwivedi in his book on Tulasidâsa explains the ten heads of Râvana had ten military commanders who were known as 'the heads', and the army divided into twenty units, was known as his 'arms'. Thus, his strength consisted in his ten heads and twenty arms, or, in other words, it was centered in a well-equipped and trained army. In the battle with Râma, it is clearly stated that as soon as one 'head' was cut off another grew in its place and the 'arms' also were similarly replaced. Tulasidasa says that 'Many times the Lord destroyed the heads and arms of Râvana but immediately new ones appeared'. He says again, 'The heads all came forward together saying "Where is Râma" and seeing them the monkeys ran for their lives. Râma laughed and wounded them with his arrows.

Another symbolic interpretation may be as follows. Râvan denotes the evil body and his ten heads are the ten organs (*indriyas*): five organs of senses—the *jñânendriyas* (eyes, ears, nose, tongue and skin); and the five organs of action—the *karmendriyas* (speech, hands, feet, anus and the generative organ) which are capable of making vices that beset humanity. If you control one organ or *indriya,* the other organs are still there and are capable of committing vices. Thus the controlled organ regain its vitality. Hence it is important to control all ten senses (*indriyas*) or organs at one time to achieve consciousness or true knowledge or *gyan* and subsequently *Brahman.* Sitâ denotes consciousness who has been prisioned by the Ego. Her womanhood denotes that it is ever dependent upon intellect or *Budhi* and looking to intellect for everything. Rama denotes intellect or buddhi. Hanumân denotes mind which is very strong and at the same time restless or fidgety as a monkey cannot sit on one branch of a tree for long. Intellect or *Buddhi* (Râma) lodged a war against the Ego to liberate the consciousness or the Queen of the land of Eternal peace (Sitâ). With the help of a strong mind (Hanuman), intellect or *buddhi* (Râma) killed or controlled all *indriyas* and restored consciousness (Sita) to her rightful place. "Senses are superior to the physical body; superior to the senses is mind; superior to the mind is the intellect *(buddhi)*; superior than intellect is He (God)" (*Bhagavata Gita* III. 42).

Tulasidasa described Ravana and other demons as criminal desperadoes and ruthless tyrants; and Rama as a saviour of the people. Symbolically, Rama's victory over Ravana signifies the victory of virtue over vice, of justice over injustice, of truth over untruth and of knowledge over ignorance.

From the Ramayana, we can further learn some important lessons as follows: One is that we ought to be content with what we possess. Running after a golden deer is symbolic of our running after material wealth and power whose true image is actually that of a demon which ultimately brings about our own ruin and destruction. Another lesson that we can learn is that as long as we do not cross our limits, we are safe. Nothing is harmful as long as it is done within bounds. The minute we step out of it, even the highest power on earth cannot help us. This is obvious from the fact that, in spite of having wanted the deer, if Sitâ had remained within the line drawn round the cottage, all would have been well. She would not have been carried away by Ravana. On return from hunting the deer Râma and Lakshmana would have found Sitâ in the cottage.

Râma set an example and took life to be duty and observed it sincerely in various capabilities—as an ideal son, as a disciple, as a brother, as a master, as an ideal husband, as a friend, as a warrior and above all as an ideal king. Once Vâlmiki asked Nârada about the qualities of Râma. Nârada enumerated 16 excellent qualities of Râma, who was well versed in the intricacies of the law of righteousness, who did not bear grievous wrongs done to him by others but magnified even the single act of kindness to him, whose thoughts, words and deeds were in perfect harmony, whose life was spotless, who always sought the highest good of humanity, who was a perennial source of delight to all those who approached him, whose senses were under perfect control, who did not lose his temper and whose heart knew no envy, hatred, spite or calumny. Ram has His self under control. He has no enemies, either in the world or in Himself. He is serene alike in weal and woe. The weak and the oppressed find in Him a ready and fearless champion. He read into the hearts of His subjects and has a watchful eye on the rights and duties of all grades of scoiety. He embodies in Himself whatever is highest and noblest. With all the uncommon virtues and qualities vested in him, it would be logical to think that Râma is a divine or superhuman person. Bharat has been praised for having considered himself as the servant of his brother, Rama and have shown a sense of duty to him. Lakshamana for brotherly affection was exemplified as true and noble brother, always ready to help his elder brother. Sita is symbolized as a devoted and chaste wife, to prove her chastity Sita leapt into fire, the God Agni restored her. Despite this, scandals about Sita, persisted and Ram was forced to banish her to the forest. King Dasaratha honours his promise true to his word in spite of the deepest suffering. Râma is the ideal son who sacrifices the best part of his life to maintain his father's promises. Hanumân plays the role of the mediating *Acârya*, the messenger of God, finding no trouble in crossing this ocean to carry the divine message of assurance. The grace of God acts like a 'bridge' built over the sea of human sorrow and in the battle with evil. Wisdom and *viveka* which is symbolized by Vibhisana rescues the soul and takes it to His permanent abode.

There are three characteristics or *gunas* of human nature. *Sâttavic* or spiritual luminosity; *râjasvic* or action-oriented and *tâmasi* or inactive. Some may have more of *sâttavic* and become the intellectual and moral leader; others have more *râjasvic* and tend to be dominating, selfish, inconsiderate, insensitive and even harsh and abrasive and have a bloated ego; and the third one *tâmasi* is inactive, cruel and ignorant. These three *gunas* are personified in Ramayana as three brothers of the Rakshasa family: Vibhishana, Ravana and Kumbhakaran. It was the *sâttavic* character of the youngest brother Vibhishana that gave him the intuition to know what is right and what is not. He was righteous and performed various deeds of mercy in Lanka. Because of his *sâttavic* character, Vibhisana sided with Ram, or on the side of *dharma* (righteousness) in a war between Ram and Ravana. Ravana was the personification of *râjasvi*, which blinds the scholarly Ravan from discriminating between right and wrong. For instance, his passion and lust led to his ruin. According to Valmiki Ramayan, Ravan was handsome, learned and brave. He had the wisdom to perform severe austerity yet he was able to acquire brilliant intellectual capabilities. He had to overpower the *devâs, asurâs, yakshas* and *nâgas.* Kumbhakaran was the personification of *tâmasi* who sleeps for months. He was also no fool, and he chides Râvan for provoking war with Râma who is God in human form. Nevertheless, he did not go into the moral aspects of the war and sided with Râvan. He acknowledged that Râma would kill him and yet in the breath roars before Râvana: 'I shall kill Râma and Lakshmana and eat up the Vânara chiefs. Enjoy your luxuries and drink your wine. Once I send Râma to his doom, Sitâ will be yours.'

2. Mahabharata

Mahabhârata written in 100,000 Sanskrit verses by Sri Vyasa, is the story of two royal families, the Pandavas and Kauravas, descendants of king Bharatha. They were cousins fighting the great war of Kurukshethra. The epic, rightly called as fifth Veda, touches upon every aspect of Hindu religious teaching, the practice, philosophy, mysticism and polity. There are numerous legendary narratives and short tales in it. In it are explained the modes and rules of good life, correct understanding of the world and the wise way to lead a disciplined life. There are various facts concerning the Indian political economy, administration of government and philosophical discussions in the Mahabharata. The Mahabharata is not a mere epic; it is a romance, telling the tale of heroic men and women and of some who were divine; it is a whole literature in itself, containing a code of life, a philosophy of social and ethical relations, and speculative thought on human problems that is hard to rival. It also contains the *Bhagavad Gita, Vishnu Sahasranâma,* significant words of wisdom in *Yuksha Prasna* and Vidura *neeti* (philosophy). Though the sentiment of heroism stands out strikingly because of the prominence given to battles, the essential note of the Mahabharata is of tranquillity of the sentiment. Lord *Krishna*, the incarnation of Sri Vishnu, appears and establishes the rules of righteousness with his super human manifestation and his teaching of Srimad *Bhâgavad Gita* in the middle of the battlefield, explaining the righteous path of *dharma* and *kama*, and the path to liberation of soul or *moksha*. The *Bhâgavad Gita* or Lord's song is the New

Testament of India, revered next to the Vedas themselves and used in the law courts like the Bible or the Koran for the administration of oaths. It may be as old as 400 BC or as young as 200 AD.

Darsanas

Darsanas are the intellectual portions of Hindu writings which explain the meaning of the Vedas by different schools of philosophy as written by the sages. There are six main schools of *Darsanas*, or institutions of truth by six different rishis, who systemized the various teaching of the Vedas in their own ways and condensed their thoughts in the form of short aphorisms or *sutras*. These six systems of Hindu philosophy are the six ways of looking at the truth and belief in the authority of the Vedas. At the same time, there came six heterodoxical system of philosophy which do not accept the authority of the Vedas. They are the materialistic and Atheistic school of Charvaka and various system of schools of Jainas and Buddhists. The six *Darasanas* are *Nyaya* founded by Gauthama Rishi; *Vaiseshika* by Kanada Rishi; *Sankhya* by Kapil Muni; Yoga by Pathanjali Maharishi; *Purva Mimamsa* by Jaimini and *Utthara Mimamsa* or *Vedanta* by Badarayana or Vyasa. They are grouped into three pairs by their rationalistic method of approach: *Nyaya* and *Vaseshika; Sankhya* and *Yoga; Purva Mimamsa* and *Vedanta. Nyaya* and *Vaiseshika* give an analysis of the world of experience and explains how God has made all material things of different categories out of atoms and molecules and show the ways to attain knowledge of God. Sankhya provides a deep study of Hindu psychology as Kapil Muni was the father of psychology. *Yoga* systems deals with the ways to discipline the body, mind and the senses, control the thought waves with meditation, and to cultivate concentration of mind to reach the super-conscious state. Some of the teachings of these texts are opposed to the Vedas and to the philosophy of Vedantha. *Poorva Mimamsa* deals with *karma kanda* and stresses the importance of recitation of prayers and rituals as the most important duty to attain salvation. It stresses prayer to the natural forces of *prakriti* whose actions can be controlled by our prayers and Vedic rituals, and it effectively marginalizes the role of God. This theory was objected and corrected in *Vedantha Darsana* which deals with *jnâna-kânda* or knowledge aspects. It explains in detail the nature of Brahman or the Eternal Being, and shows that the individual soul is, in essence, identical with the Supreme Self. It deals with the methods to remove the veil of ignorance or *avidya* and merge in the ocean of Brahman. All these schools agree that the Vedas are a record of spiritual experiences and truths observed by seers, and the work of these systems of thought is to codify, interpret and reinforce them with logical arguments.

Sectarian Scriptures

The sectarian scriptures, related chiefly to the three main sects of *Shaivism, Vaishnavism,* and *Shâktism* are known as the *agamas* or *tantras*. They are composed of four parts, dealing with the philosophical beliefs, meditative exercises, the erection of temples and making of images, and their use in worship and, finally, the conduct.

The three strands of Vedanta which embrace the full spectrum of Hindu philosophy were best encapsulated by three great Hindu saints: Shankara, Ramanuja and Madhava; and amongst them they expounded the arguments on *advaita vedanta* (non-dualism), *vishishtadvaita vedanta* (qualified non-dualism) and *dvaita vedanta* (dualism). The *atmabodha* (knowledge of the self) was written by the 7th and 8th century saint, Shankara, whose literary works include devotional songs, commentaries on the scriptures, and prose and poetry illuminating scriptural concepts.

Bibliography

Aurobindo, *The Renaissance in India,* Calcutta, Arya Publishing House,1946.

Bhandarkar, R.G., *Vaishnavism, Shaivis, and minor Religious Systems. Strassbourg,* K.J. Trubner, 1913.

Edgerton, Franklin, *The Bhagavad Gita,* New York and Evanston, Harper and Row, 1944.

Organ, Troy W. , *Hinduism, Its Historical Development,* New York, Barron's Educational Series, Inc. 1974.

Otto, Rudolf, *India's Religion of Grace and Christianity Compared and Contrasted,* London, Student Christian Movement, 1930.

Ranade, R.D., *A Constructive Survey of Upanisadic Philosophy,* Poona, Oriental Book Agency, 1926.

Schrader, F.O., *Introduction to the Panchatantra and the Ahirbudhnya Samhita,* Madras, The Adyar Library, 1916.

Weber, Max, *The Religion of India,* New York, The Free Press, 1958.

Karambelkar, V.W., *The Athurva-Veda and the Ayur-Veda,* Nagpur, Nagpur University Press, 1961.

Keith, A.B., *The Religion and Philosophy of the Veda and Upanisads,* Harvard Oriental Series, nos. 31-32, 1925, Rpt. Delhi, Motilal Banarsidass, 1970.

Singh, Ram Pratap, *The Vedanta of Shankara,* Jaipur, Bharat Publishing House, 1949.

Chakravarti Rajagopalachari, *Upanishads,* Bombay, Bharatiya Vidya Bhavan, 1982.

Griffith, Ralph T.H., *The Hymns of the Rigveda,* 2 vols. Varanasi, Chowkhamba Sanskrit Series Office, 1971.

Buhler, Georg., *The Laws of Manu,* Delhi, Motilal Banarsidass, 1975.

Hume, Robert E., *The Thirteen Principal Upanisads,* 2nd rev. ed., New York, Oxford University Press, 1971.

Radhakrishnan, Sarvepalli, *The Principal Upanisads,* London, Allen & Unwin, 1953.

Zachner, R.C., *The Hindu Scriptures,* London, J.M.Dent & Sons, Ltd. 1966.

Subrahmanian N.S., *Encyclopaedia of the Upanisads,* New Delhi, Sterling Publishers Private Limited, 1990.

List of Scriptures and their Derivation from Vedas

I. SAMHITAS:

1. *Rigveda* Samhita, Sakala Sakha
2. Sukla Yajurveda Samhita
    Vajasaneyi Samhita, Kanava Sakha
    Madhyandina Sakha
3. *Krishna* Yajurvveda Samhita
    Taittiriya Sakha
    Kathaka Sakha
    Kapisthala Sakha
    Maitrayani Sakha
4. Samaveda Samhita
    Kauthuma/ Ranayaniya Sakha
    Jaiminiya Sakha
5. Athurvaveda Samhita
    Saunakiya Sakha
    Paippalada Sakha

II. BRAHMANAS

Of the Rigveda

1. Aitareya Brahmanas
2. Kausitaki or Sankhaayana Brahmana

Of the Yajurvveda

1. Satapatha Brahmana of Sukta Yajurvveda Kanva Sakha
2. Satapatha Brahmana of Sukta Yajurvveda Madhyandina Sakha
3. Taittiriya Brahmana of Krisna Yajurvveda

Of the Samveda

1. Tandyamaha or Pancavimsa Brahmana
2. Sadvimsa Brahmana
3. Samavidhana Brahmana
4. Arseya Brahmana
5. Devatadhayaya or Saivata
6. Samhitopanisad Brahmana
7. Mantra or Chandogya Brahmana
8. Vamsa Brahmana
9. Jaiminiya Brahmana
10. Jaiminiya Arseya Brahmana

Of the Athutvveda
1. Gopatha Brahmana

III. ARANYAKAS:
1. Aitareya Aranyaka of *Rigveda*
2. Kausitaki or Sankhaya Aranayaka of Rig veda
3. Taitkiriya Aranayaka of *Krishna* Yajurvveda
4. Maitrayanika Arenayaka of *Krishna* Yajurvveda

IV. UPANISHADS: There are 108 *Upanishads*

Of *Rigveda*
*1. Aitareya
*2. Kausitakibrahmana
3. Nadabindu
4. Atmabodha
5. Nirvana
6. Mudgala
7. Aksamalika
8. Tripura
9. Saubhagyaalaksmi
10. Bahvrca

Of Sukla Yajurvveda
*1. Isavasya
*2. *Brhadaranyaka*
3. Jabala
4. Hamsa
5. Paramahamsa
6. Subala
7. Mantrika
8. Niralamba
9. Trisikhibrahmana
10. Mandalabrahmana
11. Advayataraka
12. Paingala
13. Bhiksuka
14. Turiyatitavadhuta
15. Adhyatma
16. Tarasara
17. Yajnavalkya
18. Satyayaniya
19. Muktika

Of Krsna Yajurvveda

*1. Katha
*2. Taittiriya
 3. Brahma
 4. Kaivalya
*5. Svetasvatara
 6. Garbha
 7. Narayana
 8. Amrtabindu
 9. Amrtanada
10. Kalagnirudra
11. Ksurika
12. Saravasara
13. Sukarahasya
14. Tejobindu
15. Dhyanabindu
16. Brahmavidya
17. Yogatattya
18. Daksinamurti
19. Skanda
20. Sariraka
21. Yogasikha
22. Ekaksara
23. Avadhuta
24. Katharudra
25. Rudrahrdaya
26. Yogakundali
27. Pancabrahma
28. Pranagnihotra
29. Varaha
30. Kalisantarana
31. Sarasvatirahasya
32. Aksi

Of Samaveda

*1. Kena
*2. Chandogya
 3. Aruni
 4. Maitrayani (ya) or Maitri
*5. Maitreya
 6. Vajrasucika
 7. Vasudeva

8.   Matha
9.   Samnyasa
10. Avyakta
11. Kundika
12. Savitri
13. Darsana
14. Jabali
15. Yogacudamani
16. Rudraksajabala

Of Athurveda
*1. Prasna
*2. Mundaka
*3. Mandukya
4.   Atharvaskha
5.   Brhajjabala
6.   Nrsimhatapini (Purva and Uttara)
7.   Naradaparivrajaka
8.   Sita
9.   Sarabha
10. Tripadvibhutimahanarayana
11. Ramarahasya
12. Ramatapini (Purva and Uttara)
13. Sandilya
14. Paramahamsaparivrajaka
15. Annapurna
16. Surya
17. Atma
18. Pasupatabrahma
19. Parabrahma
20. Tripuratapini
21. Devi
22. Bhavana
23. Bhasmajabala
24. Ganapati
25. Mahavakya
26. Gopalatapini
27. Krsna
28. Hayagriva
29. Dattatreya
30. Garuda
31. Atharvasiras

* Principle *Upanishads*

Smriti:

Vedangas: *dharma* Sutras, Astronomy, Astrology, Grammar, Ritual Dharmsastras: Manu Smriti, Gautama Smriti, Yajnavalkya Smriti Upa-veda : Ayur-veda, Dhanur-veda, Sthaptya-veda . (Added to Veda) Nibandhas: Rituals, Domestic rites Puranas (18 Maha-Purana & 18 Upa-Purana): Agni, Bhagavata, Bhavishya, Brahma, Brahmanda, Brahmavaivarta, Garuda, Harivamsha, Kurma, Linga, Markandeya, Matsya, Narada, Padma, Skanda, Siva, Vamana, Varaha, Vayu, Vishnu.

Epics: 1

Ramayana, 2. Mahabharata (*Bhagavad Gita*) Darsanas :. Nyaya—Gautam Rishi, Vaiseshika—Kanada Rishi, Shankhya—Kapil Muni Yoga—Pathanjali Maharishi, Purva Mimansa—Jamini, Uttra Mimansa or Vedanta— Badarayan or Vyasa, Advaita—Shankara, Vushishtadvaita Vedanta— Ramanuja Dvaita Vedanta—Madhava Agamas : Saiva Agama, Vaishnava Agama, Shakti Agamas, Smartha Sampradaya Tantras: Mantras, yantras, Mandalas, Cosmograms, Mudra, Kundalini Power, Sexo-Yogi Excercises. Other Literatures: Patanjali, Yoga Sutras, Gitagovindam, Yoga Vashishtha, Kama Sutra, Panchatantra

Chapter 4

Bhagavad Gita
(The Divine Song)

The very first English translation was done by Charles Wilkins in 1785, with an introduction by Warren Hastings, the British Governor General of India. Now there are numerous English translation of Bhagavad *Gita* written both by Indian and Western writers.

The *Gita* never commands one what to do, instead it gives the *pros* and *cons* of every issue and final decision is left oneself. Throughout the *Gita*, you will not come across even one line starting with *thou shalt not.*

The beauty of *Bhagavad Gita* is that it requires of a man complete change of consciousness rather than changes in life-styles or in outward appearances. Always remember that after the great *Bhagavad Gita* discourse, Arjuna did not become a hermit, instead he fought a very fierce war annihilating all his enemies.

When Christian scriptures are talking about *permanent hell to sinners*, the *Bhagavad Gita* proclaims *salvation for all* in various couplets (*Gita* IV:36, IX:30, 32). All of us, whether we believe in God or not, are destined to attain salvation one day. Only the time factor differs for the best and worst among us. *Gita* exhorts: *The truth shall set you free.*

If you follow the teachings of the *Bhagavad Gita* in a very logical and scientific manner, you will achieve salvation, since the *Gita* contains the unwritten laws of the universe. On the other hand, if you read it with devotion to Lord *Krishna* and if you follow the *Gita* on devotional basis, still you will achieve salvation. Both, the intellectual way and the devotional way will lead you to God.

Bhagavad Gita has been commented upon by several commentators, by constructing the meaning word by word and sentence by sentence. *Gita* does not belong to one religion. It belongs to the entire humankind. *Bhagavad Gita* is a secular scripture preaching love, understanding and unity of all His creation. *Bhagavad Gita* is a book conveying lessons of philosophy, religion and ethics. It is not looked upon as *sruti* or a revealed scripture, but is regarded as a *smrti* or a tradition. Its message of deliverance is simple. The *Gita* teaches a method which is within the reach of all, that of *bhakti* or devotion to God. *Gita* also teaches the method of combined pursuit of *jñāna* or knowledge and *karma* or duty. Neither of them by itself leads to *moksa* or freedom from birth and death.

Sri *Krishna* taught us, through the *Bhagavad Gita*, the true essence of Vedic Hindu philosophy—*karsati sarvam Krishnah*—He who attracts all or arouses devotion in all is *Krishna*. *Vedantratnemanjusa* (p 52) says that *Krishna* is so called because He removes the sins of His devotees, *papam karsayati, nirmulayati*. *Krishna* is derived from *krs* to scrap, because He scrapes or draws away all sins and other sources of evil from His devotees. Hindu religion is the purport of the *Gita*, which is a narration by the Lord Himself. He explains the importance of one's duty to the society and the true meaning of religion and rituals, emphasized not to concentrate on rituals only but as the means of achieving the goal of uniting with God. He tells us of the oneness of the Divine Force (*Brahman*) in various forms and the unity of *Âtman* and Brahman (i.e., *Paramâtman*). The basic teachings of the Vedas and *Upanishads* on Hindu religious beliefs are told once again in the *Gita*.

The Sanskrit word is *vasudevsutum* (son of Vasudev). *Vasu* stands for that which sustains life of earth. Thus food, water, airs are *devatas* (divine forces or entities) because we get life from them. So *vasudev* means the lord of the *devatas*. *Suta* means a portion. *Âtman* (soul) is a part of the *Brahman*. Therefore by *vasudevasutum* we understand the *âtman*. Prayer or *mantra* of the salutation of Lord *Krishna* states, "*Oh Lord! Son of Vasudev the destroyer of Kansa and Chanoor, bestower of the supreme happiness of Devaki, my salutations unto Thee.*" Kansa and Chanoora represent as desire and anger, both destroyed by *Krishna*, similarly by means of knowledge of the self (*atmanjnan*) desire and anger can be eliminated.

In the battle field of Kurukshetra, when the battle between the righteous Pandavas and the wicked Kauravas was about to begin, Arjuna feared the consequences of the war and refused to take part in the fight or, in other words, refused to do his duty as a warrior. Arjuna typifies the representative human soul seeking to reach perfection and peace but, in the opening section, we find that his mind is clouded, his convictions unsettled, his whole consciousness confused. For every individual there comes an hour sometime or other, for nature is not in a hurry, when everything that he can do for himself fails, when he sinks into the gulf of utter darkness, an hour when he would give all that he has for one gleam of light, for one sign of the Divine. When he is assailed by doubt, denial, hatred of life and dark desire, he can escape from them only if God lays His hand on him. Thereupon Arjuna's friend and charioteer, *Krishna*, advised him to put himself entirely in the hands of God and discharge his duty as a soldier without caring for the consequences. Well, what applies to Arjuna applies to all of us. For every one of us has his or her own duties to act. *Krishna* says, "*Who performs the duty ordained by his own nature incurs no sin*" (*Gita* XVIII.

47). Further Lord *Krishna* said, "*He from whom all beings evolved and by whom all this is pervaded—by worshiping Him through the performance of his own duty, man attains perfection*" (*Gita* XVIII. 46). In other words, True worship consists in one's discharging one's own duties faithfully and efficiently. Symbolically, the battlefield represents our own mind. The Panadavas represent our good thoughts, and Kauravas the bad thoughts. The conflict between our good thoughts and bad thoughts is constantly going on in our own minds. The *Bhagavad Gita* teaches us a very powerful approach to deal with this conflict. Just like Arjuna, we should also surrender our good thoughts to The Almighty *Krishna*. If we allow ourselves to be guided by Him, we will begin to see the battle with a new perspective. The five horses of Arjuna represent our five senses. The chariot represents our body and the wheels of the chariot represent the connection of our body to the five senses. We should allow *Krishna*, the Divine Self, to be our charioteer and then brightness, beauty and peace will come to our present life as well as after death.

The essence of the *Bhagavad Gita* is the vision of God in all things and vice versa. It is the vision of Arjuna in the *Bhagavad Gita*: "*If a thousand suns suddenly arose in the sky, that splendour might be compared to the radiance of the Supreme Spirit.*" "*And Arjuna saw in that radiance the whole universe in its variety, standing in a vast unity in the body of the God of gods*" (*Gita* XI. 12-13).

The *Bhagavad Gita* is both metaphysic (*Brahmavidya*) and theistic philosophy (*Yoga sastra*), the science of reality and the art of union with reality. The *Gita* derives its main inspiration from the *Upanishads* and integrates into a comprehensive synthesis the different elements of the Vedic cult of sacrifice, the Upanishadic teaching of the Absolute *Brahman*, the *samkhya* dualism, and the *yoga* meditation.

I. THEOLOGY (Brahmavidya)

The *Bhagavad Gita* takes up the Upanishadic conception of *Brahman* as absolute reality. It develops the theistic side of the Upanishadic teaching by giving us God who exceeds the infinite and the mere finite. In *Gita* the Supreme is at once the transcendental, the cosmic and the individual reality. In its transcendental aspect the Supreme is the pure *self* unaffected by any action or experience, detached, and unconcerned. In its dynamic aspect, it not only supports but also governs the whole cosmic action. The same Supreme that is one in all and above all is present in the individual.

Krishna represents the Vishnu aspect of the Supreme. The *Gita* makes out that *Krishna* is an incarnation (*avatar*) or descent of the Divine into the human frame. The theory of the *avatar* is an eloquent expression of the law of the spiritual world. If God is looked upon as saviour of man, He must manifest Himself whenever the forces of evil threaten to destroy human values (*Gita* IV. 7-8).

(i) Soul and Body

All creatures are composed of two eternal and eternally distinct elements, the soul and the body. The body is material and is subject to evolution, devolution, and change of all sorts; and consists of a blend of various elements or qualities. The soul is immaterial, uniform, unchangeable, without qualities and inactive. All the actions are performed by the material body upon other material bodies or substances. The soul neither acts nor is affected by action; indeed it is not affected by an influence outside of itself. It has only contemplative powers. Ordinary persons, however, confuse completely about body and soul, and imagine that their souls act and suffer. The enlightened man realizes the true distinction between soul and body; his soul is thereby freed from the bondage of connection with the body, and he attains release (*moksha*) from the cycle of birth and death.

The soul is not a material limb or organ of the body. It is not located in any particular part of the body. It permeates through the body and mind. Unless the mind is clear, which is permeated will not assume a distinct form or become known. It is one thing to see external objects and understand, whereas it is altogether a different process to perceive an entity (soul) which is permeated and hidden in our own inner being. The imperceptibility is due to our passions.

The *Bhagavada Gita* begins with the problems of life by discriminating the soul from the elements of matter and proves by all reason and argument that the soul is indestructible in all circumstances and that the outer covering of matter, the body and the mind change for another term of material existence (life) which is full of miseries. *Krishna* instructs Arjuna that he should not grieve for the soul, because it is immortal and inaccessible to the sufferings that afflict the body. *"It is declared that these bodies come to an end; but the embodied (soul) in them are eternal, indestructible, and unfathomable" (Gita II. 18). "The soul is not born, nor does it ever die; nor, once come into being, shall he ever more cease to be. Unborn, eternal, everlasting yet most ancient, soul does not die when the body is dead" (Gita II. 20). "Swords cut him not, fire burns him not, water wets him not, wind dries him not. The human soul is eternal, omnipresent, fixed, immovable, everlasting" (Gita II, 23, 24).* The soul is absolutely unitary, undifferentiated and without qualities; not subject to any change or alteration, and not participating in any action. Material nature (body) or the non-soul, is what performs all acts. It assumes many forms, and is constantly subject to change.

The variety of material nature (body) is expressed in two ways. First, it is composed of three elements called *gunas*, (i.e. 'qualities') namely, *sattva*, 'goodness, purity'; *rajas*, 'passion, activity'; and *tamas*, 'darkness, dullness, inactivity.' Mingled in varying proportions, these three 'gunas' or qualities make up all matter. Preponderance of one another of them decides the character of any given part of material nature (*Gita* XIV 5-18; Chapter XVIII). However, material nature includes the 'mental' faculties of living beings, particularly of man. This is made clear in one passage in the *Gita* (*Gita* XIII. 5,6). "Goodness (*sattva*), activity and passion (*rajas*), and darkness (tamas), these gunas, springing from material nature, the immortal soul is bound in the body" (*Gita* XIV. 5). It is only the unenlightened man to whom they can bind. When one attains true enlightenment, that is, realization of the true nature of the soul and matter and their fundamental independence of each other, then, by virtue of this perfect, mystic knowledge he attains release; his soul transcends the matter and is freed from it for good and all, and he is freed from the chain of rebirths. *"Who thus understands the soul and material nature (body) together with the gunas of the body, in whatever state he may be, he is not (to be) born again" (Gita XIII.23). "The embodied (soul) transcending these three gunas (of matter) that spring from the body, freed from birth, death, old age and sorrow, attains immortality" (Gita XIV.20). "Mentally abandoning all actions, the Embodied (Soul) sits at peace, in control, in his nine-door citadel (the body), and neither acts nor causes action at all" (Gita V.13).*

What is, then the function of the soul? It "beholds" the activities of matter, passively, and without participation. *"Passively in the sense that it is affected by them, for its true fundamental nature is just as free from the effects of action as from its performance".* *"The Lord (the soul) does not receive (i.e. reap the fruit of) any one's sin, nor yet (of) his good deeds" (V. 15). Elsewhere the soul is called the "knower" of matter: "This body is called the field (kshetra). He who knows it (the soul), and who knows the truth is called the Field-knower (kshetrajna)" (XIII. 1).* The soul, then, merely looks on and "knows" matter and it acts, but has no real connection with them.

(ii) The Nature of GOD

How does God fit into this system? Is He a sort of third principle, higher than the other two and distinct from them? So we are told at times, perhaps most clearly in the following passage: *"There are two spirits here in the world, a perishable and an imperishable one. The perishable* (i.e. material nature or body) *is of all beings. The imperishable* (i.e. the soul, spirit) *is called the immovable* (unchangeable)". *"But there is another, a supreme Spirit, called the Highest Soul, Paramâtman, the Eternal Lord who pervades into the three worlds and supports them" (XV. 16, 17). "(Five) Senses are superior to the physical body; superior to the senses is mind; superior to the mind is the intellect (Buddhi); superior to intellect is He (God)" (III. 42).*

The essential part, the fundamental element in everything, is after all One— God. Lord *Krishna* said, *"There is nothing else that is higher than I am (beyond, outside Me); this All is strung like necklaces of pearls upon a string on Me." (VII. 7) "All things and all beings have emanated from Him and subsist in Him" (IX. 4). "Also the seed of all beings, that am I. There is no being, moving or motionless, that is without Me" (X. 39). I am the taste in water, the light in the moon and sun, the sacred syllable Om in all the Vedas, sound in the ether, strength in men. The goodly odour in the earth am I, and brilliance in the fire; I am life in all beings, and austerity in ascetics. Know Me as the eternal seed of all creatures. I am the intelligence of the intelligent, the majesty of the majestic" (VII. 8-10). The splendour of the sun that illumines the whole world and the splendour that is in the moon and in fire, know that to be My splendour. Entering the earth, I support (all) beings by My power; becoming the juicy soma, I make all plants to grow. Becoming fire (as the principle of digestion, as a 'cooking' by bodily heat) I enter into the bodies of animate creatures, and, joining with the upper and lower breaths, I digest their food of all four kinds. I have entered into the heart of every man; from Me come memory, knowledge and disputation (in reasoning). I am the object of the (sacred) knowledge of all the Vedas, I am the author of the Vedanta (the Upanishads) and I am too and the sole knower of the Veda"* (XV. 12-15). So, of course, God is repeatedly declared to be the Creator, Supporter, Ruler of all, that is, the origin and dissolution of the universe, (VII. 6) "both death that carries off all and the origin of creatures that are to be," (X. 34) "both immortality and death, both the existent and the non-existent," (IX. 19) "the beginning and the middle and the end of beings" (X. 20, 32).

God is the animating principle in everything; it is He that "makes the wheels" of the universe "go around," that acts in all natural activities and processes: "The lord resides in the hearts of all beings and makes all beings go around by His mysterious power (*maya*), as if they were fixed on a (revolving) machine (that is, probably, like puppets in a puppet-play) (XVIII. 61). *"When dharma declines and adharma gains strength, God manifests Himself to protect the community"* (IV. 7-8).

(iii) Rebirth

In emphasizing the immortality of the soul he compares the successive lives of an individual to successive states (childhood, maturity, old age) in one life, or to changes of garments: *"As in this body childhood, young age, manhood, and old age come to the Embodied (Soul), so It goes to other bodies. The wise man is not confused in this"* (II. 13). *"As, laying aside worn-out garments, a man takes on other, new ones, so laying aside worn-out bodies the Embodied (Soul) enters into other, new ones"* (II. 22).

The rebirth is called "the home (or source) of misery" (VIII. 15). What results in its prolongation is, therefore, evil; what leads to release from the cycle of the rebirth which is or should be the chief aim of man. He who has obtained this release goes to the perfect state, *nirvana*.

When it comes to the details of the theory of the rebirth and release from it, the Hindu systems are less unanimous, in spite of certain family resemblance. Common to all of them is the doctrine of 'karma' or 'action, deed,' according to which, generally speaking, any action done must have its result, good or bad according to its moral quality, for the doer. It follows from this that in order to get rid of the chain of reincarnation, one must somehow or the other be released or excused from the normally inevitable consequences of his actions—even good ones. Otherwise, any action done must have its fruit in continued existence.

While different thinkers differ in their visualization of the supreme truth, by knowing which man should gain salvation, *the Gita* refers several times to such differences of method. In one passage it tells us that *"some by meditation come to* behold the self (soul, *âtman*) in the self by the self; others by the *samkhya* yoga or discipline of knowledge, and others by the discipline of action (*karma yoga*). But some others, while not having this knowledge, hear it from others and devote themselves to it; even they too cross over death, by devoting themselves to what is revealed" (XIII. 24, 25). According to this, true knowledge—here spoken of as knowledge of the *âtman*, the Self or Soul, may be gained in various ways: first, by inner meditation; then, by what is called the *samkhya* discipline; and by the "discipline of action;" and fourthly, by instruction from others, if one cannot attain it by himself. All these methods are possible; all lead to salvation, to "crossing over death," which implies also escape from rebirth, since rebirth leads to redeath.

According to Kathopanishad (II. 23, 24), "*Realization does not come by much study or by learned discussions. It comes to one whose self yearns for realization. It cannot come by mere knowledge to one whose mind has not turned away from evil and has not learnt to control itself and to be at peace with the world.*"

II. THEISTIC PHILOSOPHY (Yoga Sâstra)

The *yoga sâstra* is a discipline. It derived from the root, *yuj*, to bind together, *yoga* means binding one's psychic powers, balancing and enhancing them (*Gita* XIV. 21). The different *yogas* are special application of the inner discipline that lead to the liberation of the soul and a new understanding of the unity and meaning of humankind. Everything that is related to this discipline is called yoga, such as *jñâna-yoga* or the way of knowledge, *bhakti-yoga* or way of devotion, *karma-yoga* or the way of action. Sri Rajagopalachari once said, "*Gita is not a book for study and score marks in the examination. The book that tells men, how to regulate their activities and their minds. The Gita* is a comprehensive *yogasâstra* (treatise on yoga). *Yoga* is the name given in the *Gita* to efforts at self-improvement or discipline. *Yoga* is an effort to purify one's character. This theistic scripture gives the three fold path for salvation and gives us a religion where God is loved and not feared. These paths and the goal of union with God may be attained either by (i) *samkhya yoga* or *jñâna yoga* (the way of knowledge), (ii) *karma yoga* (the way of disciplined activities) or (iii) *bhakti yoga* (the way of devotion). Knowledge, action and devotion are complementary in both ways when we seek the goal and after we attain it. We may climb the mountain from different paths but the view from the summit is the same for all.

(i) The Way of Knowledge or Samkhya Yoga or Jñâna Yoga

Samkhya discipline is elsewhere also called the *jñâna-yoga* or discipline of knowledge. *Samkhyayoga* favours renunciation of all "works," of all activities. Some wisemen say that all actions are evil and should be abandoned (XVIII. 3). Such people choose the path of world-renouncing asceticism. To escape from the effects of action, namely continued existence, they propose simply not to act or to come as nearer to that ideal as possible.

Vedas and *Upanishads* have theorized that by perfect knowledge man can control his destiny; that the truth shall make him free. In *Gita*, Sri *Krishna* stated: *"Even the most sinful person can attain salvation in this life and even immediately if he resolves never to commit sin but only to attain salvation of self-realization. The sins of such person of firm resolve, perish in no time"* (IV. 36). The Lord further expounds, *"Even if a man of the most vile conduct worships Me with exclusive devotion, he must be regarded as righteous for he has rightly resolved and he attains eternal peace"* (IX. 30-31). *"As a kindled fire burns firewood to ashes, so the fire of knowledge burns all deeds to ashes"* (IV. 37) that is, frees man from rebirth, the effect of deeds. Doubt, the opposite of knowledge, is fatal; the ignorant doubter cannot hope for bliss (IV. 40). Man must "cut doubt with the sword of knowledge" (IV. 41, 42). He who knows God as unborn and beginningless is purged of all sins (X. 3). Knowledge is better than mere ritual religion: *"Better than material sacrifice is the sacrifice (that consists) of knowledge. All actions (karma) without the remainder are completely ended in knowledge"* (IV. 33). What Knowledge? The knowledge of the supreme religious truth which each system professes to teach. Thus, in the *Gitâ* it is most often the knowledge of God. Whosoever knows the mystic truth of God's nature is freed from rebirth and goes to God (IV. 9, 10/VII. 19/X/ 3/XIV. 1). When one realizes his identity with God, he has no affinity at all for the entire world including his body and mind, etc. So there is no question of the birth of evils such as desire and anger in him. If a striver has desire and anger even in their subtle forms, he should not consider himself a liberated soul (V. 23). But elsewhere it is, for instance, the knowledge of the absolute separateness of soul and body, the independence of the soul from the body and all its acts and qualities which brings release from rebirth (V. 16, 17).

The devotee following the discipline of knowledge discriminates between the real and the unreal. The real is eternal, all pervading, unchanging, immovable, unmanifest and unthinkable while the unreal is transitory, kaleidoscopic, movable and always undergoes modifications. Thus a devotee following the discipline of knowledge isolates himself from *prakrti* (matter) and its evolutes and realizes the Self in the self. God can be known only by the Self. To explain the existence of God, two kinds of adjectives—in the negative and in the positive—are given. The negative adjectives—imperishable, indefinable, unmanifest, unthinkable, immovable, unlimited show that God is different from *prakrti* (matter) while the positive adjectives such as omnipresent, uniform, eternal, and nouns (truth, consciousness and bliss or *Satchitânand*) show the Lord's independent existence (XII. 3-4). A striver following the path of knowledge cannot attain perfection merely by learning 'All is Brahman' so long as he has attachment in his mind, i.e. he possesses evil propensities such as desire (lust and anger, etc.). The devotees who worship attributeless and formless Brahman have evenness of mind in all persons and objects because they hold Him pervading everywhere as He is equanimous (V. 19).

In the scriptures, there are eight inward spiritual means to attain knowledge. They are: (1) discretion, (2) dispassion, (3) six traits (tranquilizing, self control, piety, detachment, endurance and composure), (4) desire to attain salvation, (5) hearing of Vedantic texts, (6) cognition, (7) constant and profound meditation, and (8) self-realization. Discretion (*vivek*) provides the ability to distinguish the real from the unreal. Renunciation of unreal or having a detachment from worldly affairs is called dispassion (*vairâgya*). Deviation of the mind from the senses is tranquilizing (*sama*). Control over the senses is *dama*. Reverence for God and the scriptures is called piety (*sradhâ*). Total detachment from the world is *uparati*. Forbearance in the pairs of opposites such as heat and cold is endurance (*titiksâ*). Freedom from doubts is composure (*samâdhâna*). The desire for salvation is called *mumuksutâ*. When the desire for salvation is aroused, a striver having renounced material objects and actions goes to the learned, God-realized preceptor. He hears the Vedantic text which removes his doubts. Then he thinks of the reality about God that is known cognition (*manana*). If he holds that the world is real and God does not exist—this is the opposite conception. Removal of this contrary conception is called constant and profound meditation. When he having renounced affinity for all the material objects, gets established in the Self, it is called self-realization. In fact, all these spiritual disciplines are practiced in order to renounce the affinity for the unreal. The renunciation is not for one's own self but the result of renunciation (God-realization) is for one's own self.

There are passages in the *Gita* itself which recommend ascetic methods, such as carefully regulating the breath, fixing the eyes on a spot between the eyebrows, avoiding the 'external contacts' of the senses with the objects of sense, holding in check the senses, the organ of thought, and the consciousness or will, and so devoting oneself solely to emancipation (V. 27, 28). *"Arranging for himself in a clean place a steady seat that is neither too high nor too low, and that is covered with a cloth and a dear-skin and kusa grass, there he should concentrate his mind, restraining the activities of his thoughts and his senses, and taking his place upon the seat should practice discipline unto self-purification. Holding his body, head and neck even and motionless, he should steadfastly gaze at the tip of his nose and not look to one side or another. Abiding in the vow of chastity, soul at peace and free from fear, restraining his mind, his thoughts fixed on Me (God), the disciplined man should sit absorbed in Me"* (VI. 10-14).

The wise striver following the Discipline of Knowledge who has realized the truth that all actions are performed by *prakrti* (nature) has no affinity for them, he is merely a witness of the activities of the senses (V. 8-9). Further a *tattvavit* (knower of the truth) is he who thinks that he (the self) is not the doer, he is different from the body, senses, mind, intellect and life-breath which perform the activities. A *sâmkhya yogi* becomes neither a doer himself nor does he make others doers. As he is not in the least attached to the body, senses, mind and intellect he cannot regard the actions done by them as his (V. 13). The Lord further pointed out the same fact when he declares, *"The man who knows the truth thinks that he does nothing at all"* (V. 8). The Lord also declares, *"The Supreme Self dwelling in the body does not act"* (XIII. 31). In fact, the *Gita*, like the *Upanishads*, tends to promise complete emancipation to one who "knows" any particularly profound religious or philosophic truth which it sets forth.

(ii) The Way of Disciplined Activities or Karma Yoga

"... better than knowledge is meditation; better than meditation is renunciation of the fruit of action; peace immediately follows renunciation." After we have attained knowledge, we can rise to the stage of meditation. Meditation is absorption in the spiritual Truth. The mind ceases to flit helter-skelter from desire to desire. Thus, meditation is the application of knowledge. There is no point acquiring knowledge if we then pay no heed to its application. Most of us are in a constant state of disturbed action. We are worried about the future fruits we might achieve or those in the past that we did not. Our minds are never on the single point of the present. We are never at peace. A striver following the discipline of action need not go to the great persons who have realized the truth nor has he to practice any other spiritual discipline in order to gain knowledge. Thus *karma yoga* (the discipline of action) as the means of Self-realization has been eulogized (IV. 38). A striver should remain equanimous during the performance or non-performance of actions. When a striver realizes the three facts that nothing is his, nothing is for him and nothing is to be done for him, he attains the state of total evenness of mind.

In the discipline of action, the renunciation of the sense of mine is important, while in the discipline of knowledge the renunciation of 'egoism' is important. If the striver renounces one of them, the other one is automatically renounced. In the discipline of action, first there is renunciation of the sense of mine and then the renunciation of egoism naturally follows, while in the discipline of knowledge, the order is reversed. If a striver has no desire for fruit, new attachment does not spring up, and old attachment perishes when actions are performed for the welfare of others. Thus, he becomes totally dispassionate. This discipline turns all action into inaction.

In general, the *Gita* is opposed to asceticism or to renunciation of action as such. The *Gita* provides a religious justification for continuing an approximately normal human life. Therein lies its strength. It does not ask the impossible, and yet it furnishes religious inspiration. It holds out the hope of salvation on terms which are not out of reach of the great mass of humankind. It provides for its scheme of salvation a philosophic background, based on commonly accepted Hindu postulates.

Gita reminds us that in the back of action lies *desire or passion* (either positive or negative, i.e. 'love' or 'hate'). It is passion that leads to actions, as we are told in the *Upanishads*, and still more emphatically in Buddhism and other classical Hindu systems. It is this that makes men interested in the results of action, it is desire, rather than action, which is man's enemy, and against which the preacher of religion must contend (III. 34, 37).

If a man acts unselfishly, without interested in the result, it leaves him free. *"The wise call him intelligent whose all undertakings are free from desire and purpose, whose actions are consumed in the fire of knowledge. Abandoning attachment to the fruits of action, ever content, independent, he performs no act whatsoever even when he sets out to act. Free from wishes, with controlled thoughts and soul, abandoning all possessions, and performing only acts of the body (not acting with the mind; that is, not feeling interest in his actions), he does not incur guilt. Contented of getting what comes by chance, superior to the 'pairs' of opposites, as pain and pleasure, heat and cold, and the like, free from jealousy, indifferent to success or failure, even when he acts he is not bound. Rid of attachment, free, his mind fixed in knowledge, acting only as performing a religious duty, all his acts are destroyed, that is, there is no binding effect"* (IV. 19-23). Therefore, one should act without interest in the result of the action, without desire or hate. *"He should not be delighted at attaining pleasure, nor should him be distressed at attaining pain"* (V. 20). He should hold alike pleasure and pain, gain and loss, victory and defeat (II.38).

The true ascetic (*sanyasi*), according to *Gita*, is he who 'renounces' not actions, but selfish interest in actions: *"Renunciation of actions due to desires is what the sages told to be (true) renunciation. Abandonment of the fruits of all actions the wise call (true) abandonment"* (XVIII. 2). Moreover, the ascetic (*sanyasi*) position is an impossible one, since *complete* cessation of action is out of the question; he who lives *must* act (III. 8; XVIII. 11). God Himself acts, though of course unselfishly; and of course He cannot be bound by action (III. 20-25; IV. 14; IX. 9). Without His action the world would not run; He keeps the universe going and thus sets an example, thus Himself setting an example for the common herd (III. 20).

"The disciplined man, renouncing the fruit of action, gains final blessedness. The undisciplined, because he acts willfully (or, according to his lusts), being attached to the fruits of action, is bound" (V. 12). If one practices this sort of disciplined activity even imperfectly, that is, without completely realizing it in life, still the effect of it is not lost but continues in future births, bringing man ever nearer and nearer to full attainment, until at last, by perfection in discipline, salvation is gained (VI. 37-45). Disciplined activity is superior not only to the "way of knowledge" but also to asceticism and to orthodox ritual religion (VI. 46).

In fact, performance of duty needs no effort, it is performed automatically. However, when a man does action for himself with egoism, attachment, desire and the sense of 'mine', it involves effort (strain). Therefore, *Krishna* said, "The action which involves strain (effort) is said to be of the nature of *passion*" (VIII. 24).

This human body has been bestowed upon us so that we may practice *karmayoga*. Nevertheless we are so much absorbed in hankering after pleasures, prosperity and honour, etc., that we do not pay heed to it. Thus it has been lost because we have forgotten it.

Everyone can easily assume that whatever he possesses is not his own but is acquired, as he has acquired the body from parents, education and knowledge from the preceptor, and so on. It means that every man, even the richest one, has depended on others in one way or the other all his possessions because has acquired them from others. This is known as *karmayoga*. No one is dependent and is unable to follow it (*karmayoga*).

In fact duty is that which can be performed easily, which must be performed and by performing which a man attains his aim. A man is not responsible for the performance of the action that he cannot perform. What is forbidden must not be done. When a person does not perform forbidden actions, either he does nothing or he performs the prescribed actions. Duty is always performed for the welfare of others without expecting any reward. The actions with the expectation of reward should not be performed because they lead to bondage. But it does not mean that actions performed without any aim cannot be performed by anyone except an insane person. There is vast difference between fruit (reward) and aim. Reward is perishable while aim is eternal. A man's aim is to attain God. He cannot realize God without performing his duty in a disinterested manner. He cannot do his duty while he indulges in the reward for actions, heedlessness and indolence, etc.

Gita teaches how one can remain without being bound by the result of one's work. Every one must do his allotted duty without being swayed by the consideration. One has to perform his duty whether it is to one's liking or not, neither seeking pleasure nor avoiding pain. By this way of doing one's work, it becomes a true renouncement of activity and makes union with God possible.

The idea is that internal joys are the only true ones; external joys, that is, those that result from the senses through external stimulants, are both transitory and illusory. *"With soul unattached to outside contacts, when he finds joy in the Self, his soul disciplined with the discipline of (i.e. that leads to) Brahman, he attains eternal bliss. For the enjoyments that spring from (outside) contacts are nothing but sources of misery; they are transitory; the wise man finds no pleasure in them. He who even in this life, before being freed from the body, can control the excitement that springs from desire and vengeance, he is disciplined, he is blessed. Who so finds his joy, his delight, and his illumination within, he, the disciplined, becomes the Brahman, and goes to the nirvana of Brahman"* (V. 21-24).

The characteristic of the "disciplined" followers of *yoga* is the moderation in all things. *"There is no discipline in him who eats too much, not yet in him who fasts completely; neither in him who indulges in too much sleep, nor yet in him who sleeps not at all"* (VI. 16).

"Ignorant one, not the wise, say that *samkhya* and *karma yoga* are different. One who devotes himself only to one of these two obtains completely the fruit of both. The goal that is obtained by the followers of *samkhya* is also reached by the followers of *karmayoga*, who so looks upon *samkhya* and *karmayoga* as one has true vision" (V. 4, 5). "Renunciation of action (the way of knowledge or the *samkhya* way) and discipline of action (*karmayoga*) both lead to supreme happiness" (V. 2).

Yet the same verse of which was just quoted a part goes on to say: "But of these two, discipline of action (*karmayoga*) is better than renunciation of action (*karma-sanyasa*)" (V. 2). And the reason, which is given a few verses later, is very interesting. "Renunciation, however, without discipline (*yoga*) is hard to attain. The sage who is disciplined in discipline quickly (easily) goes to the Brahman" (V. 6). Again, we find the *Gita* looking for the "easy way" to salvation. It allows validity to the severe, more toilsome paths of pure knowledge with ascetic renunciation of all activities, but only a few can travel that road.

(iii) The Way of Devotion to GOD or Bhakti Yoga

The *Bhakti mârga* or the path of devotion indicates the law of the right activity of the emotional side of man. *Bhakti* is emotional attachment distinct from knowledge (*jñâna*) or action (*karma*). This is a still "easier way of gaining salvation, and is most favoured of all in the *Gita*, although it is at times spoken of as bringing man to salvation indirectly by perfecting him in 'knowledge' or 'discipline' By filling his being with love of God, and doing all acts as a service to the god, man attains union with Him; that is, salvation. Sometimes God is spoken of as Himself intervening to help his devotees toward this goal. Devotion to the Supreme is possible only with a personal God, a concrete individual full of bliss and beauty. We cannot love a shadow of our minds. There is the personal need for a personal helper. The devotee "looks only on the object of his devotion, talks only about Him and thinks only of Him" (Nârada Sutras, 55). Whatever he does he does for the glory of God. His work is absolutely unselfish, since it is indifferent to its fruits. The devotee throws himself entirely on the mercy of God. Absolute dependence is the only way. Even Lord *Krishna* says, "*Merge thy mind in Me, be My devotee, prostrate thyself before Me, thou shalt come even to Me. I pledge thee My troth, thou art dear to Me. Abandoning all dharmas, come unto Me alone for shelter; sorrow not, I will liberate thee from all sins*" (Gita, XVIII: 64-66). The Lord insists on undivided devotion, cast away all forms of insufficiency and transform all into His infinite light and purity of the universal good.

For true *bhakti*, we require first of all *sraddhâ* or faith. The highest reality has to be assumed or taken on faith till it reveals itself in the devotee's consciousness (*Gita*, IV: 40). Since faith is a vital element, the gods in whom the people have faith are tolerated. Absolute devotion to God is not possible unless we give up our desires for sense objects.

The *Upanishads* taught that "knowledge" of the First Principle of the universe would lead to salvation. The First Principle of the universe is God, declares the *Gita*. It follows that knowledge of God is what brings salvation. Freedom from rebirth comes from attainment with the God (VIII.16).

Knowledge, however, whether of Brahman or of a person, God is *'hard to attain'* (VII.3,19; VIII.14). The difficulties of the intellectual method are emphasized in many places in the *Gita*. Easier for most of mankind is a more emotional scheme of salvation. This is what the *Gita* furnishes by its famous doctrine of *bhakti,* 'devotion' or 'love of God.'

The notion of *bhakti* , or devotion, enters into its scheme of salvation by a side door, without at first displacing the old intellectual theory of salvation by knowledge. At least it is rationalized in this way. It is represented that by devoted love of God one can attain knowledge (of God), and by bringing the way of devotion (*Bhakti yoga*) in our daily life actions it becomes *karmayoga*. So, indirectly, salvation comes through the way of disciplined activities (*karmayoga*) and the way of knowledge (*samkhya yoga*). "By devotion one comes to know Me, what my measure is and what I am in very truth; Then, knowing Me in very truth, he straightway enters into Me" (XVIII.55).

The starting point of prayer is either greed or fear. At some point, we have to bring devotion (*bhakti*) into our prayer. The more we are able to bring out the quality of devotion into our prayer, fear and greed fade away and are replaced by devotion. From devotion-oriented prayers, the next aspect realized is the formless form of God.

The *Gita* speaks of devotion as the immediate and all-sufficient way to final union with God. *"Whatever form a devotee seeks to worship with faith, God will stabilize his faith in that form for him"* (IX.25). *Krishna* says: *"If any worshiper shows reverence with faith to any god, I make his faith firm, and in that faith he reverences his god and gains his desires, for it is I who bestow them"* (VII. 21-22). *"Fix thy mind and devotion on Me; worship Me and revere Me. Thou shall come even to Me by thus disciplining thy soul in full devotion to Me"* (IX.34). *"Fix thy thought-organ on Me alone, let thy consciousness sink in Me, and thou shall come to dwell even in Me from now on; of that there is no doubt"* (XII.8; VIII.7; II.55). Even wicked men quickly become righteous and attain salvation through devotion to God; even low-caliber men and women may be saved in the same way; "no devotee of God is lost" (IX.30-32).

"But those who, laying all actions upon Me, intent on Me, meditate on Me and rever Me with utterly unswerving devotion, for them I speedily become the Saviour from the ocean of the round of (rebirths and) deaths, because their thoughts are fixed on Me" (XII.6,7). Therefore one should "abandon all (other) duties (or, religious practices or systems)" and make God his sole refuge; then *"I will save thee from all evils; be not grieved!"* (XVIII.66;IX.22).

A man who is the follower of divine love sees the Lord everywhere. Lord *Krishna* said, "*He sees Me present in all beings and all beings existing in Me*" (VI.30). "*He (the Yogi) through engaged in all forms of activities, dwells in Me*" (VI.31). When there is full devotion, the devotee in the form of service merges into the master and only the master (God) remains. A devotee should first have a determination that beyond ignorance there is an unaltered-One who is the illuminator, base and inspirer of all the beings. Then he should love Him from his heart. By doing so, his mind will be concentrated on Him naturally. The Lord said that the devotee sees Him in all persons, animals, birds, gods, demons, inanimate things, incidents and circumstances. When a devotee sees God everywhere, God also sees him everywhere. Thus, he is never out of his sight.

God accepts the humblest offering of His devotees, taking it in the spirit in which it is meant: "*Whoever offers Me, with devotion (bhakti) a leaf, a flower, a fruit, or a sip of water, I accept that, the pious offering of the pure in heart*" (IX.26). The Lord is satisfied with whatever little object is available for worship. In truth, we only need sincere devotion to gain access to the Lord. He accepts the offerings of His devotees as symbols of love and devotion.

We are given to understand that God may be reached (and this implies complete emancipation) in several ways. First, we are commanded to sink our hearts completely in loving devotion to God. "*However, if thou cannot fix thy thoughts steadfastly on Me, then seek to win Me by discipline of practice (i.e., by Karma yoga or disciplined activity). If incapable even of practice, be wholly devoted to work for Me; by doing actions for My sake thou shall also win perfection. But if thou art unable even to do this, resorting to My discipline then make abandonment of all fruits of action controlling thyself*" (that is, act unselfishly, as set forth in Chapter VII), (XII.9-11). The way of devotion is the favourite one to Lord *Krishna* but he admits the validity of other ways too, if for personal reasons a man finds them preferable.

It is particularly important that man should fix his mind on God at the hour of death; this has a special tendency to bring the soul of the dying man to God. Accordingly, the *Gita* does not hesitate to promise this result to one who meditates on God during death: "*He who at the hour of his death passes out and leaves his body while meditating on Me alone, goes to My state; of this there is no doubt*" (VIII.5). "*Pronouncing the single (sacred) syllable* **OM**, *which is, Brahman, thinking upon Me, he who (thus) leaves the body and dies goes to the highest goal*" (VIII.10, 13). Who can remember the name of God at the time of death? Lord *Krishna* further explained, "*Those, who realize Me in the life of the world or matter (adhibhuta), and in Brahmâ (adhidaiva) as a pure Divinity (adhiyajna), keeping their mind steady (steadfast) realize Me at the hour of death*" (VII.30). The concentration of mind on God at the time of death is a tedious task which can be accomplished only by one who has a full command over his life breath and mind.

Devotion is the focus of the *Bhagavata Purana*. The *Bhagavata Mahatmya* which forms part of the *Padam Purana* relates a dialogue between Narada and *Bhakti* in the form of a young woman on the bank of the Yamuna where she was sitting in great distress nursing her two sons (*Jñâna* or knowledge and *Virâgya* or renunciation) who looked old. Narada advised her as follows, "Why should you be so afflicted with worry? Think of the lotus feet of Sri *Krishna* and your misery will be gone. The celebrared Sri *Krishna* saved Draupadi from the tyranny of the Kauravas and the pretty girls of Vraja. You *Bhakti,* as a matter of fact, is dearer to the Lord than His own life. All this simply amounts to saying that devotion is the way *par excellence*—that it is the key-road, which controls all other roads to salvation.

Bibliography

Edgerton, F., *The Bhagavad Gita*. Cambridge, Harvard University Press, 1981.

Radhakrishanan, S., *The Bhagavad Gita*, 2nd ed. New York, Harper & Row, 1973.

Zaechner, R.C., *The Bhagavad Gita*, London, Oxford University Press, 1969.

(The above three books present three distinct points of views, Western philosophy, Advaita Vedanta and Christian theology, respectively.)

Aiyar, C.V.R., *Sri Sankara's Gita Bhashya*, Bombay, Bharatiya Vidya Bhavan, 1988.

Swami Prabhupâda, A.C.B., *The Bhagavad Gita*, As It is. Los Angles, The Bhaktivedanta Book Trust, 1985.

Swami Ramsukhadas, *Srimad Bhagavad Gita*, Sâdhaka Sanjvani. Gorakhapur. India, *Gita* Press.

Chapter 5

The Law of Karma or Action

*K*arma is usually translated in English as work, but it has a much wider and
deeper significance. In Sanskrit, term *karma* means volitional action, though
that still does not give a true picture of what *karma* is. Whatever we think, know,
watch, imagine or remember is all *karma* as long as it is deliberately or knowingly
done. If you sit or lie down intentionally in order to avoid doing work, this is
also *karma*. But we would not call it work. If we deliberately use any of the
factors in the human personality, as long as it is volitional, it is *karma*.
Involuntary and instinctive activities carried on in the human system are not
called *karma*, such as autonomic and reflex actions. While sitting, we breath and
digest our foods involuntarily, so it is not included in *karma*. If something is
brought very close to your eyes, your eyelid will automatically close, it is a reflex
action so it is not *karma*.

No human being can escape unceasing activity. Even thinking is a subtle
form of action. Action by itself is neutral. It is the will or the motive behind the
action that makes it good, bad or different or *satyavik, rajasik and tamasik*. This can
be illustrated by simple examples. Once an emperor of Chola dynasty went to
inspect a temple under construction. He asked the workers, 'What are you
doing?' The first one replied, 'Sir! I am cutting stone.' The second worker
answered, 'Sir! I am earning my living.' The third worker said, 'Sir! I am building
a great temple.' For the same action of cutting stones for the temple, the language
of each worker change in character in accordance with the motives behind the
action. Whatever you may be doing, it does not matter as long as you are doing it
with inner dedication and devotion. Another example, an old lady has some
heavy luggage on a station platform. A youngman picks up the luggage and puts
her in a train to reach her destination. This action is a noble act of service.
Suppose a porter puts her luggage in a train for a fee, then this action is no longer
called a service rendered by the porter. Take a third case where a person grabs
and runs away with the luggage. This act becomes criminal. This illustrates how
one's state of mind affects the quality of one's action. It is only a person with a
divine mind who can function *sâtyavik*.

Karma implies self-determination; it is *karma* that distinguishes human beings from all other creatures in the world. There is no *karma* on the sub-human level, because their all actions are either instinctive, involuntary or reflexive. There is no self-determination. Only the conscious, deliberate activities of human beings are signified by the word *karma*. According to the *Gita* also, the activities undertaken by the body, speech or mind are also regarded as actions (*Gita* XVIII.15). Only those actions, whether physical or mental to which a person is attached lead him to bondage. But unattached work is the best and not a cause of bondage. One should perform his mundane duty also very promptly without being attached to it. He should neither be attached to people nor to inaction. Detachment leads a striver to salvation very quickly.

From a spiritualistic point of view, a person has only four aims to achieve in life: wealth, passion (lust), religion and salvation. The materialist believes in only two, wealth and passion. They believe in accumulating wealth and enjoying life's passions to the fullest. The materialist never considers the law of *karma* or action. Western materialistic philosophers have deliberated on the mind, soul, consciousness, God and nature only. Indian philosophers have deliberated thoroughly on these but also about the law of *karma* or action. Western philosophers have not pondered *karma* although Newton postulated a law that states, "With every action there is an opposite and equal reaction." Orthodox Hindus, who accept the authority of Vedas, have propounded six philosophies— *Naya, Vaiseshika, Sâmkha, Yoga, Purva Mimâmsâ and Uttara Mimâmsa. Purva Mimâmsa Sutras* dealt with *karma kânda* of Veda. The *karmayoga* of *Bhagavad Gita* is different from the *karma* of the *Mimâmsa Sutra*. *Mimâmsa Sutra* has emphasized mostly sacrifices and oblation. It advocated sacrificial action with an aim to achieve salvation in the end, whereas *karmayoga* of *Bhagavad Gita* implies renouncing the fruit of action in order to gain final blessing. Its philosophy is of the discipline of detached action (*nishkâma karma*). *Karma* of *Mimâmsa* is the theory that one has to face the consequences of one's action—good or bad. Actions are of three kinds according to the *gunas* attending them. *Satvick* actions are without attachment, selfless and for the benefit of others, *rajasik* actions are selfish and *tamasik* actions are undertaken from delusion without heed to consequences, supremely selfish and animalistic. Mahatama Gandhi gives an interesting view of the three types of personal ties relative to the action they performed. According to him, the *tamasik* works in a mechanical fashion, the *rajasik* drives too many horses, is restless and is always doing something or other, the *satvik* works with peace in mind.

The *karma* that we do has two effects: one is an immediate, visible effect; and the other is a remote, invisible effect. If you feed a hungry man, you feel satisfaction. This is the immediate effect of *karma*. There is also a subtle, invisible effect which finds expression later. The actual experience allied with *karma* is only temporary, but the impression left by that experience is indelible and lasting. Anything you see, anything you hear, anything you do, think, or know creates internal impressions. Thus, we constantly gather these internal imppresions within us. Out of these impressions our memories grow, our likes and dislikes develop, our disposition is created. A wrong habit creates a wrong tendency; and a good habit creates a good tendency. Not only our habits, but our talents and capacities develop as a result of the accumulted impressions of *karma*. If you practice a musical intrument you develop the talent to play that instrument, or you write a little every day and you develop your capacity to be an author; practice does make a person perfect. Nobody gathers only wrong impressions, and those who perform right deeds also perform some wrong deeds; so these impressions are of a mixed character. Suppose a person, by repeated effort, succeeds in dominating his evil tendencies and performs mostly good deeds. As a result of this he will have some kind of well-being in life. He will have happiness, prosperity and a better position in life. But if the impressions are on the whole bad, they will produce some kind of disagreeable situation. You might lose honour, lose money, lose a position, lose friends,suffer from some kind of incurable disease, or meet death by accident. So these impressions, apart from creating our tendencies, talents, likes, dislikes, and memories, also serve as moral forces leading us to favourable or unfavourable situations in life. It is very important that we know what we are achieving by our conscious, deliberate actions. Still there are many of these impressions of merit or demerit that may fructify in this very life and will be in store for the future. These impressions must produce results—'As ye sow, so shall ye reap.'

It does not mean the end of his existence when a human being dies. Man is not just a physical or psychophysical being, but is really the immortal spirit or *âtman* within. When we die, there isn't a single thing in physical world we can take with us, while we carry the bundle of our *karma* with us. The mind is not separate from the departing spirit, and all of the accumulated *karmic* impressions dwelling deep in the mind go with the soul or *âtman*. We leave the world with whatever talents we may have, whatever weakness or excellences we have acquired, whatever merits or demerits we have accumulated. Death cannot nullify the influence fo *karma*. According to the law of *karma*, man has to come here to earth to reap the consequences of the past life deeds. Our present situation has been determined by our past actions, and our future will be determined by our prsent actions. *Karma* does mean that our mental and physical movements are completely fixed by our past actions, though they are determined in a general way. Past actions have created certain conditions for us, and we are working under those conditions, so naturally we have certain limitations. But we do have a good deal of freedom of movement. Sri Ramakrishna said man's freedom is like that of a cow tied to a post. Though the cow cannot go beyond the length of the rope, it can graze, lie down, stand up or sit down and do many other things within the reach of its tether. In spite of the situations created for us our past *karma*, we have a certain freedom of action, and we can modify our conditions to a great extent. Through effort, we can improve our physical and mental health. Though we are restricted in our freedom of choice, through careful use of that freedom, we can greatly change the effect of our past actions. Usually *karma* works in two distinct channels. We are born with a particular body, and with a mind containing certain latent desires and tendencies. These tendencies first lead us to certain activities, which can be counteracted by education and right association. That is the purpose of receiving moral and spiritual instruction from the *guru*. Secondly, the impressions of *karma* may lead us to sufferings or pleasures, or enjoyments. Because of these impressions, we may suffer, or lose wealth, or honour, or a loved one or may have physical disability. Or if we have done good deeds, we may enjoy a favourable situation in life with success and prosperity. Whatever situation in life we may have, we must make the best of that situation both mentally and physically because, to a great extent, we have the freedom to do so. We should not feel fatalistic. We do not lay the blame for our misfortune on God or some uncertain fate. *Karma* makes us wholly responsible for our situation in life. It inevitably produces effects, but we can mitigate these effects through our own efforts and the help of others.

Every action creates two kinds of reactions—on the mind as *vasanas* and on the body as *prârabdha*. These *prârabdhas* and *vasanas* determine your material and mental make-up in your next life and constitute what is called fate, destiny or *kismat*. Your mental and moral attitude in life depends on your *vasanas*. Physical comforts and discomforts belong to *prârabdha*.

The law of cause and effect materialism is also the law of *karma* of the spiritual world. It means that human being is the architect of his own fate. Good deeds bring him good and bad deeds bad results. He is free to choose between good and evil, and is therefore accountable for his own actions. In the final analysis, his success, happiness and progress depend on himself. Human being determines his own destiny by his own thought and action. According to Christianity, faith in the Lord; to Islam, the will of God and to Hinduism the individual's own effort, is the primary factor in shaping human destiny.

The question arises whether a person does an action or *karma* by his own free-will or it is attached with God's will or with fate of the individual. How can we say it a man's free-will action when the result of the action or *karma* is due to fate or God's will. The question then arises whether life is due to an object of human pursuit or it is united with fate. Valorous people say that what we call fate today was really a human pursuit and without human pursuit, fate cannot be made.

Although the law of causation and law of *karma* are similar, still they differ in a sense that the law of causation works in an inanimate world. The law of *karma* works with in an animate world. Nothing can come between *cause* and *effect* in the inanimate world but the consciousness comes between the *cause* and *effect* in the life of animate world. With a lack of consciousness, there is a mechanical reaction in the animate due to the law of *causation*, which we call determinism or fatalism. Due to, intervention of consciousness *karma* or action an animate remains independent along with some degree of dependence. Conscious soul comes between them to liberate the animate life, though it remains bonded with *karma*. Spiritualist has always believed in the law of *cause* and *effect* in this world—'As you sow so you reap.' But if we believe in fatalism, the result would be disastrous. It means you can do nothing but wait for things to happen to you. Thus, it would be impossible to liberate the soul from the cycle of birth and death. It is natural to try to liberate the soul towards salvation or *satchitânand* (*sat* = true; *chit* = conscious; *ânand* = bliss). How does one be bound with *karma* or action? One gets bound to punishment in this life or the next if one steals something of others or kills someone. Whatever we do in this life or have done in past lives will make an impression on our soul just as saffron leaves an impression in a cup after it is emptied. Impressions are made of every act we do in our life time. A first time offender of stealing may not be punished but he develops a tendency or inclination towards stealing which gradually leads him to incarceration. Impressions are made deeper every time we do good or bad deeds and eventually we get rewards in this life or in next life. No one deed can escape without its reward, good or bad, even if we may not get it in this life time. When a soul leaves this perishable body, it takes with it the impressions of its deeds in the subtle astral body to the next life form, where they are rewarded. The soul also carries our thoughts and experiences along with the impressions of deeds. It is like the odour of saffron that does not go away easily from a cup, even though you have emptied and cleaned it. The law of *karma* has an extension beyond the present life. We carry with us our own past. The state of human life depends upon the good or evil that we have done in the preceding lives. According to Hindu belief, God is not a judge sitting in heaven handing out punishments or rewards. Instead, our own accumulated balance of work, in accordance with the law of *karma*, performed by ourselves determines its course for the next life. The individual self (*âtmâ*) tries in every life to achieve purity till it mingles with the Universal Self or *Parmâtmâ*. The Gods are our spiritual parents and guide us through our *karma*, specially if we have established a personal relationship with them. We mould our own destiny by our actions, so the wise soul does not blame outside forces or others for his *karma* or action. Taking responsibility for our actions gives the power to face our *karma* positively. We should face our *karma* cheerfully, follow the virtuous path and perform *sadhanâ* to unwind the effects of past misdeeds. As a corollary to the law of *karma*, the effects of past actions can be strengthened, modified or even canceled by present actions. By gaining conscious control of our thoughts and attitudes, by right action, we can harness the flow of *karma* and soften its intensity. When something happens that you do not like, accept it as an effect of a past action and, rather than striking out, take the experience into the pure energies to transmute and demagnetize it forever. Yogi Vasishtha said, *"Our previous and present efforts, in case they are in contrary directions, are like two rams fighting against each other."* The most powerful of the two always overcomes the other. Whether they are the past or the present efforts, it is the stronger one that determines our destiny. Human being determines his own destiny by his own thought. He can also make those things happen which were not destined to happen. There is nothing in the world that cannot be achieved by human being by right sort of efforts.

Ancient Indian seers have assigned three categories to *karma*. The first is *sanchita*, the sum total of past *karma* yet to be resolved. The second category is *prârabdha* (fate); that portion of *sanchit karma* being experienced in the present life. It is too powerful for the realized human being to stop; it will exhaust with the extinction of its fruits. *Prârabdha karma* is the matured kind of *karma* and is therefore the current one, having taken on a physical body is a *prârabdha karma* because it is a matured one. The physical body is here and we cannot destroy it. The other two kinds of *karma*, not having come into objective existence, can be stopped and even extinguished or resolved because the favouring causes have been removed. *Kriyamana* or *agâmin*, the third type, is *karma* you are presently creating. However, it must be understood that your past negative *karma* can be altered into a smoother, easier state through *dharma* and *sadhana*. That is *karmic* wisdom. Live well and you will create positive *karma* for the future and soften negative *karma* of the past. Since human beings are dependent on action or *karma*, we are the ones who can free ourselves from the bondage of action by action. Some people are born rich, others are born poor, some are born sick, blind and/ or with other congenital defects and some are healthy. Some are born genius and others are born idiot. According to law of *karma,* they are born with the result of *karma* or action of the previous life. Spiritualist believes that people are born with their own nature, virtue and sacrament. Some are born in poverty and others in wealth. Some people are born in a rich family and have poor sacrament or ritual; others born in a poor family have kingly sacrament. Heterogeneity is the rule of nature of life. These incongruities do not agree with the social orders; rather they come by birth with soul. Since they come with birth so they have inherent qualities of *karma* of previous life.

In *Vivekacudâmani* (verse 453), Samkara says: The *prârabdha karma* is too powerful for the realized being to stop; it will exhaust with the extinction of its fruit. The other two kinds of *karma*, that resulting from previous actions (*sancita*) and that whose effects are not mature (*âgâmin*), will be burnt to ashes by the fire of knowledge. However, none of these three kinds of *karma* is capable of affecting the ascetic who has realized *Brahman* and lives in identity with it.

The question that crops up is that if person by nature takes action or *karma*, then how can he be not bonded by the action or *karma*? One can be out of bondage of *karma* when one does work without any selfish motive and with renunciation of the fruit of action. This is called *nishkâm karma*, or unselfish action, in *Bhagavad Gita*. The same idea is given in *Yajurveda*—*"Live in this world unattached, uninvolved and free from desire."* The four elements that bind us in action or *karma* are—desire or lust, anger, greed and illusion. As Lord *Krishna* said, *"To the man thinking about the objects (of the senses) arises attachment towards them; from attachment, arises longing; and from longing arises anger. From anger comes delusion; and from delusion, loss of memory; from loss of memory the ruin of discrimination; and on the ruin of discrimination, he perishes"* (*Bhagavad Gita* II. 62, 63). Further He states, *"But the self-controlled person, moving among objects, with his senses free from attachment and malevolence and brought under his own control, attains tranquillity"* (*Bhagavad Gita* II. 64).

There is a difference between inactiveness and disinterestedness. Inactive persons do not want to work whereas uninterested persons work with all zeal but are not attached to the fruit of their actions. *Nishkâma karma* also suggests that your right is to work alone; but never to the fruits thereof. Be you, not the producer of the fruits of your actions; neither let your attachment be towards inaction (*Bhagavad Gita* II.47). Renunciation does not mean you should not work. Work you must, for there can be no life without action—only keep your mind out of it and work with a sense of selflessness. Relinquish all sense of agency or doership, attachment, desire for fruits of action and later stages even the sense of enjoyment. *Nishkâma karma* or unselfish action can easily be understood by the work of a physician or a lawyer. Their patients die or clients lose their cases in court in spite of their best effort to save the life or win the case. They go on taking another patient or client without waiting to lament on the previous case. Similarly, an athlete loses a game but he does not waste time and goes on to another game. They show no attachment nor are their hearts affected by the results. Act as God's agent and obey His laws just as an ambassador carries out the wishes of his government and has no will of his own. Perform duties to which you are born according to your *swadharma*. A person must perform his duties to the best of his ability. No duty is superior or inferior to any other duty. A humble cobbler may live nearer to true life than a businessperson or political leader. Our own duty, well-performed, is the beat for our own emancipation. If we perform our duties well and conscientiously as a monarch, minister, father, son, teacher, business person, soldier, or servant we obey the law of God. In short, every one has his allotted duties to perform in whatever the walk of life, he must perform them honestly so as to exhaust his old *vasanas* and not to create new ones. All action must be *nishkâma* so as to get rid of ego and acquire humility. *Krishna* says in *Gita*, *"Better one's own duties though devoid of merit than the duty of another well performed"*, for you can attain perfection only in your own line. The path of perfection lies in the steadfast pursuit of man's own *swadharma*, in a spirit of dedication and devotion. His duty is ordained by his own nature according to *vasanas*. In the performance of his duties faithfully, he exhausts his *vasanas*. *Krishna* reminds Arjuna: "*You are a kshatriya, it is your swadharma to fight in battle. You cannot get your head shaven and become a sanyasi. It would be against your real nature.*" The field of work chosen should preferably be one's *svadharma* or inborn duties fitting with one's *svabhava* or inborn temperament and talent. In modern time, psychologist's stress on aptitude-testing—the executives changing jobs in the beginning till they settle down, are examples of the impact of this principle of *svadharma*. Work in other fields is not prohibited but it holds dangers to spiritual progress. When the results of work done in *svadharma* are dedicated to God as a matter of habit, the person becomes fit for reaching *Brahman*. One should be busily engaged in work, but that work should be based on no desire or lust. It is possible to find such desireless work when a person does the duty that falls to his lot in an attitude of dedication and sacrifice. An individual has a duty towards one's parents, one's wife and children, the extended family, friends, the clan or community, to the country or the state, to the organization where one works for livelihood, and even to the ecological environment. There may sometimes be a conflict of duties. The nature of duties to be undertaken in any given set of circumstances is not to be decided the basis of one's desires but on the basis of the guidelines given in the *dharma* or righteousness. Once the course of duty is determined, it has to be followed, irrespective of consequences and without any desire for rewards.

Increasingly people of the West are beginning to accept the law of *karma* as a sound principle. G.R.Harrison wrote in his book *What Man May Be:*

"Many religions have a doctrine of Original Sin, considering all men as having been born evil. Man inevitably takes many wrong steps and can be viewed as steeped in sin, first innocently and later as result of mixed or improper motives. Perhaps most closely related to a scientific view is the basic tenet in Hinduism and Buddhism, known as the Law of *Karma*, according to which all acts produce their results automatically, as effects follow causes. Punishment and reward are merely the automatic feed-back reactions from a universe in which all parts are inter-related. So in the *karma* theory there is implicit the concept of reincarnation, of the *âtamâ* or *jiva* going from birth to birth in a continuous chain. The external events and incidents that occur in this life are already predetermined by that portion of the *karma's* done in earlier lives."

A noted scientist, Sir Richard Gregory said in his book *Gods and Men:*

"Though science may not be able to contribute much to the ultimate problem of spiritual beliefs. It does teach that every action carries with it a consequence—not in another world but in this—to be felt either by ourselves or in the generation to come. This is the law of the natural world and cannot be transgressed without punishment, whether by saint or sinner."

William James, psychologist, wrote *"Could the young but realize how soon they will become mere walking bundles of habits, they would give more heed to their conduct while in the plastic state. We are spinning our own fates, good or evil, and never to be undone."* Emerson once said, *"Cause and effect, means and end, seed and fruit cannot be severed, for the effect already blooms in the cause, the end pre-exists in the means, the fruit in the seed."* Lord Samuel wrote in his book *Belief and Action*: 'The individual may not shift his responsibilities on to Destiny, nor yet on to God.' Destiny is a figment, and the Divine element in the world, as Plato held, is not coercive but persuasive. If God were overtly active, constantly directing, human being could be passive and nothing more. Because God is reticent, human being has scope.'

The law and divine grace are apprently contradictory. Law means the enforcement of justice, while grace means mercy. If God is all-just, how can He be all-merciful at the same time. We know the law of *karma* is conditional. As you sow, so shall you reap. If you do good deeds, you get good results; if you do evil deeds you suffer the consequences. Under this law, one is accorded what is due—punishment or reward. But the grace is unconditional; it does not consider your deservingness or undeservingness. Grace comes freely. You get it simply because you ask for it or want it. Both the law and grace operate in two different spheres of human life, there is scope for the both divine law and divine grace.

There are two distinctive functions which set human life apart. First, man has freedom of judgement. He has the capacity to judge what is right or wrong, what is good or evil, what is high or low. Secondly, man has freedom of action, he can act according to his judgement. He can act one way, or he can act the opposite way, or he can act neither way. Man is held responsible for his deeds under the law of *karma*.

As long as a person holds to the ego, he is bound by the law of *karma* and will receive only justice for his actions. But when he tries to surrender this ego to God, gradually the law of *karma* recedes and the mercy of God descends upon his life. Through this surrender to the Lord, one can leave the realm of divine law, and enter the realm of divine grace. The Bhâgavad Gitâ emphasizes that we must not be ego-centred, but try to be God-centred. Sri *Krishna* says to Arjuna: *"Even a sinful person, if he worships Me with unswerving devotion, must be regarded as righteous, for he has formed the right resolution. He soon becomes righteous and attains eternal peace. Proclaim it boldly, O son of Kunti, that My devotees never perish"* (Bhâgavad Gitâ, IX:30-31). When a person does work with the idea that he is the doer of the work, the results of his work come back to him, that is, *karma* reacts upon him. It is not *karma* that actually binds one, it is the ego-idea associated with *karma*. As long as egoism prevails a person in bound under law, but when a person gives up the ego-consciousness, he enters the realm of grace, and leaves *karma* behind. Jesus Christ also said: *"Knock, and it shall be opened unto you"* (St. Luke 11:9). Further He also said: *"Seek, and ye shall find,"* Why? Because God knows our limitations, and the greatest limitation is our defiance.

You cannot keep anything as as long as you like, or in the way you like. At best you are a custodian of things for the time being. You can lose whatever you have at any time. Even this physical body you cannot control very well. It does nor grow in exactly the way you want it to, or least in the way you would like. You cannot actually claim anything to be your own. So give up the idea of ownership which comes because you claim work to be your own. You are merely as an instrument, and a caretaker in this world. When a person gives up his ego to the Lord and works with a spirit of self-surrender, he gradually becomes free from the restriction of *karma*.

The attainment of grace is possible for anyone who can cultivate a spirit of self-surrender and accept the Supreme Being as the sole goal, the sole refuge, the sole ideal. It requires practice. God has given us freedom, though limited; so one has to utilize that freedom. Through that freedom you try to improve your material life, and by that freedom you also try to gain spiritual treasures. Divine grace is free and always waiting to enter our lives, but our egoism blocks the way. Egoism means ignoring or denial of God. We assert ourselves as the doer, as if this power belongs to us. We think, 'I am the master of my life and without God's help I can get things done very well in this world.' Grace cannot meet this spirit of defiance. Grace comes when there is humility; when there is submission. If we do something good and reap the good results, we think 'I have done this all by myself and now I am getting the benefits I deserve.' But if something goes wrong and we suffer, then we say, 'Oh, God has made me suffer.' This kind of contrasting views will not work. Both good and evil have to be surrendered completely. Lord *Krishna* says: *'Persons who surrender all their actions to Me, or perform all actions as offering to Me, regarding Me as the sole goal, knowing Me to be the sole support of the universe, and worship Me with wholehearted devotion, I rescue them from this ocean of mortality'* (Gitâ XII: 6-7). The one condition for God's grace is that a person has to surrender his ego to the Supreme Lord. God gives him not only spiritual treasures, He even gives material possessions and fulfills man's material needs. To this effect Lord *Krishna* says: *"Persons who are so devoted to Me that their whole heart and mind go unto Me wihout thinking of anything else, they who worship Me in all beings and meditate on Me, out of grace I guard what they have and I secure what they have not; their welfare is assured through Me"* (Gitâ IX: 22). Even Jesus Christ said: *"But seek ye first the kingdom of God and his righteousness; and all these things shall be added unto you"* (St. Matthew 6:33).

God's grace works in two ways: 'a person who surrenders himself to God becomes free from all attachment to the sense world and loves everything through God, as God's possession. It is our attachment to material things that compels us to do wrong deeds; when we are freed from these attachments through self-surrender, we cannot do anything wrong. Secondly, any wrong tendencies that a person has already acquired are gradually eliminated through grace.' So both ways, sin cannot be commited. Being free from attachment, a person cannot do sinful deeds, and because God's grace works upon him, his past sins are also eliminated.

Bibliography
Swami Vivekananda, *Life After Death*, Advaita Ashrama,Calcutta, 1975.

Ramanathan V., *Bhagavadgita for Executives*, Bharatiya Vidhya Bhavan, Bombay, 1982.

Chapter 6

Reincarnation

The word, *transmigration* is often used interchangeably with *reincarnation*. The word *transmigration* is derived from Latin: *trans-* = across; *migr-* = to go or move; and *-ation* = process of causing or becoming. *Transmigration* is 'the process of moving across, from one to the other.' It is used to signify the crossing of the soul from one body to another. The reincarnation word has also five Latin elements: *re-* = again; *in-*= into; *carn* = flesh; *-ate* = cause or become; and *-ion* = process. *Reincarnation* literally means 'the process of coming into flesh again' (J. Algeo, Reincarnation Explored, 1987). It implied that there is something to us that is separated from the flesh, or body, that returns after death. We refer to the belief that human beings may come back as animals, we use the word *transmigration*. *Reincarnation* usually refers to the belief that we return back in human form. Hindus have believed there are 8,400,000 species of bodies which can carry *karma* and into which the soul may migrate; and modern scientists have proposed a evolutionary hierarchy of unicellular, plants, insect, fish, birds, and mammals through which the migrating soul must go before the *âtman* (soul) has the opportunity of inhabiting a human body. The Sanskrit word for an incarnation of God is *avatâr*, which literally means descent. God descends to the earthly plane to set aright human affairs which have become chaotic through lack of morality and love. The Supreme Being is the abode of infinite auspicious qualities and they are manifested especially during His incarnations were for specific purposes and only those aspects which were necessary were manifested during each occasion. The scriptures reiterate that the two most important attributes, transcendence (*Paratva*) and easy accessibility (*Saulabhya*), were expressed during His incarnation as *Krishna*. Lord *Krishna* elaborately describes His (God) descent into this world in human form:

"Although I am unborn and Myself never deteriorates, and I am the Lord of all beings, utilizing My own energy I appear by My own potency whenever there is decline of *dharma* (righteousness), O Bhârata, at a prominent rise in *adharma* (unrighteousness), at that time I manifest Myself. For the preservation of the righteous (pious), the destruction of the wicked, and the establishment of *dharma*,

I come into being from age to age" (Gitâ IV: 6-8). In this incarnation Lord *Krishna* gave humanity the assurance that He would protect those who took refuge in Him and that He would manifest on the earth time and again for this purpose. His incarnation as Râma is significant because He showed by personal example how man should conduct himself in conformity to *dharma*.

When human beings need divine guidance, these great teachers come. Sri Ram, *Krishna*, Buddha, and Jesus Christ are worshipped by many as incarnations of God. Moses, Confucius, and Mohammad are often thought of as prophets; while Zoroaster and Lao-tse are usually considered messengers of God. Out of compassion for the suffering of human beings, God takes a human body and lives upon the earth. There are ten reincarnation (*avatâras*) of Vishnu. The Hindus speak of the *Kalki avatâr* to come, the Buddhists of *Maitreya Buddha*, the Zoroastrians of *Sosiosh*, while in Islam it is foretold that one of the Imam or great spiritual leaders will reappear. The Jews still expect their Messiah, who, we will see, some think had been Adam and later David. Do not Christians anticipate Christ's second advent?

Human beings have lived on the earth for hundreds of thousands of years. Lord *Krishna* says to Arjun, "*Many births of mine have passed as well as thine, I know them all but thou knowest not*" (Bhagavad Gita IV.5). "*Though I am unbórn, of imperishable nature, the Lord of all beings, yet, governing My Nature, I manifest Myself through My divine potency*" (Bhagavad Gita IV.6). Further Lord *Krishna* said, "*Whenever there is a decline of righteousness and rise of unrighteousness, then I manifest Myself, for the protection of the good, for the destruction of the wicked and for the establishment of righteousness. I am born from age to age*" (Bhagavad Gita IV. 7,8). According to Christian belief there is only one incarnation of God. Hinduism says that there have been many incarnations (*avatâr*) from time immemorial. The proof of incarnation is found in the Bible in the statements of Jesus Christ, "*If God were your Father, ye would love me; for I proceeded forth and came from God; neither came I of myself but he sent me*" (St. John 8:42).

The principle logic of reincarnation is due to the law of *karma*, which influence the future lives: for every action, the law of *karma* says, there is a reaction, much like Newton's Third Law of Motion. Reincarnation can be seen as the harvesting of the fruits of action: act good, get a good body; act bad, get a bad body. The biblical equivalent would be, "*As ye sow, so shall ye reap.*" Plato said in the The Repblic (617 e): "*God is blameless: man has chosen his own fate, and this by his actions.*" *Karma* provides the situation, not the response to the situation. So the living being still has free will. The logic of reincarnation dictates that if we behave like animals in this life, we can have an animal body in next time around.

After death the material body is cremated or decomposed into its five elements merge with its components. It is the non-material *âtman* (soul) that continues in a new body. According to ancient Vedic literature, living beings are essentially spiritual creatures who took birth in the world of matter due to a series of complex yet subtle desires. Such embodied souls are called *tatashtha shakti*. The word *tata* signifies the coastal zone that divides land from sea. Sometime the water covers the land, and at other times the water recedes. *Atman* (soul) is like sub-atomic particles—their existence is accepted because of the effects they produce around them. Certain sub-atomic particles are not actually seen, they are known to exist by the effect they produce. Consciousness is the most fundamental part of human experience. Can I be conscious of my body? Can I be conscious of my hand or legs or face or heart or mind? Yes, I can be conscious of any part of my body, its pains or pleasures. Can the body be conscious of itself? The answer is no. Now it is clear that there is a separation of body from the self or *âtman*, the living being within who is conscious of the body. Even it reflects in our language, for the possessive pronoun suggests that I am different than my body. Usually we say, "This is my hand or legs, etc." The body is an instrument; the conscious energy is the player of that instrument. I am no more my brain or nervous system than a guitarist is the guitar he plays. As a musician produces music with a musical instrument, so I, the thinker, produce thoughts with a thinking instrument: the brain. If an instrument is destroyed, the musician is not necessarily destroyed as a consequence. Analogically, if my body is destroyed, I am not necessarily destroyed with it. If my guitar is destroyed, I would have to get another to make music or I would have to stop playing the guitar altogether. The First Law of Thermodynamics or Law of Conservation of Energy says that energy cannot be created or destroyed. Likewise, if the *âtman* or soul exists at all, then it must sustain its existence. Physiologically, the cells of our bodies constantly deteriorate and die so that after approximately seven years the cellular structure of the body has been completely over hauled. Our whole body changes from childhood, to youth, to old age and, finally, death while the self remains in the same body.

The passions and desire are not produced by the body, but on the contrary, it is desire and passion which caused us to be born, and will bring us to birth again and again in some body on this earth. When one dies, it is the body alone that dies. The life-force within the body, called the soul, is pure energy and does not die. With the storehouse of *karmas* and *sanskaras*, it leaves the body and, at the time ordained by the Lord, reenters the body of a child about to be born. This reentry is called reincarnation, or simply rebirth. Who or what is it that reincarnates? It is not the body, for that dies and disintegrates; and but few of us would like to be chained forever to such bodies as we now have, admitted to be infected with disease. It is not the astral body that also has its term and must go to pieces after the physical body has gone. Nor is it the passions and desires. They have a very long term, because they have the power to reproduce themselves in each life so long we do not eradicate them. The *inner ego* reincarnates, taking on body after body, storing up the impression of life after life, gaining experience and adding it to the *divine ego,* suffering and enjoying through an immense period of years.

Leonard de Venice wrote: *"The soul desires to dwell in the body because without the members of that body it can neither act nor feel... The soul can never be infected by the corruption of the body, but acts in the body like the wind which causes the sound of the organ, wherein if one of the pipes is spoiled, the wind cannot produce a good result in that pipe."*

Karma is not a being but a law, the universal law of harmony which unerringly restores all disturbance to equilibrium. This theory conflicts with the materialistic conception about God who destroys or punishes that which He created. This has either caused thousands to live in fear of God or has plunged them into darkness which comes from denial of all spiritual life. In fear, man's compliance with His assumed commands is with the selfish object of obtaining reward and securing escape from the wrath. The poor, who see no refuge or hope, cry aloud to a God who makes no reply, and then envy springs up in them when they consider the comforts and opportunities of the rich. They see the rich as wicked, enjoying themselves unpunished. Turning to the teacher of religion, they get the reply to their questioning of the justice which will permit such misery to those who did nothing requiring them to be born with no means, no opportunities for education, no capacity to overcome social, racial, or circumstantial obstacles, 'It is the will of God.' Parents have beloved offspring cut off by death at an untimely hour, just when all promised well. They too have no answer to the question 'Why am I thus afflicted?' but the same unreasonable reference to an inaccessible God whose arbitrary will causes their misery. Thus in every walk of life, loss, injury, persecution, deprivation of opportunity, nature's own forces working to destroy the happiness of man, death, reverses, disappointment continually beset good and evil men alike. But nowhere is there any answer or relief save in the ancient truth that each man is the maker and fashioner of his own destiny, the only one who sets in motion the causes for his own happiness and misery. In one life, he sows and in the next, he reaps. Thus on and forever, the law of *karma* leads him. *Karma* is a beneficent law wholly merciful, relentless just, for true mercy is not favour but impartial justice.

For, Hindus *karma* and reincarnation are solid realities, simply because their minds have never been distorted by being forced into an unnatural ideas as other religions have told to believe that their sins would be forgiven because another man had been put to death for their sakes. The Hindu lives up to his beliefs without a murmur against *karma,* or what he regards as a just punishment; whereas others neither live upto its moral ideal, not accepts its lot contentedly. Hence, murmuring and dissatisfaction and the intensity of the struggle for existence in Western countries.

In modern age, people believe in inheritance. You might ask why you were born with these particular gene? Why should you be in this situation? Why do you not have a different set of genes from different parents? There is a natural selection of parents that takes place in accordance with certain laws (Law of *Karma*). If there is such a thing as a soul surviving death, there must be laws that govern the huge network of possible combinations which determine the soul's next birth. Many aspects have to be arranged—time and place of birth, parentage, social position and culture, economic situation, and so on—all of which affect, in some way, the child who is born. In this way, each person's situation is a result of action done in this life and in the past lives. In modern scientific way, we call it a problem of heredity or genetics.

Citra told Svetketu that the doers of actions from this world reach the heavens, and when the fruits of their actions are exhausted, they return to this world and are born again. They fall as rain, i.e. with the unseen seeds and essence, or the life principle present there. It, or he, then penetrates unseen the soil of this earth and becomes grains of paddy, millet and the like. 'As a worm, a caterpillar, a vulture, a human being or any other being in order of creation (reckoned at a thousand million in all); in any of these he is born in accordance with the nature of the fruits of actions yet to be spent. The food consumed by a person is turned into the sperm of the male, or the ovum of the female. The man and the woman join in love and later, this *jivatman* remaining in the womb of the would-be mother for a period for 40 weeks, is born as conditioned being, impregnated with discrimination. This could be explained on the basis of our present knowledge of gene or genetic material or DNA. He has become a mortal, having had to enjoy the fruits of his accumulated actions remaining yet unspent. There is also the supreme knowledge (*brahma-vidya*) for his emancipation, as for us all. So, he need not despair, because he can attain liberation by those means when there will be no further birth and death for him (see Law of Karma). There are some who take to the path of worship (*upasana*). They tread the path of the celestials after death, and attain the higher worlds (Kausatikya *Upanishad*).

There are four principles involved in the Hindu theory of reincarnation or transmigration: the permanence of the essential self, the operation of original ignorance, the possibility of union with the Supreme Being and the doctrine of *karma*. Without the assumption of a permanent entity, the talk of reincarnation would be meaningless. That is why the materialists, who do not believe in a permanent entity like the *âtman*, do not accept the possibility of rebirth. The operation of original ignorance or *avidyâ* is also causing misunderstanding of the *âtman* or the essential self to assume an individuality. The third principle which is basic to the belief of reincarnation, is the concept of the possibility of liberation or *moksha*, for the union with the Supreme Being. Liberation means realizing one's own true self which is already there but not realized because of the influence of basic ignorance. *Bhâgavad Gitâ* glorifies, as the highest ideal of man, the state of liberation while living in the human body, called *jivanmukti*. In that state, the individual develops an universality of outlook, a freedom from all attachments and a discernment of the truth which could come only to the liberated soul, but retains the physical body as a basis for action in this world. This is the ideal of the *yogi*. The fourth principle on which the theory of reincarnation rests is the law of *karma*. The doctrine of *karma* teaches that man himself is the architect of his life. What he did in the past life is entirely responsible for what he is in the present life, and what he is doing in the present life will shape up his next life. As a human one must work, if he acts in a spirit of passionless detachment towards the fruits of his actions, he will be leaving the road open for the soul's progress towards the ultimate goal, liberation or *moksha*.

The *soul* when embodied (human being) is subjected to the law of *karma*. All beings must reap the consequences of their actions. No action goes in vain. No effort is lost. Actions have full weight in the balance-sheet of eternity. The balance-sheet of both good and bad actions determines the destiny of the life to come. Destiny is thus the net product or effect of the actions in the previous births. Whatever a man today is, it is because of his past actions.

The soul carries with it the seeds of its *karma*. These seeds or impressions of past actions do not die when the body dies. Reincarnation, therefore, is the re-entry of a soul, together with its *karmic* seeds, into the new body. No child is born with a vacant mind. All have had past lives. This is the truth realized through direct experience by the *rishis* and *yogis* of the past and modern times as well.

Life flows as a torrent; man suffers passively the necessity of death in order that he be born and die again and again. This is the basis of Hindu belief, the frightful retributive accountability. But there is an essential corollary: by his actions man can direct his destiny. According to *Manu-Smriti* (XII. 3-9): *"Action, which springs from the mind, from speech, and from the body, produces either good or evil results; by action are caused the various conditions of man, the highest, the middle, and the lowest. A man obtains the result of a good or evil mental acts in his mind, that of a verbal act in his speech, that of a bodily act in his body." "As a consequence of many sinful acts committed with his body, a man becomes in the next birth something inanimate, as a consequence of sins committed by speech, a bird, or a beast, and in a low class"* (Manu-Smriti XII. 11).

The ignorant says: '*Karma* does everything. It is all destiny. I am destined by my *karma* to be all this or that. Why then I should exert?' This is a fatalist view. This will bring inertia, stagnation and misery. Human beings, unlike other creatures, are gifted with intelligence, ability of reasoning, wisdom and will-power to exercise judicious discretion and measure up to the challenge of destiny. Man has the capacity to choose his action in this life. Man has the faculty (*viveka*) to discriminate between right and wrong, and adopt the path of his choice. Through self-effort (*purshârtha*), he is in a position to change the result of the influence of his destiny—the effect of his past actions. Right thought and right action can reduce or neutralize the destiny. Thus, the freedom to modify the effect of the past and create a future, better or worse, depends on man's self-effort.

The law of *karma* is purely mechanical. From the stand point of *karma*, your cancer or any other ailments may be a result of either past *karma* performed long ago or more recently. It may be due to any reasons—food habit, smoking or infection—all of which can be viewed in terms of either immediate or remote past. If you win a lottery and call it good luck, or you lose something and call it bad luck—all of this may be past *karma* at work. In spite of all your efforts and plans, situations that we call bad luck keep happening. *Karma* may be unfolding everyday, what is happening right for you now may be due to past *karma*. You just cannot see it.

How can we neutralize the effects of past, both immediate and remote past? Along with efforts we require enthusiasm, courage, knowledge, resources, and the readiness and capacity to face obstacles. Even with all these, we still can have the same misfortune, we need help from God, which we will get if we pray sincerely. We cannot get His help if we only sit and pray without the above six qualities present.

Man has to pay for all his deeds. This explains why even a person leading a noble, pious and chaste life has to suffer, maybe for something he had committed in earlier births though he might have been ignorant of the same. But his ignorance cannot prevent the operation of the law of *karma*. *Karma* and *asmsakara* are considered as inseparable in many passages in the *Upanishads*, e.g., "*Whatever he does in this world, he comes again from that world because of his action*" (Brhadaranyaka Upanishad IV.4.6). "*Accordingly, those who are of pleasant conduct here—the prospect is, indeed, that they will enter a pleasant womb, either the womb of a Brahmin, or Kshatriya, or Vaishya. But those who are of stinking conduct here—that the prospect is, indeed, that they will enter a stinking womb, either the womb of a dog, or the womb of a swine, or the womb of an outcast*" (Chandogya Upanishad V.10.7). "*Some go into a womb for the embodiment of a corporeal being, others go into a stationary thing, according to their deeds, according to their knowledge*" (Katha Upanishad V. 7). "*The individual self roams about according to its deeds*" (Shvetashvatara Upanishad V.7). "*Whatever being (object) a man thinks of at the time of death when he leaves the body, that alone does he attain, O Kaunteya, being ever absorbed in the thught there of*" (Gitâ VIII: 6).

The idea of reincarnation has also been expressed in the *Katha Upanishad*: "*He, however, who has no understanding, who is unmindful and ever impure, reaches not the goal, but goes on to reincarnation*" (Katha Upanishad III.7). "*As the indweller (âtman) in the body experiences childhood, youth and old age in the body, he also passes on to another body. The wise man (enlightened one) does not affected about this*" (Gitâ II: 13). "*As man discarding worn-out clothes put on new ones, so the embodied soul, casting off worn-out bodies enters into others which are new*" (Gitâ II: 23). "*As a goldsmith taking a piece of gold reduces it to another newer and more beautiful form, just so this soul, striking down this body and dispelling its ignorance, makes for itself another newer and more beautiful form*" (Katha Upanishad IV. 4.4).

"*At the end of many births, the man of wisdom takes refuge in Me, realizing that this is God. Such is a great soul is very rare indeed*" (Gitâ VII: 19). "He who thus knows *purusa* (spirit) and *prakrti* (Nature) together with the *Gunas* (modes) is never born again, in what ever way he may live" (Gitâ XIII: 23). "*That Supreme soul is said to be the light of all lights, entirely beyond darkness (ignorance). He is knowledge, the knowable, the goal of knowledge and is seated in the hearts of all*" (Gitâ XIII: 17).

The doctrine of reincarnation helped solve some of the difficulties inherent in the doctrine of *karma*. The *rishis* recognized that some of the fruits of a life did not appear to be the harvest of seed sown within a particular incarnation, and some of the karmic seed sown in an incarnation did not appear to reach fruition within the incarnation. But when *karma* was linked with *samskara*, then the *karmic* seeds and *karmic* fruits could be considered to be distributed over many incarnations.

Reincarnation is not punishment for sin. An incarnation according to the Hinduism of the *smriti* tradition is the natural consequence of acts. Divinity is not necessary to control and direct *karma*, although some sects have introduced a divinity for such purposes. The hypothesis of reincarnation has suffered in the hands of both its believers and its non-believers. One of the serious misunderstandings is that reincarnation must include the continuation of consciousness, whereas the significance of the doctrine is to be found in the area of the conservation of values rather than in the ability to remember previous incarnations. Hinduism as a *sadhana* is a programme for self-perfection, not a technique for displaying feats of memory reaching back into earlier embodiments of the human spirit. The most common Western misunderstanding about the concept of reincarnation is that it is chiefly concerned with the continuation of consciousness, i.e. that one will, therefore, be able to remember previous existence.

Intelligent people have always believed in reincarnation. The greatest thinkers of ancient Greece—Pythagoras, Plato, Socrates, Plotinus—all believed in it. Pagan Rome produced two great philosophers. One of them was a crippled slave, Epictetus; the other was an emperor, Marcus Aurelius. Neither of them wrote about reincarnation, but they both believed in it. We know they believed in reincarnation because they were both Stoics, and all Stoics believed in reincarnation—it was a tenet of their philosophy. Like Cathari, later, they taught that you are born again because you are a spiritual being and you have to purify yourself of materiality. The largest group, other than Hindus, that believed in reincarnation was called the Cathari. In France, they were called the Albigenses. The Cathari believed they had to be born until they had purged themselves from the taint of this material world, reborn and reborn again until they became pure spiritual beings, so that they could once more be one with God, as He had made them to be. It took twenty years of fierce fighting by non-believers to destroy the Catharis. Hundreds of thousands of them were slaughtered by Catholics. But even after they had wiped out the powerful centers of Cathari in France and Italy, the Church still could not get rid of the belief in reincarnation. Though the Renaissance was a couple of centuries away, enlightenment was growing, and more and more people were beginning to think for themselves and to question the authority and teachings of the Church. All over Europe, there were people who believed in reincarnation.

The movement of the soul from one body to another was accepted by the early Christian Church (John Makenzie: Two Religions, 1950). Even Lord Jesus himself believed in it. He says in the Bible: "Before Abraham was, I am." Amazingly, the best of these passages that suggest reincarnation consists of statements made by Jesus, or describes incidents in which He took part. Jesus was Eliseus in a past life, and the Jesus' *guru*, John the Baptist, was Elijah (Elias), in the former life. Referring to John the Baptist, Jesus said, "and if ye will receive it, this is Elias, which was for to come" (Matthew 11: 14). Elias' later incarnation as Jesus was foretold several hundred years before the event, because he was destined to fulfill a divine plan of God's. That prophecy is told eight centuries before Christ: "Therefore the Lord himself shall give you a sign: Behold, a virgin shall conceive, and bear a son, and shall call his name Immanuel" (Book of Isaac, 7: 14). St. Matthew, recording the event of Christ's birth, stated: "Now all this was done, that it might be fulfilled which was spoken of the Lord by the prophet, saying, Behold, a virgin shall be with child, and shall bringing forth a son, and they shall call his name Emmanuel, which being interpreted is, God with us" (Matthew 1: 22-23). The Old Testament had predicted that Elijah would return before the appearance of the Messiah and at the end of the world. A part of the very last statement in the Old Testament is this one in Malachi: "Behold, I will send you Elijah the prophet before the great and terrible day of the Lord comes." Jesus said, "Elijah does come, and he is to restore all things; but I tell you that Elijah had already come, and they did not know him, but did to him whatever they pleased. So also the Son of man will suffer at their hands." Then the disciples understood that he was speaking to them of John the Baptist (Matthew 17: 9-13). In another place in Matthew, He said: "Truly, I say to you, among those born of women there has risen no one greater than John the Baptist.... and if you are willing to accept it, he is Elijah who is to come. He who has ears to hear, let him hear" (Matthew 11: 11-15). One thing is certain, Jesus said, " John is Elijah." Its a very hard-to-explain incident if Jesus and His disciples did not believe in reincarnation. The most conclusive incident of all is the well-known story of John, where Jesus heals the man born blind from birth. ... His disciples asked him, "Rabbi, who sinned, this man or his parents, that he was born blind?" Jesus answered, "It was not that this man sinned, or his parents, but that the works of God might be made manifest in him" (John 9: 2, 3). Many incarnations ago He created us as He created Jesus. In the Gospel of St. John we find Jesus himself declaring: "Is it not written in your law, I said ye are gods" (John 10: 34). Jesus was made of the image of God, as are we; and he conquered delusion showing us how to do likewise. If you conquered delusion in this life, you will go back to God and reincarnate no more. "Him that over cometh will I make a pillar in the temple of my God, and he shall go no more out" (Revelation 3: 12).

The Pharsees were among the largest group who believed in reincarnation. They also had a belief in the after world of heaven and hell, angels and demons we are familiar with. The influence of ancient Persian religion, Zoroastrians, is quite interesting. Today relatively few Zoroastrians remain—mainly the Parsees in India. The Jews brought Zoroastrians back from their captivity in Persia. Then Christianity, naturally, developed its notions from the Jewish belief, and Mohammed, seven centuries later, got its notions of the after-life from his association with Jewish rabbis, Christian, Zoroastrian teachers and missionaries who wandered about the Arabian deserts.

Those who do not believe in reincarnation always argue that it is ridiculous to think that the soul, if it survived death, would not remember its former life. Regarding our loss of memory from life to life, there is now a growing body of scientific evidence suggesting there is ample reason for such forgetfulness. The large quantities of one of the hormones of posterior pituitary gland, oxytocin, produces loss of memory in laboratory animals and causes even well-trained animals to lose their ability to perform otherwise easy tasks. Normally, the Oxytocin increases the contractions of the uterus during childbirth and prevents subsequent bleeding. Because a woman's oxytocin floods her child's system during the later stages of pregnancy, it is not unreasonable to suppose that this natural drug flushes away memories of former incarnations along with conscious remembrance of birth (J.Fisher, 'The Case for Reincarnation,' New York: Bantam Books, 1984). Besides, it is undoubtedly an act of mercy to instill forgetfulness in a soul who takes a new birth; imagine the hardship of trying to live one life while plagued with memories of previous life. It would cause needless confusion to have to live with the problems of more than one life at a time. However, some children do remember their former life which can not be explained on the basis of genetics or environment.

Dr. Ian Stevenson of the Department of Psychology and Neurology, University of Virginia, has made his lifework the scientific investigation of stories of reincarnation. He has extensively studied some 3,000 cases as of 1987 from all parts of the world, where somebody says, "I remember my former life". He has studied cases in many different countries, among them are India, Lebanon, Sri Lanka, Turkey, Thailand, Burma, Brazil, Alaska, etc. Interestingly, many Eskimos and American Indians believe they had former lives, which they can remember distinctly. He has found 90 per cent of their memories to be accurate. Stevenson, after complete and detailed investigation of these cases, has published a book called 'Twenty Cases Suggestive of Reincarnation'. Thus far, four large volumes of his case histories have been published by the University of

Virginia Press. A distinguished psychiatric journal, The Jou*rnal of Nervous and Mental* Disease, featured his lengthy article 'The Explanatory Value of the Idea of Reincarnation'. It is difficult to believe anybody could read his books and articles and still not get convinced that there are people who remember their former lives. We are all more likely to remember recent events than those of the distant past; we are more likely to remember events with which we have some familiarity, and events we can associate with something in our present life. This happened to them to remember things from one life to another when there was a short time between death and rebirth and also when they were of the same sex in both lives. But to continue on this point of rejecting reincarnation because you cannot remember a former life, I question people, "How much of this life do you remember?" Even the few remaining Stevenson critics, however, cannot explain how these children, who are often so young that they are just learning their native tongue, can, in these rare cases, speak fluently a language with which they are otherwise unfamiliar. Stevenson now joins hundreds of scientists and millions of laymen who believe that "reincarnation could account for certain behaviour not explained by genetics and early environmental influences" (G.Zukav, 'The Dancing WuLi Masters: An Overview of the New Physics,' New York:Bantam Books, 1980).

Men are born with different *samskara* of their own from previous life, such as these famous people have exhibited it. John Stuart Mill started to write the history of Rome at the age of six; Mac Call started to read and write at the age of three and, at the age of seven, he wrote a poem. Paschal (1623 – 1662) had done 32 chapters of mathematics book in his early childhood without anybody's help. It seems that it has nothing to do with the inheritance of talents from their parents. Similarly, we know that great poets such as Byron (1788 – 1824) was lame and Milton (1608 – 1674) was blind. But it does not mean that every blind and lames are not going to be a poet unless his *samskara* has that talent.

Xenoglossy is the phenomenon where someone speaks or writes in a language unfamiliar to him, which he has never studied, and with which he has no prior acquaintance. Dr. Frederick H. Wood, in his book, 'After Thirty Centuries' and in other books and articles, has reported many instances of such unaccountable occurrences. H.Harvard wrote in his book, 'Reincarnation', that a man named George Carlton from the Royal Iris Rifles abruptly started speaking a language that no one could understand. After sometime, his army unit was transferred to Burma, then people could find out that the language which Carlton was speaking was none but Burmese. Stevenson in his book,' Evidence for Survival from Claimed Memorials,' wrote that an English lady started speaking Norwegian language abruptly. This and other examples of xenoglossy provide a proof of remembering language of previous lives.

Among the ancients, Plato and Virgil wrote descriptions of the after-world. Both of them believed in reincarnation, and both of them described the soul as retaining the memory of this life until the time comes for its re-entry into our world. Then the soul drinks from the waters of the river called Forgetfulness, all memory disappears and the soul is ready to be incorporated in another body. According to Plato's theory of reminiscence, our present knowledge is a recollection of what was learnt or known by the soul in a previous life. One will say, it has no knowledge of its previous lives. But what person remembers every day of this life? As the psychologists tell us, lost memories are recoverable. For the memory appears to be a palimpsests, from which nothing is ever obliterated. If we have forgotten most days and incidents of our present lives, it is natural that memories of previous lives should fail us. Yet from infancy every forgotten day and hour has added to our experiences, to our growth and capacity, made its contribution to the mind and soul. So may it be with former lives, each of them but a day in our past history.

We are born with unequal talents and abilities. This has seemed especially to be true in a field like music. Creative talent of a musician or a composer would not depend on the prior accumulation and retention of great stores of detailed information, such as might be needed, say, by a historian or an engineer. As a performer, a musician may need the ability to hold whole pieces of music note by note in his mind, but his creative power depends more on a sense of rhythm and a feeling for melody and harmony. These do not depend on memory, but are clearly imbedded in the unconscious layers of our being. We just say, " He was born with these qualities," which is true. Training may sharpen them.

Christians and Muslims believe in heaven and hell which last forever. Most of the eastern religions believe that, in order to gain the state of spiritual perfection that is the goal of existence, you have to come back here on earth and make your overcoming here. According to Hinduism, it is called 'moksha' or *turiya*, and Buddhists call them *nirvana* or *samadhi*. We believe even the gods are also under the law of *karma* and they have to reincarnate sooner or later and work out the *karma* which made them gods. With Vishnu are associates, the *avataras*, the incarnations of the god on earth at different periods under the guise of an animal or a human being. These periodic descents of the god on earth are intended to save our world from some great peril (Bhagavad Gita IV. 7,8). There are ten reincarnations (*avataras*) of Vishnu.

Eventually, we may come to the understanding that reincarnation is a fact for all human beings, regardless of their cultural or religious backgrounds; that reincarnation is a gift to us if we have not learned the lessons in one lifetime. We are always given a second, and another chance, and another chance, until all of us are able to graduate, to return to the Source and Creator of all life.

Bibliography

Algeo, John, *Reincarnation Explored*, Wheaton, III, The Theosophical Publishing House, 1987, pp. 133-4

Leonardo da Vinci's Note-Books translated by Edward Mac Curdy, New York, Empire State Book Co., 1935, pp. 47-48.

Cranston, Sylvia. (ed), *Reincarnation—The Phoenix Fire Mystery*, Theosophical University Press, Pasadena, 1994.

Freeman, J.D., *The Case for Reincarnation*, Unity Books, Unity Village, M.O., 1986.

O'Flaherty, W.D. (ed), *Karma and Rebirth in Classical Indian Traditions*, Berkley: University of California Press, 1980.

Rosen, Steven, *The Reincarnation Controversy*, Torchlight Publishing, Inc. Badger, CA. 1997.

Stevenson, Ian, *Twenty Cases Suggestive of Reincarnation*, 2nd Ed. (Revised), Charlottesville, V.A., University of Virginia, 1978.

William Walker Atkinson, *Reincarnation and Law of Karma*.

Siddhyatâlankar, Satyabrat, *Scientific Exposition of Vedic Thought*, New Delhi: Goindaram Hasânand, 1981.

Eliade, Mircea, *Yoga: Immortality and Freedom*, translated by Willard Trask. 2nd ed. revised and enalarged Princeton, Princeton University Press, 1969.

Berg, Philip, *Reincarnation: The Wheels of a Soul*, Jerusalem, Israel, New York, Research Center of Kabbalah, 1982.

Zukav, Gary, *The Dancing Wu Li Masters: An Overview of the New Physics*, New York, Bantam Books, 1980.

Fisher, Joe, *The Case for Reincarnation*, New York, Bantam Books, 1984.

Moore, Clifford H., *Ancient Beliefs in the Immortality of the Soul*, New York, Cooper Square Publishers, 1963.

Chapter 7

Life and Death

What is an urge? It is an urge, a thought of the Brahman. The creative urge is inherent in Brahman—everything is inherent in infinity. "Brahman—the Creator, has the urge, combines it with consciousness, to create life, and He created the pair 'matter (*prakrti*) and energy' (*purusha*) which by mutual interaction, life forms of the many different types were to produce" (Pranopanisad V.4). These perceive objects, thereby creating the five elements. In Hindu scriptures, there are many stories about the creation of life but this approach is one most closely echoed by modern scientific ideas. God is depicted as a diffused form of energy that becomes condensed into active forms of energy, including the creative force Brahman. Other parts of this energy become transformed and are thickened into matter. Some matter, when infused with soul, becomes life forms; and some life forms, when imbued with Consciousness, become higher living creatures, including man. Other forms of active energy become forces that are personified as the gods, the renewing and preserving principles of the world as well as its many other natural laws. "From this life born life, mind, and all the senses, space, air, light, water, and the earth which is the support of the Universe" (Kaivalopanisad 15).

The *Shvetashvatara Upanishad* (VI.2) speaks of *prakrti* (matter) composed of five pure elements that appear in the course of creation—namely, earth, water, fire, air and ether. The *Taittiriya Upanishad* (II.i.1) also enumerates these five elements, and holds that all these have emerged from Self one after the other. The gross bodies are the products of these elements. These are classified into three groups: those born from eggs (*andaja*), those born from germs (*jivaja*), and those born from sprouts (*udbhija*). The various organic bodies affect the souls differently. The earlier *Upanishads* are silent about the alternating courses of creation and dissolution of the world. However, the *Shvetashvatara Upanishad* (III.2; IV.1) alludes to both in more than one place. The basis of the five-fold classification of the elements is the five-fold character of sense-organs whose distinctive objects—namely, sound, touch, colour, taste and odour—are, respectively, the distinct features of ether, air, fire, water and earth.

The Gita seeks to trace all physical things to an ultimate material cause, *prakrti*, which is described as divisible into eight elements, viz., earth, water, fire, air, ether, mind, intellect and ego-sense (*Gita* VII.4). *Prakrti* is inherently characterized by three qualities, i.e., *sattva*, *rajas* and *tamas*. All these three qualities bind down in the body of the immortal and ageless self. It is in such a state of bondage that the soul gets bewildered and becomes incapacitated for discerning the true from the false. While it is the three qualities of *prakrti* that are ever determining his behaviour, the deluded person thinks, I am the agent. The knots of bondage tend to become stronger and stronger with each act of indulgence in sensuous delights.

According to *the Samkhya*, the process of evolution starts when *prakrti* comes in contact with *purusha*. *The Samkhya* speaks of eleven organs, derived from the ego principle, for example, mind, the five sense organs and five motor organs. These organs are followed by five *tanmatras* that are the generic essences of sound, touch, colour, taste and smell. These gross physical elements that spring from *tanmatras* arise in a systematic manner, and they are well-marked stages of differentiation. These elements arise in this way: "From the essence of sound (shabd*atanmatra*) is produced *akasha* with the quality of sound perceived by the ear. From the essence of touch (*sparshatanmatra*) accompanied by sound, arises air having sound and touch as its attributes. From the essence of colour (*rupatanmatra*), accompanied by sound and touch, there arises fire with the properties of sound, touch and colour. From the essence of taste (*rasatanmatra*), combined with sound, touch, and colour, is produced water with the qualities of sound, touch, colour, and taste. The essence of smell (*gandhatanmatra*), combined with the other four, gives rise to earth that has all the five qualities of sound, touch, colour, taste and smell. The five physical elements—ether (*âkasha*), air, light, water, and earth—possess, respectively, the specific properties of sound, touch, colour, taste, smell.

The Subala Upanishad (II.1) traces the ultimate source of all things to the Transcendent Spirit. Thus the beginning is made when earth dissolves in water, water dissolves in ether, ether in the senses, the senses in the *tanmatras*, the *tanmatras* in the element of *mahat* or intellect, the element of *mahat* dissolves in Unmanifest, and the Unmanifest dissolves in the Imperishable. The Imperishable dissolves in the *tamas*. The *tamas* becomes one with the Transcendent. Beyond the Transcendent there is neither being nor non-being, nor both being and non-being.

The beginning is made when the three *gunas*, *sattva*, *rajas* and *tamas*, enter into a state of mutual strife. The three *gunas* jointly produce a tremendous commotion in the infinite bosom of *prakrti*, and with this the process of differentiation and integration sets in. Gradually, things of various magnitudes begin to appear as a result of combination and permutation of the three *gunas* in various proportions. The first to emerge in intellect (*mahat or buddhi*) and because of its importance occupies the highest position. It is nearest to the *purusha* and is able to reflect it in making all right decisions. In making its appearance on the cosmic scene, it indicates the preponderance of the *sattva* element in *prakrti*. The next to arise is the ego-sense (*ahamkara*), often manifested in identifying itself with different pursuits and things of the world. The third element to emerge is mind, also known as the sixth sense. Several hymns of the tenth book (*samhita*) of the *Rigveda* deal with the creation or evolution of the cosmos through entities or divinities newly devised to account for it. Among such entities we meet a Golden Embryo (*Hiranyagarbha*) out of whom the universe emanated a god called All-Maker (*Visvakarman*), a feminine entity called Voice (*Vac*), and Time (*Kala*). The first two divinities were consolidated into a new god called *Prajapati*, the Lord of Progeny, conceived as the father of the gods and of all things whatever (*Rigveda* 10.129). The Primal Being, feeling lonely, decided to divide itself and produced *Viraj* (Shining Forth), a feminine entity (*Rigveda* 10.90). A later verse, found in the *Brhadaranyaka Upanishad* (1.4), informs us that the mating of *Purusa* and *Viraj* produced a second *Purusa*, and after him the gods. At this time, even before the universe existed, the gods decided to sacrifice to their father, the first *Purusa*. As the victim they chose his eldest son, the second *Purusa*. He was slain and dismembered, and from the parts of his body the universe, including its human inhabitants, was fashioned. "The *brâhmana* was his mouth, of his arms was made the warrior, his thighs became the *vaisya* (peasant and trader), and of his feet the *sudra* (serf) was born. The moon arose from his mind, from his eye was born the sun, from his mouth *indra* and *agni*, from his breath the wind was born. From his naval came the air, from his head there came the sky, from his feet the earth, the four quarters from his ear, thus they fashioned the worlds." With Sacrifice the gods sacrificed to Sacrifice—these were the first of the sacred laws. These mighty beings reached the sky, where are the eternal spirits, the gods. This is written in the well-known *Purusasukta*, "Hymn of the (Primeval) Man" (*Rigveda* 10.90). The *Purusasukta* represents the triumph of a sort of sacrificial mysticism. The universe was created not out of the body of a primeval man slain in battle not as in the Hymn of the Golden Embryo, by the bursting of a primeval egg floating in the ocean of chaos, not by a mighty process, almost indescribable in words, as in the Hymn of Creation, but a sacrifice. The conclusions drawn from these premises are significant.

At Janak's court, Yajnavalkya was questioned by another sage Jaratkarava Artabhaga. He answered all Jaratkarava's questions until the last one.

"Yajnavalkya! when a man dies, his voice enters fire, his breath enters the wind, his eyes the sun, his mind the moon, his ears the quarters, his body the earth, his self (*âtman*) space, the hair of his body the plants, the hair of his head the trees, and his blood and semen repose in the waters. Where is that man then?" (*Brhadaranyaka Upanishad* III.2.13).

Yajnavalkya is questioned by another sage, Jaratkarava Astabhaga about what happens to man after death. They discussed it privately. What they discussed was *karman*, what they praised was the doctrine of activities or *karman*. The results of action, *karman*, produce rebirth. "By good works a man gets good (*punya*), by evil works, evil (*pâpa*)." If we take this passage at face value then it becomes evident that the doctrine of *karman* was discovered by Yajnavalkya. In *Brhadaranyaka Upanishad* (IV.3.1) Yajnavalkya elaborates this doctrine and proposes it explicitly. Yajnavalkya then elaborates further: "The person consists only of desires. As is his desire, so is his will; and as is his will, so is the deed he does, whatever deed he does, that he attains." (*Brhadaranyaka Upanishad* IV.4.5).

To whatever his mind and character are attached to, that a man goes with his works. He reaps the reward of deeds he does on earth and comes back again to the world of action (but), he who is free from desire ..., being Brahman itself, goes to Brahman...When all desires in the heart are released, then the mortal becomes immortal and he attains Brahman (*Brhadaranayaka Upanishad* IV.4.6-7). He who has desires continues to be reborn. The person free from desires realizes *Brahman* even here: *sa ca vidvân âpta-kâmah âtma-kâmatayâ ihaiva brahmabhûtah*. What the blind need is to receive sight. Sight is not change of place or transporting into another world. One need not wait for the death of the boy, *na sarîra-pâtottara-kâlam*. Freedom is the cessation of ignorance, *avidyâ-nivrtti*. He in whom desire is stilled suffers no birth.

Another key text on the origin of the doctrine of transmigration is contained in a latter portion of the *Brhadaranyaka Upanishad* (VI.2). It is repeated, with a few variations, in the second oldest of the *Upanishads*, the *Chandogya Upanishad* (V.3-10)

A chieftain named Pravahna Jaivali, a kshatriya, puts a number of blunt questions to the young brâhmana, Svetaketu, ..."Do you know how beings go away in different directions when they die? ...Do you know how that world up there is not filled up by all the many souls that are constantly departing from here? ... Do you know how to get to the path of the Gods or the path of the Fathers?" (*Brhadaranyaka* VI.2.2). Svetaketu had to admit that he could not answer any of these questions. He asked his father, Uddalaka Aruni, to answer these questions. Uddalaka could not answer them either. He asked Jaivali politely. The teaching of Jaivali is rather too lengthy to quote verbatim, and much of it is not immediately relevant. It is summarized in what follows (*Chandogya Upanishad* V. 5-10).

The birth of a child takes place as result of a process interpreted as a series of sacrifices. In heaven the gods offer their faith and produce *soma*. In mid-space they offer *soma* in the rain—clouds, which are thought of as fiery because they contain lightening. On earth they offer the rain, and thus food is produced. In man they offer food, and semen is produced. In woman they offer the man's semen, and the child is produced. He lives his life and dies. Then his body "is carried off to the pyre, to go to the allotted place whence he came" (*Brhadaranayaka Upanishad* VI.10-15).

In *Brhadaranyaka Upanishad* (IV. 4.4), we are told that the self or the soul is like a looping caterpillar, which draws itself up at the tip of a blade of grass in order to pass to another, or like gold used by a goldsmith who forges a new and more beautiful object from an old and broken one.

The souls of those who understand this mystery, as well as "those who in the forest revere faith as truth," merge in the flame of the pyre. After rather complicated peregrinations, the souls reach the sun, and then in the flashes of lightening, they are led to the World of Brahman. "For them there is no return."

On the other hand, the souls of the righteous dead who do not know the mystery, but who perform sacrifice, alms giving and penance, go through similar peregrinations and find their way to the World of the Fathers, heaven. Thence, when their stock of merit is exhausted, they pass into space, from space to the wind, from the wind to the rain, and with the rain they come back to earth and "they turn into food." "Then they are again in the fire of man, then in the fire of women and then they are born to face the worlds once more; and so, over and over again, they are caught up in the cycle" (*Brhadaranyaka Upanishad* VI.2.16; and *Chandogya Upanishad* V.10.6). The soul, returning to earth in the rain, enters a plant. Ultimately the plant is eaten by a man or a male animal, and the soul is transferred to a woman through the semen. Thus it is reborn as a living being.

The Chandogya version adds further (V.10.7-8): "Those who have pleased the gods by their conduct are reborn in one of the three higher (twice-born) classes. Those whose conducts have been evil enter "a foul and stinking womb, such as that of a bitch, a pig or an outcast." Small creatures like flies and worms do not enter either of the two paths. "Theirs is a third condition, to be born and die" (*Chandogya Upanishad* V.10.7-8).

The doctrine of the *Brhadaranyaka Upanishad* appears again, in a much elaborated form, at the beginning of the early *Kausitaki Upanishad* (I.1-7). Here there are several striking differences. The souls of all the dead go to the moon in the waxing half of its cycle and leave it again in its waning half. The moon asks the soul, "Who are you?" And if the right answer is not given, the soul returns to earth in the rain. The soul has to choose whether it wishes to return or go on further through the heavenly realms. Appropriate formulas are given, to be pronounced in the case of either choice. The final password to the higher realms is the answer to the moon's question, "Who are you? The correct password being 'I am you.' This, however, is only the beginning of the soul's journey. It must undergo many tests and ordeals until at last it reaches the throne of the god Brahman. Ultimately, the soul identifies itself with Brahman and is never again reborn.

In the *Katha Upanishad* (I.20), the boy Nachiketâ asked a question from Yama, the god of death: 'When a man is dead, there is this doubt—Some say, He is dead, some say, He is not.' I want you to instruct me about this. Yama replied: "There are two kinds of people in this world; one who believe both body and *âtman* (soul) perish. Others believe that soul (*âtman*) is independent of the body which is perishable but soul (*âtman*) is immortal." Both types of believers have their separate way of life (*Kathâ Upanishad* II. 2).

With many analogies and figures of speech, in beautiful verse, Yama declares the secret of life after death. This self is the owner of, and passenger in, the chariot of the body. Its charioteer is *buddhi* (consciousness and awareness). *Manasâ* (generally translated as mind, the sixth sense) forms the reins, which coordinate the other five senses that are the horses. The *buddhi*, through the mind, must learn to control the vicious refractory senses to achieve the highest state. He who always lacks discretion, unmindful, impure, does not reach that highest state and goes back into the cycle of birth and death. He who is always fastidious, mindful and pure, reaches that state from which he will not be born again (*Kathâ Upanishad* III. 3, 4).

Modern physiologists, anatomists, pathologists and materialists hold a view that the body or the combination of matter produces thought, intelligence, consciousness, mind or soul. They teach that thought, intelligence or consciousness is nothing but a function of the brain. Moreover, they say that every special form of thought is a result of the activity of a special portion of the brain. When we see things, or think of the seen objects, the optical convolutions of our brain are active. A certain portion of the tympana's lobes is active when we hear and so on. If the brain functions stops, the mind, intelligence, consciousness and all the mental phenomena will instantly stop. They say that there is no such thing as soul, consequently, there can be no question regarding its existence after death. They deny the existence of the soul altogether.

In *Gitâ* (II. 23—24) Lord Krishna made it very clear to Arjuna that soul (*âtman*) does not perish when body perishes after the death of a person; *âtman* is the life, not the body; body perishes, *âtman* is immortal. The snake casts off his old slough and gets a new slough; and a person puts on new cloths and discards the old torn-off cloths. Similarly, *âtman* or the *soul* gets out of the old body and enters a new one (*Gitâ* II. 22-25). If a person understands this truth, he knows *Brahman* and not what people here adore. "That which is not thought by the mind, but by which they say the mind thinks; that which is not seen by the eye but by which the eyes see; that which is not expressed through speech but that by which speech is expressed; that which is not heard by ears but by the ears hear; that which is not breathed by life, but by which life breathes; that verily know thou, is *Brahman* and not what people here adore" (*Kena Upanishad* I. 5- 9).

Krishn urges Arjuna not to grieve for the dead, he says that death is not extinction. The individual form may change, but the essence is not destroyed. Until perfection is obtained, individuality persists. However repeatedly the mortal frame is destroyed, the inner individuality preserves its identity and takes on a new form. Beaconed by this faith, man has to work for self-knowledge. Lord *Krishna* said: "Death is certain of him who is born and rebirth is certain of him who is dead. Over this unavoidable affair, therefore, you should not grieve." (*Gita* II: 27). He further said, "What happens to body and soul when they are separated by death." He told about body: "Even as a person discards worn-out clothes, and puts on new ones, so the embodied soul casts off worn-out body, and enters into others which is new." (*Gita* II:22). "O Bhârata! All beings are unmanifested before they were born and will become unmanifested again when they are dead; they are manifested only in the intermediate state. What is the point then to grieve about?" (*Gita* II: 28). He explained the characteristics of the soul (*âtman*). "Weapons can't cut the soul, nor can fire burn it, water can't drench it, nor can wind make it dry." (*Gita* II: 23). "This soul cannot be cut, nor burnt, and neither can be wetted nor dried. It is eternal, all-pervading stable, constant and everlasting." (*Gita* II:24). "This soul is unmanifested, unthinkable and immutable. Therefore, knowing it as such, you should not grieve." (*Gita* II: 25). "O Mighty armed! Even if you regard this soul as constantly undergoing birth and death, you should not grieve." (*Gita* II: 26). Sir Edwin Arnold translated them into the following:

"Never the spirit was born; the spirit shall cease to be never,

Never was time it was not; end and beginning are dreams,

Birthless and deathless and changeless remainth the spirit for ever,

Death hath not touched it all, dead thouth the house of it seems."

Some of the learned persons from the Western countries also think in same way about death as Hindus do. Following is a stanza quoted from the book, "Song of Creation," written by J. Miller (1841—1913):

Death is but a name, a date,

A milestone by the stormy road,

Where you may lay aside your load,

And bow your face and rest and wait,

Defying fear, defying fate.

Beaumont and Fletcher wrote a poem about death:

To die

Is to begin to live, It is to end

And old, state, weary work and to commence,

A newer and a better.

Cicero (106 to 43 BC) wrote:

The last day does not bring extinction,

But a change of place.

Even Shakespeare wrote in his famous book, 'Julius Caesar,' that we all know so well.

Cowards die many times before their death;
The valiant never taste of death but once.
Of all the wonders that I yet have heard;
It seems to me most strange that men should fear;
Seeing that death, a necessary end,
Will come when it will come.

Confucius, the Chinese philosopher said when he was asked about death, "How can I say anything about death when I do not, as yet understand life?" He further explained, "Let us not trouble ourselves with supernatural things and beings, while we do not know how to serve men."

All of us are born to die. It is the nature of birth. The seeds of desire left from previous lives have pushed us into this world and they will affect the manner in which we die. These unmanifested desires (*vâsanas*) are the blueprint of our destiny. How we use it is up to us. If you have a difficult destiny because of your past actions you will need much of self-effort to achieve, but it is not impossible. It is the difference between a smooth, fast-flowing river, and one that is stagnant and full of obstructions that will take you a shorter distance for the same degree of effort.

Bibliography

Basham, A.L., *The Origins and Development of Classical Hinduism*, New York, Oxford University Press, 1989.

Griffith, R.T.H., *The Hymns of Rigveda*, 2 Vols, Varanasi, India, Chowkhamba Sanskrit Series Office, 1971.

Muller, Max F., *The Upanishads*, Vol & II, New York, Dover Publications Inc.

O'Flaherty, W.D., *The Rig-Veda, An Anthology*, Harmondsworth, Middlesex, Penguin Book, 1981.

Radhakrishnan, S., *The Principal Upanishads*, London, George Allen & Unwin Ltd., 1974.

Radhakrishanan, S. and Moore, C.A., *A Source Book in Indian Philosophy. Princeton, N.J.*, Princeton University Press, 1967.

Singh, Balbir, *Indian Metaphysics*, New Jersey, Humanities Press International, Inc. 1967.

Chapter 8

Man and God

What is the difference between man and God, between the saint and the sinner? Only ignorance. What is the difference between the highest man and the lowest worm that crawls under your feet? Ignorance is the difference. The infinite divinity is unmanifested; it has to be manifested. This is spirituality, the science of the soul.

The Upanishad states, tat tvam asi, 'that art thou.' this mean that "God is myself" even as my soul is the self of my body. God is the supporting, controlling principle of the soul, even as the soul is the supporting principle of the body. God and soul are one, not because the two are identical but because God dwells and penetrates the soul. He is the inner guide. God is not recognized by the soul so long as the soul does not acquire the redeeming knowledge. We acquire this knowledge by serving God with our whole heart and soul.

MAN

Man is made up of body and *âtman*. Further the body consists of the physical body, mind and intellect (*buddhi*). Five sense-organs (*jñâna-indriya*) such as eyes, ears, nose, tongue and skin, and five organs of action (*karma indriya*) such as, mouth, hands, feet, anus and genitalia are located in the physical body of a man. Mind is the focal point of all *indriyas* (all the sensory and motor organs) activities. Man makes contact with the world through these ten organs only. All the stimuli from the world of objects can reach the mind through the five sense organs that merely serve as vehicles through which the mind perceives objects. It also experiences emotions like joy, sorrow, lust, passion, greed, jealousy, love, kindness, pity, etc. Without mind, the eyes cannot see, ears cannot hear, nose cannot smell, tongue cannot taste and skin cannot feel. In deep sleep, when the body, mind and intellect are not functioning, none of the above function is felt. The effects of all these stimuli assail the mind as five vices (*vikâras*): desire (*kâma*), anger (*krodha*), greed (*lobha*), attachment (*moha*) and ego (*ahamkâra*). It is these vices that constitute all the sorrows of man.

Intellect is the judging capacity and mind is the doubting capacity in man. The intellect, depending on its own previous experience, decides as to the action to be taken, thereby showing power of reasoning and discrimination, and passes its decision on to the mind for action through the five organs of action (*karma indriya*). If the data provided by the mind is correct, the intellect will make good decisions; if the data is inaccurate and prejudiced or selfish and full of likes and dislikes, the decisions are bound to be selfish, and result in selfish acts. However intellect may, on its own, initiate desires. Thus intellect has the controlling influence on the mind. Intellect dictates good or bad actions. The mind may, on occasions, acts its own reaction, this is called instinct. Only animals act by instinct. Eating, sleeping, mating, fear and life are common to man and animal. Man is different from animal in the intellect. When man cannot make use of the intellect, he acts on instinct like an animal. Men are not considered human when they are not able to discriminate between good and evil. The mind is impetuous, the intellect has sobering effects on the mind. There is always conflict between the impetuosity of the mind and the intellect. The mind wants to eat sweets, the intellect says, "Don't, you are suffering from diabetes". These doubts exist at every step in our life, thus there is always conflict within us. Maladjustment between mind and intellect can result in distorted or imbalanced personality. Integration of the mind and intellect is a big step towards a good life and bliss. Real happiness is possible only in proportion to the amount of integration that the individual has gained within himself. That integration can only be possible by religion or *dharma*. How often have you had second thoughts? Every time a thought has arisen in your mind? It is an integrated mind that allows itself to be guided by the intellect. A tranquil and poised man is one whose mind and intellect work in co-ordination. Intellect, being closest to the âtman, best reflects the attributes of the *âtman*. In the *Katha Upanishad*, the intellect has been called the charioteer of the *âtman* (soul), senses are horses and the body is chariot. He whose horses are well broken, and whose reins are strong and kept well in the hands of the charioteer (the intellect) reaches the goal, which is the state of Him, the Omnipresent. But the man whose horses (the senses) are not controlled, nor the reins (the mind) well managed goes to destruction.

Sage Kausitaki said: 'The *prâna* or *âtman* or soul is the Brahman unto whom the other sense organs carry their offerings, i.e. the knowledge and various experiences relating to the world of names and forms.' 'The prâna or âtman is the Brahman, and it prevails over the mind as the overload' (*Kausitaki Upanisad*). When the vocal-organ speaks, the *prana* speaks in unison. Similarly, when the eyes see, the ear hears, the mind ideates. That is, when each one of these organs functions jointly with the vital energy inherent therein, then all of them together function likewise in unison, each inhibiting for the time being its own characteristic function. Thus, it establishes its identity with the prâna at the time of cognition. When any one of the organs loses its vitality (whether of perception, or of action), then that alone ceases without detriment to the function of the others. But on death, and with the departure of the *prâna or âtman*, the functions of all the others too cease.

Evidences of the existence of the soul is not only given in the Hindu scriptures, but one can experience himself with the perception by the senses. In our sleep we see, hear, and experience fear and run. This act of seeing without eyes, hearing without ears, and running without legs are accomplished by none other than the soul. Another example, when man dies, his eyes, ears, legs and other organs are still present, but he cannot see, hear, run or do other vital functions without the soul. *Yogis* or ascetics can take the soul elsewhere separate from this body.

Atman (soul) provides energy and consciousness (*cetanâ*), i.e. life to the body. Without *âtman*, the body cannot function. It is like electricity for a radio, TV, bulb, heater, etc. Like the electricity, *âtman* is present in all living beings. *Atman* energizes the intellect to assimilate experiences, to provide understanding and discrimination from good and evil, and to give ideas and desires. The same *âtman* energizes the mind to think how to implement these desires, and to experience emotions. *Atman* also provides energy to the body, to carry out thoughts into practice. When *prakriti* of a man such as, body, mind and intellect are impregnated by the *âtman or purusha* (spirit), it becomes a viable man. Although the matter (*prakriti*), i.e. body, mind and intellect are themselves inert and insentient, they become sentient when in contact with *âtman* , i.e. spirit or *purusha*.

A body without *âtman* is nothing but filth consisting of filthy excretory matter and raw flesh covered in skin. Hence it is said. "Beauty is skin deep." On departure of *âtman*, even the dearest and nearest relatives, whom you are so fond and proud of, will be anxious to get rid of you. This is the real worth of your body without *âtman*. Therefore, it is the *âtman* you should worship. This is the 'self realization'.

Being subtlest of the subtle, *âtman* cannot be perceived by sense organs. *Atman* is a part of Supreme *Atman*. Unless one destroys the ego completely and its bondage to the world, one cannot recognize the Supreme *Atman* (*Pramatman* or God). When the egoism is destroyed by spiritual advancement, what remains is pure *âtman* which recognizes the Supreme *Atman*, i.e. God.

It is said that God is farther than the farthest, nearer than the nearest. Farthest because He cannot be apprehended by our sense organs, yet He is nearer than the nearest, for He is the very life in us abiding in every cell of our body, in me, in you and in every thing around us. Without Him, the body would be a dead lump.

As the same sun reflects on the hills and planes of all the continents of the world and as the same fire manifests itself through different kinds of wood, the Self (*Pramâtman*) is manifest in all beings. The true Self in man is God. To realize the Self (*Pramâtman*) is to realize God. Souls (*âtman*) are limited to bodies, whereas Self (God) is all-pervading. Soul (*âtman*) enters into the body and departs. Self (God) is the soul of all the souls (*âtmans*). Soul is a spark of God. Self (God) is eternal and so is soul (*âtman*), being a part of the Self. As the fire pervades a metal when it is made hot, same way Self encompasses the soul within and without.

Souls (*âtmans*) are divided into three categories due to their association with nature: *Sâttavic jivas* or pure souls, *râjasic jivas* or souls with attachment, and *tâmasic jivas* or souls with gross ignorance. When the *âtman* enjoys the wakeful state, it uses the *sthula sharira* or gross body. In the dream state, the *âtman* is experiencing the astral or the subtle state body known as *sukshma sharira*. In *turiya*, or the transcendental state, the *âtman* is in the presence of the pure Self (*Pramâtman*). Therefore, it enters into pure consciousness or *samadhi*.

Atman is enveloped by five sheaths or *koshas*. They are known as *annamaya kosha* or the food sheath, *pranamaya kosha* or the vital sheath, *manomaya kosha* or the mental sheath, *vijñânamaya kosha* or the intellect sheath, and *ânandamaya kosha* or the bliss sheath. These five sheaths constitute the triple bodies known as the gross, the subtle, and the causal. The food and vital sheaths are in the gross body; the mental and intellect sheaths are in the subtle body; and the bliss sheath is in the causal body. One attains Self realization by negating the triple bodies of the five sheaths. This is the *jñâna yoga* or discipline of knowledge. Yama, the teacher, says to Naciketâ, the young student, "This *âtman*, (being) hidden in all beings, is not manifested to all. But it can be realized by all who are trained to inquire into subtle truths, by means of their sharp and subtle *buddhi* (intellect) or pure reason" (*Katha Upanisad* III.12).

Meditation is the door that leads to the Self (God). In meditation, the faculty of intuition operates and intuition alone can reveal the Self. This makes the soul (*âtman*) withdraw from sinful thoughts and deeds and it experiences joy and strength in its work coming directly from the Self (*Pramâtman*). In its gradual realization of the Self (*Pramatman*) within, the *âtman* receives the support and protection of the Self in both visible and invisible ways. And finally, the *âtman* identifies with the Self (*Pramâtman*) and realizes that all this is the play (*lilâ*) of the *Pramâtama* (Self), and that the Self is the true enjoyer of this cosmic play. When the *âtman* reaches this state, it attains joy and peace. Experiencing God within, the *âtman* (soul) experiences God everywhere and in everybody. This experience destroys all desires (*kâma*), dispels all doubts, and the soul (*âtman*) finds its eternal freedom from all desires and adjuncts. This freedom is salvation (*mukti*). This is Self realization.

Lord *Krishna* said, "When the lord (*jivâtmâ*) or the individual soul takes up a body and when he leaves it, he takes (the sense and the mind) and goes (with them) as the wind takes scents from their seats (flowers)" (*Gita* XV. 8). As essentially the wind is unconnected with the smell (scent), so is the (*âtmâ*) soul unconnected with the mind, senses and body but it, by assuming them as Its own, attracts them towards it. As wind, in spite of being the evolute of ether, carries smell (perfume), a fragment of the earth, so does the soul, in spite of being a fragment of God carrying the transitory body, the evolute of Nature migrate to the different wombs. The wind being *matter* (insentient) does not possess the discrimination that it should not take scent from its seat. But the embodied soul has the discrimination and power to renounce affinity for the body. Every human being has been bestowed upon independence by which he can either get attached to the insentient body or renounce this attachment. In order to rectify the error he should accept the reality, by changing the assumption that he (the soul) has no affinity for the physical, the subtle and the causal bodies, the fragment of Nature. Then he can be easily liberated from the bondage of birth and death. The soul commits three errors: (1) It regards itself as the master of the mind, intellect and body but actually becomes their slave; (2) Having become the master of insentient objects, it forgets its real master, God; and (3) It does not renounce its assumed affinity for the insentient objects though it is independent in renouncing them. God has provided independence to the soul (âtmâ), to make proper use of objects such as the body, mind and intellect in order to attain salvation rather than to become their master. But by an error, the soul, instead of properly utilizing such objects, regards itself as their master but really becomes their slave.

He who loves becoming a master cannot attain God because he forgets who is the real master. An boy in childhood cannot live without his mother but when he matures and marries, he becomes house-holder and becomes the master of his children and wife; he forgets his mother, so does the soul (âtmâ) forget its real master when it becomes the master of insentient objects such as the body, etc. So long as this forgetfulness continues, i.e. it has a disinclination for God, it will go on suffering.

A man (soul) has got two kinds of power: (I) life-breath power; and (ii) will power (power of desire). The life-breath power decays every moment and when it comes to an end, it is called death. Attachment to the insentient leads a man to have a desire to act and to acquire. If this desire to act and to acquire is wiped out while possessing the life-breath power, the man is emancipated. But if he gives up the body while possessing desire, he has to be reborn with the will (desire) power of the previous birth while he receives new life breath. The life-breath power should be spent in wiping out desires. The desire can be easily wiped out by being engrossed in the welfare of all beings without any selfish motive.

GOD

There are five gross elements of nature—namely, earth, fire, water, air and ether. These are both within and outside of all living beings in this world, and the same way, God has no shape or form, is limitless, pervading everywhere—

there is no place where He is not. God is omnipresent, He is both inside and outside this existence, and those who are His devotees can realize this. If God had form, who made that form? Our conception of God being the prime cause, prime creator, would fail. Thus, God is omnipresent and also omnipotent like electricity in the electronic world; but electricity cannot help us unless we make a contact with it through a finite switch which connects the bulb with the electricity. As soon as the contact is made, light appears. Hence, one has to bring about the connection between the human soul and God.

Forms: *Nirguna* and *Saguna* are two forms applied to God. *Nirguna* literally means without qualities, shape or form, hence cannot be recognized by any of the five *indriyas* (sense organs), mind or intellect. *Saguna* means having qualities. According to *Saguna* or anthropomorphic conception, people have considered God as a human form and more particularly like a male. Yogic philosophy does not consider God as an anthropomorphic form, because we use secular words to describe the celestial qualities of God. The human being is illusioned by His transcendental form; if He is a man who is above the mundane. In *Svetasvatara Upanishad* (III.19), it is stated, "God is without foot or hand, yet swift and grasping. He sees without eyes, and He hears without ears. He knows whatever is to be known; of Him there is none who knows. They call Him the Primeval, the Supreme Person." According to Vedâs, God is not an individual, it's energy but it is not an inanimate power or unconscious like electricity, rather it has animate energy or conscious power. This means He (God) may not have a human form and who live somewhere up in the sky. God is that mysterious power which is responsible for the creation and maintenance of the universe and its variegated phenomena. *Ekam sat viprâ bahudhâ vadanti* or "truth is one; while men call it by different names" is the teaching of the *Chandogya Upanishad*. We call Him Ram, *Krishna*, Jesus, Mohammad, etc. These are qualities of God which are denoted bythe above names. Unlike the many gods of the Vedas, there is only one God in the Vedânta, and that one is *Brahman*, the only one true God. The *âtman* or soul that is in you is *Brahman* Himself. "This is my self within the heart, this is *Brahman*" (*Chandogya Upanishad* III, XIV.4). So God is right within you. Worship the God that is within yourself. That is what the *Upanishads* teach. U*panishads* say in bold terms: "Seek not favour from any divinity. Reality is not the divinity which you are worshipping—the guardian of order is not outside, but it is right within you".

There is one and only one God unchanging and indivisible and the One God functions everywhere just as the one Sun can be reflected in many water pots at the same time. Break the pots, the sun remains the same. On the death of man, *âtman* remains unaffected.

The diversity of deities is part of the earliest Vedic history of the Hindu tradition. In the *Rigveda*, the various gods are elaborately praised and in their individual hymns, each is praised as Supreme. *Indra* may in one hymn be called the "sole sovereign of men and of gods", and in the next hymn *Varuna* may be praised as the "supreme Lord, ruling the spheres". It is not monotheism nor really polytheism. To describe the deities of Hinduism, Muller coined the word *kathenotheism*—the worship of one god at a time. Each is exalted in turn. Each is praised as creator, source and sustainer of the universe when one stands in the presence of that deity. There are many gods, but their multiplicity does not diminish the significance or power of any of them. Each of the great gods may serve as a lens through which the whole of reality is clearly seen.

In the *Rigveda*, thirty three gods were described. Now people believe, there are three hundred thirty million or 33 crore gods in Hinduism, meaning thereby that there are innumerable gods. In the *Brhadâranyaka Upanishad* (III.9.1), a seeker named Vidagdha Sâkalya approaches the sage Yâjnavalkya with a question, "How many gods are there, Yâjnavalkya?"

"Three thousand three hundred and six," He replied.

"Yes," said he, "but just how many gods are there, Yâjnavalkya?"

"Thirty three".

"Yes", said he, "but just how many gods are there, Yâjnavalkya?"

"Six".

"Yes", said he, "but just how many gods are there, Yâjnavalkya?"

"Three".

"Yes", said he, "but just how many gods are there, Yâjnavalkya?"

"Two".

"Yes", said he, "but just how many gods are there, Yâjnavalkya?"

"One".

This conversation makes us conclude that even though there are many gods, in reality there is only ONE. One God appears in a thousand different forms to devotees according to the way they perceive that Supreme Power.

The phrase, 33 gods, occurring in the Vedas, is explained in the *Shatapatha*. They are 8 *vasu* or the abodes of creatures (derived from *vas* = to live), i.e. the earth, water, fire or light, air, sky, sun, moon, and planets; 11 *rudras* or vital processes (derived from **ru** = to weep, as on the disappearance of these vital forces from the body, it ceases to live, when the relatives of the deceased weep), i.e. in-breath (*âpana*), out-breath (*prâna*), energy (*vyâna*) or motive power, swallowing power (*udâna*), bracing or recuperative power, circulation (*sâmana*), belching (*nâga*), twinking (*kurma*), hunger or craving (*kirkala*), yawning (*devadatta*), decomposing power (*dhananjaya*), and the ego (*jivâtma*); 12 *adityas* or the signs of zodiac (derived from from *ada* = to take), i.e. the sun's (*aditya's*) course through these constellations takes away or reduces the life of creatures, *Indra* or electricity, derivatively meaning a great cause of power and prosperity, *Prajâpati* or the lord of creatures or *yajna* (work) sacrifices; as it is a cause of purifying the air; water, rain and plants. It also gives an opportunity to respect the learned, and it is the mother of inventions and various kinds of manufacture. These are the 33 gods, denominated from their having wonderful properties mentioned above. The 14th chapter of the *Shatapatha* distinctly says that the Supreme Being is the Lord of all these objects and the greatest of all. Yjnavalkya reduced the 33 to one God, that is *Brahman*. The 33 crore gods are not gods *per se*, they are manifestations of the one Supreme *Brahman*, who alone is true God. The Hindu idea of God is that He is everywhere—in the rocks, plants, animals and human beings. He pervades the whole universe. Even the illiterate Tamil labourer says, "God is in a pillar as in a piece of fiber (*thurumbu*)". According to the *Upanishads*, God is not conceived of dwelling in Heaven. "Our Father in the Heaven" is a Christian idea. The *Upanishads* say that both *Brahman* and *âtman* (soul or self) are one and the same. *Brahman* is neither masculine nor feminine, although in popular language *Brahman* is referred to as 'He'. He is sometimes referred to as 'That' as in 'Thou art That'(*Tat tvam asi*) or 'You are God.' The Bible says, 'I and My father are One', the Hindu scripture says, 'I am Brahman' as well as the Sufi claims 'Ana al Haq', and the statement 'I am that I am' of the old Testament. All reflect the same idea of the oneness of Ultimate Reality and Man as essence, the difference being only one of degree and not of kind.

Man is a copy of Ultimate Reality as he is not a mere physical entity but a *mind-matter* unity. Theology with only a narrow anthropomorphic conception of divinity, invest God with hands and feet, like man. In the Hindu concept, God is attributed a thousand heads, hands, legs and eyes! Taken literally, such a creature will be a fearsome ogre indeed! However, it is only meant to convey the all-knowing, all-powerful and all-seeing nature of the Supreme. The Hindu have gods and goddess in charge of every function in the universe, and any person can aspire to attain these positions by hard penance.

According to *Upanishads*, God is conceived of in four ways. Firstly, when the absolute God is by Himself, i.e. before the creation of the universe, He is called by *Brahman*. Secondly, when He has manifested Himself as the universe, He is called *Virât*. Thirdly, when *Brahman* is conceived as the universal spirit, He is called *Hiranya Garbha*. Fourth, when He, in *sagun* aspect, does the triple function of creation, preservation and dissolution of the universe, He is known as *Eshwara*. Hinduism has personified the three functions into three separate Gods—*Brahmâ, Vishnu* and *Shiva* respectively. These three are fundamentally one though conceived in a three-fold manner. *Brahman, Vishnu* and *Rudra* may be considered as three different aspects or powers of the Supreme God. For example, the same individual is a son to his parents, a husband to his wife, a brother to his brothers and sisters, and a father to his children. He treats them all differently. The four words: son, husband, brother and father do not denote four different persons, but four roles of one and the same individual. Even though, the one God is, as creator, known as *Brahman*; as preserver, known as *Vishnu*, and as destroyer, known as Rudra. Thus, they are not different gods, but three aspects of the same Supreme God. Some aditional power (*sakti*) is needed for these Gods; and this *sakti* is personified as the wives and goddesses. Sarswati,

Lakshmi and Parvati are so called consorts of *Brahma, Vishnu* and *Shiva* respectively. Similarly, *Ganesha* and *Skanda* (called also *Kartikeya* or *Subrahmanya)* are so called sons of Shiva and Parvati. These too represent some functions. Subrahmanya is supposed to be the generalissimo to assist gods, the Forces of God, by putting down the demon of unrighteousness and establish *dharma* or righteousness in the world (see chapter, Idol Worship). In the *Upanishads*, there is only one Supreme *Brahman*, and He is neither male or female and so neither married nor marriageable, and therefore no sons or daughters.

In Vedanta, the Supreme Ultimate Reality is known as *Brahman*. It is also known as *Satchidânanda* and is of the nature of *sat* (truth) or existence, *cit* or consciousness and *ânanda* or bliss (*sat cit ânanda*) which are absolute, that is, not contingent on anything else. These true existence, consciousness and bliss are also primal in the sense that these are features of man which are all derived from *Brahman*. These are not attributes of Brahman, rather Brahman is these aspects. It is compacted of them whole and entire as sugar candy is sweetness all over. Sweetness cannot be separated in thought or reality from the sugar candy. There is no candy independent of the sugar and qualified by it. *Sat, cit* and *ânanda* are not different to each other rather *sat, cit* and *ânanda* are all one in substance.

The word '*Brahman*' is derived from the Sanskrit root '*brh*' which means to 'grow big' without limit and it can be an oblique reference to an explosion. Hence, it is perhaps also called '*Shabda Brahman*' in the Scriptures as *Brahman* manifests itself as a '*Sphota*' or explosion. *Brahman* being the one and only Reality, represents everything, including even the state of singularity before the Big Bang, as well as the whole manifested universe after it. As the point of singularity, *Brahman* is the impersonal absolute of pure timeless existence. As all creation emerges from *Brahman* with the Big Bang, its only symbol is the single syllable '*OM*' (*shabda Brahman*). *Brahman* has no form because a form is a restriction of an object in space. Since it is the all and everywhere, it cannot have a specific form bounded by physical contour. It has no qualities. It is *nirguna*, it does not have any shape or colour. For, if it is said that it has a particular quality, say a red colour, then it means that it does not have any other colours, which will put a limitation on *Brahman*. That will go against the universality of *Brahman*. *Brahman* is not exclusive of anything; it is all-inclusive. In fact, it is the All. As it is the All, there is nothing outside it for it to attain. As it is the permanent substratum of the universe, it can undergo no change. Being the Ultimate Reality, it is perfect and pure, and so does not stand in need of any purification. Brahman being the All, it is the infinitesimally minute and the infinitely mighty. It is the stuff of everything in the universe, the inner core and essence of all objects— living and lifeless—which are its manifestations or appearances. We have a prayer with this effect: "*Om poornamadah poornamidam poornât poornamudachyate; poornasya poornamâdâya poornamevâvashishyate. Om shântih shântih shântih.*" The meaning thereby is that the invisible is the infinite, the visible too is the infinite.

From the infinite, the visible universe of infinite extension has come out. The infinite remains the same, even though the infinite universe has come out of it. Om peace peace peace. We cannot say what Brahman is; we can only say what it is not (*neti neti*). "The Supreme Being cannot be seen with the eyes. Nor words can express Him. Indeed, non of the senses can actually perceive Him. He cannot be reached by the performance of deeds or the practice of austerities. Hands cannot grasp Him. The mind fails to comprehend Him. When the mind is purified through the clarity of understanding, the aspirant realizes Him, the subtle one, through deep meditation." (Mundak Upani*shad* III: 1.8)

The Brahma Sutra of Vyasa is the basis of Vedantic philosophy, widely followed by all Hindus. Several great achâryas or teachers have given commentaries and interpretations of Hindu philosophy based on srutis. We have the systems of Shankra, Bhaskara, Ramanuja, Madhava, Vishnuswami, Nimbarka, Vallabha, Chaitanya and the northern and southern schools of Shavism. Among them are the Advaita by Shankra, the Vishista-Advaita by Ramanuja, and the Svaita by Madhava are commentaries on Brahma Sutra.

1. **Advaita or Monism**: During 780–820 AD, Sankarâcharya or Shankra interpreted the *Upanishads* and the *Vedanta Sutras* as teaching monism or idealism Shankra's *advaita* is an elaboration of vedic text, "*Ekâm Sat, Viprâ Bahudhâ Vadânti*", a great word in *Chândogya Upanishad*. *Advait* literally means 'No-twos'. God (*Brahman*), the Soul (*âtman*) and the world are one and the same. The *Advaita* as taught by Sankra is a rigorous and absolute teaching. Whatever is, is Brahman. It is absolutely homogenous by itself. *Brahman*, the absolute, alone is real; the world is unreal; and the *jiva* or self (individual) soul is non-different from *Brahman*. *Brahman* is not an object, as it is *adrishya*, beyond the reach of our vision. Shankra's Brahman is *nirguna*, without attributes, formless, without special characteristics, immutable and eternal. It is impersonal. It becomes a personal God or *Saguna Brahman* only through its association with *mayâ*. They are not two opposite entities. In the Advaita philosophy, the same *Nirguna Brahman* appears as *Saguna Brahman* for the pious worship of the devotees. It is the same truth from two different points of view. The former is transcendental and the latter is relative. The world is not real. It only appears to be so, because of the veil or *mayâ*. The soul is not a part of God but God Himself. Because of veil or *mayâ*, the soul thinks it is different God. For man's salvation, he should remove this curtain of *Mayâ*. Man should follow *jnâna yoga*. When *jnâna* has dawned, the soul (*âtman*) realizes its past ignorance and its present true nature of godliness. This means freedom from the misery of rebirth and union with *Brahman*. This union (*sakshatkâra*) means *moksha* or *mukti* or eternal bliss.

2. **Visishta—Advaita** or Qualified Monism: After about 300 years Ramanujâcharya or Ramanuja (1017–1137 AD) interpreted the *Upanishads* and *Brahma Sutras* as teaching *Visishta—advaita* or qualified monism. In this system, there are three distinct realities. God is *Vishnu—Narayan* and is the Supreme Reality. The souls which are myriad and the world are also real but distinct from God. At the same time, souls and the world cannot be separated from God as the soul cannot be separated from the body. This internal relationship among the three entities is called *Aprthaka siddhi,* a doctrine fundamental to *Visishta advaita*. According to the *Brhadaranyaka Upanishad*, the world is the body of God and God lives in and rules the world from within. The soul is a part of God, but not God Himself. The primary way to salvation is devotion or *bhakti* to God with complete self-surrender or *saranagati* to God; this is the important doctrines of this school. After a man's death, the soul that has released itself from rebirths goes to Heaven (*Vaikunta*)*,* and enjoys the presence of Gods there but does not unite with Him, as in the *Advaita*. God and His incarnates and *sakti* must be worshipped in the form idols or icons.

3. **Dvaita or Dualism:** Between 1119–1278 AD Madhva-âcharya or Madhva interpreted the *Upanishads* and the *Brahma Sutras* as being theism and realism. Madhva's system of *dvaita or dualism* is really pluralism. In this system, the soul and the world are very real and eternal like God. They are distinct and absolutely separate from one another. According to this doctrine, there are five real and eternal differences: (1) between God and individual souls; (2) between God and matter; (3) between individual souls and matters; (4) between one soul and another; and (5) between one particle of matter and another. God, in spite of these differences, is Supreme and all the others are subordinate to Him. The pathway to salvation, as in all *vaishnava* school (visishta *advaita* of Ramanuja), is *bhakti* or devotion and self-surrender.

The question that comes to mind of everybody is whether or not one can see God face to face. We should not take parochial views rather take augmented view of getting a glimpse of God. We can only infer the existence of God like butter in milk, like a tree in a seed. The fact is that we cannot see God with our eyes, but if we take meditation as a sixth sense of knowledge, we would see. We can see God when we reach *turiya* or the transcendental stage of meditation. There is a distinction between existence, manifestation and realization. Terrestrial objects have existence and they also have manifestation and realization. God has existence, and realization but no manifestation. The novel creation of the universe and its realization is the manifestation or demeanour of God. When materialists say that there is no God, only Nature exists, they really thereby mean that these materialistic matters such as, earth, water, fire, air and ether are Nature. Though these materialistic matters are the building blocks of creation of the universe, however the universe is not self-creating. Even with the materialistic points of view the implication of Nature is to the power or energy by which the universe is created utilizing the materialistic matters. Materialistic matters of the creation can be seen but can the power or energy by which it is being created cannot be seen. Analogously, we can see the glowing of a light bulb, we can hear radio and a T.V., and see the working of many electric appliances but can we see the electricity by which these appliances work. How can we expect to see the supreme power or energy, i.e. God. It would be fruitless to ponder it. Materialists consider the energy as the basis of Nature. Spiritualists consider it as consciousness. Neither of the two would get a first hand glimpse of God.

God is not a person, as are we in our narrowness. Our being, consciousness, feeling, volition have but a shadow of resemblance to His being (existence), consciousness, and bliss (*Sat, chit, ânand*). He is a person in the transcendental sense. He has an impersonal and absolute aspect, but we should not think He is beyond the reach of all experience—even our inner one. He comes within the calm experience of men. It is in bliss-consciousness that we realize Him. There can be no other direct proof of His existence.

The nature of God and soul is holy, immortal and righteous. But God's actions are the making of the world, its preservation, and its destruction, the keeping of all things in their respective spheres. The functions of the soul are the propagation of the species, and the preservation of the offspring, and the doing of good and evil. The attributes of God are eternal knowledge, happiness, omnipotence, and other infinite powers. The qualities of soul are the desire to obtain things (*ichha*); hatred of pain and other evils (*dwesha*), strife (*prayatna*), pleasure (*sukha*), bewailing and sadness (*dukha*), knowledge and discernment (*jnana*) (*Nyaya* II, 10 and *Vaisheshika* III,ii.4). The soul also has out-breath (*prana*), in breath (*apana*), closing of the eyes (*mimesh*), opening them (*unmesha*), consciousness (*mano*), motion (*gati*), senses (*indriya*), hunger, thirst, joy, sorrow and other affections (*antarvikara*); these qualities of the soul are distinct from those of God. These qualities are manifested as long as the soul dwells in the body. This is like the light which is not found in the absence of the sun and the lamp, but is always present when they are present. The knowledge of God and the soul is possible only through the characteristics of the soul. Further distinction between God and the soul are: God, the Supreme Being is infinite, all pervading and omniscient. The Supreme Being is eternal, holy, ever wakeful, absolute by nature, but the soul is sometimes free and, at other times, subject to the influence of her actions. The Supreme Being is ever above ignorance or confusion, being omnipresent and omniscient; but the soul is sometimes illumined with knowledge and, at other times, it falls into ignorance. God never suffers the pains of birth and death, which the soul endures.

The relationship amongst man, world and God is beautifully illustrated by the example of a piece of damask cloth in which some patterns have been woven by the same thread. The cloth represents the universe and the thread is God. Now has this piece of cloth an existence other than the thread? If the thread were to be removed there would be no cloth. The thread and the whole universe depicted on the cloth would become one. Similarly, without God the world, its beings and things, could not exist and, like the cloth, the total concept of the world would fall.

When one sees the night sky, one naturally raises questions about the stars, how they are situated, who lives there, etc. In an answer to such an inquiry, the author of *Srimad-Bhâgavatam* says that the God is the origin of all creations. There are people who do not believe in the creator. The modern scientist creates rockets and satellites which are thrown into outer space to fly or stay in there under the control of a scientist far away. All the universes and the innumerable planets within them are similar to such rockets and satellites, and they are all controlled by the God. If a man's mind can produce rockets spaceships and satellites, it is conceivable that a mind higher than man's can produce superior things, such a stars.

The chief engineer of a big complicated construction project does not personally take part in the construction but it is he who knows all the nooks and corners of the construction project because everything is carried out under his instructions only. In other words, he knows everything about the construction. Similarly, God, who is the supreme engineer of this cosmic creation, knows very well what is happening in every nook and corner of the cosmic creation, although activities appear to be performed by someone else.

When one argues that God is no more expert than the producers of a complicated piece of electronic equipment or simple watch which has so many delicate parts, we have to say that God is a greater mechanic than the watchmaker or electrical engineer because He simply creates one machine in male and female forms, and the male and female forms go on producing innumerable similar machines without the further attention of God. If a man could manufacture a set of machines capable of producing other machines without man giving the matter any further attention, then man could be said to equal the intelligence of God. This is not possible. Each and every man's imperfect machines has to be handled individually by a mechanic.

Some religions teach that God created the universe out of nothing and within six days man appeared on the scene. The Hindu view is that God projected the universe out of himself and the process of evolution took place till the emergence of man. It took millions of years to evolve human being. Recently our satellite pictures reaffirm the theory of Big Bang on the origin of universe. Here science can be used to resolve the tangle, for all its weight is on the side of the doctrine that everything in the world has evolved from a single source and has taken ages to do so.

The two most important arguments are given here amongst the many. For creation of the universe, there is a conscious power for creativity, there is a regulated system, there is a purpose and aims, there is a coordination in diversity, there is a vastness, and there is a stability in undurability. These traits are found universally in all plant and animal life. Hence, it is impossible to have all these characteristic features without an universal conscious power. Different pleas have been given by different Indian philosophies, such as, *Vaisheshika, Nyaya, Sânkhya, Yoga,* and *Vedânt,* for the existence of God. Each one has given its own views. Among these Indian philosophies, *Purva Mimâmsa* expounded the rite of religious treatise equal to or in place of God. But how does the inanimate world work like consciousness? How does one get the results of an action by itself? It does not have any appropriate answer to these questions. All other important Indian philosophies support theism and the existence of God.

Sri Kris*h*na, in the *Bhagavad Gitâ,* did not make it obligatory for common folk to believe in God or acquire knowledge of Him. By dividing the human society broadly into four classes, teachers, warrior-administrators, businessmen and workmen, man reaches the perfection by each being intent on his own duty. One can notice here that belief in God and knowledge of him are among the most important duties of only those who take to religion as a full-time occupation. Moreover, as we have seen, belief in god, even worship of him, does not, by itself, make any one good or holy. The sages of India declared that God reveals himself only to those who seek Him whole-heartedly, by all the means at their command and through all their activities.

To believe that God is the root of the entire universe is knowledge; while realization is that, in the entire universe, there is nothing besides the Lord. By knowledge and realization, a devotee comes to know his real and eternal affinity for God.

Krishna told Arjuna in the *Gita*: "By the delusion of the pairs of opposites arising from attachment and aversion, O descendant of Bharata, all beings are fallen into deep delusion at birth, O scorcher of foes. But those men of virtuous deeds whose impurities have been destroyed—they, freed from all the delusions of pairs of opposites, worship Me with firm resolve" (*Gita* VII, 27-28).

A.C. Morrison, Physicist and former President of New York Academy of Sciences, has given, in his book, " *Man Does Not Stand Alone,*" several reasons why he, as a scientist believes in God: (1) by unwavering mathematical law we can prove that our universe was designed and executed by a great engineering intelligence, (2) the resourcefulness of life to accomplish its purpose is a manifestation of all-pervading intelligence, (3) animal wisdom speaks irresistibly of a good creator who infused instinct in otherwise helpless little creatures, (4) man has something more than animal instinct—the power to reason, the intellect, (5) provision of all human beings is revealed in such wonderful phenomena as the genes. So unspeakably tiny are they that if all of them responsible for all the living people in the world could be collected together, there would be less than in thimbleful. Yet these ultra microscopic genes and their position in the chromosomes, inhabit every living cell and are the absolute keys to all human, animal and plants characteristics. This is an example of profound sagacity that could emanate only from a Supreme Intelligence, (6) the economy of nature is such that only Infinite Wisdom could have foreseen and prepared with such astute husbandry, (7) the fact that man can conceive the idea of God is in itself a unique proof.

Erwin Schrodinger, winner of Nobel Prize in Physics, writes in his book 'Mind and Matter': "No personal God can form part of a world model that has only become accessible at the cost of removing everything personal from it. We know, when God is experienced, this is an event as real as an immediate sense perception or as one's own personality. I do not find God anywhere in space and time, that is what the honest naturalist tells you. For this he incurs blame from him in whose catechism is written: God is spirit."

Charles Sherrington, Nobel laureate and a neuro-physiologist wrote in his book, 'Man on His Nature': "Biologist cannot go far in its subjects without being met by mind. Though living is analysable and describable by natural science, that associate of living, thought, escapes and remains refractory to natural science. In fact, natural science repudiates it as something outside its ken. A radical distinction has therefore arisen between life and mind. The former is an affair of chemistry and physics; the latter escapes chemistry and physics."

J.B.S.Haldane, a distinguished biologist, wrote in his book, "The Sciences and Philosophy": "It is only a narrow view of what is natural that prevents our recognizing the presence of God everywhere within and around us. Nothing is real except God, and relations of time and space are only the order of His manifestation. Nature is just the manifestation of God, and evolution is not mere biological or physical phenomenon, but the order in time relations of His manifestation."

C.J. Herrick, noted biologist, writes in his book, 'The Evolution of Human Nature': "...there are, in my opinion, no scientific or philosophic grounds for denying the possibility of an All Knower, the regulating agency of the natural cosmos. Faith in divine power, wisdom and guidance is for many people their stringent motivation for moral conduct and sustenance of spiritual values. It is unseemly for any man of science or any philosopher to condemn that faith, even though he himself may not entertain it... We may render to God the things that are God's and to science only those things that are nature's."

Loren Eisley, an anthropologist writes in his book, 'The Unexpected Universe': " I would say that if dead matter has reared up this curious landscape of fiddling crickets, song sparrows and wondering men, it must be plain even to the most devoted materialist that the matter of which he speaks contains amazing, if not dreadful powers, and may not impossibly be, as Hardy had suggested, 'but one mask of many worn by great Face behind."

A.H. Compton, Nobel Laureate writes in his book, '*The Cosmos*'. "When we pray to our God, it is common experience that we receive courage and strength to do deeds of friendliness towards His children. It is hard to think of receiving strength without imagining a Being that gives us the strength."

Warren Weaver once said, "You can no more convince me that there is no such God than you can convince me that a table or a rock is not solid; in each case, the evidence is simple, direct and uniform."

Alexis Carrel, Nobel Prize winner in medicine, said in his book, '*Reflections on Life*': "The existence of God explains, better than any other hypothesis, the results of prayer, the phenomena of mysticism and the sense of the holy. It is prudent to consider the need of the divine, not as illusionary but as the expression of structural characteristics of the human spirit which are more or less developed according to the individual. Since the universe is a coherent system, the fact of there being such a need makes us anticipate a means of satisfying it in the external world. For example, the cells of the organism would not be aerobic if there were no oxygen in the atmosphere. Equally, the need of water, fat, sugar or protein implies the existence of these substances in the external environment. It is permissible to attribute the same significance to a more or less obscure need felt by a great number of human beings to communicate with an invisible and sovereignty powerful spirit: a spirit at once personal and immanent in all things, which is manifested to us through intuition, revelation and the natural laws."

Bibliography

Carman, John B., *The Theology of Râmânuja*, New Haven, Yale University Press, 1974.

Kumarappa, B., *The Hindu Conception of the Deity as Culminating in Râmânuja*, London, Luzac and Co., 1934.

Kramrisch, *The Hindu Temple*.

Van Buitenen, J.A.B., *Râmânuja on the Bhagavadgita*, Delhi, Motilal Banrasidass, 1966.

Part II

Chapter 9

Soul, Body and Ego

Man is born with the body-idea; he thinks he is a physical being. At the most, if he believes in soul (*âtman*), he thinks that he has a soul. However, the real standpoint is that a person is soul (*âtman*), and has a body. You are not really a body possessing a soul (*âtman*), you are essentially pure spirit with a body for a covering. But unfortunately, man thinks of himself as physical or psychophysical being. As such, he is subject to heat and cold, hunger and thirst, birth, growth, decay and death. Shankara says: 'How can the body, being a pack of bones covered with flesh, a bag of filth, highly impure, be the self-existent *âtman*, the knower, which is ever distinct from it?' (Shankarâcharya, *Vivekchudamani*, v.158, pp.160, Madhavananda, S. Translator, Calcutta, 1921.)

There is an old fable about a student who once complained to his teacher about this idea of Shankara. 'Just see how Shankara condemns the body!' the student said. 'How strange! This body so charming, so attractive, he refers to as 'a bag of filth!' The teacher replied, 'Is it not really a bag of filth?' Is not filth coming out of your nose, your mouth, your ears, out of your eyes even, what to speak of your lower apertures? Filth is coming our of every pore of your body constantly. What else is it?' Still the student would not accept the teaching. 'I can't agree with this. Shankara takes too pessimistic a view of the human body.' Finally, the teacher asked him, 'Go out and find the most filthy thing you can find, worse than filth. Bring me something which you know to be the worst.' So the student searched here and there, for this and that, because he did not know which thing was the filthiest of all. At last he found some human excreta, and decided, 'I don't find anything filthier than this, it will have to do.' But when he went to pick it up with some sticks, the excreta cried out, 'Don't touch me, don't touch me!' 'Why?' asked the student. 'Yesterday I was a delicious food. Being in a human physical body, I have become reduced to this repulsive mess. Now everyone shuns me. Don't touch me! I don't know what will happen to me now if you touch me again!' At this, the student's mind was changed, and he returned to his teacher to tell him he now understood.

So what is the effect of this body-idea, of our identification with our physical selves? Man tries to satisfy the demands of the body and the sense organs in whatever way possible. Shankara severly condemns how foolish a person is to think of himself as a physical or psychophysical being, constantly in the grip of sense desires which cannot be satiated. Man devotes his wealth, his intellectual knowledge, his physical power, his mental resources all to the satisfaction of the senses, and all because he identifies himself with this body.

Then what is a human being really? You are a person who cognizes; that is your main function. The organs themselves do not cognize. You may sit here with your eyes wide open, and still you will not see. Your ears may be open, and still you will not hear. There is another factor in the human personality which must join with the organs. That factor is mind. Even the hands, organs of action, will not function of themselves. You cannot read a book or do any good work if your mind does not function. So beyond this physical being, beyond these senses, organs of action and organs of perfection, there is the human mind. That mind must join with your organs, and then perception and action can take place.

Though the mind must be joined with the organs, still the mind is not the perceiver, the doer. There is one basic factor which perceives and works through all the organs: it is the 'I,' the ego. You say 'I think, I hear, I feel, I imagine, I am happy, I am unhappy.' Functioning through the organs in the waking state, this ego is your apparent self. Yet even this ego is not centre of human personality, for behind it is the principle of consciousness. Through the 'I,' a person identifies himself and relates to external objects. 'My name is such and such; I hold this job; I live in this city; I have this many children; I like this; I do not like that.' But the 'I' or the ego is not real man; even the mind and thought are not real man; all these are constantly changing. Body is also changing every minute. Your appearance, your abilities, your family and residence, your tastes, and even your name, can and do change from day to day, year to year. Both body and mind belong to nature and must obey nature's laws.

I or ego is the greatest paradox in life. We always say 'I, mine, my son, my house, my car' etc. but we do not know—who am I ? When the soul leaves the body at the time of death, the dead body does not say 'I am here' neither the departed soul says 'I am here outside the body'. Yet when body and soul join together, we hear 'I' all the time. Don't you think that is a great paradox ? The 'I' or 'ego' feelings make our lives miserable. If I tell you that 1000 houses were demolished by a car bomb in a remote village in some part of the world, you will shake your head as if nothing happened. But if I tell you that there is a small fire in one of the houses in your street, you immediately become concerned and perhaps panicky. But at the same time, if you increase your ownership from the *limited* to the *unlimited*, you feel free. When you think about your son, you are worried about his welfare but when you think about all the children of the world, you have no worry and indeed you are very happy. It is said that a God-realized man sees the 'I' as the universe and the universe as 'I'. So when the *limited ego* becomes the *universal ego*, we achieve everlasting happiness. Of course, to transform *limited ego* to *universal ego* is not an easy job, but by continued practice of different methods of God-realization, we can achieve that Herculean task in front of all of us.

In the midst of all the activities of these changeful, fickle ego, mind, thought, and body, there is one central principle of conciousness or unity of self (*âtmâ*) which is ever constant and unchangeable. Because of this you recognize yourself amidst all changes. 'Yesterday I was happy; today I am unhappy. Before I was young; now I am old.' Who say this? Behind all the changing conditions of body and mind, is the one, ever-present spiritual principle. So Shankara says: 'How can the body, being a pack of bones covered with flesh, a bag of filth, highly impure, be the self-existent *atman*, which is ever distinct from it?' It is the *atman*, the central principle of consciousness, which is the source of all knowledge, the source of all your power. Because of that central principle, the mind functions, the organs function, the body functions. It coordinates all the factors in the psychophysical constitution. The object of cognition is bereft of the power cognition, of consciousness; but the one cognizing principle cognizes all the changing conditions of the body, the organs, and the mind. It is ever-present, ever-distinct from all the objects of cognition, all conditions of body and mind.

That constant, central priciple of consciousness in man is self-evedent. No one has to prove the existence of his own self or *âtmâ*. Through the senses he requires proof of the existence of everything else, but not of himself, because he is essentially changeless, self-luminous—the central principle of consciousness. Even a child says 'I am'. You may require proof of the existence of God, but never of yourself.

Once a teacher brought ten different types of pots and asked the student: 'what you find in these pots?' The student said that it was filled with nothing but space. Teacher broke the pots and then asked: 'Where did the space go?' Space within the pot merged with the outside space and became one, was the answer of the student. It could not go anywhere as it did not come from anywhere. Only earthen pots separate the inner space from the outer space. That's the relationship that exists between the *âtmâ*, and *Pramâtmâ*. Just like the pot encloses the space which is a part of outer space, the inner *âtmâ*, which is a part of *Pramâtmâ*, is enclosed by the human body. The body and pots are made of five elements and in the end again it goes back to five elements. The teacher again asked: 'What are the colour and smell of space inside and outside?' The student answered: 'There is no colour and smell of space either inside or outside. Both are colourless and odourless. Teacher said: 'Every pot has the same space without any difference in colour and smell whatsoever.' Same way there is no difference in *âtmâ* of anyone in this world and each one of them is a part of *Pramâtmâ*. Our outer appearances of bodies which enclose *âtmâ*, are different inside is the same. The *âtmâ* is nameless because it is formless. It takes the form of the vessel it fills. If it is not in Space, either of two things is possible. Either the *âtmâ* permeates space or space is in it. God is omnipresent. He is the formless, the deathless, the eternal. The idea of God came. He is the lord of soul (*âtmâ*), just as my soul is the Lord of my body. If my *âtmâ* left the body, the body would not be for a moment. If He (God) left my *âtmâ*, the *âtmâ* (soul) would not exist. He is the creator of the universe; of everything that dies He is the destroyer. There is no you and me. Everyone is either you and I. If an educated person cannot find the similarity between individuals, what can we expect from the common people. All ritual performances in the temple or home do not mean anything unless we understand the concept that we are a part of *Pramâtmâ* and love every one as you love yourself.

God manifests himself in human form. In the beginning, before creation, God was invisible, but He wanted to become visible, and to enjoy His infinite nature through many forms. He created this universe. Electricity is in the air around us, but we don't see it. It is unmanifested and impersonal, but when it is brought into a bulb, it becomes visible; when it is brought in a T.V. or radio, we can see and hear, even though it is the same electricity. So it is with God. We are all gods, not our body but our soul (*âtmâ*)—the part of *Pramâtmâ*, the Divine Electricity made visible in the body-bulbs—though we don't know it. The relationship of a *jivâtmân* and *Pramâtmân* is like a drop of water and the ocean. In fact both are water though one is a dot like drop and other is unfathomable and vast ocean.

This *mantra Tat Tvam Asi*—(Thou art That) and *Sarvam khalu idam Brahman*—(Everything is Brahman), appear in many ancient memory songs, sung well before the time. This *mantra* itself remains current in the later Vedic, past-Vedic and modern era. It was quoted in *Chândogya Upanishad* (*Chanddogya Upanishad*, IV: 8.7.). Besides, its many variants current in Hindu thought have also found indirect repetition of this statement in other Vedic literatures—for instance, in the Brihadâryanaka *Upanishad*, we have: *Aham Brahmâsmi*—(I am Brahma, the infinite) and *Ayam Atmâ Brahman*—(This Self or soul is *Brahman*). This can be explained in the following way: Both the 'dead body' and 'living body' are identical, but the 'living body' has something that 'dead body' does not have. That which is missing in the 'dead body' is spirit, *Brahman*, and at the same time, when *Brahman* is present in the body, it creates the greatest illusion (*maya*) that 'I am the body.' '*Tat tvam asi*' means that *thou art that*, subtle essence is the self of this entire world.

In earlier days, people used to greet each other by saying *Tat tvam asi*, with palm pressed together, raise hands on head becomes a common form of greeting, to salute and celebrate the flame of divinity that each acknowledge in the other— *tat tvam asi* (Thou art That). It is passed on to the modern age a '*namaste*', even though the pressed palms are raised not always to level of the forehead, but often stay below the chin of even at the breast. 'Thus I do homage to the God in each and all of you' (Sindhu Putra explains 'Namaste')

Isa Upanishad also recaptures the *mantra* which was current in the age of Sanathana Dharma, when it says: *Yas tvam asmi so'ham asmi* (you are indeed that I am). Again, *Isa Upanishad* expresses itself in the thought and words of the pre-ancients when it repeats 'Soham' (I am He, that am I). *'ham aham sah'* means 'I am He, He is I'. This *mantra* came from the word *hamsa. Hamsa* means swan. It is a symbol of Brahman. Hence those who attained cosmic consciousness are often call 'Paramahamsa'—the great swan.

The *Mândukya Upanishad* also reflects the words of the ancients of Sanathana to say, 'Idam sarvam asi (Thou art all this). Again in the *Mândukya Upanishad* is the reappearance of the words, 'Brahma eva idam visvam (This whole world is Brahman). Further it is stated that *Brahmavid Brahmaiva Bhavati*—(Realising Brahman, you indeed become Brahman).

The Vedas teach us that the soul (*âtmâ*) of man is immortal. The body is subject to the law of growth and decay; what grows must decay. But the indwelling spirit (*âtmâ*) is related to the infinite and eternal life; it never had a beginning and it will never have an end. Lord Krishna has said: 'The *âtman* is neither born nor does it die. Coming into being and ceasing to be do not take place in it. Unborn, eternal, constant and ancient, it is not killed when the body is slain' (*Bhagavad Gîtâ* II: 20.). 'Weapons do not cleave the *âtman*, fire burns It not, water wets It not, wind dries It not.' This Self is uncleavable, incombustible and neither wetted nor dried. It is eternal, all-pervading, stable, immovable and everlasting' (*Bhagavad Gîtâ* II: 23, 24.). He further said: 'As a man casting off worn-out garments puts on new ones, so the embodied (*âtman*), casting off worn-out bodies enters into others that are new' (*Bhagavad Gîtâ* II: 22.).. Lord Jesus also said: 'Is it not written in your law, I said, Ye are gods?' (*John X:* 34) Further He said: 'Know ye not that ye are the temple of God, and that the Spirit of God dwelth in you?' (*Corinthians III:* 16.) Though God has made a personal representation of Himself in each human being. Some deflect His light more than others. These are great saints and *avatars*.

Shankaracharya has described the nature of *âtman* as follows: 'If you realize it, you will be freed from thebonds of ignorance, and attain liberation.' 'There is a self-existent Reality, which is the basis of our consciousness of ego. That Reality is the witness of the three states of our consciousness, and is distinct from the five bodily coverings. That Reality is the knower in all states of consciousness— waking, dreaming and dreamless sleep. It is aware of the presence or absence of the mind and its functions. It is the *âtman*. That Reality sees everything by its own light. No one sees it. It gives intelligence to the mind and the intellect, but no one gives it light. That Reality pervades the universe, but no one penetrates it. It alone shines. The universe shines with its reflected light. Because of its presence, the body, senses, mind and intellect apply themselves to their respective functions, as though obeying its command. Its nature is eternal consciousness. It knows all things, from the sense of ego to the body itself. It is the knower of pleasure and pain and of the sense-objects. It knows everything objectively—just as a man knows the objective existence of a jar. This is the *âtman*, the Supreme Being, the ancient. It never ceases to experience infinite joy. It is alwaysthe same. It is consciousness itself. The organs and vital energies function under its comand. Here, within this body, the pure mind, in the secret chamber of intelligence, in the infinite universe within the heart, the *âtman* shines in its captivating splendour like a noonday sun. By its light, the universe is revealed. The *âtman* is distinct from *maya*, the primal cause, and from her effect, the universe. The nature of the *âtman* is pure consiousness. The *âtman* reveals this entire universe of mind and matter. It can not be defined. In and through the various state of consciousness waking, dreaming and sleeping—it maintains our unbroken awareness of identity. It manifests itself as the witness of the intelligence' (Shankaracharya, *The Crest-Jewel of Discrimination*, translated by Swami Prabhavananda and Christopher Isherwood, Hollywood, Vedanta Press, 1947.).

Unfortunately, man forgets that self-existent *âtman*, and identifies himself with his body. Hence Shankara says: 'It is the foolish man who identifies himself with the mass of skin, flesh, fat, bones and filth, while the man of discrimination knows his own self, the only entity that there is, as distinct form the body. The identification with the body alone is the root which produces the misery of birth, etc., of people who are attached to the unreal; therefore, destroy thou this with utmost care. When this identification caused by the mind is given up there is no more chance for rebirth' (Shankarâcharya, *Vivekachudamani*, v.159, pp. 164.).

Again and again the *Upanishads* have declared that the way a person goes beyond birth, growth, decay and death is by realizing the changeless Self. There is no other way. Anything you acquire in this world is temporal; God alone is Eternal in the midst of the non-eternal. Whatever you gain, you will undergo reincarnation until you realize God. Jesus said, 'That which is born of the flesh is flesh.' As long as you identify yourself with the physical body, the 'mass of skin, flesh, fat, bones, and filth,' you will have no escape from the cycle of birth, death and rebirth. And physical rebirth means you are subject once again to pain and pleasure, hope and fear, love and hatred, good and evil, and all the other dualities that make up this worldly existence. You cannot enter the Kingdom of God beyond dual experience unless you gain consciousness of your spiritual self.

There are three things which are rare indeed and are due to the grace of God—namely, (i) a human birth, (ii) the longing for liberation, and (iii) the protecting care of a perfected sage. Our soul or *âtman* has got this rare form of a human body to wish for and work for getting liberation (*moksha*), that is, the soul or *âtman* will not have to take birth again and again and go through all the pain and pleasure and the dualities of life. The self-realization and God-realization can easily be achieved with the help of right *guru*. So do not miss this rare opportunity

The *Brihadâranyaka Upanishad* tells us of the visit of the sage Yajñavalkya to the king Janaka. The sage avoids discussion with the king but eventually allows him to ask questions. 'What is the light of the Spirit of man?' asks the king. Yajñavalkya test the persistence of the king and the depth of his question by responding with evasive answers. First the King is told that the sun is the light of the Spirit of man; next that the moon is the light; then fire; then voice. Each reply leads the king to question more deeply until he finally asks: 'But when the sun is set, *Yajñavalkya*, and the moon is also set, and the fire sinks down, and the voice is stilled, what is then the light of the Spirit of man?' The soul then becomes his light; he answered. What is the soul? It is the consciousness in the life-powers. It is the light within the heart. The soul of man has two dwelling-places; both this world and the other world. The borderland between them is the third, the land of dreams. The soul of man wanders through both worlds, yet remains unchanged.

Leaving the bodily world through the door of dream, the sleepless soul views the sleeping powers. Soaring upward and downward in dream-land, the god makes manifold forms. Then clothed in radiance, returns to his own home, (he) the gold-gleaming genius, swan of everlasting. From this state, called *Sushupti*, when the body is in deepest slumber and the soul path hurrying back to his former dwelling-place in the world of waking. Then as a wagon heavy-laden might go halting and creaking, so the embodied soul goes halting. When it has gone so far that a man is giving up the ghost. When he falls into weakness, then like as a mango is loosened from its stem, so the soul of man is loosened from these bodily members. When he falls into a swoon, as though he had lost his senses, the life-powers are gathered round the soul; and the soul, taking them up together in their radiant substance, enters with them into the inner heart. Then the point of the heart grows luminous. The soul becomes conscious and enter into c onsciousness.

Like as the skin of a snake lies lifeless, cast forth upon an ant-hill, so lies his body, when the spirit of man rises up bodyless and immortal, as the life, as the eternal, as the radiance. As a goldsmith, taking an ornament, moulds it to another from newer and fairer; so in truth the soul, leaving the body here, and putting off unwisdom, makes for itself (in the heavenly state) another form newer and fairer: a form like the forms of departed soul, or the seraphs, or of the golds.

Through his past works he shall return once more to birth, entering whatever from his heart is set on. When he has received full measure of reward in paradise for the works he did, from that world he returns agin to this, the world of works, according as were his works and walks in (another) life, so he becomes. He that does righteously becomes righteous. He that does evil becomes evil. He becomes holy through holy works and evil through evil.

Because the soul exists in all times, therefore time is not the cause of the bondage (of the soul). Because the soul can exist in any country or anywhere, therefore locality cannot be the cause of the bondage. Because age is the property of the body, and not of the soul, therefore age cannot be the cause of the bondage. Because the soul is independent of matter, therefore matter cannot be the cause of bondage. Because the soul is by nature free is subject to so many desires, even that is not the casue of bondage. The transmigration of soul is not the cause of bondage. Bondage is not caused even by the conjunction of the body and the soul, but by the wrong knowledge as to the nature of their conjunction and the proper functions of body and soul. The real cause of bondage is non-discrimination or misunderstanding the nature of the soul and the body, and not finding the true purpose of life. Just as darkness is removed by its natural opposite, light, so non-discrimination is removed by true discrimination. The seat of bondage is in the mind; it is (only) by way of expression we call it the bondage of the soul. When the mind becomes purified like a mirror, knowledge is revealed in it. Care should therefore be taken to purify the mind.

The soul makes its entry into matter as a spark of omnipotent life and consciousness within the nucleus formed by the union of the sperm and ovum. As the body develops, this original 'seat of life' remains in the medulla oblongata. The medulla oblongata is therefore referred to as the gateway of life through which the soul make his entrance into the bodily kingdom. In this 'seat of life' is the first expression of the incarnate soul's fine perceptions, imprinted with the *karmically* designed pattern of the various phases of life to come. By the miraculous power of *prâna*, or intelligent creative life-force, guided by the faculties of the soul, the zygote develops through the fetal and embryonic stages into a human body. In other words, the *prâna* in the spermatozoa and ova guide embryonic development according to a *kârmic* design. The creative faculties or instruments of the soul are astral and causal in nature. When the soul enters the primal cell of life, it is wearing two subtle bodies, a causal form of thought, which is turn is encased in an astral form of *prâna*. The casual body, so named because it is the cause of the two soul encasements, from which is formed the astral body of nineteen elements and the physical body of sixteen gross chemical elements and thus a total of 35 ideas or thought-forces. The 19 elements of the astral body are intelligence (*buddhi*), ego (*ahamkara*), feeling (*chitta*), mind (*manas*, sense consciousness), five instruments of knowledge (*jnâna-indriya*), five instruments of action (*karma-indriya*), and five instruments of intelligent creative life force (*prâna*), i.e. assimilating, eliminating, metabolizing, circulatory functions of the physical body, and empowering performance of the crystallizing.

When the soul descends into body consciousness, it comes under the influence of *maya* (cosmic delusion) and *avidya* (ignorance, which creates ego consciousness). When deluded and tempted by *maya*, the soul becomes the limited ego, which identifies itself with the body. The soul, as the ego, ascribes to itself all the limitations and circum-scriptions of the body. Once so identified, the soul can no longer express its omnipresence omniscience, and omnipotence. It imagines itself to be limited. In this state of delusion, the ego takes command of the bodily kingdom. Instead the soul consciousness saying '*Aham Brahamâsi* (I am Brahman , the infinite),' the deluded soul, the ego consciousness says, 'I am the body; this is my family and name; these are my possessions.' Though ego thinks it rules, it is in reality a prisoner of the body and mind.

The body and mind rightfully belong to soul or *âtman* and his noble subjects of virtuous tendencies. But ego and his kinsmen of wicked, ignoble tendencies cunningly usurp the throne. When the soul arises to reclaim his territory, the body and mind become the battle ground. Every spiritual aspirant, aiming to establish within himself the rule of soul, must defeat the Ego and his powerful allies. And this is the battle that takes place on the field of Dharmakshetra Kurukshetra.

The battle of Kurukshetra described in the *Gitâ* is therefore the effort required to win the battle on all three portions of the bodily field: (1) the material and moral struggle, (2) the psychological war, and (3) the spiritual battle. These three parts of the bodily field, according to the manifestation of the three *gunas* or influencing qualities inherent in *Prakriti* or Cosmic Nature. The three *gunas* are (1) *sattvik*, (2) *rajasik*, and (3) *tamasik*. Thus, *sattvik*, the pure and enlightening qualities of Nature, is the predominating attribute in the territory of Dharmakshetra. The first portion of the bodily field of actions consists of the periphery of the body which includes the five instruments of knowledge or *jñâna-indriya* (ears, skin, eyes, tongue and nose), and the five instruments of action or *karma-indriya* (mouth, hands, feet, anus and genitalia). This outer surface of the human body is the scene of continuous sensory and motor activities. Hence, it is called Kurukshetra, the field of external actions where all activities of the outer world are accomplished. The second portion of the bodily field of action is the cerebrospinal axis with its six subtle centres of life and consciousness (medulla, cerevical, dorsal, lumber, sacral and coccygeal), and its two magnetic poles of mind (*manas*) and intelligenece (*buddhi*). This cerebrospinal axis with the six subtle centres is called Dharmakshetra Kurukeshtra, field of subtle energies and superamental forces as well as of grosser action. The third portion of the bodily field is in the brain. This is called Dharmakshetra, and consists of the medulla and the frontal and middle upper parts of the cerebrum, with their astral centres of the spiritual eye and thousand-petaled lotus, and corresponding states of divine consciousness. This Dharmakeshtra portion of the bodily field upholds man's being through which forces the soul (*âtman*) ultimately quit the body and return to the spirit (*Pramâtman*).

Designated specific areas of the body and its activities are affected by its ruler, such as the soul and the ego. First the body under the reign of soul: the centres of superconsciousness in the cerebrum and medulla, the soul bestows his beneficence of bliss, wisdom and vitality throughout the body. The soul with his discrimnative tendencies located in the medulla, cervical and dorsal centres under the influence of *buddhi* (intelligence) the discriminatory power, reveals truth and is attracted to the spirit (*pramâtman*). The common sensory powers of *manas* (mind or sense consciousness) seated in the lumber, sacral, and coccygeal centres become obedient to the wise influence of the *buddhi*, the intelligence.

The ordinary man is primarily under the influence of the sense-conscious mind (*manas*). Sense consciousness works through the three lower spinal centres. When man's life comes under the guidance of the soul, the senses operating through the three lower centres become obedient to the discriminative tendencies in the upper cerebrospinal centres of consciousness. Thus, it may be said that the worldly person predominantly lives in the lower centres of consciousness in the lumbar, sacral, and coccyx, with mind (*manas* or sense consciousness). The spiritual man lives in the upper centres of consciousness in the dorsal, cervical and medulla, with descriminating intelligence (*buddhi*). The creative 'Mother Nature' in the coccyx is calm and controlled under soul, bringing health, beauty and peace to the body. At the command of the *yogi* in deep meditation, this creative force turns inward and flows back to its source. Yoga refers to this power flowing from the coccyx to spirit as the awakened *kundâlini*.

The physical tracts of the body come under the influence of ten sensory powers, which reside in their respective sensory organs. These are the five senses of knowledge or *jñâna-indriya* (sight, sound, smell, taste and touch) and five sensory power of execution or *karma-indriya* (the power of speech, of locomotion in the feet, of manual dexterity, of elimination in the anus and excretory muscles, and reproduction in the genital organs). The senses are all noble and good, in tune with the discriminative, harmonious power of the soul or *âtman*. Bodily dependent discrimination and mental (sense) tendencies, the discrimination, and the pure sense organs are the beneficiaries of the blessings and wise guidance of the soul. Thus, the thoughts, will and feelings are wise, constructive, peaceful and happy. The conscious, intelligent, molecules, atoms, electrons and creative life sparks (*prâna*) are vital, harmonious and efficient. As a result, happiness, health, prosperity, peace, discrimination, efficiency and intuitive guidance pervade the body.

The three *gunas* are (1) *sâttvik* (2) *râjasik*, and (3) *tâmasik*. *Sâttvik*, the pure and enlightening qualities of Nature, is described in *Bhagavad Gîtâ* as follows: 'Fearlessness, purity of heart, steadfastness in knowledge and yoga, almsgiving, control of the senses, *yajñâ*, study of the scriptures, austerity and straight-forwardness,' 'non-injury, truth, absence of anger, renunciation, serenity, aversion to fault finding, compassion to all living beings, uncovetousness, gentleness, modesty and absence of fickleness,' 'Vigour, forgiveness, fortitude, purity, absence of hatred, absence of pride, these belong to one born for a divine state (under the influence of soul), O Bharata' (*Bhagavad Gîtâ* XVI: 1-3).

The *rajasik* qualities are defined as follows: 'Ostentation, arrogance and self-conceit, anger and also harshness and ignorance belong to one who is born for a demoniac state (*asura* or egoistic), O Pandava' (*Bhagavad Gîtâ* XVI: 4). The *tamasik* qualities are described as follows: 'The demoniac know not what to do and what to refrain from; neither purity, nor right conduct nor truth is found in them.' 'Filled with insatiable desires, full of hypocrisy, pride and arrogance, holding evil ideas through delusion, they work with impure resolve' (*Bhagavad Gîtâ* XVI: 7, 10).

The body under the reign of ego (*ahamkâr*), the delusory force that induces the human being to believe himself to be separate from God is also called the pseudosoul, for it imitates the authority of soul or *âtman* and tries to dominate the entire body. Ego likes material desires, emotions, habits and undisciplined sense inclinations under the influence of ignorance. These insurgents close the doors of the medulla, cervical, and dorsal centres. The lower chambers, the lumbar, sacral and coccygeal centres are open. Ego works under the influence of ignorance which goes for material desires, emotions, habits and undisciplined sense inclinations. When the discriminative intelligence (*buddhi*) that reveals truth and is attracted to the spirit (*âtman*), it is over-powered by ego and the accompanying influence of ignorance (*maya* and *avidya*), then sense consciousness (mind, *manas*) predominates—*manas* obscures truth and links conciousness (*manas*) to matter. The physical body under the ego is often fallow and unhealthy from epidemic of diseases and premature aging. The senses identify themselves as pleasure-seekers, indulgent and self-centered and they fall into evil ways and self-destructive habits.

SENSES UNDER THE SOUL (ATMAN) AND EGO

(1) **Vision**: The soul perceives in all beauty the expression of Divine Beauty and feels a blissful expansion of consciousness and love through that exprience. Man sees only the good in everything—good objects, nature's wonders, exquisite scenary, holy faces, spiritual expressions of art, etc. The soul perceives in all beauty the expression of Divine Beauty and feels a blissful expansion of consciousness and love through that experience.

Under the influence of ego, man is attracted to beautiful objects and faces, which leads to material attachments and sensual indulgences. Evil-awakening, sense-rousing art, sensuous, materialistic suggestions are poured into the brain to degrade the natural good taste.

(2) **Hearing**: Under the influence of soul, the sense of hearing loves the voice of beneficial truth, which guides man's thoughts to the goal of wisdom.

Under the influence of ego, man prefers to hear nothing but artificially sweetened, poisonous untruths, leading the thoughts to a false consciousness of self-sufficiency and self-importance. Many persons willinglingly sacrifice their time, money, health, reputation and character just to receive constantly the honeyed praise of 'parasitic' friends. In fact, most people prefer flattery to intelligent criticism. They also like to hear praise for accomplishments and promises of devotion from loved ones.

(3) **Smell**: Under the influence of soul, man loves to entertain with the natural scents of flowers and pure air; devotion-arousing temple incense; and the aroma of health-producing savoury foods.

Under the influence of ego, the thoughts and cells crave and indulge in heavy, sensuous perfumes; and their appetite is aroused by the smell of unhealthy, malnutritious, rich or too-spicy foods. When the sense of smell is enslaved of ego, it loses its natural attraction to simple foods that are good for the body. Man also finds enjoyment in odours of alcohol and cigarette smoke.

(4) **Taste**: Under the influence of soul, man has natural attraction towards right foods possessing all the necessary elements, especially fresh raw fruits and vegetables with natural flavours and undestroyed vitamins. These natural foods nourish the body cells, helping to make them immune to disease, and aiding in preserving their youth and vitality.

'The foods that augment vitality, energy, vigour, health, joy and cheerfulness, which are savoury and oleaginous, substantial and agreeable, are liked by *sattvika* (*Gitâ* XVII: 8).

Under the influence of ego, man is tempted to over eat unnatural, overcooked, devitalized and injurious foods which subject the body to indigestion and sickness. 'The foods that are bitter, sour, saline, overhot, pungent, dry and burning are liked by the *râjasika*, and are productive of pain, grief and disease' (*Gitâ* XVII: 9.). 'That which is stale, tasteless, stinking, cooked overnight, refuse and impure is the food liked by the *tâmasika* (*Gitâ* XVII: 10).

(5) **Touch**: Under the influence of soul, the bodily sense of touch loves moderation in climate, food and the real necessities of life. He loves warmth of sun and the sensation of a cool breeze. Healthy and wholesome bodily habits— promptness, cleanliness, alterness and activity results in peace.

Under ego's, control the sensuous touch makes the body attached to comforts and luxuries, and to sensuous feelings that rouse sexual desire.

(6) **Intellect (Buddhi)**: 'The intellect which knows the paths of work and renunciation, differentiation of right and wrong action, fear and fearlessness, bondage and liberation -that intellect *is sattvika*, O Parth' (*Gitâ* XVIII: 30). The intellect or *Buddhi* is under the influence of soul (*âtma*).

'The intellect that makes a distorted grasp of *dharma* and *adharma*, of what ought to be done, and what ought not to be done—that is *Râjasika*, O Partha.' 'That which, enveloped in darkness, regards *adharma* as *dharma* and views all things in a perverted way, that intellect is *Tâmasika*, O Partha' (*Gitâ* XVIII: 31,32).

(7) SPEECH: Under the influence of soul, speech entertains the thoughts of harmony and of melodious words. Peace-producing, heart-melting speech, vital words of truth, educate and inspire the thoughts toward divine activities for the elevation of one's self and others.

Under the influence of ego, the speech creates ugly vibrations, angry, or vengeful words which are not of peace, friendship and love. And it is despicable to gossip and spread unkind rumors.

(8) HANDS: Under the influence of soul, the hands reach out for beneficial things, for constructive work and service, for doing good deeds and sharing with others, and for soothing and healing.

Under the ego's influence, the hands are almost busy in performing misdeeds, grasping for more possessions, taking more than one's share, thieving, killing, striking out in anger or revenge. All actions make for the inharmony and ruin.

(9) FEET: Under the influence of soul, the human feet seek places of inspiration, temples, spiritual services, good entertainments, nature's scenic places, and the company of worthwhile friends and holy people.

Under the ego's influence, the footsteps are urged toward places of noxious amusements, gambling dens, bars, and to rowdy, distracting company.

(10) PROCREATION: Under the soul's influence, creative impulse guides the sex inclination, enabling parents to bring on earth a noble spiritual human being like themselves.

Under the influence of ego, the body is constantly excited and restless with morbid impulses of sex temptation. The insatiable lust imparted to the thought, subject the body to moodiness, depression, irritability and suffer debility etc.

Paramahansa Yogananda has suggested the following five methods for the soul to attain victory over the ego: (Paramahansa Yogananda, *The Bhagavad Gîtâ*, Self-Realization Fellowship, Los Angeles, 1995). (1) By meditation the aspiring person's resolve is strengthened to find God through self-realization. (2) He tries to find consciousness free of all external attachments; (3) It still clings tenaciously within to body consciousness when he tries to meditate on God. By deep concentration on *yoga* techniques, the person next tries to silence the internal and external body-sensations, so that his thoughts may focus solely on God; (4) By the right technique of life-force control (*pranayama*), the person learns to quiet his breath and his heart; he withdraws his attention and his life energy into the spinal centres; (5) When the person can quiet his heart at will, he enters super-consciousness.

The ego experiences joy and relaxation when it feels in peaceful sleep the subconscious mind. In the sleep state, the breath and heart still work while the senses are asleep. In meditation, the *yogi* consciously withdraws his attention and energy from his heart, muscles, and senses, these all remain as though asleep, but he has passed beyond the subconscious sleep-state of mental awareness into superconsciousness. Such conscious sensory-motor sleep bestows on the *yogi* a joy greater than that of a ordinary dreamless sleep. In the state of superconsciousness, man's perceptions are internalized rather than externalized. In superconscious meditation, the heart is calmed, and the yogi can stimulate at will the spiritual centre of the medulla or point between the eyebrows, he can control the inner and outer searchlights of perception. When he switches off the lights of the gross senses, all material distractions vanish.Then the ego automatically turns to behold the forgotten beauty of the inner astral kingdom. The heart-quieted yogi in superconsciousness becomes able to see visions and great lights; to hear astral sounds; and to become identified with a vast dimly lighted space—alive with glimpses of beauties hitherto unknown. In the external conscious state, man does not see God's active manifestation as the beautiful Cosmic Energy that is present in every point of space, and that constitutes the luminous building blocks of every object; he perceives only the gross dimensional forms of human face, of flowers and of other beuties of nature. The soul coaxes man to turn his attention inward to behold, through its astral vision, the ever-burning, ever-changing, multicoloured lights of the fountain of Cosmic Energy playing through the pores of all atoms. The physical beauty of a face, or of nature, is fleeting; its perception depends on the power of the physical eyes. The beauty of Cosmic Energy is everlasting, and can be seen with or without the physical eyes.

The deeper the *yogi's* meditations, and the more he is able to hold on to the after effects of awakened soul-virtues and perceptions and express them in his daily life, the more spiritualized his body becomes. His unfolding self-realization is the triumphal reestablishing of the reign of soul and his noble courtiers of intuition, peace, bliss, calmness, self-ccontrol, life-force control, will power, concentration, discrimnation and omniscience rule the bodily kingdom. The *yogi* who has won the battle of consciousness has overcome the misguided ego's attachment titles, such as, 'I-ness', and has released the prisoner of his attention from all limiting delusion. In ordinary man, the ego or the pseudosoul, foats down the current of sense pleasure, finally wrecking itself in the torrents of satiety and ignorance. In a self-controlled man, the entire current of life force, attention and wisdom moves floodlike toward the soul; the consciousness swims in a sea of God's omnipresent peace and bliss.

In God's diverse creations such as plants, worms, birds and animals, human being should be considered as extremely privileged as he is endowed with the rare faculty of reasoning and discriminating between good and evil, thus giving him also the rare opportunity to rise to the level of the divine. The principal purpose of man's birth is to give him a chance to realize the nature of the soul. Realization of the self results in the total reversal of this identification when the aspirant identifies himself with the *âtman* and is fully aware that the body is only an adjunct to his Self. The result to this identification is that there is no more delusion about the ephemeral nature of his body which he understands to be the effect of *karma*. Human being learns to identify with the features of the self—consciusness which is eternal, independent, all-pervading, changeless, the experiencing subject and non-doer and non-enjoyer (*akarta, abhokta*). The transition from the first to this stage is a process of internalization of the knowledge which one has learnt in the first stage.

Chapter 10

Idol Worship or Murti Puja

Of the principal religions of the world, such as, Hinduism, Buddhism, and a certain denomination of Christianity (Orthodox Catholics) freely use images: icons and anicons; only two religions, Judaism and Islam, refuse such worship. Buddha himself, however, did not teach idol worship. Yet after his death, his followers made his images and started worshiping him.

In the Vedic time, there was no idol worship. Neither the *Vedas* nor the *Upanishads* teach idol worship. Iconography, which was abundant from the 7th or 8th century AD, supplements what literature has to teach us regarding details of mythical stories and the symbolism of divine acts and attributes. The pre-Aryan in all likelihood Dravidian origin of the most noteworthy ritual of Hindu religion would appear quite to be reasonable to assume. In the present day texture of Hindu culture and religion, the warp appears to be Dravidian and weft Aryan. The acceptance of pre-Aryan ritual meant also the acceptance of the conception of the divinity and the mythological figures of the gods and goddesses that were current among them. The more puissant and personal gods, and more profound, cosmic and philosophical in their conception become established. There is a good deal of compromise between the Aryan and pre-Aryan practices. Take, for example, the distinctive Hindu ritual of *puja*, by which we mean the worship of an image or a symbol of the divinity. They treat gods as a living personality and show grateful worship by offering flowers, the produce of the earth, and incense, and by waving lights in front of it and playing music and singing before it. This is something quite different from the Vedic rite of the *homa*, in which wood fire is lighted on an altar. Certain offerings of food, butter and milk are offered to the gods. Gods are supposed to dwell in the sky and to receive these offerings through the fire. The whole objective of worship is to become perfect, to become divine, to reach God and be God.

The variety of names and forms in which the divine has perceived and worshipped in the Hindu tradition is virtually limitless. There are at least one thousand God's names that are compiled in a book called 'Sahasra Nâma'. Really speaking, as God has no shape or form, He has no name and all these names are based on the action He has performed. Krishna says in Gita, 'All names are mine, I have no preference for any one.' *Nirguna* and *Saguna* are two forms applied to God. *Nirguna* literally means without qualities, shape or form, hence cannot be recognized by any of the five *indriyas* (sense organs), mind or intellect. *Saguna* means with qualities. In a gold ornament a woman admires the shape and form, but the goldsmith sees the gold of which the ornament is made, and its purity. According to *Saguna* or anthropomorphic conception or formed deities, people have considered God in a human form. For each form, we recite some verse called *dhyāna sloka*, which describes every aspect of that form. We worship *sagun* form of God to look at but we really meditate on its *nirguna* or subtler meaning. For example let us look at the meaning of a *dhyāna sloka* of Lord Vishnu:

Sāntākāram bhujagsayanam padmanābham suresam
Visvādhāram gaganasadrsam meghavarnam subhāngam
Loksmikāntam kamalanayanam yogirbhir dhyānagamyam
Vande vishnu bhavabhayaharam sarvalokaikanātham.

The first word of the verse explains the true nature of Vishnu. He is *sāntākāram*—natural absolute peace. Therefore, it means that the Lord (the Self) is abiding in His own absolute nature. *Bhujagasayanam* means the one who is reclining on the snake. The snake is also called *sesa* i.e. which remains when everything else is gone. *Sesa* refers to time; when all things that are born disappear, time alone remains. Here the snake also represents the time that kills everyone and he survives. Lord Vishnu reclining on snakes represents the Supreme Self existing as the cosmic time factor. *Padmanābham* means the lotus (*kamal*) coming out of naval or centre of all creation of the Lord Vishnu. The meaning of *kamal* is 'the dirt of water' But it really refers to that which comes out from oneself. Lord Brahma shown sitting inside the lotus (*kamal*) has four faces. Subjectively, we find that for everything we create and in every action, there are four stages. The first face of Brahma represents mind where a thought arises, which is also referred as *sankalpa*. The second face of Lord Brahma reflects the stage of decision, *nischaya*, by which one decides to do anything. Due to a memory of the past, we make a decision in the present; for example, if we have seen or experienced some beautiful thing before, we would like to see it again. Memory or *smrti* is represented by the third face of Lord Vishnu. Then, finally we determine to take an action. This final determination of the will is called *ahamkāra* (ego) and is represented by the fourth face of Lord Brahma. The sequence given so far is as follows: First, the pure consciousness in its absolute nature is described as *sāntākāram*. The Lord is described as *bhujagasayanam* lying on the bed of snake. Then the lotus of 'I-consciousness' (*ahamkāra*), along with the four aspects of the mind, arises from that pure consciousness and begins the process of creation; here He is called *padamanābham*. The last word in the first line is *suresam*, which means Lord of *Suras*, the gods. The next line starts with *visvâdhâram* and means that Lord Vishnu supports the Universe. *Ganganasadrsam* means 'like all-pervading space'. Just as space is all-pervading yet unseen, and though it gives accommodation to everything, it remains unpolluted, untouched (*nirmala*), the same is true of the pure consciousness, which is *Brahman*. *Meghavarnam* means 'the (blue) colour of a water-bearing cloud.' Blue is the colour of infinity, just as the sky and the vast expanse of oceanic waters appear blue; the eyes cannot see the limit of sky or ocean or the Lord. Though the Lord may take a particular incarnation as Rama or Krishna; His true nature remains infinite. *Subângam* means the one whose body (limbs) is auspicious and pure, because He is, by nature, absolute purity without any stain of ignorance. *Laksmìkântam* means 'the beloved Lord of Lakshmi.' Lakshmi is none other than the Lord's power of creation, *sakti*. Lakshmi never stays where Lord Vishnu is not present. This indicates that the creative power cannot exist or function without the presence of Lord, the pure consciousness. *Kamalanyanam* is 'the lotus-eyed one,' whose eyes are fully blossomed and beautiful. *Yogibhir dhyânagamyam* means the true nature of the Lord is only experienced by *yogis* in meditation. *Vande Vishnu* means I salute Lord Vishnu. Etymologically *Vishnu* means 'all-pervading.' *Bhavabhaharam* means one who relieves others' troubles and fear. *Sarvvalokaikanâtham* means He who is the Lord of the universe. I reverently salute the Lord who has all these qualities. Through it we can know the nature of the absolute Reality beyond all names and forms and can understand the entire creation along with its various states. If we understand and appreciate this profound verse with its deeper meaning and implications, then we can fully understand the Supreme Reality or God. Once we know that such wonderful truth is being depicted in the picture or idol, with this understanding we should worship and meditate on any idol.

The assertion that Hindus are polytheists is not correct. Hindus do not believe in a group of gods who together share in divinity. In Hindu worship, there is always one God in view, even though there is general recognition that God takes different forms at different times. Ordinary human beings can only grasp a God in human form. They resort to different forms of worship to different deities, even though they are all actually worshipping one God. To elaborate further, let us take mother as an example. Her son looks at her as his beloved mother and spouse look at her as a life partner, with whom he can share everything in life; her parents look at her as their little girl, who still has a lot to learn. And if she is a teacher, her pupils look at her as a teacher who gives them knowledge. We are speaking of one person, but every body is experiencing that person from different points of view, and all of them are right in their perception of that person. So even if we worship hundreds of gods, we are actually worshipping one Supreme Being, one God. It is difficult for some people to understand this ideology. Some people have stated that Indians are animistic, in that they seem to worship rivers, mountains, trees, rocks and animals. Again this characterization misses the point, for it is not the natural objects themselves that are worshipped, but the hidden reality that lies within is in some way symbolized by these objects. Hindus have a transcendental idea of the divine, it is precisely because divine is so radically different that they feel free to use a variety of symbolic forms in their worship of it.

What other religious critics contemptuously call the weakness of polytheism in Hinduism is really a source of its strength. Polytheism is a powerful aid to personal religion and caters exclusively to the spiritual needs of individuals according to their temperaments and levels of culture, but a polytheistic view is entirely optional. If one can do without many gods, one is at perfect liberty to set them aside and go the higher way (*jñâna*). In some cases, individual God (*ishtadevatâ*) becomes a source of inspiration, sacrifice and powerful living. Through prayer, meditation and *japa* a person comes into an intimate relationship with a deity and is finally absorbed into it. So one can have a personal God but try to see one's personal God in all the forms of God. One can worship in a Christian church, Jewish synagogue, a Muslim mosque or a Buddhist vihârâ and see a personal God in all those places of worship. By doing so, one establishes the oneness of God and eradicates his ego that is a stumbling bloc in ones spiritual progress.

To explain the importance of idol-worship, the Indian sages used to point out that the idols that are worshipped remind of one God who is formless and eternal. It is the same as a toy-fruit or a toy-elephant reminds us of the real fruit and living animal. *Agamas* or sectarian scriptures are text written by sages who obtained them by their intuitive powers of meditation. They explained the various aspects of the Ultimate Reality or *Sagun Brahman*, so that the common masses can comprehend and develop the mental powers necessary to elevate themselves to understand the Almighty and practice faith. It is the first step of the faith before knowing the philosophy. It also gives the devotional forms of worship or the *bhakhati marga*. *Agamas* reaches the illiterate and the devout masses.

The worshippers worship God first who is endowed with attributes and form (*Saguna*), so long as His form is not fixed in their minds, they assume, 'God exists and He is ours.' The firmer His form is fixed, the higher their adoration is regarded. At last when they are able to behold Him, talk to Him, touch Him and receive blessing from Him, their worship attains perfection. The worshippers of an attributeless (*nirguna*) God think of Him as One who pervades everywhere. The subtler their disposition grows, the higher their worship is regarded. At last when their attachment and egoism are completely renounced and no feeling of 'I'ness and 'You'ness is left but only pure consciousness remains, their worship attains perfection. Thus, both devotees after attaining perfection become one and attain the same God. The worshippers of the God endowed with attributes and forms (*Saguna*) by His grace also realize the Lord who is without attribute and form (*nirguna*).

Practically every deity of the Hindu pantheon has three modes of expression or manifestation: (i) the idol (*murti*), the three-dimensional form which can be sculptured; (ii) the *yantra*, a two-dimensional or geometric pattern which can be drawn; and (iii) the *mantra*, the sound form or the thought form, which is uttered in contemplation. The *murti* is usually describe in the appropriate *Dhyânasloka* (verse chanted at the beginning of meditation, to call up the form of deity into the mind) and dealt with in greater detail in the iconographical works.

When all mental processes fail to grasp the reality of an object and when that objects is away from one sight, in order to represent the object, and somehow retain it, one is driven to use symbols. It is just like learning geography. A student is looking at the maps that are only representations, how much more is one required to lean on appropriate symbol-systems for the arduous task of delving into the very subtle spiritual reality?

Idols are not only visual theologies, they are also visual scriptures. Many myths of the tradition are narrated in living stone. For example, in the West, the great carved portals of the Charters Cathedral presented the stories, the ethics and the eschatology of the Christian tradition for the vast majority who could not read. Even earlier, Pope Gregory I had recognized the didactic value of images: 'For, that which is a written document is to those who can read, that a picture is to the unlettered who looks at it. Even the unlearned sees in that what course they ought to follow; even those who do not know the alphabet can read there.' Similarly, the great temples of Hindu India often displayed as relief portrayals of myths and legends.

The ultimate aim of the spiritual pursuit is to go beyond mental intelligence to supra-mental awareness. Here again the use of symbols is of great aid to the mind during *dhyana* (meditation). During, meditation, the mind is totally centred on the symbol, and when gradually the form of the symbol vanishes from the mind and is totally absorbed, it is said to be in *samadhi*.

Understanding of the nature of the divine idol that we Hindus see has two principal attitudes that may be discerned in the worship of idols. The first is that the idol is primarily a focus for concentration, and the second is that the idol is the embodiment of divine.

Can a person attain *mukti* (liberation) by image worship? Swami Vivekananda said, 'Image-worship cannot directly give *mukti*; it may be an indirect cause, a help on the way.' Image-worship should not be condemned, for many, it prepares the mind for the realization of the *advaita* (non-duality) which alone makes a person perfect.

The idol is a kind of *yantra*, practically a 'device' for harnessing the eye and the mind so that the one-pointedness of thought (*ekagratâ*) which is fundamental to meditation can be attained. The idol is a support for meditation. As in the

Vishnu Samhita, a spiritual *agama* text puts it: 'It is difficult to meditate upon God without a form.' If (He is) without any form, where will the mind fix itself? When there is nothing for the mind to attach itself to, it will slip away from meditation or will glide into a state of slumber. Therefore, the wise will meditate on some form, remembering, however, that the form is a superimposition and not a reality (*Vishnu samhita* 29: 55-57).

The *Jabala Upanishad* goes even a step further, intimating that such an idol, while it may be a support for the beginner, is of no use to the *yogi*. 'Yogis see Shiva in the soul and not in images. For the ignorant person, idols are meant for the realization of God (*J. Upanishad* 3: 59).

It is the second attitude toward idols that most concerns some of us, that is, the image is the real embodiment of the deity. It is not just a device for the focusing the human vision, but is charged with the presence of the God because of intense belief. The emotional attitude toward idols emerged primarily from the devotional (*bhakti*) movement. This adores the personal God 'with qualities' (*saguna*) which show the idol as one of the many ways in which the Lord becomes accessible to persons evincing their affections.

In the early theistic traditions of the *Bhagavatas* or *Pancaratras*, which emphasized devotional worship (*puja*) rather than the Vedic sacrifice (*yajna*), the idol was considered to be one of the five forms of the Lord. These five are: the Supreme form (*para*), the emanations or powers of the Supreme (*vyuha*), the immanence of the Supreme in the heart of the individual and in the heart of the universe (*antaryamin*), the incarnations of the Supreme (*vibhava*) and, finally, the presence of the Supreme Lord in a properly consecrated image (*arca*). Later, the Vaishanavas used the term *aracavatara* to refer to the 'idol-incarnation' of the Lord: the form Vishnu graciously takes so that he may be worshipped by his devotees. Indeed, the very theology of the Vaisanava community, as articulated by Ramanuja in the 11th century, is based on the faith that the Lord is characterized both by his supremacy (*paratva*) and his accessibility (*saulabhya).*

God has become accessible not only in incarnations, but also in idols. In the *Bhagavad Gita* (*Gitâ* IV.11), Krishna tells Arjuna: 'In whatever way people approach me (*bhajami*), in that way do I show them favour (*darsayami*).' He further said: 'God does not only rescue those who resort to Him in the shape of one of his *avataras* by descending into that shape alone, but He reveals Himself to all who resort to Him, whatever the shape in which they represent Him.'

Another theologian of the Vaishnava movement, Pillai Lokacharya, writes of the grace by which the Lord enters and dwells in the idol for the sake of the devotee: 'This is the greatest grace of the Lord, that being free He becomes bound; being independent, He becomes dependent for all His service on His devotee..... In other forms, the man belonged to God but behold the supreme sacrifice of *Isavara*, here the Almighty becomes the property of the devotee... He carries Him about, fans Him, feeds Him, plays with Him—yea, the Infinite has become finite, that the child soul may grasp, understand and love Him.'

Young has clearly demonstrated that ten theological nuances to the Srivaisnava understanding of the Lord's incarnation in an icon are contained in Râmânuja's (*Bhagavad Gita Bhâsya* IV:11): (1) the fullness of God in the image form; (2) easy accessibility; (3) God's gracious condescension; (4) mutuality of God : human relationship; (5) reversal of relationship between God and humans; (6) universality of eligibility; (7) equality inherent in surrender to God; (8) identity of means (*upâya*) and goal (*upeya*); (9) dependence of the Lord's variety of forms on the desire and imagination of the devotees; and (10) God incarnations unrestricted by time, space and eligibility (Young, Râmanuja on *Bhagavadgita IV: 11:* The Issue of Arcâvatâra, pp.95-104).

Even one God does not necessarily have only a single form, but may appear in a variety of traditional poses that reveal the different aspects of that God's nature or episodes in the God's mythology. Shiva, for example, may be depicted in an iconic *linga* form, as a dancer (Nataraja), as a meditating ascetic (Daksinamurti), as the husband of Parvati (Kalyanasundara), as the destroyer of demons (Tripuranataka), as the half-woman God (Ardhanarisvara), or as the one who emerges bodily out of the *linga* (Lingodbhava). The *sastras* enumerate the various poses and specify the details for each one of them.

The diversity of deities is part of the earliest Vedic history of the Hindu tradition. In the Rig Veda, the various gods are elaborately praised, and in their individual hymns everyone is depicted as Supreme. Indra may in one hymn be called the 'Sole Sovereign of Human Being and of Gods', and in the next hymn Varuna may be praised as the 'Supreme Lord, Ruling all Spheres'. It is not monotheism, although there certainly is a vision of divine supremacy as grand as the monotheistic vision. It is not really polytheism, at least if one understands this as the worship of many gods, each with partial authority and limited sphere of influence. The monotheistic God stands with human being as a father and a patriarch, while in a *Rig Veda* hymn to Agni is called: 'My father, my relative, my brother and my friend.' Monotheism aptly contemplates the Divine in heaven and polytheism contemplates the Divine in the universe. Polytheism believes in the assembly of gods, each possessing a character of his own. These western terms do not quite fit in the Hindu situation. To describe the deities of Hinduism, Max Muller coined the word *kathenotheism*—the worship of one God at a time. Each is exalted in turn. Each God is praised as a creator, as a source, and as a sustainer of the universe when one stands in the presence of that deity. There are many gods, but their multiplicity does not diminish the significance or power of any of them. Each of the great gods may serve as a lens through which the whole of reality is clearly seen. To celebrate one deity, one sacred place or one temple does not mean there is no room for the celebration of another. Each deity has its hour. Traditionally there are three gods: Brahman, Vishnu and Shiva. But it is clear from their hymns and rites that these deities are not regarded as having partial powers. Each God is seen, by devotees of that God, as Supreme in every sense. In the *Brhadaranyaka Upanishad*, a seeker named Vidagdha Sakalya approaches the sage Yajnavalkya with a question, How many gods are there? Yajnavalkya responds that there are many gods. There is Shiva, and there are Vishnu, Ganesh, Durga, Lakshami, Saraswati, Hanuman and many other gods. But, of course, there is really only one. There are two basic ideas underlying the Veda—*Satya* (truth) and *Rta* (eternal order); and every God or goddess exemplifies and represents these two ideas. As Abibash Chandra Bose says, it Vedic theism based on moral values that may be upheld in a non-theistic way. In India, it is not the atheist who is denounced but the person who repudiates *sharma*, moral law. (*Rig-Veda* X.85.1) states that the earth is sustained not by the will of God but by truth, and of this truth God is the supreme exponent, revealing Himself through *Rta* (eternal order). Examining the Vedic hymns as a whole, one discovers a doctrine, not of oneness, but of one divine substance pervading all. It is stated that the One Being is contemplated by the sages in many forms (*ekam satyam bahudha kalpayanti*) (*Rig-Veda*, X.114-5). It may also be observed that the Vedic ritual or *yjna* is a uniform ceremonial; whatever deity is worshipped, the ritual is the same. For every deity there is a *dhyâna sloka*, which is to be meditated upon with its deeper implications, meaning and appreciation. Once we know that such wonderful truth is being depicted in the picture or idol and we worship on it with understanding, it will be a heavenly experience.

Many of the deities are made of multiple arms, each hand bearing an emblem or a weapon, or posed in a gesture called a *mudra*. The emblems and *mudras* indicate the various powers that belong to the deity.

Devi Durga has ten arms, and in her hands she holds the weapons and emblems of all the gods who turned their weapons over to her to kill the demon of chaos. Multiple faces and eyes are common. The creator Brahman, for example, has four faces, looking in each of the four directions. Shiva sometimes has three faces, (*trimurti* or triple form) each with a different countenance to indicate the various aspects of the one God. Triple Form represents cumulatively Brahma the creator, Vishnu the preserver and Shiva the destroyer. Shiva's third eye indicates the omniscience of the one God. The bodies of the gods sometimes convey multiplicity in oneness. For example, during the medieval period Shiva and Vishnu were depicted together in one body, each half with the emblems appropriate to its respective deity. The androgynous image is one breasted, dressed in one half in male garments and another half in female—*ardhanârisvara*. *Ardhanârisvara* is half Shiva and half Parvati, representing the union of the God with his *shakti*, the strength or potency of her male counterpart. As Shiva is worshipped in the *linga* or phallic emblem, so is Durga worshipped in the female emblem, or *yoni*. In similar way, Radha and Krishna are sometimes shown as entwined together in such a fashion that, while one could delineate two separate figures, they appear to the eye as inseparably one.

In any idol, it is the combination and juxtaposition of these gestures and emblems which Hindus have seen in the deity. Shiva holds both the drum and the flame; the Goddess Kali simultaneously wears a gory garland of skulls, and gestures to provide protection; Vishnu appears with Shiva's emblems in his hands. This idol-world of India is what Betty Heimann has aptly called 'visible thought.'

Sukraniti Sara mentions that any idol or representation of the gods falls into three classes: the first is *sâtvik* where a sitting posture in the attitude of meditation is adopted, which exudes an atmosphere of peace. The second is *râjasik* as in seen when gods or goddesses are seen riding in a vehicle. Such idols express love, happiness and heroism as are seen in Mahâlakshmi on the lotus and Durga riding a lion. The third type *Tâmasik* is disguised to create a sense of terror and utter helplessness of the individual as in *Narasimha* (Half lion and half man) and *Kâli* with the tongue out, adorned with a string of skulls, with fearsome expression.

Hindu philosophical ideas are propagated through mythological stories. To meet the needs of less evolved minds, a symbol or a form or an idol is created which helps everyone to see, understand and remember what all it stands for. This helps the illiterate to grasp the truth as is enshrined in such idols and helps them to evolve spirituality. This is how *saguna*, with attributes, and worship finally leads to *nirguna*, without attributes or worship.

AVATARAS

The *avâtâras*, or reincarnations of Vishnu are *Matsya, Kurma, Varaha* and are considered to be allegorical representations of the stages of human evolution, and finally reaching perfection in the human as Rama-*avatara*, Krishna and Buddha. The struggle towards the sanctifying of the earth or the revealing of the God-ideal has passed through several stages in the evolution on earth. The ten *avâtârs* of Vishnu mark out the central steps. The growth in the sub-human or the animal level is emphasized in those of the fish,the tortoise and the boar. Next we have the transition between the animal and the human world in the man-lion (Narasimha *avâtâr*). *Narasimhavâtâr* is the incarnation of the Lord Vishnu, who is distinct and unique, ferocious and dazzling. No one ventured to approach Him for mitigation of his aggressive posture after the death of the cruel giant, Hiranyakasipu, for fear of being destroyed, except His genuine devotee par excellence, Prahlada, the son of Hiranyakasipu. Atrocities of Hiranyakasipu aroused the Lord to become the protector of the meek and gentle, the sole succour of His devotees who surrender to Him totally without any reservation whatsoever. The development is not completely fulfilled when we came to the dwarf (Vâmana avâtâr). Vâmanâ avâtâr expounds the omnipresent and omniscient nature of the Lord. Nothing can defy his power. His will is law. But at the same time He willingly binds Himself to the established laws of *dharma*. It is for 'Lokasangraha.' The first stage of man is that of the brutish and violent Prasurâma with his axe, who devastates the rest of humanity. Lord Parasurama is the sixth *âvatâr* of the Lord Vishnu who made His powerful presence felt at a time when the Kshatriyas, entrusted with the well-being of the world, became cruel and evil violators of *dharma*. Thus they became the eyesore of the meek and gentle, sages and saints. Later we get the divine spiritual Râma, who consecrates family life and affections. Lord Rama is the redeemer. He wiped out Râvana and assured safety for all the followers of *dharma*. The Ramâ avatâra is Dharmâvatâra. He is the very personification of *dharma* itself. Lord Rama is the ideal son, spouse, monarch and superman, the Purushottoma, to be worshipped and attained. Then Lord Krishna avâtâr exhorts us to enter into the warfare of the world. Lord Krishna was Lord Vishnu in full manifestation. He descended to the world in an age to rid it all vicious forces that reigned supreme at the time and to ensure safety and prosperity for the innocent and virtuous people. Krishna stands for one's conscience. He said that the *atman* is indestructible whereas the body is destructible. After Krishna, Buddha, who full of compassion for all life, works for the redemption of mankind. Lord Vishnu was born as Lord Buddha to redeem the world from the evil of dogmatism, ritualism, and the nepotism of the few who belonged to the priestly class. At the time when Buddha was born, the world was full of human beings of intellectual sterility. Buddha sought to purify his person by diverse modes of austerity and penance and inculcate the same values in all others. The *Upanishads* and the *Vedas* were confined to a few. The spirit of the *Vedas* and the *Upanishads* was lost. Outward show had won over internal virtue. There was a need for the complete overhauling of the system with emphasis on morality, truth and universal love. Lord Buddha was born to make the humans human, moral, truthful and courageous armed with nonviolence in thought, word and deed. Buddhism is an emphasis on Ethics, Love and Service by which human being becomes God. The tenth *avâtâra* (Kalki) is still to be born during this time who will fight evil and injustice. When men and women are living a life of gross immorality. Their only aim in life is to satisfy their lust. They have become slaves of their senses and will not observed the related ties of mother, sister and daughter in their lustful behaviour. They are worse than animals in this respect.

VISHNU

The word Vishnu itself means the great omnipresent. Vishnu, the Supreme Being is functioning as the sustainer, protector and preserver of the universe. In idols, Vishnu is either standing or reclining. He is reclining on Ananta on the milky ocean. Ananta or the snake stands for cosmic energy. The ocean of milk stands for *Ananda* or beatitude. Vishnu has blue colour like the sky, indicating His infinitude. He is *Achyuta*, because there is no rise or fall for Him. The four-faced Brahma rising from His navel is symbolic of his creative power. Brahma has four heads because he is the creator of the entire universe. He has four hands. The *chakra* or discus in one of the upper hand of Vishnu symbolizes the cycle of time (*kala-chakra*) whose whirliging brings in consolation as well as revenge, according to *Varaha Purana*. It is also described as the *dharma-chakra*, maintaining orderliness and proper functioning of the universe. The *shankha* or conch in the other upper left hand symbolizes the destroyer of ignorance (*avidya*), represented by darkness and silence. Others say that *shankha* represents *Nada-brahma*. In one of the lower hands Vishnu holds the club or sometime *asi (sword)*. The sword is meant to cut the knot of *samsara* which human being has woven round himself through numberless births. It is a weapon of detachment. If He is holding a club, it is for setting right the irregularities of the world, *dushtanigraha* and *sishta paripalana*. With the other hand, He is blessing everyone. The lotus flower He holds with a long stem in one hand signifies the beauty and freshness of the cosmos.

Sri Krishna, an incarnation of Vishnu is revealed in the *Gitâ* to Arjuna. Sri Mahâlakshmi is the consort of Vishnu. Vishnu appointed *Garuda* or an eagle as His vâhana or vehicle. Garuda is the monarch of all flying creatures. Garuda with his ability to fly at unlimited speed is a most apt carrier of Lord Vishnu, who is the All-pervading protector cf the universe. Garuda is also represented as a destroyer of evil, as symbolized by the serpent which he holds in his two claws. The Eagle or Garuda kills the serpent.

SHIVA

The worship of Shiva has been in existence from pre-historic times. Roughly resembling Shiva and His bull are the idols that have been unearthed at Mahenjo-daro and Harappa. From very ancient times, Shiva was worshipped as the Supreme God. About 2000 BC in *Rig Veda*, Shiva—then called Rudra is mentioned. Shiva has been worshipped both in the subtle (*linga*) and the gross embodied (human) forms.

Concerning the range and extent of the practice of *linga* worship, Shri Babu Siva Prasad in his book, *Prithvi Pradaksana* or Round the World, has claimed that the worship of the *linga* prevailed in ancient times all over the world. In support of his claims of *linga* worship, Siva Prasad described *linga* worship under local names even today in Egypt, Greece, Scotland, Austria, Hungary, Assyria, Mecca, Iran and America.

Some people worship the *sakala-niskala* form, some worship in the heart, or in the *linga* or in the fire. Some people worship the *sakala* form along with their spouses and sons. Some people call him one, another calls him one with two *gunas* (*prakriti* and *purusa*). Some call him Triguna (Brahma, Vishnu and Rudra). Others, the knowers of the *Vedas*, speak of him as the cause of the universe (*linga purana* I.75.32,37 & 39).

It is a living idea that the universe is like an egg, of circular or oval shape. Even an ordinary human being, when he looks at this universe, cannot miss its circular shape. The idea of its circular shape is also depicted in the *Manusmriti*. Modern astronomers, too, have concurred that this infinite universe is a huge solid mass of circular shape. The basic form of the *linga* that has manifested everything, from the most subtle atom to the biggest universe is circular in shape. For all races, the circular shape has been the emblem of the infinite and the eternal. The *linga* is adored as a symbol of God in the shape of the universe.

Unlike other idols, which are in human or animal forms, the *linga* is glorified as two folds: gross and subtle. As a subtle form, *niskala* (attributeless or formless) it has no head or feet since He is identical with the Supreme Brahman; and is the embodiment of Unmanifest Absolute, the cosmic energy immanent in the macrocosm. The gross *linga* is made of clay, wood, stone, crystal, etc., and is meant just to create a feeling of devotion in the gross minded people. In fact, Lord Shiva is like the ether, an indivisible centre whose division into *sakala* (attributes) and *niskala* (attributeless) forms as of the ether into *ghatakasa is illusory* (*linga Purana* I.75). He is also *sakala* (attribute) as He has an embodied the form known as Shiva. The subtle form is not perceptible to the deluded person who conceives things only externally. The creatures in the heaven and on the earth are re-evolved out of the five elements (water, soil, wind, fire and ether). Still they are seen in multiple forms as different species and individuals. In the primordial beginning, the first human being must have witnessd the light and rain descending from the sky, might have implied the existence of some abnormal power in the sky. Lest it be enraged against him, out of fear and devotion, it is quite likely that he, superimposing God-hood upon the sky and preparing in its circular shape *linga*, might have worshipped him. Man's desire is to pour water on the *linga*, which is an emblem of the sky, because there is water in the sky. The custom of performing *abhisekha* (pouring water over the linga) might have developed. To facilitate draining water poured upon the *linga* that is circular in shape, a *jalahari*, or a channel-like thing in the shape of a cow's mouth are made. It may thus be implied that the idea of *linga* and its shape has evolved eventually.

The word *linga* has been used extensively in several *Upanishads*. It normally means a sign, a symbol or emblem of something. *linga* refers to *linga-sama suksma-sarira*, the entity consisting of *budhi, ahamkara, manas, indriyani, tannatrani* (Svetasvetara Upanishad: VI.9; Katha Upanishad: II.3.8; and Maitri Upanishad: VI.10). In the *Sivapurana*, the *linga* is described as the embodiment of *OM*. 'The *OM* that grants all accomplishments is itself *linga*. The three letters, *A,U,M* represent respectively, *Linga's* base (*pitha*), the cow's mouth (*gomukha* or water drain) and globe (*golaka*).' If the *linga* is taken in this sense, it means that the Supreme needs no subtle body as it is not subject to death and rebirth (*Katha Upanishad:* V.3.9).

We usually can say we smell a flower, when really what we smell is not the flower but the perfume within it. Though we normally adore God in the shape of the universe, but we actually adore is the Universal soul and not the universe. Therefore, the universe is the means, and the Universal soul, the goal. To disown the means is neither proper nor fair while seeking to attain to the goal through the means. It would not be right to say that we want only the perfume and not the flower, we cannot say we want the Universal soul and not the universe, or only the soul and not the body. Perhaps we may not realize the soul without the body or the universe or the mean.

We have to go beyond the idolistic idea of the sky as God, and worshipping the *linga* as its representation, in order to realize that Shiva, the holder of Ganga, is an idea of spiritistic worship.

There is considerable lore about the origin of the Shiva *linga* in which form Shiva is usually worshipped. Birth, following the union of sexes, and the coming of a new being into the world was regarded as a mystery and a manifestation of the Supreme. Since the earliest of times, there was connection between the postures of yoga and of sexuality. Lord Shiva is beyond the *Pradhana* and *Purusa*. In his one half, (*ardhanarisvara*) he is devoid of qualities (*niskala*) but his other half (*sakala*) is characterized by the three attributes: *sattva, rajas* and *tamas* that are personified as *Brahmâ, Vishnu,* and *Rudra*. The male form (*purusa*) enters into the womb of the female form (*prakriti*) and lays the golden seed (*hiranyagrava*). The seed is of the nature of fire, the creative force and is permeated by a creative potency. According to the *linga Purana,* (*Linga purana* I.20.73) this creative energy is personified as *Brahmâ*; the recipient of the seed, the fetus, is named *Vishnu* while the sower of the seed is Lord Shiva himself. Thus, the half-man and half-woman form of the Lord is both the efficient and the material cause of the universe. The entire phenomenon of creation is symbolized by the phallic icon (*linga*) of Lord Shiva. A *linga* is as a column, arising out of a *yoni* (vaginal passage) is set up in temples dedicated to Shiva. The creation of the Universe is not a permanent feature. For all creations end in dissolutions, which in turn give place to recreation. At the appearance of recreation after dissolution, Lord Shiva is present in two forms, *Prakriti* and *Atman*. Lord Vishnu adopts the body of *Prakriti* and lies on the yogic couch in the midst of the primordial waters. Then *Brahmâ* is born of his umbilical lotus. *Brahmâ* asks Shiva to grant him power to recreate. This icon or enigma was therefore worshipped as the *linga* or phallus that is in essence a symbolic expression of the union of sexes. The worship of the *linga* by Shaivites is not accompanied by any act suggestive of sexual union. Emphasis on this fact is further expanded upon that Shiva is enemy of *Kâma Deva*, the God of Love, because He once burnt *Kâma Deva* to ashes with a mere look of His third eye. Although the erect phallus is, of course, a sign of the God of male generative power, in Indian culture it is a symbol of chastity as well. 'He is called *urdhvalinga* (erect phallus) because the lowered *linga* has shed its seed, but not the raised *linga*. (Bharati, A., *The Tantric Tradition,* London, The Ocher Robe, 1961).' The basic Sanskrit expression for the practice of chastity is the drawing up of the seed (*urdhvalinga*). The seed is often confused with the *linga* itself, which is raised in chastity. The raised seed is a natural image of chastity. Thus Shiva is both the god whose seed is raised up and the God whose *linga* is raised up. Shiva is a pillar (*sthânu*) of chastity, yet the pillar is also the form of the erect *linga*. It is in this form of the Lord of Yogins that becomes *sthânu* or of *linga* form. Since, in the context of the Hindu attitude toward sexual power, Shiva's chastity is power of eroticism. The erect phallus can represent both phases. The ethyphallic condition has been attributed by some not to priapism but to the *tantrik* ritual of seminal retention. Iconographically, the image of the androgyny (*linga and yoni*) is the symbol of sexual union but also representative of a situation in which union is physically impossible. This also suggests that innocence is not the absence of the erotic but its fulfillment. Hermaphroditic imagery suggests that there is a state of consciousness in which the erotic no longer has to be sought or pursued, because it is always present in its totality (Watts, A.W. : The two hands of God: The myths of polarity. Vol.iii of Patterns of Myth.ed. Alan W. Watts, New York, 1963). The conquest of desire is the satisfaction of desire: 'In the life of sentient beings, only the state of total sexual consummation is desireless, hence again the symbolism of *linga* (Bharati, A:The Tantric Tradition. London: The Ocher Robe, 1961).'

In the temple at Tiruvanaikoil, in the district of Trichinopoly of Tamil Nadu, is a unique Shiva Lingam with five faces. This is the rarest type of Shiva Lingam and probably the only one of its kind in the whole of India. All the five faces differ from each other. Four faces face the cardinal points of the compass and the fifth is on the top, facing the sky. The Vedic names of these are *tatpurusa* facing east, *vamadeva* facing west, *sadhyojata* facing north, *aghora* facing south, and the fifth *èsâna* on the top, facing the sky. They are all depicted quite correctly in keeping with Vedic description of such in '*dhyâna slokas.*'

Lord Shiva is the Supreme Being functioning as the destroyer of ego and illusion, and the material universe at the end of each cycle of creation. The gross embodied form of Shiva is worshipped as *Natarâj*, the Cosmic Dancer, whose dance sustains and energizes the entire universe. The icon of *Natarâj* reveals the many aspects of this God in one visual symbol. The genius of Indian thought found a marvelous unity of religious, art and science fervour in the sculpture of the Dancing Shiva, *Natarâj*, the Lord of the Dance. In this image, Shiva is conceived as the embodiment of Eternal Energy, engaged in the five-fold activity (*pancha-kriya*) of creation, preservation, annihilation, concealment or obstruction, and liberation or salvation. It indicates cosmic activity. The inflaming ring in which he dances is the circle of creation and destruction and is called *samsara* (the earthly circle of birth and death) or *maya* (the illusory world). The four-armed Shiva dancing in a ring of flames, the *prabha mandala*, the dance of nature all initiated by the Self in the centre, all emanating from Him, and all dissolving within Him. The Lord who dances in the circle of this changing world holds in the two of his upper hands, the drum of creation and the fire of destruction. The upper right hand holds aloft the *damaru* or drum, representing *nada*, the sound, the evolution of the universe. From sound came all language, all music, all knowledge. The shape of the drum, with its two triangles, tells us of nature and energy which unites all creation. The upper left hand is in the half moon gesture, holds a tongue of flame. Why does Shiva hold the hope of creation in one hand, and the flame, the fire that destroys, in the other? For, creation and destruction are the counterparts of His own Being. There are the two aspects of our life, as we are surely born, so do we die. He displays his strength by crushing a struggling dwarf, a human being who is the embodiment of all that veils truth from falsehood, the *apasmara purusha*, made up of ignorance and forgetfulness, under the foot. This is the *purusha* within us, which prevents us from realizing our own essential divinity. It is for us to firmly crush out the ignorance if we are to attain the supreme eternal bliss that we call God. Simultaneously, He shows his mercy by raising his palm to the worshiper in the 'fear-not' gesture and, with another hand, by pointing to his upraised foot, where worshiper may take refuge. The left foot is raised, telling the human being that as the dancer raises his foot, so can human being raise himself and attain salvation. It is a wild dance, for the coils of his ascetic hair are flying in both directions, and yet the facial countenance of the Lord is utterly peaceful and his limbs in complete balance. Around one arm twines the *naga*, the ancient serpent, which he has incorporated into his sphere of power and wears now as an ornament. In his hair-locks sit the mermaid River Ganga, who landed first on Shiva's hair when she descended from the heaven on to the earth. Driving away *maya*, burning *karma*, crushing the ego and raising Jeeva by grace—these are said to be the works of the Lord's dance during the *pradoshas*. Its deepest significance will be felt when it is visualized that it should take place in our heart. Then will the realization come that the Kingdom of God is within and God is everywhere. Such an idol of the dancing Shiva catches the eye and extends one's vision of the nature of this God. In the right ear is the ornament 'makara kundal' that is an ornament worn by males while the left ear bears the 'tatanka' or 'patra kundala,' an ornament worn by females. The wearing of both categories of ornaments indicates the 'ardhanâriswara' idea, which is a combination of the male and female aspects of life signifying the dual aspect of creation.

The allegory of the dance has to be understood about the place of the dance. The platform of the dance is the cremation ground where all the individual bodies, names and passions that once rocked them and all that makes up one's world are burnt away and only pure consciousness devoid of all attachments and devoid of illusion alone remains.

What is perhaps most significant of all in the image is the combination of this God ascetic, the solitary one, master of meditation, with the frenzied dance—the *yogi* and the artist. A dancer becomes the being that he impersonates on the stage. The dance is aroused the entire energy of body, mind, intellect and soul. It is a complete surrender to God. Thus, a dancer is similar to the *yogi,* who gives his all to the Lord.

A noted physicist, Fritj of Capra wrote, (Fritj, *The Tao of Physics.*): 'The dance of Shiva is the dancing universe; the ceaseless flow of energy going through an infinite variety of patterns that melt into one another. Modern physics has shown that the rhythm of creation and destruction is not only manifest in the turn of the seasons and in the birth and death of all living creatures, but is also the very essence of inorganic matter. According to quantum field theory, all interactions between the constituents of matter take place through the emission and absorption of virtual particles. More than that the dance of creation and destruction is the basis of the very existence of matter, since all material particles 'self-interact' by emitting and reabsorbing virtual particles. Modern physics has thus revealed that every subatomic particle not only performs an energy dance, but also is an energy dance—a pulsating process of creation and destruction... For the modern physicist, then Shiva's dance is the dance of subatomic matter, a continual dance of creation and destruction involving the whole cosmos, the basis of existence and of all natural phenomena. The metaphor of the Cosmic Dance thus unifies ancient mythology, religious art and modern physics. It is indeed, as Coomarswamy has said, 'poetry, but science nonetheless.' The Hindu religion which was postulated thousands of years ago is a cosmology that only today is being invented and appreciated by science through the ponderous progress of reason and empirical proof. Our religion knew the truth of the source and organization of the universe long before Newton and Einstein confirmed the validity of our world view.

In some idol(s), Lord Shiva has the river Ganga flowing from his head. It means the flow of knowledge coming out his head is as pure as water of the Ganga river. Why does Lord Shiva have the Ganga on His head? This could mean that one should keep his head cool as water. On Shiva's forehead is the crescent moon and in His neck is blue due to poison. The crescent moon represents the nectar of life. It is said that the nectarine rays of the moon fall on earth and nourish the entire vegetable kingdom. But poison is just the opposite—it brings death! Lord Shiva holds both the moon and the poison, yet is ever in meditation. It indicates that our lives are filled with opposites: life and death, joy and sorrow, success and failure, etc. We should be able to bear these opposites with calmness of mind and not let them destroy our mental equilibrium. His neck became blue because He took the poison and drank it. The poison came out of the fight between the gods and demons and none of them were ready to take it. So they called Lord Shiva to take it. However He did not swallow the poison. He kept it in His throat without letting it go down into His stomach. It means that only a great and wise person will be able to swallow all the poison in life without letting it go into body system. Lord Shiva is adorned with the snake garland. The snake represents time (*kâla*). The snake of time also bites every created being and people die. Time and death are frightening to us, but Shiva is fearless and He is the Lord of time. Lord Shiva bears the ashes of the cremation ground smeared all over His body. By these Lord Shiva shows us that our bodies are already dead and will turn to ashes one day. Therefore, we should rise above our identification with the body while we are alive. Lord Shiva has three eyes. The third eye is located between the eyebrows, and is the eye of wisdom. The other two eyes represent love and justice. When the Lord deals with this world, He is both loving and just, and He looks at this world with the vision of knowledge that destroys all ignorance and passion. He has four hands. In the right hand He has a *trisul* or trident that represents the three *gunas* or qualities, namely, *sattva, rajas,* and *tamas* (purity, passion and inertia). Lord Shiva rules the world through these three *gunas.* The *damaru* or little drum in His left hand represents Om, from which all sounds, languages, all music and all knowledge originate. The shape of the drum, with its two triangles, tells us of nature and energy which combine for all creation. He also holds a deer in another hand. The deer jumps from place to place very swiftly. The mind also jumps from one place to another with lightening speed. Sometimes the deer is shown in one of his hands which indicates that He has removed the restlessness of the mind. The mind is equated to it; control of mind is suggested by it; control of mind is thus taught. The fourth hand is held out to bless and protect us. He wears the skin of an elephant, indicating that He has overcome pride. Sitting on a tiger skin tells us that we must strip ourselves of *ahankâra* or pride or lust which is equated to the tiger. Thus the Lord is telling us that He has thereby conquered lust. The *vrishabha* or bull that Shiva rides is *dharma*. The Nandi before Shiva temples signifies that we are all *pasu* and Shiva is *pati* (lord), hence the name *Pasupatu* for Shiva. It's looking towards Shiva indicates *Pasu,* e.g. *Jiva* should seek union with *Pati,* i.e., *Paramatman.* Shiva as *Dakshinamurti* is another beautiful idea. He becomes the cosmic preceptor. His *chinmudra* where the right thumb and first finger meet while the other three stand away has great philosophical significance. The thumb represents God, the forefinger represents the individual self, and the other three fingers are delusion, toil and egoism. The meaning is that one is relieved or separated of three *doshas* as the individual self unites with the Cosmic Self.

It is quite possible that the concept of Shiva has evolved from that of the sky. Since there are in the sky three modes of light—the sun, the moon and the fire (lightning)—by personification Shiva is made the three-eyed one with the sun, moon and fire (lightning) as his three eyes. The sky cannot be clothed; even so, Shiva cannot be clothed. Shiva holds the Ganga just as there is water in the firmament. Parvati means *prithivi,* or the earth. Just as the sky is supposed to be the lord of the earth, Shiva is believed to be the Lord of Parvati. Thus, it may be seen that the animistic concept of the sky as God has evolved into the spiritistic concept of Shiva.

The salutation for Shiva is the 'pancâkshara' *mantra* i.e., the five letter *mantra*—*OM NAMA SIVAYA* (*Na* = feet; *Ma* = navel; *Si* = shoulders; *Va* = face; *Ya* = head), i.e. the salutation covers from head to foot.

JAGANNATHA

The name *Jagannatha* means the 'Lord of the Universe.' The idol of Jagannatha does not easily correlate with the human form and symbolizes both the formless (*nirguna*) and the physical (*saguna*) aspects of divinity. The round eyes of Jagannatha characterized as a black spot surrounded by white circles signify the existence of *Brahman*, the omnipotent creator, and his creation, the universe (*Biswa Brahmanda*). He extends both his hands to embrace his creation and bless them. The idol of Jagannatha has no legs and feet. According to *Purusha Sukta*, he has thousands of feet extending to the different *lokas* of the universe. The ordinary devotees see a half-built idol, but self-realized person can visualize His divine body and limbs in all their glory. Lord Jagannatha is worshipped in 'Srimandir' at Puri with Balabhadra, Subhadra, and Sudarshana. Their idols are sculptured from Neem wood.

SARASWATI

In the Hindu pantheon, *Sati* or energy, the female aspect of creation is worshipped in many forms. The important are: Saraswati, Lakshmi, Durgâ, Kâli and Annapûrneswari.

Saraswati is the goddess of speech learning, and wisdom. She gives (*ti*) the essence (*sâra*) of our own self (*sva*). Saraswati is pure white, shining like jasmine, moon, camphor and snow. The goddess wears spotless white *sari* that means an educated person should have spotless or blemishless character. Ignorance is signified by dark colour and knowledge by white. That is why She is depicted as pure white in colour. She rides on a swan that has the rare ability of separating milk from its admixture with water, in the same way as pure intellect can distinguish truth from falsehood in this world. The swan also symbolizes purity and tranquillity and also able to discriminate good from evil. It means that an educated person be firmly situated on the purity and tranquillity. She has four hands. She holds a *veena* with her two hands, a rosary and a book in other two hands. The *veena* shows the need for the cultivation of fine art. The *veena* produces pure, melodious, divine and resonating sound. It is sweet and soothing to the soul and mind as well. The educated person should be sweet in words and disposition. The book represents all areas of secular sciences. The *book* also signifies wisdom. Real wisdom is to know who are you and where you come from, that is, to know *âtman* and *prâmâtma*, and where you have to go ultimately. In short, she is the goddess of wisdom and far-sightedness, of arts and culture. *Srotriyam* means one who knows the philosophy of the *Upanishads* well, and *Brahmanishtam* means one who is well established in the subjective experience of the Self—these two are the qualities of a true teacher. The rosary symbolizes all spiritual sciences. Educated or wise people should have a blemishless or spotless character and have the ability to separate good from evil, they should have serenity, and a sweet disposition and also have faith in God. Thus one can achieve the highest level of knowledge and Supreme Reality. Worship of Saraswati removes 'avidyâ' or ignorance and gains 'vidyâ' or true knowledge that helps one to attain liberation from the cycle of births and deaths, i.e. *moksa*.

Saraswati is venerated by both Buddhists and Jains. Buddhism spread to China, Japan and Tibet. Saraswati was also accepted by the people there.

LAKSHMI

The *Vedas* describe Mother Lakshmi as the Goddess of wealth and prosperity, and as the consort of Lord Vishnu, the preserver of humanity. She is 'prakrti' and Vishnu is 'purusa" and a union of these two becomes the universe. Lakshmi provides eight types of blessing sought by human beings, i.e. wealth, health, courage, victory, fame and fortune, family, peace and happiness as well as spiritual wealth. Lakshmi is portrayed as 'sweta varna' or having a white complexion, and as a noble and graceful person, with four hands and a richly decorated crown either standing or sitting on an open lotus. Two upper hands are seen holding lotuses, one in each hand. A full-bloom lotus flower represents fullness in all aspects, both material and spiritual. The lower left hand shows the *mudra* or sign of offering succour to the worshipper. The lower right hand is ever showering wealth and prosperity on those who sincerely pray for her help. Lakshmi is seen as being richly dressed. She wears golden ornaments. The elephant at her side represents pomp and grandeur. According to the scriptures, if the goddess Lakshmi travels alone, she travels on an owl and, if she travels with Lord Vishnu, she travels on the Garuda (Eagle). An owl is supposed to be blind during the day and a wealthy person without the right kind of intellect cannot see beyond his richness. Therefore, whenever Lakshmi travels without Vishnu she makes the person whom she visits metaphorically blind. However, when the goddess of wealth Lakshmi travels with Lord Vishnu, she travels on a Garuda (Eagle) who is the symbol of wisdom.

SHAKTI

Shakti, the dynamic aspect of the Supreme Being, worship either as Pârvati, Lakshmi, Annapurneswari, Drugâ, Kâli is fairly widespread in all parts of India. Pârvati is the manifestation of Shakti. Shakti's various representations are symbolic of the passions of human beings as jealousy, hate, greed, anger and love.

Shakti or Supreme Mother of the universe is the creative power of Lord Shiva. Shiva and Shakti are inseparable, like fire and heat. Female deities are source of energy, providing strength or potency to their male counterparts. *Shakti* means energy and has been represented by many biological and allegorical truths. *Kali* is *Shakti's* destructive aspect. She is Time personified. In Lalita form, *Shakti* assumes her tender aspect. The noose in her upper hand is symbolic of attachment (*ragaswarupa—pasadhya*) to the world; the *ankush* or hook she holds in the other upper hand represents the power of righteousness (*krodha-karonkusojwala*). The sugarcane-bow in her left lower hand signifies that when one begins to acquire knowledge and knows things properly, life becomes sweeter. It is like sugarcane that is immature and insipid at the top, but is mature and sweet at the bottom. The other hand holds five arrows in a sheath. Each of these arrows represents one of the sense organs of knowledge through which all human beings perceive the world, i.e. the senses of sight, hearings, smell, taste and touch. These five sense perceptions reflect Nature.

The *Sapta-shati* is an allegory on the liberation of human consciousness during its evolutionary process from illusions, limitations and attachments of the lower order. Her killing of Shumbha is destruction of the ego.

KALI

The idol of the goddess *Kâli* is indeed deep blue or almost dark in colour. The word 'Kâli' virtually means black as ink. The new-moon night of Deepavali, the Indian festival of lights, is considered to be a very special occasion for Her worship. *Kâli* has four hands and has a sword in the upper left, while the lower left hand is seen holding a head that has been severed from a body. The upper right hand makes the sign that is meant to remove all fear in Her votaries, while the lower right hand has the gesture of granting the wishes or conferring boon to those devoted to Her. The idol of *Kâli* has a posture indicative of some movement—with the hands raised, tongue out, a garland of skulls around Her neck, a skirt made up of cut-off hands and a sword stained with blood. It signifies the destruction of the demoniac qualities in us. *Kâli's* sword symbolizes *jnâna* or knowledge by which one can cut *âjnâna* or ignorance. The heads that are severed indicate the seat of *tatvajñâna*, i.e., true knowledge—the truth— signifying freedom from attachment. The severed hands are symbols of the principal instruments of doing work *(Karma)*. The corpses point to the *'Nirguna Brahma'*—the absolute substratum of all attributes and actions. We have many vicious qualities in us, such as anger, violence, a harsh tongue, and so on. If we are to follow the divine path, then all these obnoxious qualities must be destroyed. It is through the help of Mother Kali that we can destroy them. This also obviously depicts action or dynamism, and is thus a natural symbol of *shakti*, the primordial energy, the cause of all creation as well as of destruction. It is symbol of Mother Nature Herself. Her Consort Shiva, on whom she is standing—or moving—is lying still and motionless. The idol of Shiva here is actually much less conspicuous to an ordinary viewer, as if He is in the background, though supporting and providing inspiration to the Goddess. Shiva symbolizes cosmic energy in its passive form, and Shakti symbolizes the dynamic form. The eyes of the Goddess, if carefully observed, would be found directed towards those of Shiva. In other words, the symbol here we worship represents an integral vision with the inactive Purusha, the Conscious soul as the Lord, and the Nature-soul as His executive energy. As Sri Aurobindo observes, the relation of the two is the same as that between the poles of rest and action. When energy is involved in the bliss of conscious self-existence, there is rest; when the Purusha evolves itself in the action of energy, there is creation and the enjoyment or *anand*. In order to emphasize that *Shakti* and *Brahman* are inseparable, Sri Ramkrishna used the following analogies: 'The relation of Brahman to Shakti is that of fire to its burning property. ...*Maya* is to Brahman what the snake in motion is to the snake at rest... Force in action is *Maya*. Force in potency is Brahman... 'Some say that Mother Kali wants us to sacrifice animals as an offering to Her.' This is nothing but sheer ignorance. The Divine Mother wants us to sacrifice the 'animal' that is hidden within us as the cunningness of the fox, the cruelty of the tiger, the gluttony of the pig, and the venom of the scorpion. Mother Kali helps us to destroy these beastly qualities within us. When these are destroyed or sacrificed, the divine qualities of love, compassion, truth and purity will grow in their place.

DURGA

Durga is the destroyer of evil and protector of the good. She represents the war-like aspect of *shakti*. She possess the power of all the gods and wielding all of their weapons in her many arms. Mother Durga rides on a lion. By riding on a lion, She asks us to follow her example. We have to have complete control over the vicious lion qualities within us. It means conquest of ourselves over ourselves. This also means that we must remove lust, anger, greed and cruelty. She also holds a *chakra* or disc in one hand that is constantly spinning. She uses this disc to keep the balance and orderliness of the universe. She assumes the forms of wars, floods, earthquakes and famines. This is her way of keeping up the balance and preventing over-population. Creation and destruction are the processes that go on side by side. In some pictures of Durga, she has ten hands showing that her powers are enforceable in all the ten directions. She also holds a number of weapons, suggesting her omnipotence. She is the killer of Mahisha (buffalo) *asura*, i.e. ignorance. Her sons are Ganesha—wisdom, and Kartikeya—talented leadership. Lakshmi and Saraswati—wealth and learning —pay homage to her. So if we worship Durga in this form, our ignorance will be removed and we will become wise, rich and learned.

GANESHA

Ganesha, the son of Shiva and Pâravati, is worshipped as the remover of all obstacles, and as the God of wisdom and success. All Hindus worship Lord

Ganesha, regardless of their sectarian belief. He is both the beginning of the religion and the meeting ground for all Hindus. Lord Ganesha is the personification of the material universe. The universe in all of its varied and various magnificent manifestations is nothing but the body of Lord Ganesha. The bulky body of Ganesha stands for the cosmos in its entirety. The Lord in spite of being the Lord, of the Cosmos, attends to our earth that is but a speck of dust in the universe. Elephants are very wise animal. Wearing the head of an elephant denotes that Lord Ganesha is full of wisdom. Ganesha's lotus position is an auspicious sign. Four hands for gods, in general, are meant to signify supernatural powers. The fifth hand of Ganesha includes the trunk, which makes him more powerful than the other gods. The long trunk has the strength of being able to uproot a tree; yet at the same time it picks up a tiny needle from a haystack, as we believe that, in spite of His great power, the tiniest creature does not pass unnoticed by the Lord. His trunk represents the *Pranava* or *Aum*, the sound-symbol of Cosmic reality. In his upper right hand, Ganesha holds a goad or *ankush*, this assures that in his role as guardian of the threshold, he is armed to prevent the passage of miscreants. The *ankush* or hook is for goading forward the recalcitrant. Ganesha propels us forward on the Eternal Path with his goad. The goad may be seen as the force of fear by which all things are repelled from us. When Ganesha determines to remove obstacles in our path, He is exercising the power of goad. With the goad He can strike and repel obstacles. He is called the remover of obstacles, but He also places obstacles in our way, for sometimes we are going in the wrong direction, and His obstacles block our progress in the wrong direction and guide us back on the straight path. So if you decide to step out of the boundaries of your immediate *karma*, Lord Ganesha is there to block your way. when you evolve a relationship, a personal relationship, with the deity Lord Ganesha, He will not allow you to use your free will to get into difficulties. Guiding you carefully and protecting you along your way in your natural *karma* through life is His concern. The noose, usually held in Ganesha's left hand, is unlike the more warring weapons of the other deities. The noose is a gentle implement, used to capture and then hold obstacles or difficulties, for pulling human being along the right path. With the noose He can hold you close, or hold obstacles close. He can capture and confine both blessings and obstacles. In this manner Ganesha helps us in overcoming obstacles and ensures us our success. When Ganesha seeks to maintain obstacles for our benefit, He is exercising the powers inherent in the noose. The broken tusk that He holds like a pen in one of his lower hands and is considered a symbol of sacrifice. For the elephant, tusks are beauty and pride and strength. He broke his tusk for writing the Mahâbharata. Thus it proclaims that nothing is too costly, much less so is beauty, for the sake of intellectual progress. The rosary in his other hand suggests that pursuit of knowledge should be continuous. The ladoo or cake he holds in his trunk indicates that, beneath the outer layer of sordid self, lays the *atman* that is sweet and must be discovered by everyone. The fan-like ears of Ganesha convey to us that he is all ears to our petitions. The snake that runs round his waist is indicative of Energy in all forms. He is riding on a mouse. A mouse is a small creature. The elephant is the biggest of all the terrestrial animals. Riding on a mouse and wearing the head of an elephant indicates to us that God is the creator of all creatures, from the biggest elephant to the smallest mouse. Riding on a mouse also shows that He is humble enough to ride on the lowest of creatures. He has destroyed vanity, selfishness and pride. It also denotes the process of evolution. The little mouse gradually evolves into an elephant and finally becomes a human being. In olden times, whenever abundance came as well stocked granaries, the mouse was there. Thus, the mouse is traditionally associated with abundance, which the seers refer to as the fifth *shakti* or the power of Lord Ganesha, the success of bringing Him into our life.

KARTIKEYA or SUBRAHMANYA

Kartikeya is the second son of Absolute Reality, Shiva and the Transcendental Reality, Pâravati. He is the leader of the army of gods to destroy the evil and protect the good. A significant name for Kartikeya is *Guha* meaning cave, that suggests God as the dweller of the human heart. The word Subrahmanya means one who tends the spiritual growth of the aspirants. Kartikeya or Subrahmanya represents the highest state of evolution. He has six heads corresponding to the five senses of knowledge or *jnana-indrias* and the mind. When these six heads function harmoniously, the human being becomes perfect or God—that is the lesson. Sometimes the six heads are equated to the *shatchakras* or plexuses in the body through which *Kundâlini* is said to pass in yoga. Other icons would have six faces to represent the five senses and the mind so when all these functions harmoniously, human being becomes God. His twelve hands holding different weapons are collectively held to represent the manifold functioning or collective possibilities of the human spirit. His two spouses indicate God's *jñâna-shakti* (knowledge power or intelligence) and *kriya-shakti* (creative power). His supreme weapon vel or the luminous spear is known *medha*, or supreme power of knowledge that pierces the darkness or ignorance. When applied to man, these three suggest will, emotion and cognition, which should function together for success. His vehicle, a peacock, represents pride or ego which is to be sat upon or suppressed. The peacock is shown as belabouring a snake with one of its legs. The snake represents lust or desires. By controlling the ego or pride, human being can become perfect.

HANUMAN or ANJANEYA

Hanuman has the appearance of a monkey. He is, however, not like the monkeys we see today. His mother Anjani was pure and known for her beauty. She was the wife of the Kapi chief, Keshari. Because of a curse, she was born as a

Vânara woman. The Vânaras were a tribe with monkey-like features. The wind-God, *Vayu*, was pleased with her and blessed her with a son who was named, Hanumân.

Sri Anjaneya is more commonly known as Hanumanta or Hanumân. Anjaneya on being hit on his *hanu*, i.e. cheek, by Indra, become known as Hanuman. He became very powerful due to the boon granted by Lord Vishnu and Brahma. But his learning was not affected due to this power. He learned all the *Vedas* and Sâstras. Sri Râma, the incarnation of Vishnu, met him at the Rsyamuka mountains as a minister of Sugriva and recognizing his qualities, enrolled him as a great ally in his search and recovery of his wife Sita. Hanumân was an adept in *hath yoga*, by which, according to Pâtanjali, a person who subdued his senses and controlled his breadth and had full faith in God would make his body light and fly fast in the air or sail effortlessly. Thus, Hanumân crossed the sea to reach Lanka from the southern end of India. On his way, he became very small in the face of a formidable obstruction and pushed aside the minor obstacles. Nothing could stop Hanumân in his mission. As the envoy of Râma, Hanumân contacted Sita at Asokavana in Lanka and found out the strength and weakness of Ravan. He performed such acts such as setting fire to Lanka, killing Râvan's son, his ministers and other stalwart warriors. During the war, the dead and wounded were all restored to health by Hanumân who went to the mountain and gathered the medicinal plants. Hanumân was so devoutly attached to Sri Râma that hardly anyone thought of Sri Râma without Hanumân.

We should never forget that God is not a mere glorified human being clothed with all the virtues of our human conception in perfection. We should therefore always be on our guard and say to ourselves 'Not this, not this (*neti neti*), but far more, of which we have no conception'. Not only should we thus remember the highest teaching of the *Upanishads*, but we should also visualize for ourselves the innumerable galaxies in boundless space each containing millions of stars which probably are planetary systems like our own solar system. We think of God not only as the Almighty Creator of all these but also as their all pervasive spirit.

As Swami Vivekananda states if images and imagination are adopted in the right spirit, they help us to evolve inwardly, leading us ultimately to the infinite spirit. *Upâsanâ* the worship and contemplation of the various gods, is the means by which we become conscious of our divine heritage, and then achieve the dissolution of our soul or self in the Universal Self or Godhead. A knowledge of these various gods of the Hindu pantheon will endow us with the ability to know the Power behind them.

Bibliography

Sayings of Sri Ramkrishna, Sri Ramkrishna Math, Madras, 1954.
Sri Aurobindo, *The Secret of the Veda*, Sri Aurobindo Ashram, Pondicherry, 1971.
Swami Harshananda, *Hindu Gods and Goddess*, Ramkrishna Math, Madras, 1983.

Swami Nityabodhananda, *Myths and Symbolism and other Essays*, Ramakrishna Math, Madras, 1983.

Ghosh,A.S., *Symbolism and Spiritualist Wisdom: India's Life-breath,* Bharatiya Vidya Bhavan, Bombay, 1990.

Coomaraswamy, Ananda K., *The Dance of Shiva*, The Noonday Press, New York, 1974.

Eck, Diana L., *Darsan: Seeing the Divine Image In India*, Anima Books, Pennsylvania, 1981.

Parthasarathy, A., *The Symbolism of Hindu Gods and Rituals*, Bombay, Vedanta Life Institute, 1983.

Rao, T.A.G., *Elements of Hindu Iconography*, Vol II. Motilal Banarsidass, 1914.

Ananda Coomarswamy, *The Dance of Shiva* New York, Farrar Strauss & Co. 1957.

Banerjee, J.N., *The Development of Hindu Iconography*, Delhi, Munshiram Manoharlal, 3rd Edition, 1974.

Stella Kramrisch, *Indian Sculpture*, London, Oxford University Press, 1933.

Anncharlott Eschmann, *Hinduization of Tribal Deities in Orissa*.

Albert C. Moore, *An Introduction of Iconography of Religions*, Philadelphia, Fortress Press, 1977.

O'Flaherty W.D., *Shiva: The Erotic Ascetic*, Oxford, Oxford University Press, 1973.

Chapter 11

Hindu Customs and Belief

Rites and ceremonies, myths and legends, traditions and institutions are of course necessary for every religion. As Ramakrishna profoundly observed, rites and ceremonies are the husk of religions but, without the husk, the seed will not germinate and grow. But rites and ceremonies, myths and legends are not religions, they are only the instruments of religion. They are the means by which religious truths are preserved and taught to the people. They are concrete forms of abstract ideas. As long as they are understood to be the means to religious ends, and not as the ends in themselves, they serve a highly necessary and useful purpose. But when they lose touch with religious experience and assume an independent existence of their own, they become a danger to true religion. This is what has often happened in the history of every religion.

Prayer

Ramana Maharishi, in *Upadesa Saram*, describes prayer as three different forms of action (*karma*): physical (*kayika*), oral (*vacika*) and mental (*manasa*). Ritual is in itself a physical form; singing (*bhajan*) in praise of the lord is an oral form; and chanting a *mantra* silently is a mental (*manasa*) form of prayer. There are two types of results of prayer: one is immediate (*drstaphala*) and another is the unseen result (*adrstaphala*) of prayer. The immediate (*drstaphala*) is praying for something, such as mental clarity. You recognize another power, a higher power than yourself, and you accept the limitations of your power and knowledge. This is a pragmatic view, you may call it psychological or anything that you like. It is not easy to sit down and pray, but when you do, a kind of rendering happens. Otherwise, the ego would not let you sit and pray. The unseen result (*adrstaphala*) is where faith comes in. The action and the expressed desire bring about a result which is purely subtle in nature, and unseen. This unseen result will manifest itself in time and is what we call grace.

Prayer consists of the silent recitation (*japa*) of sacred formulae (*mantras*) which are repeated indefinitely. The *mantras* are composed of from one to a hundred or more syllables. It may consist of a simple mention of *OM* or the divine name, such as *Rama! Rama! or Krishna ! Krishna! or Shiva ! Shiva*! This type of prayer is an aid to mental concentration and is thought to bring about the desired effects of protection, fulfillment of promise and/or expiatory virtue. Other elements of personal worship are the study of the scriptures, and above all, meditation. Strengthened by *yoga* exercises, meditation can lead to such a paroxysm of tension that the exercisers can accomplish the ultimate aim, a state of union with the Absolute. Three times a day prayers (morning, noon and evening) are accompanied by offerings to the gods, to the sages, and to the ancestors.

Since the human senses of perception cannot conceive of the Absolute of the *Upanishads*, idols are made for concentration and worship. While reciting prayers or *mantras* before any idol, it must always be borne in mind that they are all offered to the ultimate being—Brahman—not to the God represented by that image. This is what is known as *pratikopâsana*.

All rituals have meaning. They are solemn and impressive. A ritual is sensuous in that it makes full use of all the senses—seeing, touching, smelling, tasting and hearing. The eye sees the image which, with all decorations, is made enchanting, the hands touch the deity and also touch the limbs of one's own body to establish the presence of the deity, the ear hears the devotional songs, the nose perceives the sweet smell of flowers and incense made as offerings, the tongue is active in repeating the prayers and the mind contemplates. All of these senses are effected in ritualistic worship. The rituals vary from the simple to the most gorgeous and elaborate and can be performed in houses and temples. The essential features of the rite consists of welcoming the God as a distinguished guest. Bathing the God with water and milk, dressing him, adoring him and applying scent, feeding him, putting flowers around him and worshipping him with moving flames and lamp accompanied by music and song; the sipping of sanctified liquid offerings, the eating of consecrated food—these are the basic constituents of Hindu worship (*puja*). The primary function of worship is the realization and experiencing of the Divine by the one who offers worship (*puja*). In performing the *puja*, one feels close to God. In the temples, an atmosphere conducive to such worship exists.

The access to God through prayers is easy and is given by the Lord Himself in the *Bhagavad Gitâ*, 'With devotion, the pious offering made by the pure in heart, whether it be a leaf, a flower, a fruit or water, I accept' (*Gita* IX. 26). One need not make any precious offering to the Lord to win His favour, but with *bhakti* (devotion), anything offered as token of love, He accepts.

We worship without fully understanding the real meaning behind the whole process. Once we understand the real meaning behind each of the symbolic items and activities involved in worship or *puja*, it will have profound impact on our lives. This will bring eternal and absolute truth in us.

It is very difficult for us to describe the divine experiences on the basis of limited human knowledge and intellect. Therefore, a variety of symbols is used to convey the deep and intricate meanings in our religion. Rituals were developed for the purpose of expressing meaning to our worship. *Puja, arti, yajna* and *pradakshina* are some of such rituals which carries many deep spiritual meaning with it.

Worship or *Puja*

Throughout the entire early Vedic literature, the *puja* ritual with flowers, etc., offered to an image or symbol is unknown. The word *puja*, is not found in any Aryan or Indo-European language outside India. Professor Mark Collins suggested that the Sanskrit word *puja* was nothing but a Dravidian *pu* 'flower' plus the root *ge* 'to do' (palatalized to ji), which is found in Tamil as *chey*, in Kannada as *ge* and in Telgu as *che: puja, puge, puche* was thus a 'flower ritual', a 'flower service', a *pushpa-karma*. Jarl Carpenter of Sweden derived *puja* from a Dravidian root *pusa* meaning 'to smear', as a smearing of sandal paste an important item in the *puja* ritual. In any case, the pre-Aryan and, in all likelihood Dravidian, origin of this most noteworthy ritual of ancient Hindu religion would appear to be quite reasonable to assume. In the present day texture of Hindu culture and religion the warp appears to be Dravidian and the weft Aryan.

The Hindu ritual of the *puja* is worship of an idol after it has been consecrated, as a living personality, by bringing before it, as before a living being, cooked food, vestments, ornaments and other offerings which are usable by a man, and by showing grateful worship by offering to it flowers, the produce of the earth and incense, and by waving lights in front of it and praying and singing before it. This is something which is quite different from the Vedic rite of *homa*, in which a wood fire is lighted on an altar and certain offerings of food in the shape of fat, butter and milk, cakes of barley and other cereals are offered to the gods, who are not at all symbolized by an image, but are supposed to dwell in the sky and to receive these offerings through the fire.

The worshiper submits himself to considerable preparation: preliminary ablutions, food restrictions which may extend to fasting, corporal postures and gestures of the finger (*mudra*), control of the breath, 'possession' (*nyasa*) by the God of the body of the worshiper, etc.

Puja is an integrated activity involving the five aspects of Nature. The physical being does the physical functions. The emotional being is engaged in summoning up the emotions in the way we approach God, as mother, father, friend or beloved. The intellect derives satisfaction in appreciating the idea of the various phases of the *puja* and the sum total of the meaning of the complete process. The symbolism of the idol is understood. Psychic satisfaction is fulfilled by the feel of what is not apparent. The spiritual being obtains satisfaction in meditation which is enhanced by true worship when realization takes place.

Kâma (desire), *krodha* (anger), *lobha* (covetousness), *moha* (infatuation), *mada* (intoxication) and *mâtsarya* (competition) are the bad qualities that hide the real attributes of the *âtman*. When these are removed, the *âtman* shines forth in all, as it has been told and felt by the great *rishis*. Just as the light of the lamp removes the existing darkness, so also when prayers are offered continually, all that is evil disappears from the mind and the light of the unsullied *âtman* shines forth. It is with that view that, in order to obtain such a state, one should constantly repeat God's name or names as prayers. Thoughts about God clear the way for contemplation about *âtman*.

Whether it be *puja*, prayer or contemplation, all are religious observances. Progressively, one is superior to the other as prayer is considered to be superior to *puja* and contemplation more rewarding than prayer. For a *puja*, various articles are necessary but, for prayers and contemplation, only concentration of mind is necessary. Krishna advises, 'Oh Parantapa, better than material offerings (those used for *puja*), *jñâna yagna* (intellectual sacrifice) is superior' (*Gitâ* IV. 33).

Husked coconuts are often offered during the worship of God. The coconut offering has several symbolic meanings. The breaking of coconuts at the time of worship symbolizes the shattering of ego, which must be surrendered before God or it will obstruct true worship through its desires and intrigues. Breaking the rough, hard shell of the coconut to reveal the ripe fruit within is likened to the shattering of our brittle shell of ignorance to reveal the sweet spiritual truths inside.

Flowers, incense and light waving indicate progressive types of *âtmarpana* or personal offering to God. The materials of worship for God are *durva* grass, *arka*-flower and leaves, etc., which are least coveted by common people; each offering has a lesson. No part of creation is repugnant to God. He is as much pleased with the lowliest of creation as with the highest. God accepts the humblest offering of His devotees, taking it in the spirit in which it is meant. In the Bhagavad *Gitâ* Lord Krishna said: 'Whoever offers Me, with devotion (*bhakti*) a leaf, a flower, a fruit, or a sip of water, I accept that, the pious offering of the pure in heart' (*Gita* IX.26). The Lord is satisfied with whatever little object is available for worship. In truth, we only need sincere devotion to gain access to the Lord. He accepts the offerings of His devotees as symbols of love and devotion.

Lighting camphor before God symbolizes that, if we burn our illusion or ego with the fire of true knowledge, we shall merge with God, leaving no residue. The camphor is nothing but solidified fragrance, and is called *vâsa* (smell) or *vâsanâ*, and it represents the ego manifests in the form of desires, or likes and dislikes. When camphor is burnt up, nothing remains to be seen. When we perform *aarti*, a small flame is burned on a wick which we rotate around the deity. The *aarti* reminds us of the greatness of God, because the flame that rotates around it is symbolic of the Cosmos (sun, moon, stars) revolving round Him, thereby making us obedient to Him. Hindu philosophy teaches us that we should burn our desires, because they are the root cause of all our problems. By burning the flame, this reminds us that our desires are burned away along with the flame as we go through the rhythmic movement of *aarti*. Another interpretation of *aarti* is as follows: when *aarti* is rotated around the idol or deity, this is a means getting His power in the flame; and when we take *aarti* with both hands open and then touch our eyes, head and chest; this symbolizes that we want to keep permanently before eyes and heart that light in which we saw the Lord. Consequently, we have this new vision of the Lord everywhere. The first verse of *Isâ Upanishad* states: *isâvâsyam idam sarvam*—All this, whatsoever moves in this universe, is dwelled, pervaded and enveloped by the Lord. Usually, we put some donation into the plate as the camphor-flame or *aarti* is being passed around. It means that when we gain this greater vision of the world we will become generous.

At the end of this ritual, food or *prasâda* is distributed. We receive this small amount of sweet or *prasâda* as a gift from the Lord, and we experience in our heart peace, joy and bliss. No matter whether it tests sour or sweet (not good for diabetic patients), we still accept it gladly after we have performed our daily worship (*pujâ*) with love and devotion. In the same way we should accept any result, fruit or *prasâda* that comes to us as a result of our daily sincere work or action. In *Bhagavad Gita*, Lord Krishna said: 'Your right is only to work; but never to the fruits thereof. Be you not the producer of the fruits of (your) actions; neither let your attachment be towards inaction' (*Gita* II: 47).

The third eye of God stands for omniscience or wisdom. When Hindus wear *kumkum*, or sandal-paste, on their forehead, it is to remind themselves of their latent power of wisdom of which they should awaken. The *Shaivas* (*Advaitas* included) wear holy ash (*bhasma* or *vibhuti*) on their foreheads, arms and chest. The ascetics smear their whole body with the ash. This ash, *vibhuti*, connotes purity and is perhaps to remind oneself and others that the world is nothing but ash, nothing but empty, just as modern scientists say that the world—the matter—on reducing, is full of only empty space. Therefore, one's aim should be to strive after higher values of life and not just the materialistic ends. Sankaracharya of Kanshi says: 'When the things of the world are burned, what remains is white ash or *bhasma* which persists even when it is burned. The consummation of all objects is *bhasma*. *Bhasma* in the material world corresponds to Shiva in the spiritual world. When we test anything in the fire of *jñâna* or knowledge, the residue is ash. We smear our bodies with sacred ash to remind ourselves of Shiva who is the ultimate goal of life.' The ash reminds us of the transistory and precarious of life. Men apply the *vibhuti* as *tripundra*, or three horizontal lines drawn across the full width of the forehead. These three lines signify the burning away of the three bonds: *ahamkâra* (ego), *karma* (effects of past deeds) and *mayâ* (the world). Women generally wear a light film of holy ash over the entire forehead (not the *tripundra*).

'This creation was created by Me (God) and has shame, delusion, and fear as its soul; for the gods and sages are born naked, and all the other men in the world are born without clothing. People with unconquered senses are naked even if they are clothed in silk, for, if one is enveloped in unconquered senses, no garment can hide him. Patience, forbearance, non-injury, passionless indifference to honour or dishonour—this is one's best garment. Let a man smear his body with ashes and meditate upon *Bhava* in his heart, and then even if he does a thousand things that one ought not to do, by bathing in ashes he will cause all of that to be burnt to ashes as fire burns a forest with its energy. Therefore, if anyone makes a great effort always, even throughout the three times, to bathe with ashes, then he becomes a leader of My hosts, receives all sacrifices, and grasps the supreme ambrosia. Brahmananda Purana.

Saivite Hindus wear *pottu*, or dot, along with *vibhuti* on the forehead as identifying emblems honouring their religion. The *pottu*, or dot, can be either sandalwood paste (saffron in colour), or *kumkum* powder (bright vermilion-red). Men wear the *pottu* made of *sandal* paste or with *kumkum* on top of the sandalwood at the centre of the lowest line of *vibhuti* or just below it between the eyebrows. Women wear the red *kumkum pottu* slightly higher on the forehead. School girls usually wear the vermilion *pottu* with a short, single stroke of *vibhuti* just above the eyebrows. They also wear just sandalwood pottu. Wearing *pottu* inbetween the eyebrows, or over the third eyes, draws our focus to our higher spiritual faculties and insight. Sandalwood paste has its own fragrance, which is quite soothing for the wearer as well as to the people near by. *Kukum pottu* is made of vermilion; chemically, it is either lead oxide or mercury oxide which has the properties of a germicide or an insecticide. *Kukum* helps in getting rid of lice, if it is infested in the women's hair.

We worship God by rapping at our forehead and temples with our knuckles three times and pulling at the ear-lobes with crossed hands help psychic power in proper tune for the worship. Esoterically, this act is said to stimulate certain nerves within the head for the benefit of catalyzing the flow of nectar, *amrita*, which floods down through the nerve system and gives an *abhishekam* (bath) to God. It is also a gesture of submission, humility and surrendering of the ego.

The *pradakshina* (circumambulation) or going round a deity's idol is making salutation in action, reminding us to concentrate on it, or practice it. Prostrating before God signifies complete surrender of self including the five *Jñanendriyas* or organs of sense or knowledge (eyes, ears, mouth, nose and skin) and five *karmendriyas* or organs of action (speech, hands, feet, sex organs and anus) to God's will.

The devotional songs that we sing, the continuous repetition of a *mantra* and the swaying movement of Hindu prayer have rhythmic techniques, and these tend to make the mind cling to the *mantra* thereby making the mind still. According to *Katha Upanishad*, 'When the five senses and the mind are still, and reason itself rests in silence, then begins the path supreme.' The most powerful *mantra* amongst Hindus is the *Om*. The vibrating sound of the *Om* encompasses the universe and, by chanting it continuously with a certain technique, we can be put in tune with the Cosmos.

The beads of *rudraksha* Shiva wears represent the solidified tears of pity He sheds at the woes of his *bhaktas*. Wearing *rudrakshas* then, on our body, reminds us of Shiva's concern for us and the need for deserving his grace by our steadfast devotion to Him.

FASTING

Attunement to the Lord through meditation is fasting. While contemplating, it is an agony to eat. For intellectual work, eating food and indulgence in the world outside is detrimental. Food means satisfaction for the senses. You need to starve the senses to uplift them senses to contemplation.

Hindus fast, i.e. do not eat food, on certain days of the month, such as *Purnima* or full moon, *Ekadashi* or the 11th day of the fortnight, and any day of the week depending upon individual choice. Fasting is a sort of self-discipline, it regulates your diet and gives rest to the digestive system. Almost everybody is aware of dieting or fasting for the sake of good health. Similarly, Hindus do not take salt on certain days of the week as we now know that excessive amount of salt or sodium content in the body can cause hypertension or elevation of blood pressure; but Hindus have given religious connotation to it.

Since the human body is composed of 80 per cent liquid and 20 per cent solid, almost the same compositin as the surface of the earth, the gravitational force of the moon on a full moon night on the human body is the same as on earth, which affects the high and low tides in the ocean. On a human being, the gravitational pull affects the fluid contents of the body which causes emotional imbalances, making some people tense, irritable and violent. Hence the term lunatic derived from the word *'luna'*, meaning moon in Latin. As a matter of record, most females menstruate during the full moon or new moon day. The wise founder of the Hindu system found that light food on these days will lower the acidic content in our body which helps the human beings to retain their mental balance. By praying on this day, a man would not allow his emotions to run wild. By fasting, he feels comfortable physically and psychologically, and may not be prone to irritation and outburst of temper. Each day of the week is governed by a planet even by western astrological system: Monday by the Moon; Tuesday by Mars; Wednesday by Mercury; Thursday by Jupiter; Friday by Venus; Saturday by Saturn; and Sunday by the Sun. According to Hindu beliefs, the planets influence the subconscious stage of man. By worshipping them, man is attuned to their influences, thereby helping him to gain a control over his mental activity.

PRANAYAMA

The *yogis* have developed, over centuries of study, certain methods of charging the mind and nervous system with *prâna* through techniques of life-giving breath. This particular method of breathing referred to as *pranayama* (*prâna* absorbing rhythmic breathing). *Pranayama* is, by definition, the science of the regulation of breath for the purpose of controlling directing, and applying the *prâna* or vital/energy force. *Pranayama* is largely concerned with rhythmic breathing consisting of stages of inhalation, retention and exhalation of the breath in prescribed rhythm. In addition to modern physiological knowledge concerning the two great branches of the nervous system, viz., the cerebrospinal and the sympathetic nervous system, the Hindu sages teach an additional knowledge of the human nervous system, known as *kundalini* or 'the serpent power'. For an understanding of this power, *yoga* teaches us that in each human body there is stored up a supply of *prâna*, and that this supply is constantly in touch with the universal supply of *prâna* which abides throughout all space. In other word the human body is regarded as a little inlet of *prâna* which is connected with the great ocean of *prâna* from which an infinite supply may be drawn or it shows the real connection of contact of the individual existence with the universal existence, and of the power which abides in each.

In the rhythmic breathing of *pranayama* comes a tendency of all the molecules of the body to flow in the same direction. And when the mind changes into will, these currents change into a motion similar to that of electricity in an exact manner that the nerves show polarity under the action of electric currents. For our understanding, this shows that will evokes within the nerve currents an action very similar to electricity. When all the motions of the body have become perfectly rhythmical, the body will have become a gigantic battery of will. This is the true *will power*. This bring about a rhythmic action in the body and helps us, through the respiratory centres, to control other centres. Thus the aim of *pranayama* is to arouse the coiled-up power in the *muladhara*, which is called *kundalini*. All the sensations and motions of the body are being sent to the brain, and sent out of it through the wires of the nerve fibers. The column of sensory and motor fibers in the spinal cord are the *ida* and *pingala* of the *yogis*. They are the main channels through which the afferent and efferent currents are travelling. But why should not the mind send the news without any wires? Using the analogy of electricity, we find that man can send a current only along a wire; but nature requires no wires to send her tremendous currents. Indeed, western science will eventually find the means of transmitting electricity without wires. The mind can do it now. This proves that the wire is not really necessary, but only our inability to dispense with it compels us to use it. The *yogis* say that if the mind can send the news without the wires of the nerve fibers, then one has removed the bondage of matter.

AHIMSA OR NON-VIOLENCE

Ahimsa is loosely translated in English as 'non-violence.' In the Vedic tradition, the word possesses a much broader meaning: 'Having no ill feeling for any living being, in all manners possible and for all times, is called *ahimsa*, and it should be the desired goal of all seekers' (*Patanjali Yoga Sutras*, 2, 30). *Manusmriti* says: 'Without the killing of living beings, meat cannot be made available, and since killing is contrary to the principles of *ahimsa*, one must give up eating meat' (*Manusmriti* 5, 48). If a person realises that every soul (*âtmâ*) is a part of God (*Prmâtmâ*), he will never trample on its right. This will lead him to show compassion towards all living beings, resulting in harmony and peace in the world. Non-violence is the recognition of equality of all beings. From time immemorial, non-violence had occupied the highest place among the Hindu cardinal virtues for the individual action. *Ahimsa Paramo Dharmah*—non-violence is the highest virtue—is written in Hindu scriptures. The principle of non-violence in Jainism embraces not only humans but also animals, plants and creatures of the earth, in air and in water.The doctrine of *ahimsa*, though originally a Hindu or Upanishadic doctrine, came to be emphasized, in a later period, and to a greater extent in Jainism and subsequently in Buddhism. If *ahimsa* disappears, Hindu religion disappears. We have Hinduism of the *Gitâ*, the *Upanishads*, and Patanjali's *Yoga Sutra* which is the acme of *ahimsa* and oneness of all creation.

The following are but a few of the thousands of Vedic injunctions against meat-eating: 'One who partakes of human flesh, the flesh of a horse or of another animal, and deprives others of milk by slaughtering cows, O King, if such a fiend does not desist by other means, then you should not hesitate to cut off his head' (*Rig Veda* X:87.16). 'You must not use your God-given body for killing God's creatures, whether they are human, animal or whatever' (*Yajur Veda*, XII: 32). 'One should be considered dear, even by the animal kingdom' (*Atharva Veda*, XVII, 1.4). 'By not killing any living being, one becomes fit for salvation' (*Manusmriti*, VI: 60). 'The purchaser of flesh performs *himsa* (violence) by his wealth; he who eats flesh does so by enjoying its taste; the killer does *himsa* by actually tying and killing animal. Thus, there are three forms of killing. He who brings flesh or sends for it, he who cuts off the limbs of an animal, and he who purchases, sells or cooks flesh and eats it—all of these are to be considered meat-eaters' (*Mâhâbhârata*, Anu. 115:40). 'Those who are ignorant of real *dharma* and, though wicked and haughty, account themselves virtuous, kill animals without any feeling of remorse or fear of punishment. Further, in their next lives, such sinful persons will be eaten by the same creatures they have killed in this world' (*Bhâgavatam*, XI: 5. 14).

The moral view point of the vegetarians' belief is based on the theories of *ahimsa* (non-violence). *Ahimsa* believes in non-aggression and non-violence on any living being and creature, and the way of disciplined activities or the law of *karma* proclaims that we are the builders of our own destiny and that from good deeds, joy shall come, and from evil deeds, suffering comes. Mahtma Ganndhi wrote (*Mahatma Gandhi*, M. Harijan 1939, pp.185-196): 'Man as animal, is violent, but as spirit is non-violent. The moment he awakens to the spirit within, he cannot remain violent.' Man, however, is still an animal. His brutal instinct cannot, therefore, be suppressed by this doctrine completely. So, in spite of this doctrine, the majority of the Hindus continue to be meat-eaters. Since meat-eating would necessitate the slaughter of animals, which is a violation of the *ahimsa* theory, vegetarians do not indulge in non-vegetarian food as they do not want to increase their *karmic* debts by partaking of flesh.

The waste products of the animal body are normally taken away by the blood stream to discard it through urine, but when an animal is killed for meat consumption, the waste products are retained in the decaying flesh. Meat-eaters absorb those toxic waste products into their own bodies. Nowadays meat is loaded with preservatives: DDT, arsenic (used in cattle feed as a growth stimulant), sodium sulfate (used to give meat that 'fresh' red colour) and a synthetic hormone, DES, which is known carcinogenic or metastasizer of cancer. Meat-centred diets are linked to many types of cancer, most notably cancer of the colon, breast, cervix, uterus, ovary, prostate and lung. In a two-pounds of charcoal-broiled steak, there is as much benezopyrene as contained in the smoke from 600 cigarettes (Lijinsky & Shubik, *Science*, 145: 53, 1964). It has been found that meat contains approximately fourteen times more pesticides than plant foods. In America, the highest meat-consuming nation in the world, one person out of every two will die of heart or related vascular diseases. The Journal of the American Medical Association reported in 1961 that a vegetarian diet can prevent 90-97 per cent of heart disease. Seventy-two per cent of the deaths were due to artherosclerosis (hardening of the arteries), a disease strongly linked to meat-eating. Recent reports from England about the 'Mad Cow Disease' or *Bovine Spongiform Encephalopathy* (BSE) is a terminal neuro-degenerative cattle disease casued by toxic, virulent and mysterious infectious proteins called *prions*. An outbreak of this disease in England in 1996 had stricken about 160,000 cows. Evidence pointed to the British practice of mixing the remains of sheep, including their brains and bones, into cows' feed as the cause of the outbreak. It is now theorized that cow-eating humans may be the next victims of this horrible disease. *Prion*-based diseases often have incubation periods that takes decades, much like AIDS, so we are only beginning to see the long-term consequences of this dreaded disease.

According to the *Isa Upanishadic* teaching, God is not only in all human beings but is also in all living creatures; for there is no reason why men should think they alone should live in this world. Other creatures have as much right to live here in this world as do humans. According to this doctrine, this rule of conduct implies that: no innocent living beings should be killed; no injury, no harm should be done to them.

Plants synthesize amino acids from air, earth and water, but animals cannot. Animals are dependent on plants for proteins, either directly from plant or indirectly by eating an animal which has eaten and metabolized plant components. There are twenty-two known amino acids. Fourteen are 'non-essential' and eight are 'essential'. The essential amino acids that human, cannot manufacture, are leucine isoleucine,valine, lysine, tryptophane, threonine, methionine and phenylalanine. The foods from the plants have the added advantage of combining amino-acids with other substances that are essential to the proper utilization for the body development and maintenance: carbohydrates, vitamines, minerals, enzymes, hormones, chlorophyll and other elements that only plants can supply. When we eat, our body breaks the protein into its constituent amino acids and these are either utilized individually or reassembled into new proteins needed by the body. Protein obtained from nuts, pulses, grains, and dairy products is relatively pure as compared with meat, which has fifty-six per cent impure water content.

Some who argue about eating plants say that both plants and animals have soul, and question about the ethical significance between plants and animals. Plants have no evolutionary need to feel pain, and completely lack a central nervous system. Nature does not create pain gratuitously, but only when it enables the organism to survive. Animals, being mobile, would benefit from having a sense of pain; plants would not. Most of the vegetarian diets contain fruits from the trees, seeds harvested after the plants have dried up in the field, and some green vegetables and leaves. We destroy some plants while being vegetarian, but by eating animals for food, many more plants are destroyed indirectly to raise the animals. So vegetarianism causes the least amount of harm to sentient beings, and one who thinks deeply about all of the issues involved will surely see the sense of the vegetarian alternative. For propagation of the plant species, Nature had made fruits to be consumed by the animals and/or humans so that seeds can grow back into a new plant. So Nature has made them for this purpose.

There are few scientific facts for the human beings to be vegetarian than non-vegetarian. (1) The *yogis* claim that a vegetarian diet is conducive to meditation, may be because the five senses (sight, hearing, sound, smell and touch) are less active of the mind and this is a very important prerequisite for a person who wants to maintain equanimity of mind. (2) Recent biological research tends to show that flesh eating is not essential for good health and some researchers are even of the opinion that flesh eating persons are more susceptible to illness, such as cancer, etc., than are vegetarians. (3) Human physical and physiological constitution is more akin to plant-eater or herbivores, such as monkeys, elephants, cows and horses, than to carnivores, such as dogs, lions, tigers, leopards and snakes. Carnivorous animals have the following characteristics: (i) Animals like lions, tigers, dogs etc., have newborn babies that often open their eyes after 5 to 7 days of the birth, whereas herbivores' newborns are born with open eyes; (ii) carnivorous animals leak water with their tongue, herbivorous drink water or liquids in by suctions through the teeth; (iii) carnivores do not sweat through their skin; they perspire with the extrusion of their tongue to control the body heat, whereas the herbivores have sweat pores for heat control and the elimination of impurities and as such they perspire with the whole body; (iv) carnivores have claw shaped nails, the herbivorous have flat nails and palms; (v) the teeth of the carnivores are long, cylindrical and pointed at the tip for holding and killing prey; but herbovorous like cow, horse and others have flat teeth for chewing; (vi) the jaws of the carnivores only open in an up-and-down motion; those of herbivorous animals move up and down as well as sideways for chewing food; (vii) carnivorous animals have shorter intestines than the herbivorous animals, including human beings; (viii) the saliva of carnivores contains no ptyalin and cannot predigest starches; that of herbivorous animals contains ptyalin for the predigestion of starches; (ix) meat eater animals secrete large quantities of hydrochloric acid to help dissolve bones; herbivorous animals secrete little hydrochloric acid; (x) the physiological reason is that meat increases the acidic content in our blood which results in the lowering of the amount of carbon dioxide. Eating vegetables has the opposite effect; the acidity is reduced and carbon dioxide pressure in the lungs is increased, thereby reducing the amount of oxygen going to the brain. Looking at the above characteristics humans naturally come under vegetarian category, and I don't know why human beings eat meat?

The older the religions, the closer to vegetarianism, with exceptions of a few. One of the most ancient religions, Hinduism, is a strong supporter of vegetarian principle, Judaism, about 4,000 years old, has a large tradition of vegetarianism, Buddhism and Jainism are essentially Hindu heterodoxies, and so fully share the vegetarian principles, Islam, the youngest of the world's major religions, is not strong supporter of the vegetarian ideal and Christianity offers a bit more evidence for the practicality of the meatless way of life. Some modern denominations of Christianity do promulgate vegetarianism, such as Seventh-Day Adventists, Quakers and Mormons have meatless contingent. Sufis, among the Muslims, and the Baha'i Faith also endorse vegetarianism.

The Kirgese, an Eastern Russian people that at one time lived chiefly on meat, rarely survived past the age of forty. The average life span of Eskimos, who live primarily on meat and fish, rarely exceeds thirty years. On the other hand, there are tribes such as the Hunza, who live in the Himalayan mountains, or groups like Seventh-Day Adventists, primarily vegetarians, tend to live between 80 and 100 years.

Researchers cite vegetarianism as the reason for their excellent health and longevity. Moreover, the world's invaluable rain forests tend to be victimized by the lumber and meat industries. Much of Central America was transformed into a giant pasture to provide cheap beef for North America, while in South America, the Amazon rain forests were cleared and burned to make room for cattle grazing, largely to supply the beef needs of England and Europe. These ideas, developed by Jeremy Rifkin in his book *Beyond Beef*, make it a clear connection between meat-eating and the degradation of the environment, explaining that the earth will not support us in our avarice and ignorance. Rather, he says, quoting Gandhi, 'The earth can supply everything for man's need, but not for his greed.'

Mahatma Gandhi wrote in his autobiography, 'My uniform experience has convinced me that there is no other God than Truth and the only means for the realization of Truth is non-violence. A perfect vision of Truth can only follow a complete realization of *ahimsa*. God can never be realized by one who is not pure of heart. Truth without non-violence is not truth, but untruth.' Further he said, 'God grant me the boon of *ahimsa* in mind, word and deed. Gandhiji said, '*Ahimsa* is the basis of the search for truth. I am realizing every day that as the basis' (Mahatma Gandhi, M., *The Story of My Experiments with Truth*, 1945).

His common experience was that '*Ahimsa* and Truth are so intertwined that it is practically impossible to disentangle and separate them. They are like the two sides of a coin. Nevertheless *ahimsa* is the means: Truth is the end.' Mahatma Gandhi was convinced that there is no other God than Truth. And when you want to find Truth as God, the only inevitable means is love, i.e. non-violence. "Since I believe that ultimately the means and the end are convertible terms, I should not hesitate to say that God is Love" (Mahatma Gandhi, M., *Young India*. 1931, p.327) Mahatma Gandhi has emphasized that there should be no exploitation of any kind of weaker classes, races and nations by stronger ones.

Mahatma Gandhi extended *ahimsa* to communities and nations and developed a suitable technique of action for it, called *satyagrah*, which is non-violent defence of what one considers to be truth. Gandhiji explains *satyagraha* (Mahatma Gandhi, M., *Satyagraha in South Africa*, 1928, pp.178-179) as follows: '*Satyagraha* expects the *satyagrahi* to love the opponent; at least hatred of the opponent has no place in *satyagraha*, but is a positive breach of its ruling principle. In *satyagraha*, there is not the remotest idea of injuring the opponent.' His message was not meant simply for Hindus or India, but for the whole world. Though his activities were confined to the political sphere, he repeatedly declared that they were only a means to the realization of Truth, *moksha*. According to him, Truth is God and non-violence is the means of reaching it. Perfect non-violence is perfect self-realization.

Can Hinduism, following the doctrine of *ahimsa* consistently teach people to defend their country's freedom by force? Can it teach, 'Meet force with force'. The answer is 'Yes'. The classical example in Hinduism is the example of Rama and Krishna who used force most reluctantly and, as a last resort; when all their attempts to bring about a just, amicable settlement had failed, then they used force. In the larger interest of·the society, it is our belief to maintain *dharma* (righteousness) we may have to kill men in battlefields in self-defence. Dr. S. Radhakrishnan once said: 'When submission to evil is wrong, when resisting it by love is impossible, then resistance by violence is allowed, and the warrior classes are told that it is their duty to resist aggression by force without hate and out of a sense of duty, and not in a vindictive mood' (Radhakrishnan, S., *Heart of Hindusthan*, p.18). K.M. Munshi gave the following answer on *Ahimsa* to a correspondent. *Ahimsa* is not only non-killing. It is removal of vengeance, anger, hatred and malice from our mental makeup. If animals and even men become incurable danger to life, killing them would not be *ahimsa*, if it is done from a pure motive of saving *dharma* (righteousness) or life' (Munshi,K.M., *Bhavan's Journal*, June 26, 1940). Even Gandhi once said, 'When there is a choice between cowardice and violence, I would advise violence' (Mahatma Gandhi, M.,*Young India*, dated 11-8-1920).

Mahatma Gandhi said: '*Ahimsa* is not the crude thing as it has been made to appear. Not to hurt any living thing is no doubt a part of *ahimsa*. The principle of *ahimsa* is hurt by every evil thought, by undue haste, by lying, by hatred, by wishing ill to anybody. It is also violated by our holding on to what the world needs' (*The Words of Gandhi*, Selected by R. Attenborough, Newmarket Press, 1982).

YAJNA

We perform *tajna* by lighting the fire and putting in it purified butter, wheat, rice, barley and sesame seeds, etc. This important ritual can have profound impact on our lives, provided we understand its significance and meaning, and attempt to relate it to our way of life. Each of the products used in *yajñâ* has special meanings. The first such term is fire. Fire has many special characteristics. The flames unlike water always rise up and towards its origin—the Sun. The fire motivates people to raise their consciousness. Once human consciousness has acquired religious orientation, it begins to move toward new spiritual heights. This can be accomplished by bringing one's life closer and closer to such symbols as fire which constantly remind us that we must aspire to upgrade our thinking and to acquire our ultimate destination in life. Another characteristic of fire is that it burns everything that comes in contact with it. In *yajna*, it means that it burns only impurities. For example, gold is put in the fire to remove its impurities. It is in the same way when we do something in the presence of fire, it removes such impurities of life as ignorance, greed, anger, ego, hatred and lust, etc., and brings us out in our purest form. Still another characteristic of fire lies in that its flames disappear into the unknown after flickering for only a very short period of time. It is in the same way that one experiences the enlightened consciousness only for a little while and then submerges into the supreme absolute, the Brahman. The individual does not feel his independent existence and becomes liberated forever. Thus fire is the symbol of higher levels of consciousness in man. In ancient times, the saints kept active fire in their *'yajñâshala'* as a reminder to all that they must aspire to enhance their consciousness. Why is oblation offered in the fire? It symbolizes personal sacrifice, on the one hand, and throwing away one's ego which is the main hindrance in achieving the goal and is also the basis of inter-personal conflicts, on the other. Small amounts of grains are used in oblation. The grains, if sown, can be turned into large quantities of grains. These sacrificed grains symbolize ego. If the ego is allowed to grow, it generates anger, greed, lust, hatred, mental restlessness and conceit, thus making life miserable. One must sacrifice one's ego in the same way that grains are offered as oblation in the fire. Periodic analysis and introspection would enable one to crush one's ego before it becomes destructive. People who want to serve God, must be free of egoism. Another important symbol is purified butter. When purified butter is poured into fire, flames grow and become clearer and powerful. Butter helps to burn various offerings. In life, one should burn evil with the power of goodness. One such power lies in love. Purified butter is an important symbol also because, unlike wheat, it is not a direct product of nature. Egoism and wickedness are very much a part of human nature, but goodness takes time and effort to cultivate. Egoism is very much like purified butter where several processes are involved before it is produced. It is easy to be mean, obnoxious, dishonest and greedy. Therefore, people have to be determined to develop honesty and selfless service for other. Eventually even the goodness, just like evil should also perish. Just as the purified butter burns along with grain, to attain freedom, man must strive to free himself from the temptations of the world of materialism. Thus purified butter is full of interesting secrets. This action of burning gives life upward direction and perishes itself leaving a familiar fragrance in the environment. We should all learn from this example.

Lord Krishna said, 'The ladle with which the oblation is poured into the fire has been called *arpanam*, that is God. Sesame seed, barley and melted butter which are poured as oblation into the fire are God. He who performs the sacrifice is God, the fire into which the oblation is poured is God and the act of pouring oblation is also God. He who sees God in the doer, the instrument, the action and objects, all of them become God for him. Actions have no existence of their own apart from God. When he views everything as no other than God, he attains Him' (*Gitâ* IV. 24).

FESTIVALS AND SACRED DAYS

Festivals and sacred days are special parts of the Hindu way of life. In the spiritual endeavour of the Hindu, there is hardly a month when we do not have a sacred day or a festival. The festivals are illustrative of the body of religious ceremonies commanded by Hindu law or convention, dealing with our custom, apparel, popular belief, conduct and character, and the mode and manner of eating and drinking, living and social relationships that we engage in. In life, there are always ups and downs. When one attains success, one becomes happy and starts singing and enjoying. One cries or becomes miserable with his failures. Then one remembers God and takes refuge in Him. One offers a pledge to a deity upon fulfillment of success of one's desire or lust. One endures torment for one pledge by fasting or other penance; listens and chants the praises of the almighty God. One purifies one's soul by acknowledging the differences between divine and demonic instinct through the stories from the scriptures. Thus one's soul is uplifted.

On the occasion of Hindu festivals and sacred days people, get together and exchange their greetings and views. They organize festivals for their cultural unity and mutually advance the friendly sentiments, and condemn animosity and hostility against each other. They gain inspiration from each other by participating in their sorrow and happiness. It helps them in understanding the difference between human and animal natures of themselves and lets them get acquainted with the divine and demonic culture. They also understand the ancient culture of the country and develop pride and inspiration to protect it. Charity and righteous action are taken after understanding the importance of the human being. It establishes the sentiment of well-being for the public welfare in their heart. Thus their philosophy of life is brightened upward and the filth of life is cleansed. How important is religion for society? What is the responsibility of society to keep religion alive? These questions can only be answered by celebrating our festivals and sacred days. Our life is insipid or uninteresting without participating in these cultural activities.

Our philosophy of life has been changed for the better by devout austerity, worship, fire sacrifice, pilgrimage, and association with pious men. On the basis of this some people became saints and finally became divine beings by their spiritual endeavor. Future generations remember their character and good deeds on the festive days. People try to emulate the ideals of saints in their life. Even in *Bhagavad Gitâ*, Lord Krishna said, ' Whatever a great man does is followed by others; people go by the example he set up' (*Gitâ* III. 21). Thus, the occasion for the performance of religious rites of our society becomes stronger.

The main purpose of these rituals or the stories of popular festal days is to reform the society. The purport of this is not merely craving for pledges or vows. The soul is purified by these vows; the mind becomes emancipated from sinful feelings; and sobriety is increased in life. Spiritual power blooms. Various diseases are spontaneously annihilated.

It seems now that the foremost events of our life—the folk festal days—have been effaced. In this scientific age, the faith in festivals and festal days has been eroding, but we cannot say that the folk festal days are devoid of power. Festivals do have scientific values and are an important component of our life.

This is a foremost ingredient for elucidating the Indian culture. A ray of our social life is evident from these festivals. With this view in mind this chapter is presented here.

GURU (TEACHER)

Just like for acquiring *bhautikya jñâna* (materialistic knowledge) we need a teacher to show the way to earn money or wealth going into a different professions, similarly for *adhyatamic jñâna* (spiritual knowledge), we need a *guru*,who can show us the way to achieve the knowledge of spiritualism. Many people remain engrossed in worldly activities and fail to realize their goal of life. Life is like a dense forest in which man faces bewildering situations. Once a prince, accompanying the king, lost his way and landed amidst hunters. He was brought up by the hunters for years, he forgot his identity and acquired their customs. Ultimately he was found by chance by a man from the palace who revealed to him his real identity and helped him by restoring him to his rightful place. So too, aspirants who find themselves bogged down by worldly affairs, will be guided by a spiritual mentor or *guru*, and shown the path to salvation. The teachings of the great *guru* are not for a day or two and to be forgotten the rest of the week; they are to be practiced daily. Mere belief is not sufficient; self discipline, control of moods, is also essential. The training given by the *guru* is meant to show the disciple how to be unconditionally happy, untouched by suffering and change. Through the *guru's* pure perception, God teaches the devotee. For God has taken a vow of silence, and He does not address the disciple directly until that devotee has attained a considerable degree of spiritual development. If one is sincere in one's search for Truth, God helps him to find a book or a *guru* to inspire and encourage him. A *guru* is a God-knowing person who has been divinely appointed by Him to take the seeker as a disciple and lead him from the darkness of ignorance to the light of wisdom. The meaning of *guru* is: *gu* means darkness and *ru* means remover, that is, the one who removes the darkness (of ignorance) and brings the light of wisdom.

Although numerous *gurus* in the form of *rishis* and ascetics have taken birth time to time, God has also taken *avatâra* or incarnations to teach us. In His incarnations, the Lord Râma unfolds before humanity the way of leading an ethical life and to enable them to reach His divine domain. Râma concealed His identity and behaved like an ordinary man. He laid before humanity the easier way to obtain His grace by adopting the simple procedure of unconditional and total surrender. Râma came to teach us boundaries, boundaries of discipline in life and compassion. He has shown boundaries in every walk of life. He taught by personal example the path of *dharma*, the way of right living and excelled in the noble virtues of truthfulness, performance of duty, love, justice and valor. On the other hand, Lord Krishna has taught the way, rules and power of God. He also taught the perfection in every action, the path of selfless love and total surrender to God. In a way Krishna and Râma are complementary to each other. We need to assimilate and act upon the teachings of both *avatâras* to achieve our goal, *moksha*. Swami Sri Yukteswar wrote in 'The Holy Science': 'To keep company with the *guru* is not only to be in his physical presence, but mainly means to keep him in our hearts and to be one with him in principle and to attune ourselves with him.'

BIBLIOGRAPHY

Renou, L (ed.), *Hinduism*, The Eaton Press, Norwalk, CT.

Mahadev Desai (Trans.) Gandhi, *An Autobiography*, Navajivan Press, Ahmedabad.

Swami Tejomayananda, *Hindu Culture: An Introduction*, Chinmaya Publications, 1993.

Unto Tahtinen, *Ahimsa , Non-violence in Indian Tradition*, London, Rider and Co., 1976.

Manusmriti V: 48.

Tom Regan (ed.), *Animal Sacrifices: Religious Perspectives on the Use of Animals in Science*, Philadelphia, P.A., Temple Univ. Press, 1986.

John Cook, *Diet and Your Religion*, New York, Woodbridge Press, 1976.

Swaran Singh Sanehi, *Vegetarianism in Sikhism*, Madras, The Vegetarian Way, 1977.

Christopher Chapple, 'Noninjury to Animals: Jain and Buddhist Perspectives,' in *Animal Sacrifices, Religious Persectives on the use of Animals in Science*, ed. Tom Regan, Philadelphia, PA, Temple Univ. Press, 1986.

Reay Tannahill, *Food in History*, New York, Stein and Day Pub., 1973.

Richard Schwartz, *Judaism and Vegetarianism*, New York, Exposition Press, 1982.

Steven Rosen, *Diet for Transcendence: Vegetarianism and the World Religions*, Torchlight Publishing, Inc. 1997.

Philips Handler, *Science, Food and Man's Future*, Borden Review of Nutrition Research, Vol. 31:No.1, 1971.

Chapter 12

Religiosity or Dharmikta

A question may be raised as to why, when we have been practising religion for thousands of years, we are still in this imperfect conditions? What is it that prevents us from realizing God's truth? We think we are religious so long as we perform a set of mechanical rites. We go to temples, mosques or *gurudwaras;* we chant hymns; but all these lie on the surface of our minds. They do not enter the depths of our being. They do not transform our nature. An authentically religious man is not one who merely performs rites or utters hymns or preaches dogmas. Great religions ask us to practice austerity, asceticism, etc. Many people, even after studying classic works on religion and philosophy, do not know what they should do in practice in order to attain the goal of life. All these may not be necessary although it may help in achieving the goal of life. What is necessary is self-search or self-realization. Four essential factors are necessary to be religious: (1) Feel the presence of God within yourself, (2) Oneness of the spirit in all, (3) Spiritualisation of one's activities and (4) Cultivation of virtues.

1. FEEL THE PRESENCE OF GOD WITHIN YOURSELF

As a drop of water and a fathomless ocean contain water, so do *âtman* (soul) and *pramâtman* contain the same 'God'. One is a tiny dot and other is vast ocean.

So far as our theory is concerned, we affirm that there is God. But when it comes to practice, we behave as if there were no God. So long as this divorce is there, the present moral crisis will also be there. The only way to overcome the crisis is to examine yourself, ask yourself whether you are drawing nearer to the ideals you profess or departing from the ideals you profess.

In order to feel the presence of God within yourself, the Hindus believe from the pre-historic period of Sanathana Dharma that man and God are akin—that all creation is a manifestation of God—that we are all fellow-workers of God—that all humanity stems from a single root and in all humanity is *Brahman*, the infinite spirit, and none can say where man ends and divine begins—that we all belong to the real and the real is reflected in us all with no barriers between the self and Universal Spirit—that there is only one single, indestructible, abiding, imperishable reality, and truly He is I, as I am you, and you are Him. *Tat Tvam Asi* (Thou art That)—that the human soul is coexistent with God Himself, not as an emanation from Him, not as a part or effect, but as an eternal verity, birthless, ageless, and undecaying.

This *mantra Tat Tvam Asi*—Thou art That, and *Sarvam khalu idam Brahman*—Everything is Brahman, appear in many ancient memory songs sung for ages. This *mantra* itself remains current in the later Vedic, past-Vedic and modern era. It was quoted in *Chândogya Upanishad* : IV: 8.7.

Besides, its many variants current in Hindu thought have also found a pride of place in other Vedic literature—for instance, in the Brihadâryanaka *Upanishad*, we have: *Aham Brahmâsmi* (I am Brahma, the infinite and *Ayam Atmâ Brahman*) This Self (soul) is Brahman. (This statement is an indirect repetition of *ta tvam asi* (you are that). This can be explained in the following way: Both the 'dead body' and 'living body' are identical, but the 'living body' has something that 'dead body' does not have. That which is missing in the 'dead body' is spirit—*Brahman*, and at the same time, when *Brahman* is present in the body, it creates the greatest illusion (*maya*) that 'I am the body.'

In earlier days, people used to greet each other by saying *Tat tvam asi*, with palm pressed together, hands raised on head. This became a common form of greeting, to salute and celebrate the flame of divinity that each acknowledged in the other—*Tat Tvam Asi* (Thou art That). It is passed on to the modern age a '*Namaste*', even though the pressed palms are raised not always to level of the forehead, but often stay below the chin of even at the breast. 'Thus I do homage to the God in each and all of you' (Sindhu Putra explains 'Namaste')

Isa Upanishad also recaptures the *mantra* which was current in the age of Sanathana Dharma, when it says: *Yas tvam asmi so'ham asmi* (you are indeed that I am). Again, *Isa Upanishad* expresses itself in the thought and words of the pre-ancients when it repeats '*Soham*' (I am He, that am I). '*Ham Aham Sah*' means 'I am He, He is I'. This *mantra* condensed in a word *Hamsa*. *Hamsa* means swan. It is a symbol of Brahman. Hence those who attained cosmic consciousness are often called '*Paramahamsa*'—the great swan.

The *Mândukya Upanishad* also reflects the words of the ancients of Sanathàna to say, '*Idam sarvam asi* (Thou art all this). Again in the *Mândukya Upanishad* is the reappearance of the words, '*Brahma eva idam visvam* (This whole world is Brahman). Further it is stated that *Brahmavid Brahmaiva Bhavati*—Realizing Brahman, you indeed become Brahman.

The *Vedas* teach that the soul of man is immortal. The body is subject to the law of growth and decay; what grows must decay. But the indwelling spirit (soul) is related to the infinite and eternal life; it never had a beginning and it will never have an end.

The sage Patanjali formulated the *yoga* system, the science of oneness—oneness of the soul with God, into eight steps for achieving the goal: (1) *yama* (moral conduct) avoid unrighteous behavior; (2) *niyama* (religious observances) follow certain moral and spiritual precept; (3) *âsana* (right posture) learn to be still in body and mind, for where motion ceases, there begins the perception of God; (4) *pranayama* (control of *prâna*, subtle life current) while concentrating on the state of peace, practice control of the life force in the body; (5) *pratyahara* (withdrawal of the senses from external objects) when your mind is your own, that is, under your control through *pranayam* then you can give it to God; (6) *dhârana* (concentration); first, concentrate on one of God's cosmic manifestations such as love, wisdom, joy; then begins meditation; (7) *dhyana* (meditation) What follows in meditation is an expansion of the realization of God's infinite omnipresent nature; (8) *samâdhi* (superconscious experience) when the soul merges as one with God, who is ever-existing, ever-conscious, ever-new Bliss, that is the goal. The first two steps are not enough to know God. After adopting the right methods of living, you must learn to quiet the body and mind, and this begins with right posture. Always sit upright, with the spine straight. This is particularly essential for meditation. Mastery of the restlessness of the body produces great mental power. The fourth step is to switch off the life force from the body, so that the attention is freed for inner contemplation on God. When the life force is shut off from the muscles and senses, sensations cannot reach the brain to disturb one's inner concentration. Whence comes the peace you experience in sleep at night. That peace felt in sleep, during muscular and sensory relaxation comes from God. So the sage has said we should practice *pranayama* to control the life force in the body. Through *pranayama*, switch off the five sense telephones of sight, smell, taste, touch and sound. After successful *pranayama*, you will find your mind fully alert and concentrated within, ready to enjoy the divine peace and presence of God in deep concentration and meditation, the sixth and seventh steps. The last or eighth step is *samâdhi* or oneness with God as light, or cosmic *aum*, or joy, or love, or wisdom—and not only oneness, but expansion of that oneness from the limitations of the body to boundaries of eternity.

Paramahansa Yogananda said, 'In the night time, when you are free from your material duties, look to your spiritual welfare. Meditate, pray—pray again and again. Practice the meditation techniques to master the restlessness of the mind.' Follow the great *gurus* of this path: through these teachings they found God. Knowing God—this is what the Self Realization teachings are all about. Sincerity is a transparent diamond through which the light of God shines in our lives (Paramahansa Yogananda, *The Divine Romance*, 1986). In order to feel the presence of God within yourself, one of the steps suggested by many ascetics is the chanting of God's name constantly.

2. ONENESS OF THE SPIRIT

Lord Krishna said, 'He who perceives Me everywhere, and beholds everything in Me, he never loses sight of Me, nor do I ever lose sight of him' (*Gitâ* VI: 30). Kena *Upanishad* says, 'The living man who finds Spirit, finds Truth. But if he fails, he sinks among fouler shapes. The man who can see the same Spirit in every creature, clings neither to this nor that, attains immortal life.' 'Spirit is known through revelation. It leads to freedom. It leads to power. Revelation is the conquest of death.'

God is personal as well as impersonal. God created human beings, and is their originator. He could not be wholly impersonal. God had given us not only the power to appreciate the thoughts and feelings of others but to respond to them. The Lord is surely not devoid of the spirit of reciprocity. When we permit it, our Lord can and will establish a personal relationship with each of us. God is spirit, invisible and impersonal. This whole universe is the body of God but as soon as He assumes the role of Creator, He becomes personal, and He becomes visible. If there were no blue sky, no vast space, no beautiful scenery, no moon or twinkling stars in the sky, we would never have suspected the existence of God at all. The wonders be hold in this universe suggest to us the imminence of God. He is visible everywhere, in everything He has created everything animate or inanimate and the working of His intelligence governs all creation.

When we see pictures of tragedy and drama and commedy on a movie screen, we forget that all the characters and their characteristics are nothing more than vibratory forms of electric light. So it is when we see all the different things about us—the earth, the sky, the trees, other human beings, and myriad creatures—we forget that they are nothing but God, the Cosmic Electricity. We must realize that all of us are playing a drama of good or evil in this world, and that our flesh, the bulb and the electricity that illuminates it, the vast ocean, the wood, the iron—all are made of God. Do not forget this. Everything is composed of the subtle vibrating cosmic energy of God.

The visible universe is thus a vast personal representation of the invisible Spirit. Everything is a part of Him, even the smallest speck of dust. The wood that appears to be inert matter is the living light of God. In seemingly empty space there is one Link, one Life Eternal which unites everything in the universe—animate and inanimate—one wave of Life flowing through everything. The wave is the same as the ocean, though it is not the whole ocean. So each wave of creation is a part of the eternal Ocean of Spirit. The Ocean can exist without the waves, but the waves cannot exist without the Ocean. Therefore, God is both personal and impersonal. He is the Uncreated Absolute; and He is manifest in creation, peering at us through the twinkling stars, breathing to us His sweet fragrance through the flowers, and talking to us through his saints.

Now, just behind the universe is the infinite presence of God. And because God cannot be bound by any form, even His personal aspect in the universe is also infinite. So what we call finite and infinite are both right before our eyes. But our eyes deceive us, because they cannot see all there is, what we call finite and infinite in essence. Therefore, we cannot conceive the depth of the space. The space in this room is about 10×15 feet, measured by what confines it; but space itself cannot be seen or measured. At a clear night we see only a few thousand stars, but uncounted trillions more lie beyond our vision. The light of the distant stars takes aeons to reach the earth. and what is beyond the farthest star? Man does not know, space is infinite. The ordinary human mind cannot comprehend this truth.

God is visible as these created forms, yet that very visibility makes Him invisible: Gross vibrations hide His infinite nature, His omnipresent invisibility in which everything has its beginning and end. To illustrate, steam is invisible, but when condensed it becomes visible as water; condensed further by freezing, it becomes ice. Steam is a gas; ice is a solid how different, and yet the same. Similarly, the impersonal God is personal, and the personal God is impersonal. All matter is Spirit, and Spirit has become matter. There is no essential difference.

In the beginning, before creation, God was invisible, but He wanted to become visible, and to enjoy His infinite nature through many forms. Electricity is in the air around us, but you don't see it. Unmanifest, it is impersonal. But when it is brought into a bulb, it becomes visible, even though it is the same electricity. So it is with God. The Divine Electricity made visible in body-bulb (body + *âtman*). God has taken the forms of more than billions beings on earth. Although He has made a personal representation of Himself in each human being, some reflect His light more than others. These are His great saints and *avatars*.

The animals cannot reason, but man can. All the attributes that God has—consciousness, reason, will, feeling, love—man has too. In these qualities man may be said to be made in the image of God. If you register the consciousness of God in your body. You will realize that flesh is nothing more than a physical manifestation of the five vibratory elements of earth, water, fire, air and ether. The whole universe—which is God's body—is made of the same five elements that also compose man's body. The star-like shape of the human body represents the rays of these five elements. The head, the two hands, and the two feet form the five points of the star. God manifests motion in creation. Man has developed legs and feet because of the urge to express motion. The toes are materialization of the five rays of energy. So in this way, we are made in the image of God. *Upanishad* states that, '*Tat Tvam Asi*' means, '*Thou art that*' that is to say, 'thou, the individual, art identical with the ultimate principle of things (Supreme).' When you concentrate at the point between the eyebrows, the current in the two eyes reflects as one light, and you behold the spiritual eye. This single orb is the 'eye of God'. We have developed two eyes because of the law of relativity that prevails in our dualistic universe.

God has assumed a human body so that He might be the refuge of all men; but they (men) do not know Him as He is. Those who consider him to be a man like are ignorant of God's supreme state of being which is boundless receptacle of compassion, generosity, goodness, love, etc., and is characterized by its human shape. God's body is the universe, God is the sacrifice, the libation and oblation offered to nourish the deceased ancestors, etc.

From the metaphysical point of view, the self (*âtman*) is eternal and never dies. Therefore, in considering the question of death, all that one has to consider is the body which has fallen to one's lot according to one's destiny (*prâralabdha*). This body is perishable in any case. This perishable human body is the only means by which one can perform whatever is to be performed in this world for the benefit of the *âtman* to merge with *Pramâtmâ* (Brahman).

Based on the oneness of the spirit, humanity must be recognized as one in nature. If you do that, then you are truly religious man. Not when you harbour greed, passion, love of power, love of putting down the other man; you may talk of religion, but you are not a truly religious man. You are a fraud, so to say.

I or ego is the greatest paradox in life. We always say 'I, mine, my son, my house, my car', etc. but we do not know—who am I ? When the soul leaves the body at the time of death, the dead body does not say 'I am here' neither the departed soul says 'I am here outside the body'. Yet when body and soul join together, we hear 'I' all the time. Don't you think that is a great pradox? The 'I' or 'Ego' feelings make our lives miserable. If I tell you that 1000 houses were demolished by a car bomb in a remote village in some part of the world, then you will shake your head as if nothing happened. But if I tell you that there is a small fire in one of the houses in your street, you immediately become concerned and perhaps panicky. But at the same time, if you increase your ownership from *limited* to the *unlimited,* you feel free. When you think about your son, you are worried about his welfare but when you think about all the children of the world you have no worry and indeed you are very happy. It is said that a God-realized man sees the 'I' as the universe and the universe as 'I'. So when the *limited ego* becomes the *universal ego,* we achieve everlasting happiness. Of course to transform *limited ego* to *universal ego* is not any easy job, but by continued practice of different methods of God-realization, we can achieve that Herculean task in front of all of us.

Lord Krishna said in *Gîtâ,* 'He who has no egoism, whose intelligence is not tainted by good or evil, even if he kills the whole world, he neither destroys nor is bound by the action.' What is needed of a sincere devotee is that he should feel that the entire universe is a manifestation of the Lord.

The first end of life is knowledge; the second end of life is happiness. Knowledge and happiness lead to freedom. But not one can attain liberty until every being has liberty. Not one can be happy until all are happy. When you hurt anyone you hurt yourself, for you and your brother are one. He is indeed a *yogi* who sees himself in the whole universe and the whole universe in himself.

Once the *guru* was teaching his disciples that everything in the universe was *Brahman* and said: *Guru Brahma, Sishya Brahma, Sarvam Brahma.* Usually every day on his arrival, the disciples were accustomed to greet the *guru* respectfully. But after this particular event, one of the disciples did not do so and never got up from his seat. The *guru* questioned him on this strange behaviour. The disciple replied that the previous day, the *guru* had said that everything was *Brahman* and therefore there was no difference between them. The *guru* wanted to teach him a good lesson. He wrote on the board 'Guru Brahma' as two different words. He also wrote 'Sishya Brahma' and 'Sarvam Brahma'. When you look at these three, though *Brahma* is occurring as the same in all the three, the *Guru, Sishya* and *Sarvam* are different. Only when these words also become one, you can say that all are one. Thus, until you are able to experience this oneness of all in practice, the student will remain a student and *guru* will remain a teacher, and there is no escape from the need for the student having a respect the teacher. The basis is one but the containers are different.

Once again a devotee heard his *guru* say, 'God is in everything and everyone.' As he walked away pondering this wisdom, an enraged elephant appeared on the road ahead. 'Run! Run! Run!' shouted the *mahout.* The man thought to himself, 'I am God and the elephant is also God, why should I be afraid?' The charging elephant knocked the man in the ditch. Bruised and upset, the man set off to see his *guru* to complain. After hearing the story, the *guru* said,'You are right that both you and the elephant are God. But why didn't you listen to the *mahout,* who is also God, and get out of the way.'

Sufi poem translated by Professor Browne of Cambridge:

> Beaker or flagon, or bowl or jar,
> Clumsy or slender, coarse or fine;
> However the potter may make or mar,
> All were made to contain the wine:
> Should we seek this one or that one shun,
> When the wine which gives them their worth is one?

A south Indian folksong says:

> Into the bossom of the one great sea,
> Flow streams that come from hills of every side,
> Their names are various as their springs,
> And thus in every land do men bow down
> To one great God, though known by many names (Gover, *The Songs of South India*, 1871, pp.165).

3. SPIRITUALISATION OF ONE'S ACTIVITIES

One should feel he is an instrument in the hands of God and realize that 'God's will be done.' It will be wise to remember the verse of the *Gitâ*, 'whatever you do, eat, offer in sacrifice, give or practise as austerity, do it as an offering unto the Lord.' To retain the vision of the Lord in our mind, the *Gitâ* contains a powerful plea to be submitted to Him to grant us asylum in His Kingdom. Arjuna asked, 'My heart is overpowered by the taint of pity; my mind is confused as to the duties. Tell me decisively what is good for me.' To this, God replied, 'Abandoning all duties, take refuge in Me and I shall liberate you from all sins and hence do not grieve.' The *Gitâ* enjoins us to offer all our actions and also their fruits to God. 'He who has no egoism, whose intelligence is not tainted by good or evil, even if he kills the whole world, he neither destroys nor is bound by action.' What is needed of a sincere devotee is that he should feel that the entire universe is a manifestation of the Lord.

The paramount importance for the success of various spiritual exercises are ethical discipline and perfection. In a pure heart, serenity, tranquility, tolerance, humility and divine light will descend. Cheerfulness, equilibrium, solace and self-restraint, all constitute mental discipline.

(4) CULTIVATION OF VIRTUES

Mere belief in God is not sufficient; self-discipline, control of moods, is also essential. Hindu religion shows us the dicipline how to be unconditionally happy, untouched by suffering and change. Most people are victims of moods, and unless one controls them, they will control him. He who masters his moods becomes a more balanced individual. Do only those things which your discrimination tells you are good for you.

If a person gets established in one virtue, all other virtues will be accured to him. First, we have to be self-controlled, be charitable and be compassionate, and other virtues such as non-injury (*ahimsa*), truthfulness and impeccable character, will be acquired. For this, one should cultivate purity of thought, word and deed. A truly religious man must bring about an inward transformation of his being and must control himslef of any kind of anger (*krodha*), greed (*lobha*), hatred, etc., and and must look upon the whole world as his kindred. He is a religious man who has rid himself of passion and has become truly dispassionate.

All the Sâstras contain the advice that desire (*kâma*), anger (*krodha*), avarice (*lobha*) are enemies of man, and that unless they are fully conquered, neither he nor society will in any way be benifitted; as stated in the *Bhagavad Gitâ* and also in Mahabharat (*Bhagavad Gitâ* (XVI: 21) and also in Mahabharat U. 32.70.).

trividham narakasyedam dvâram nâsanam âtmanah
kâmah krodhas tathâ lobhas tasmâd etate trayam tyajet

i.e., '*kâma*, *krodha* and *lobha* are the three gateways of hell; and they are destructive agents, they must be eschewed'.

a. ANGER (Krodha)

You are an image of God, you should behave like a God, but what happens? First thing in the morning, you lose your temper and complain, 'My coffee is cold!' Why be distrubed by such things? Have that evenness of mind wherein you are absolutely calm, free from all anger. That is what you want. Don't let anyone or anything get deprive you of peace. Let nothing take it away from you. Blame no one else for your unhappiness; blame yourself. If you are mistreated by others, seek the fault in yourself, and you will find it much easier to get along with everyone. Look at your enemies as little children. If a child hits you, you don't hate him for it. You forgive him, realizing he didn't know better.

In speaking about anger (*krodha*), Bhâravi says that (*Kirât-kâvya* I: 33):

amarsasunyaena janasya jantunâ
na jâtahârdena na vidvisâdarah

i.e., 'If a man does not get angry or annoyed when he has been insulted, it is just the same whether he is your friend or whether he hates you!' Vidulâ has said that from the point of view of the warrior (*ksatriya*) religion:

etâvân eva uruso yad amarsi yad aksami
kshamâvân niramar sas ca naiva stri na punah pumân

(*Mahabharat* U. 132. 33)

i.e., ' He who gets angry (on account of injustice) and who does not submit (to insult), is truly a man. He who does not get angry or annoyed is neither a woman nor a man'. It has already been stated above that in order that the world should go on, there must not be either anger or valour at all times, or forgiveness at all times.

b. AVERICE (Lobha)

The same law applies to avarice (*lobha*). Even if a man is a *sanmyâsi* (ascetic) yet he has avarice (*lobha*) to want a release (*moksa*). Vyâsa has stated in various stories in Mahâbhârata that the various virtues of valour, courage, kindness, probity, friendship, impartiality, etc., are, in addition to their mutual oppositions, also limited by considerations of time and place. Whatever the virtue may be, it is not equally appropriate in all circumstances.

c. DESIRE (Kâma)

Lord Krishna has described his own form in the following words: '*dharmâviruddho bhutesu kâmo smi Bharatarsabha* (*Gitâ* VII:11), i.e. 'O. Arjuna I am that *kâma* (desire) which exists in the hearts of living things, being consistent with law (*dharma*)'. Therefore, that *kâma* (desire) which is inconsistent with *dharma* is the gateway of hell and other kinds of *kâma* are not proscribed by the Lord; and even Manu said: *'parityajed arthakâman yan syâtâm dharmavarjitau'*, i.e. 'that wealth (*artha*) and desire (*kâma*) which are inconsistent with justice (*dharma*) should be eschewed' (*Manusmiriti* 4.176). If tomorrow all living beings decide to say good-bye to the Lord Kâma, and to observe celibacy the whole of their lives, the entire living creation will come to an end within fifty or hundred years, and the silence of death will reign everywhere. In order to save from that creation and destruction, the Blessed Lord takes incarnations every now and then. *Kâma* and *krodha* are enemies, it is true, but when? It is only when you allow them to become uncontrolled. Even Manu and other seers have accepted the position that *kâma* and *krodha* are extremely essential, within proper limits, in order that the world should go on (*Manusmriti* 5. 56). It is stated in the Bhâgavata that:

> *loke vyavâyâmsamadyasevâ*
> *nityâsti jantor na hi tatra codanâ*
> *vyavasthitis tesu vivâhayajñâ-*
> *surâgrahairâsu nivrttir istâ.*

> (*Bhâgavata* XI:5.11)

i.e. 'In the world, it is not necessary to tell anyone to indulge in the enjoyment of sexual intercourse or in eating flesh or drinking wine. These are things which human beings want naturally. And it is in order to systematize these three impulses, that is to say, in order to give them a systematic basis by subjecting them to limitations or restraint, that the writers of the Sâstras have ordained marriage, and the *soma-yoga* and the *sautrâmani-yajñâ* respectively for them; but even with reference to these matters, the most excellent course is renunciation (*nivrtti*), that is to say, desireless action'. It must be born in mind, the word *'nivrtti-karma'* means 'Action which is to be performed desirelessly'. The word has been used clearly in those meanings in the Manu Smrti and in the Bhâgavate-Purâna (*ManuSmrti* 12.89; *Bhagavate-Purâna* XI:10.1 and VIII: 15.47).

In conclusion, it is also important to understand that a human beings consist of a physical, an emotional, a spiritual and intellectual quadrant. When these four aspects of the human being are in a total harmony, without any negativity, namely without any fear, guilt, and shame, only then we are all wed to return to the unobstructed world, where we do not have to reincarnate or to take rebirth. Hence self-realization is an arduous and protracted process. Aspirants must make painstaking and patient efforts to reach the goal.

Part III

Chapter 13

Steadfast Wisdom

In all *ashrams* and institution which were started by Mahatma Gandhi, the last 19 verses (54 to 72) of Chapter two of *Bhagavad Gita* were chanted every day in the evening prayer at 1900 hours. This was and still is the practice. Following is the script of those verses.

Definition of Steadfast Wisdom

Arjuna asked Krishna: 'How can one identify realized soul, stable mind and be established firmly in perfect tranquillity of mind (*samadhi*) ? How does the man of steadfast wisdom, the illumined soul, speak? How does he sit? How does he walk? (Gita II.54)

Lord Krishna answered: 'Arjuna! when a man puts away all the desires of his mind, and when his spirit is content in itself, through the joy of the self, then he is called a man of steadfast wisdom' Gita II: 55. These are the two marks of man. Firstly, he has become desireless, having destroyed all desires. Secondly, he has learned to take joy from himself.

The next two verses (Gitâ II:56-57) deal with the manner in which an enlightened (God-realized) soul speaks. 'He whose mind is no shaken by adversity, who does not hanker after happiness, who has become free from attachment, fear and anger, is indeed a man of steadfast wisdom' (Gita II: 56). Lord Krishna answers it attaching importance of feelings and understanding because an action is performed according to the feelings and understanding. There is no end of sorrows and unfavorable circumstances in this world. But the man of wisdom is not perturbed by anything. He is neither perturbed by happiness nor by sorrow. His life is devoid of such things as attachment, fear, anger, jealousy and sorrow. It is because the aim of his life is to discharge his duty to the best of his ability and capacity without having any desire for its fruit. 'He who is unattached everywhere, who is neither delighted at receiving good, nor dejected at receiving evil, is poised (stable) in wisdom' ((Gita II:57). He speaks without fear and remains undisturbed.

How does he sit? 'Having controlled all the senses, a striver should sit for meditation (*yoga*), devoting his heart and soul to Me. For his wisdom (mind) is stable and his senses are under control.' After controlling the senses and the mind, he sits, contemplating the Supreme. Self-discipline is not a matter of intelligence. It is a matter of will and emotions. Self-discipline is easy when there is vision of the Highest.

How does he walk? This means: how does he live or move everywhere in the world? 'He who abandons all desires and acts free from longing, without any sense of mineness or egotism, he attains peace (Gita II: 61). He freely and readily acts himself without measure.

How does he live? Lord Krishna gives illustration that explains the mental state of the man in the following slokas. 'Rivers flow continuously into the ocean, But the ocean is never disturbed. Desires flow into the mind of the seer, but he always remains undisturbed (Gita II: 70).' Wave upon wave of emotion assails him, but they all die away. Like the ocean, he remains undisturbed.

How does he think? 'O Arjuna, one who renounces or permanently uproots desires and moves in the world unattached, having abandoned ego and selfishness, he is peaceful (Gita II: 71).' He is free from desires. He has neither attachment, nor ego, and for him, there remains nothing except taking joy from the self. This is knowledge, and this is the yoga of steadfast wisdom.

Lord Krishna explains two types of human beings: the enlightened whose senses are completely restrained from their objects, and an ordinary unenlightened (ignorant) person and their nature. 'The enlightened mind remains wide awake in that state of divine knowledge and Supreme Bliss which is dark night to the ignorant. And that, the ever-changing, transient, worldly happiness in which the ignorant keep awake, is night for the enlightened (Gita II:69).' The enlightened person is always wide awake for divine values and unenlightened (ignorant) remains awakened for evils, clinging onto and embracing them. For him, the good, divine, moral virtues are non-existent: such a person is asleep towards good things, while remaining awake for evil ones.

Method of Achieving Steadfast Wisdom

(a) Destruction of Desire

Lord Krishna has provided definition of steadfast wisdom, shown the path and illustrated methods to achieve the wisdom to have perfect life. Krishna said: 'When a person puts away all the desires of his mind, and when his spirit is content in itself, then he is called stable in wisdom.' Or when a person abandons all cravings of the mind, and is satisfied in the self through the joy of the self, then he is called a person of steadfast wisdom.' (Gita II.55). Two points are made here, and they fit together perfectly. First, he is a *yogi* (one who has mastered steadfast wisdom) has *no desire whatsoever*; secondly, he *derives contentment from himself*.

It is a hard and arduous task to eradicate desires. No one can ever satisfy all desires. Gita describes 'desires have been likened unto fire'. Here a person is adding more and more oil or fuel to the fire and he thinks that he is putting it out. The flames will only blaze forth, and not die down. The thing to do is to neglect the fire (of desire) to die a natural death. Desires are rooted deeply in the nature of human being, and they must be uprooted completely and destroyed uncompromisingly. Desires have to be burned down to ashes to ensure that they cannot germinate again. Can desires be completely destroyed ever?

Krishna further said: 'He who draws away the senses from the objects of sense on every side as a tortoise draws in his limbs (into the shell), his intelligence is firmly set in wisdom' (Gita III.58). As a tortoise withdraws its six limbs—four legs, a tail and a forehead—into the shell to protect itself against possible dangers, similarly an enlightened person also withdraws his five senses and one mind from sense objects. If an animal such as the tortoise can control itself; why can person not do the same? Lord Krishna explains in the next verse that mere withdrawal of the senses from the sense-objects is not the mark of the person of steadfast wisdom. 'Sense objects cease for him who does not enjoy them with his senses, but the taste for them persists. This relish also disappears of the person of stable mind when he sees the Supreme (Gita II:59).' This *sloka* has two parts. One is about the control of the senses. But the control of senses is never complete as long as desires *persist*, which live in the human mind. Here Krishna explains the difference between outer abstention and inner renunciation. We may reject the objects but desire for them may remain. Even the desire is lost when he sees the Supreme (God). By seeing the Supreme, a person becomes fearless concerning desires, which disappear for ever and are destroyed. Seeing the Supreme means seeing the Self. Does seeing the Self means seeing the physical self? No! It means self-realization and its experience. When such an experience comes to a person once in his life, then desires flee from his mind. Until then, the person should continue his practice regularly, punctually and consistently. God has brought us into this world and He has given us two things: wisdom or discriminatory power, and striving-power. We have to use these two powers.

(b) Control of Senses

The *Upanishads* discuss about who is greater—senses, mind or intellect. They fail to demonstrate the proof that the functioning of the body depends on him. But when the soul begins to leave the body, the eyes cannot see, the ears can not hear, the tongue can not taste or make speech and so on. All the senses began to cry out, 'Don't leave us! The senses are thus nothing but horses or mules ridden by desires. Therefore, from the beginning, Arjuna, you must control your senses, then kill this evil and wicked thing that destroys wisdom and discriminative knowledge and obstructs realization of the *âtman*.

'The senses are said to be greater and higher than body or sense objects, but greater and higher than the senses is the mind. Intelligence is higher than mind. What is higher than intelligence is the *ātman* itself, the life divine in man. Thus, Arjuna knowing him who is above the intelligence, and subduing or controlling the mind through reason and spiritual discrimination, you must destroy the elusive enemy in the form of lust and desires that is hard to get at and to overcome (Gita III. 41-43).

Krishna said: 'Thus, Arjuna, knowing that which is above the intelligence, you should subdue the mind through reason and spiritual discrimination. Then smite and destroy your elusive enemy who wears the form of lust and desires, and is so hard to get at and overcome' (Gita III.43). It is a mistake to assume that the eradication of desire is a simple task; it is a hard and arduous task. Human Being does have the power by which to subdue the senses and control the mind. That's why Krishna addresses Arjuna 'Mahabaho,' meaning 'mighty-armed.' Human Being has been endowed with the powerful weapon of spiritual discrimination and understanding with which to control the senses, to destroy the desires, and so to obtain enlightenment.

Consequence of Uncontrolled Senses

'The man, thinking about sense-objects, develops attachment for them; from attachment springs up desire and addiction, and from desire unfulfilled or addiction thwarted ensues anger. From anger arises infatuation; from infatuation confusion of memory; from confusion of memory, loss of reason; and from loss of reason, the man goes to complete ruin' (Gita II: 62-63).

It is obligatory for a striver following the discipline of action to control his mind and senses. But what happens to the person who has not controlled his mind and senses, is explained in this verse. 'Where there is no control of the senses, there is no understanding. Without understanding, there can be neither concentration nor meditation. Without concentration and meditation, there can be no peace. And where there is no peace, there is no happiness' (Gita II: 66).

God has bestowed upon person this human body to attain Him. So a person should firmly resolve to attain God-realization. This resolution removes his attachment for pleasures and makes his intellect determinate. But what happens if the intellect does not become determinate, has been described here. 'Just a the wind carries away a ship on the water, the mind that yields to anyone of the wandering senses takes away the discrimination of man.' (Gita II: 67). In 60th verse Lord explained that senses carry away the mind, while in this verse it is explained that the mind carries away discrimination. It means that both senses and mind are impetuous. So a striver should control both of them. 'The turbulent senses, O son of Kunti, forcibly carry away the mind of even a wise man who is practicing self-control' (Gita II: 60).

Now in the next verse Lord Krishna describes the condition of the striver who has controlled his senses. 'Therefore, O mighty-armed (Arjuna), his intellect is stable, whose senses are completely restrained from their objects' (Gita II: 68). He says here that the intellect of the person whose mind and senses are completely free from the worldly attractions, is stable.

Following *slokas* is explained the consequences of mastery over the senses. 'The man of steadfast wisdom moves in the world of sense-objects with all his senses free. For, having gained power over his senses, he goes forth in peace' (Gita II: 64). 'When one attains peace, one's sorrows die away. When peace has been attained by the person of steadfast wisdom, the understanding becomes clear and unwavering to him' (Gita II: 65). The Lord here describes peace and the results of peace. The first thing to note is that wherever there is peace, there is no sorrow, there is happiness.

Methods for Controlling Senses

Second component of the definition of the yoga of steadfast wisdom is this, '*Have contentment from your own self.*' No one can give us happiness. We cannot bring contentment, at any price, from any other person. Yogic practices exist to help us eliminate and uproot desires from life and achieve self-contentment. Krishna said: 'The sage whose mind remains unperturbed by sorrow, whose pleasures have altogether disappeared, and who is free from desire, is called a man of steadfast wisdom, a seer, or an illumined. He who is unattached to everything, and neither rejoices nor weeps on meeting with good nor bad fortune. I call him a man of steadfast wisdom, an illumined' (Gita II. 56, 57).

Arjuna asked: 'Krishna, what is it that compels a person do evil, even against his will, as though driven to it by force' (Gita III. 36). Krishna answered him as follows: 'It is craving, desire, lust, and wrath. It is born of the mode of passion (*rajogunna*), and it has two faces: rage and lust. It is insatiable, ravenous, all-devouring, deadly, grossly wicked, most sinful. Recognize these as the enemy here' (Gita III. 37). There is no difference between desire and anger. Anger is a result of a desire unfulfilled. Anger is desire in a different form. Anger takes birth from the ego, I-consciousness, when a person declares: 'I am going to do this and that... I am going to show others where power lies, etc. Krishna further said: 'As fire is enveloped by smoke, mirror covered by dust, and embryo hidden by womb, so knowledge is hidden by it (desire, lust)' (Gita III. 38). 'So, Arjuna, knowledge or wisdom is covered by hungry and insatiable fire of desire, the constant and eternal enemy of the wise' (Gita III. 39). 'The senses, mind and intelligence are said to be its seat. Veiling or hiding wisdom and knowledge by these, it (desire) deludes the embodied soul' (Gita III.40).

One thing is certain and must be understood: results are not in human hands. If results were to be controlled by persons, the consequences would have been dreadful. Our job is only trying to work hard and making every effort; but the results are not in our hands. One should neither get fuddled with happiness, nor die of sorrow, anger or jealousy. By continual practice, a person can become a master of the *yoga* of steadfast wisdom. We should do our duty and do it right. At the end of a duty well done, if the result is unfavorable, don't become angry. And if the result is favorable, don't have attachment or longing for that either. One should not be affected by the result. Always keep your mind balanced. Never allow your mind to waver, or to be perturbed. A story of a businessman, Tuladhar, demonstrates this. He always concentrated on the beam of the scale, keeping it balanced for everyone. Another simile has been given of a vehicle coming down a steep hill. If the driver loses control, the vehicle will be smashed, and the driver and passengers may perish. The thing to do is to keep a firm grip on the *self*, never permitting oneself to become over joyed to the extent of losing one's self control or ignoring one's responsibility. We should avoid becoming intoxicated by senses because there are future successes for which we have to work. One's progress in life stops, if one accepts his success as being last and final. The athlete's spirit should be pondered and cultivated. When a good athlete loses one game, he neither retires nor accepts that game as final. The athlete takes a lesson from it so that next time he becomes more alert and plays the game more skillfully. He prepares well before the second season starts.

Person takes a lesson from defeat and encouragement from victory. Person gets wisdom from defeat, inspiration from victory; so that, in victory or defeat, progress is made. In victory or defeat, we must go on striving for more and more progress as long as we live. This approach gives us steadfast wisdom. By continual practice, when person creates this habit or makes this his way of life or nature, then he is a *yogi* of steadfast wisdom, and nothing can stop or hinder his future progress. Followings are the suggested five methods controlling senses:

1. Yogic Way or Meditation

There are four steps in yoga: *yama, niyaama, asana and pranayam*. These four steps are the external steps. These are disciplines: (1) the don'ts, (2) the do's, (3) the *asanas* or postures, and (4) breathing. Then begin the internal steps that are also four: *pratyahara, dharna, dhyana,* and *samadhi*. Pratyahara is the art of drawing the senses back from the sense-objects. Dharna is concentration. No one can meditate without first having mastered the Pratyahara, the arts of withdrawing sensess from the sense-objects, and of *dharna* or concentration. There are ten senses in humans. These senses cannot let the practitioner meditate. Imagine a person sitting in a narrow box linked by ten nails pricking him. How can he concentrate? It is impossible and impractical.

The practical steps in concentration are: first, try to silence the mind, and then the art of withdrawing the senses from the sense-objects is rehearsed, and eventually mastered. Sit down in silence. Close your eyes and lips. Then try to listen by chanting the sacred syllable, *Om,* is to chant in silence. Firsts chant it loudly. When you listen to word, you skip it and fail to hear it. Try again to pick it up, but soon you lose it again. Try again and again. This gives you practice, and as often as you hear that word, you are automatically withdrawing your senses from sense-objects. Krishna told Arjuna, 'Even though a person may ever strive (for perfection), and be ever so discerning, O son of Kunti (Arjuna), his impetuous (turbulent) senses will carry off his mind by force' (Gita II: 60). So the practitioner should go beyond the name. Go deeper and deeper, and deeper still. Keep asking yourself: 'Where is the sound coming from? What is the source of the sound?' This becomes concentration (*dharna*). Becoming one with the sound is meditation. The final merging with the source is called *samadhi*. This is *yoga*.

2. Devotion

Bhakti or devotion is the way by which we can easily realize God. The control should be both on the body and the mind. Liberation from the tyranny of the body is not enough; we must be liberated from the tyranny of desires also.

The desires cannot be completely burned and destroyed until and unless the Supreme has been seen, as has been mentioned in *sloka* II: 59. One should carry on practicing *yoga* until one sees the Supreme.

Our goal is to see, realize and experience the Supreme, and not the mastery of sense-control. Sense-control is the means to achieve the goal. To see the Supreme, devotion (*bhakti*) is essential. So there are some preludes to devotion: (1) control of the senses, (2) destruction of desires, (3) faith, not blind belief, (4) ego and (5) prayer.

'The turbulent senses, O son of Kunti, forcibly carry away the mind of even a wise man who is practicing self control' (Gita II:60). The turbulent senses of even a wise person carry away his mind towards pleasures. The reason is that so long as the mind is not permanently established in God, the past influences of the enjoyment or pleasures attract senses and mind towards pleasures, forcibly. Even some sages could not control this temptation. Therefore, a striver should never believe his senses and should be always on his guard. Control of the senses does not bring about the destruction of desire, so we should continuously strive to achieve desirelessness. The practitioner should keep a balanced mind and carry on striving harder and harder till he achieves it. We cannot control the mind without destroying desires.

'As the wind carries away a boat upon the waters, in the same way, by their force, the uncontrolled senses take away the mind and the understanding' (Gita II: 67) Further, Lord said: 'When all his senses are completely controlled regarding sense-objects, O, Arjuna, a man gets steadfast wisdom' (Gita II: 68).

3. Faith

Faith that follows conviction and understanding is real faith otherwise it is blind belief. There are scientific and natural sequences of events for developing faith. First, we hear of an event. Second the desire to know more about it is aroused within us. Third we make efforts to satisfy the desire to know. Fourth, we have faith that insures permanence in the practice. If faith preceedes knowledge, it is no longer a faith; it becomes a belief. Belief is always blind. There is no longer room in the mind of such a person for understanding, reasoning or the use of discriminating power. The aspirant should have faith in own understanding and knowledge, not in someone else, but in himself. For example, When our sisters and mothers cook, they add a pinch of salt, a dash of garlic, sprinkling of pepper, and so on. How are they able to cook along these lines? It is because they have faith in their knowledge. Therefore, they add the ingredients with confidence and faith. Realization can bring the confidence, knowledge and understanding, that is faith. When we possess this kind of faith, nothing in the world can change us from our path.

Senses and mind are controlled permanently (not destroyed), but the desires are destroyed. Senses and mind are going to live with us as long as the body is alive. The desire to see thing remains when a person is blind. Similarly, a person practicing celibacy, the desires for sex remain within him. An alcoholic stops' drinking but his desire for a alcohol remains. The roots of desires grow deep. A person should never think that by controlling the senses, the desires are uprooted permanently and perfectly. Krishna described it as man being 'even though a person may ever strive (for perfection) and be ever so discerning, O. Son of Kunti (Arjuna), his impetuous senses will carry off his mind by force' (Gita II:60). Further He explains how to control the turbulent senses that forcibly carry away the mind of a wise person in whom the taste for sense objects still persists. 'Having brought all (the senses) under control, he should remain firm in yoga intent on Me; for he, whose senses are under control, his intelligence is firmly set.' For, he whose senses are controlled, becomes a person of steadfast belief' (Gita II: 61). But what about those who don't devote themselves to God? The answer is provided in the next two verses. 'Brooding on the objects of senses, a man develops attachment for them; from attachment springs up desire; from desire (unfulfilled) ensues anger. From anger arises delusion; from delusion, confusion of memory; from confusion of memory, loss of reason; and from loss of reason (discrimination), he goes to complete ruin' (Gita II: 62-63).

We need the help of devotion to control the senses and the mind when we have used both attributes, striving and wisdom, within our power.

4. Destruction of Ego

When a person discovers that all his efforts, strength, and wisdom are not sufficient for accomplishment of a given objective, then his ego melts and person turn to God. He cries to Him from his heart and full emotion. That cry is real until then person is full of ego that controls him. It is the story of an elephant who was overpowered by a crocodile. The elephant cried for God and God came to rescue him. By the fear of death, at the point of death, the elephant realized: My power is no power, my strength is no strength and now I am about to die. The ego disappeared completely, and the real name of the Lord comes to the mind of the person. It comes from the heart: 'Hari! O God! O God!!' As long as the human mind is full of ego, it is impossible to get God's grace. The strongest part of man is the mind. It is most egotistic, most powerful. It is only when ego disappears from the mind that the mind comes to God, but not before that. When person uses all his God-given power, making all efforts with wisdom and experience, then only he has earned the right to ask God for help. The kind-hearted Lord, whose kindness, compassion, and love incarnate, is waiting for that moment to help. He comes running to such devotees. All they have to do is think of God, and He comes running to them. This is a spiritual truth, a divine truth.

5. Prayer

Lord Krishna enjoined to fight at every step of the Divine discourse. He did not say: 'Arjuna, I am going to kill all these people for you. Now that I am here, you don't have to do a thing. Put your arrows back into the quiver, and sling your bow across your shoulder.' No! Instead He charged him: 'Fight, fight and fight! And after understanding the lesson, become an instrument in My hand.' The correct way is explained by Lord Krishna in the Gita. God has given you the strength and power, first you completely use it up, then and only then you earn the right to pray. The prayer should be true, sincere, and honest. Saying: 'O. God, help us! There is no one else in the world to protect and save me or give me refuge. You are the only one, God!'

There is a story in the *Upanishads* of a devotee of the Lord who was purifying his mind by remembering God continuously. When the mind became purified, God appeared and asked him: 'What do you want?' The devotee replied: 'O my Lord, You must know what is good for me, seeing You are goodness itself. I do not know what is good for me. You are everything to me and You know everything about me. It is for You to decide what is good for me, and give some to me.' This is the correct way to pray.

Importance of the Spiritual Person

In the end of Chapter 2 of the Gita, Lord Krishna described the person having spiritual illuminations as a result of being free from desire, thirst for enjoyment, attachment and egoism. 'Such is the state of the God-realized soul. Having attained this state, he overcomes delusion. Being established in this state even at the end of life, he attains Brahmic Bliss (*Brahmishiti*) (Gita II:72).

Delusion is born of egoism, attachment or desire. To remove this delusion, Lord Krishna has talked about two kinds of discrimination—discrimination between the real and the unreal (Gitâ II:11-30) and discrimination between discharging one's duty and abandoning it (Gita II:31-53).

Chapter 14

Nama Japa

'You cannot come to a knowledge of any particular form, even if placed on the hand, unless the name is known; but if, without seeing the form one meditates on the name, the form, too flashes on the mind as an object of passionate devotion' (Râmâyan BalKanda. 200: 3). In the world we meet many people. If you ask a person, 'do you know him?' He may say, 'I know him only by name.' How many aspects are there of any man? *His name*, his *emotional nature*, and his *intellectual accomplishments*. So the man is one and the same, but when we say, 'I know him only by name,' or 'I know him to be a good-natured person, but I do not understand his way of thinking', what we know about that man is only one aspect of him. Even though we take the whole name of the person, the entire personality of that man is not known to us. We have to know the person's name, his nature and his accomplishments, then we really know that person. Similarly, nâmajapa of a God is fruitful, if we know Him by understanding the meaning of it, His nature, etc., and go through several stages of it.

OM

By analogy, Om is *Brahman*, but the entire personality of that *saguna Brahman* is not known to us. If our understanding of Om is limited, confined to the *gross physical world*, the result of our *upâsanâ* (prayer) will also be limited. But if the universality of that Om is known, then we can understand our oneness with the universe; we also recognize the *nirguna* aspect of it. Then we become totally one with it, identical with it. We attain identity with it. The result of the *upâsanâ* with partial knowledge of Truth is one thing, and with total knowledge, it is different.

The person who has a real longing for this knowldge is the qualified student. But, the *upâsanâ* will be at different levels. *One level* of *upâsanâ* will be the Om *chanting;* one chants Om, Om, Om. Thereafter, that student's level increases, and he comes to *understand the meaning* of it, but the total aspect of that Om can be understood only by a person of very high calibre. Thus, the *Omkar upâsanâ* is very easy and at the same time very difficult.

Om is a sound symbol. Anyone can chant it, but only a highly qualified student, who has learned the scriptures at the feet of his teacher, can meditate on Om as one's own true nature. However, we do not have to wait for all that; we have to make a beginning and start with the Om chanting. This is why *Om* has gained so much prominence, and all our *mantras* begin with Om.

To prepare the devotee's mind for the practice of meditation on the form of the deity, various modes of worship—physical, verbal, and mental—have been prescribed. The repetition, preferably inaudible, of the symbol *Om*, or of any other sacred word or formula, is considered very efficacious in this respect. According to sage Patñjali, the repetition of the symbol *Om* and contemplation of its meaning are conducive to the comprehension of the innermost self and the elimination of all obstacles to its realization. Those who do not have faith or devotion adequate for the worship of the divinity are instructed to practice *karma yoga*; that is, to perform their duties, domestic, social or humanitarian, dispassionately, caring for inner purification rather than secular gain, here or hereafter. Even this cannot be practiced until the aspirant's mind discerns the futility of the temporal values and turns to the spiritual idea.

Rama

Upanishadbrahmayogin attributes special significance to the name of Râma: 'The reason for this is the traditional interpretation of Râma as combining the *astâkshra* (*Nârâyana-mantra*) and the *pañcâkhsara* (*Siva-mantra*). In the former, *Om namo nârâyana*, the fifth syllable **râ** is the life, for if we take out that syllable, the *mantra* would become *nâyanaya*, meaning 'not for salvation.' Similarly, if we take out the syllable **ma** from the *Shivapañcâksha* (*Om namah Shivâya*), that *mantra* becomes '*Om na Shivâya*,' 'not for good.' Thus, Râma stands really for both the *Nârâyana-mantra* and the *Siva-mantra*, of which it is the vital essence.' Tulsidasa also said in Ramâyana: 'I do homage to Râma, the name of Raghunathana, the source of all light, whether of the fire, or Sun, or the Moon; essence of Brahma, Hari (Vishnu), and Hara (Shiva); vital breath of the *Vedas*; the impersonal, the unique, the treasure-house of all perfections' (Râmâyan Bal Kanda. 18: 1). By its primary and secondary meanings, the syllable **râ** signifies respectively God-consciousness (primary) and pure existence, consciousness and bliss (secondary); similarly the syllable **ma** means the consciousness in the form of the *jiva* (primary) and the consciousness of the inner soul (secondary). It is the identification of the two in their secondary meanings that gives the unity to *tat* and *tvam*.

The practice of *Râma-nâma* has several stages. *First*, the name is contemplated in the *gross form* (Râma as *Vaisvânara* or *Virajâ*). Then the practitioner proceeds to the subtle stage, where the name Râma repressents *Hiranyagarbha*. The *third level* is the *Bijâmsa*, the seed-level, where the name venerated as the source of everything. The highest and proper level—the *nâma-artha-* is reached when Râma is seen as identical with Brahman-consciousness. At that level the name Râ—ma is explained as standing for the two words *tat* and *tvam* in the *mahâvâkya 'tat tvamasi'*. 'Of the two letters of the name, Râma, one gleams like a royal umbrella ( ) and the other like a crest-jewel ( ) over all the letters of the Devanâgari alphabet.' (R.Bk. 20:).

Krishna

'*Karsati sarvam Krishnah*', He who attracts all or arouses devotion in all is Krishna. *Vedantranemanjusa* (p.52) says that Krishna is so called because He removes sins of His devotees, (*pâpam karsayati, nirmulayati*). Krishna derived from '*krs*' means to scrap, because He scraps or draws away all sins and other sources of evil from His devotees.

One should worship Krishna, not as the cowherd boy, but the Krishna, the indefinable, inscrutable, divine principle that is born in the naval of the body (Mathura) as the product of the energy (*Devaki*), that is then transported to the mouth (Gokulam) and fostered by the tongue (Yasoda) as its source of sweetness. Krishna is the visualisation of *âtmâ*, that the repetition of the name grants the vision that was gained by Yasoda. You must foster that Krishna on your tongue; when he dances on it, the poison of the tongue will be rejected completely, without harming any one, as happened when as child he dances on the hoods of the serpent, Kâlinag.

When Krishna has broken the curd's pot and hides, Yasoda traces Krishna to the place He hides in, by the foot-prints He leaves. This is a symbolic story to illustrate how the Lord breaks our identification with the body and leads us on to Himself by signs and signals that He provides all around us. These signs are ever present in the nature around each one of us, in the beauty of the rising Sun, ecstasy of the rainbow, the melady of the birds, the lotus-spangled surface of lakes, the silence of snow-crowned peaks. It's only that we have to find Him. Welcome Him into your heart. He will come to you by means of joy He imparts, and live with you every moment and take your offerings, your *dhyâna*, your *pujâ* and *japa*. That will open the doors of *jñâna* and of liberation. This is the mark of the wise, while those who are otherwise, wander in the wilderness, filling their moments with meaningless trifles, toys and geegsaws.

Shiva

The salutation for Shiva is the '*pancakshara' mantra*, *i.e.* the five letter *mantra—Om Nama Shivaya* (*Na* = feet; *Ma*= navel; *Shi*= shoulders; *Vaya*=head) , i.e. from head to foot the salutation covers.

NAME VERSUS FORM

For the Advaitin, the Name becomes *one not with the deity which it stands for*, but with *Brahman* itself. Thus the repetition of the Name becomes a means of attaining oneness of *âtman* and *Brahman*. It is *upâya*, instrument, at the beginning, but becomes *upeyam*, the very object of the effort itself, in the end. The Name, then, is not the Name of something, but is itself the Highest. '*Râma* is no longer a Name of a *rupa*, but the *rupa* itself.' *Upanishad*-Brahma-Yogin speaks of a two-fold nature of the name: *nirvisesa* and *savisesa nâman*, the first meaning the Abolute itself, the second a particular name of personal deity. In Ramânyan also Tulsidasa said: 'There are two forms of the *Brahman*—impersonal (*Nirguna*) and personal (*Saguna*); both these aspects are unutterable, fathomless, without beginning and without parallel. To my (Tulasidasa's) mind the Name is gretear than both, for by its own power it has made both subject to itself' (Râmayan Balakand 22:1). 'The glory of the Name is thus immeasurably greater than of the attributesless Brahman (Absolute); and Tulasidasa declares that in my judgement the Name is greater than Râma too.' 'as Râma assumed the form of man to help the faithful and endured misery to make the pious happy; but votaries who lovingly repeat the Name easily become abodes of joy and blessings' (Râmayan Balakanda, 23: 1). 'The mystery of Name and form is unutterable; it is delightful to those who understand it, but it cannot be expressed. The Name bears testimony to the impersonal (*nirguna*) and the personal (*saguna*) alike; it is a clever interpreter revealing the truth of both' (Râmayan Balakanada, 20: 4). 'As their tongues repeat the Name, ascetics awake, free from passion, all detached from the Creator's world, and enjoy divine felicity, unequalled, uneffable, unsullied, without either name or form' (Râmayan Balakanda, 21: 1).

'It is presumptuous to ask which of the two (name or form) is the greater and which is the less; When they hear the differences between them, the wise will understand. Form is found to be subordinate to name; the form cannot be known apart from the name' (Râmâyan Balakanda, 20:2). 'Between Name and Form, the former is even superior to and subtler than the latter. While 'form' stands for the physical features of the world of phenomena, 'name' stands for the physical characteristics' (Chandogya Upanishad VI: iv.1). (The 'form' does not condition us so much as the 'name'. The spell of 'name' is even harder to get over than the hold of 'form'. Hence the divine name is said to be more efficacious than the divine form in extricating the devotees from the trammels of worldliness. There are several stories in the *Puranas* to illustrate this point. On more than two occassions, Hanuman proved to his Lord Râmachandra himself that the name 'Râma' was more powerful than the phsiycal form of Râma. On the coronation ceremony of Râma, Satrughan was welcoming everyone by putting *chandan tilak* on their forehead. Somehow Durvâsâ Muni was left alone and he felt insulted. He told Râma about his feeling. Râma promised him to bring out the head of the person who insulted him. Satrughan took selter under Hanumâna. Râma told Hanumâna to let him fulfill his promise. Hanumâna said: 'No! He too has promised Satrughan to protect him. Take my head first before Satrughan. Râma started shooting arrows on them. To encounter, Hanumâna started reciting

Râma, Râma, Râma. Both the arrows and the power of Name got tangled in the middle. It became a big problem. Finally, Durvâsâ Muni told Râma that he foregave Satrughan. Thus the power of the name, Râma, was established beyond doubt over the God Himself. Another time when the bridge was under construction to cross over Lankâ. Everybody were bringing stones to put on the sea. When Râma puts stones on the bridge they sink under the sea. So he asked Hanumâna: 'Why stones brought out by others float and his stones sink?' Hanumâna replied: 'Râma was written on every stone that was brought by others except yours.'

Highlighting the efficacy of the 'name', it is said that the mere utterance of the 'name' leads to the highest level, although the utterer may not even know the meaning. The classical story of Ajâmila illustrates this. The worst sinner in life, Ajâmila, called his son's name, *Nârâyana*, in the last moments of his life. Unintentionally uttering the Lord's name, Ajâmila was absolved of all his sins, and he went to the kingdom of Heaven, *Vaikuntha*. In this context it is said: 'Unknowingly or knowingly, the chanting of the supremely praise worthy Name burns away man's sin, as fire reduces fuel to ashes' (Bhagavata Purâna VI: ii, 18). The following verse of a *Purâna* says: 'The Name of *Hari* has such a power to remove sin that even the most sinful man cannot do enough sins!'

> *nâmnosti yâvati saktih*
> *pâpanirharane hareh*
> *tâvat-kartum na saknoti*
> *pâtakam pataki janah.*

Ayyaaval addresses the Great Lord Shiva in a hymn, *sivabhaktikalpalatika*, and says: 'Are you not the supremely compassionate one! O Lord, you are on the look-out for some pretext to save people; when words such as *'ahara'* (bring), *'parahara'* (take away), and *'samhara'* (destroy), containing the letters, *ha-ra*, are spoken by them, you think that they are uttering your name and you save them!'

Sri Shankara in his *Sahasra-nâma-bhasya*, cited, 'Of all *dharmas*, *japa*, indeed, is said to be the supreme *dharma*; with non-violence towards all beings, *japa-yajña* proceeds.' Lord Krishna also declared in Gita (Gita X:26). 'Of sacrifices, I am *japa-yajña*.'

When devotion is expressed through words, i.e. speech, it is called *stotra*. *Stotra* is of two kinds: (i) expatiating on, and praising the auspicious and glorious attributes of God; and (ii) uttering the Names of God which *manifest His attributes*. The latter is easier, but is, a in way, less efficacious. This is the path that is best suited to, and specially designed for, *kali-yuga*. (Vishnu Purana V:ii,17) teaches that what is gained through meditation in *Satya-yuga*, through performing sacrificial rites in *Treta-yuga*, and through ritual worship in *Dvapara-yuga*, is obtained by chanting the names of God in *Kali-yuga*. The four *yugas* need not necessarily mean successive ages in physical time. The *yugas* are in the minds of men. The spiritual ascent is from the *Kali* to *Satya yuga*, from the least evolved state of consciousness to the near-perfect state after which the mind itself will cease to be, and there will be only the non-dual experience. Since the least evolved state is characterised by the impurities imported by passions, etc., what can serve to elevate the vast majority of people who are in that state. That state is the Divine Name. In Brhamardiya Purana it is stated: 'The name of *Hari*, the name, verily the Name is my life; in *Kali-yuga* there is no other means, no other, indeed no other' (Brhamardiya Purana I:xli, 15).

harer-nâmaiva nâmaiva
nâmaiva mama jivanam
kalau nâstyeva nâstyeva
nâstyeva gatir-anyathâ

Of the Tantrika technique of worship, the central principle is the gradual susbstitution of subtler for grosser modes of devotion. The grades are indicated in the following verse:

prathamâ pratimâ-puja
japastotrâni madhyamâ
uttamâ mânasi puja
soh'am pujottamottamâ

'The first stage is image worship; the next consists of *japa* and prayer; still higher is mental worship; the highest is of the form 'I am He'.' It will thus be seen that the repetition of the divine names and sacred formulas occupies a crucial place in the scheme of spiritual disciplines.

In the *upâya* state the 'name' has four stages: *sthulâmsa*, *sukshâmsa*, *bijâmsa*, and *turia*. The first connotes annihilation of sins, the second freeing from *karma* produced by good deeds, the third brings about four kinds of liberation (*sâlokya*, *sâmipya*, *sârupya*, and *sâyujya*), and the fourth is identical with union with Brahman.

Practice of Name

According to *Upanishad-brahmayogin* everybody is qualified to practice the Name; there is no restriction on *varna* or *âsrama*. 'Name is the universal redeemer from sin.' *Nâmârta-rasâyana* offers six reasons for showing that the utterance of the Divine Name is superior to the other discipline taught in the scriptures. In the first place, the repetition of the *Nâma*, which is open to all, irrespective of caste, stage in life and sex, involves no injury to any living being. Secondly, it does not stand in need of any ancillary aid. Thirdly, in producing its result, it does not require the intercession of a third person. Fourth, its practice is not conditioned by the time factor; *nâma-japa* can be performed at any time. Fifth, there are no restrictions in regard to place. And sixth, there are no ritualistic regulations for practicing the repetition of the Divine Name. Although there are extraneous restrictions in regard to the practice of *nâma-sâdhana*, the *sâdhaka*, however, should not be guilty of certain offences, which are offences against the Name itself (*nâma-aparâdha*). As many as ten of them are listed as follows: (i) Insulting those who are good, and speaking ill of others, is contrary to the practice of *nâma-japa*. (ii) The devotee should not make any distinction between Shiva and Vishnu, in respect of either their attributes of their name. (iii) Disrespect shown to the preceptor is also a grave offence. (iv) So also, devision of the *Vedas* and other sacred literatures. (v) The Divine Name should be regarded always as the supreme truth; it should not be looked upon as *arthavâda*, mere eulogy. (vi) It is true that the repetition of the Name will remove all sins; but, on that account, one should not use the Name as cloak for the commission of sins. (vii) The cultivation of virtues such as non-injury, truth, non-stealing, etc., should not be neglected. (viii) Observance of religious vows, etc., should not be given up nonchalantly, imagining that the Name will do. (ix) Those who are devoid of faith should not be initiated into the practice of *nâma-japa*. (x) He who believes in the greatness of the Name should not behave in a way which is devoid of love; he should not be governed by the conceits of 'I' and 'mine'.

Alwars and other saints have expressed the sentiment that they would chant His names and glory while they were in good health. We do not know how our minds would function when the end approaches. It can be understood how important it is for ordinary people who have not attained control over their minds to remember and pray to God in daily life.

Chapter 15

Om or Aum

The chant *AUM* (commonly known as *OM*) has an extraordinary effect on human beings. Only by chanting it ourselves can we understand why so many people throughout the ages have found harmony, peace and bliss in this simple, but deeply philosophical sound.

Aum does not belong to one language or culture. All religions seem to know it. Some pronounce it as Amen, or Omen or Amen, or just Om or hum or omniscient, omnipresent, etc. *Aum* is not a word but rather an intonation which, like music, transcends the barriers of age, race, culture and even species. *Aum* is chanted in meditation, and before and after all the prayers and teaching. It is the sound symbol for the Absolute and Infinite Truth, known to the Hindu as Brahman. Brahman is not knowable by any of our human faculties. It cannot be grasped intellectually, emotionally or physically. So we need a symbol—an idol—to help bring us to realization of the Unknowable.

Sound symbols are the most subtle idols, those closest to the spiritual realm, because only one of the five senses can perceive them—the ear. At the other extreme are the stone idols (*murti*) which can be perceived by all five sense organs and are therefore the grossest of the idols. For this reason, verbal teaching, chanting and music have always played a predominant role in Vedic philosophy.

Om is the supreme name of God. The word *Om* has the power of expressing various ideas and qualities. *Om* represents the *saguna* (anthropomorphic conception) as well as *nirguna* (formless or shapeless) reality. There is the *absolute reality*, which is nameless, formless, and attributeless, but that alone manifests itself as the cause of this entire world, which in Vedic language is called as *Saguna Brahman*. The absolute Reality is called *nirguna Brahman*. *Om* represents both these aspects and that is why it is called *Pranava*, to mean that it pervades life and runs through *prâna* or breath. *Pra* means 'remarkable,' and *nava* means 'novel or new.' With the help of *Pranava* one can praise or meditate on the deity of one's own choice, either the manifested aspect of reality which is *Saguna*, or on the absolute reality which is *nirguna*.

The word Om or *Aum* which is in itself a *Mantra,* and is otherwise known as *pranava,* is invariably prefixed while chanting any other *mantra,* as it is considered that without it no *mantra* has its power in full.

When we meditate, our mind should chant *Aum.* The momentary silence between each chant symbolizes Brahman. Mind moves between the opposites of sound and silence until, at last, it ceases the sound. In the silence, the single thought—*Aum*—is extinguished; there is no thought. Mind and intellect are transcended as the individual self merges with the Infinite Self in the sacred moment of realization. When we chant *Om,* it represents the entire manifested world. When one chant is over, what remains is silence. That silence represents the *nirguna,* the attributeless. From the silence, which is produced, and again when the sound is gone what remains is silence. In the background of silence, sound is heard, therefore silence is there all the time, when we speak and when we don't speak. That is why *Om* represents both *nirguna* and *Saguna.*

In making a sound, we use the larynx and the palate as a sound-board. The preeminent *Om* is the most natural and articulate sound from which all other sounds are manifested. *Om* (Aum) is the basis of all sounds. In order to say A (ah), we have to open our mouth without touching any part of the tongue or palate. Thus, 'A' is also the first letter of the alphabet of all languages. Thus 'A' is the root of all sound and signifies the beginning of or the creation of the Universe.

When saying 'U' (oo) the mouth is still kept open, the lips are curved and the tongue rolls from the very root to the end of the sounding board of the mouth. This signifies the quality of maintaining, preserving and sustaining.

'M' is pronounced with the lips fully closed and m m m m (vibrating sound). 'M' represents the last sound in the series. Thus, *Om* represents the whole phenomenon of the sound-production. As such, it must be the natural symbol, the metric of all the various sounds. It denotes the whole range and possibility of all the words that can be uttered.

Saying or calling out of a particular name or object produces a vibration in us. Food, wine, fruit, and tea, these are the names of certain objects, and we know that when we utter these names, different ideas occur in our mind and we have different sensations in our body. Snake, war, ugliness, flowers or earthquake produce a different sensation in our system. They are not merely words, they are vibrations that are conveyed to our system by a particular word or phrase; and *Om* is also a vibration, not merely a word or a sound. *Om* is a vibration, a universal vibration with which creation commenced, as they say. When we chant *Om,* we try to create within ourselves a sympathetic vibration, a vibration that has a sympathy with the cosmic vibration, so that, for the time being, we are in tune with the cosmos. We flow with the current of the cosmos when we recite *Om,* and it produces a harmonious vibration in our body and psychological system. Instead of thinking independently as individuals, we start thinking universally as God. Instead of thinking in relation to objects segregated from one another, we think in terms of nothing at all. There is thought thinking itself, as it were. Can you imagine the thought thinking itself? This is God's thought. When a thought thinks of an object, it is an individual's thought. When the thought thinks only of itself, it is God's thought. We do not think at that time; it is God who thinks through this mind of ours. We, as persons, cease to be for the time being. We exist as the thing-in-itself. God, who exists by His own stature, mind, and status does not exist as an individual in terms of other objects. We always exist in relation to something else. God exists with relation to no one else. We try by this means of the recitation of *Om* to flow into God's Being like rivers trying to flow into the ocean. By the inclination of the vibration of Om, we enter the universal form of God. When we recite *Om* properly, we enter into a meditative mood. We are not merely reciting a sound or a word or a phrase, we are creating a vibration. This vibration melts all other particular vibrations, puts an end to all desire, extinguishes all cravings, and creates a desire for the Universal. As fire burns up straw, this desire for the Universal burns up all other desires.

The word *Aum* expresses the three great qualities of God. On this basis God is known to us by three other names. 'A': Brahma (Creator), 'U': Vishnu (Preserver) and 'M': Shiva (Destroyer). When we pronounce the word *AUM*, the vocal organs express these qualities of God.

Thus we know that God is the creator, preserver and destroyer of this universe. This natural Law of God has been in practice for an infinite period of time and will continue to be for an infinite period of time.

According to the Mandukya *Upanishad*, 'A' stands for waking state (*jagrata*), 'U' for the dream state (*swapna*), and 'M' for the sound-sleep state (*sushupti*). Note further that when the word *Om* is uttered, it does not end abruptly, who but rather the sound rolls over a little longer as **MMMM......**(following a ringing pattern), before zeroing down, at which this portion is considered as the fourth part of the word, and it represents the state known as *tureeya* (transcendental). The fourth state is the pure consciousness of unmanifested Brahman. In other words, *Om* signifies the *totality* consisting of both the manifested and unmanifested, just as the sound A-U-M is pervaded by silence. Out of silence come these tones, within silence they exist, and into silence they merge. Similarly, the waking-dreaming-deep sleep state arises out of the unmanifested Brahman, and exists within It and merge back into It.

The word '*Aum*' also has two special meanings—*Omnipresent* and *Protector*. God is present in every particle of the atom and there is not a place imaginable where His presence is not to be felt. Being omnipresent, He is protecting this universe through His power, knowledge and His laws. God is also the protector of His devotees.

'Let a man worship the syllable *Om*' (Chandogya *Upanishad*). It may seem impossible at first sight to elicit any definite meaning from this word and from much that follows after. Meditation on the syllable *Om* consists of a long-continued repetition of that syllable with a view to dissolve the thoughts away from all other subjects, and thus concentrating them on to some higher object of thought of which that syllable was made to be the symbol. This is concentration of thought, *ekagrata* or one-pointedness, according to Hindus. Our minds are like kaleidoscopes of thoughts in constant motion; and to shut our mental eyes from everything else, while dwelling on one thought only, has become to most of the westerners almost as impossible, just as it is comprehend the sound of one musical note without harmonics. Hindus adopt all kinds of contrivances in order to assist them in distracting away their thoughts from all disturbing impressions and to fix them on one subject only. Repetition of *Om* is indeed of great help in making the mind one-pointed.

By repetition, the sum total of the impressions of *Om* stays in mind. They may become more and more latent, and they remain there until they get the right stimulus to come out. We know that atomic vibration never ceases. Each atom performs the same function as the large molecules do. So even when the vibrations of the *chitta* (mind) subside, its atomic vibrations sustain; and when they get the impulse, they come out again. It is the greatest stimulus that can be given to the spiritual *samskaras*. The repetition of *Om*, and to ponder meaning are the same as keeping good company with your mind, a power of association which builds a ship to cross this ocean of life. By repeating *Om* and understanding its meaning, the light will come to you and Self will become manifested. The first effect of the repetition and contemplation of *Om* is that the introspective power will manifest itself more and more; all the mental and physical obstacles will begin to vanish. When by means of repeating the syllable *Om*, people can arrive at a certain degree of mental tranquillity; the question arose what was meant by this *Om*, and to this question various answers were given from above. And thus the mind has to be led up to higher and higher objects.

Om is the beginning of the Veda, or as we have to deal with an *Upanishad* or the beginning of the Sama-veda, so that he who meditates on *Om*, may be meditating on the whole of the Sama-veda; but that is not enough. *Om* is said to be the essence of the Sama-veda, which, being almost entirely taken from the Rig-Veda, may in itself be called the essence of the Rig-Veda, and more. The Rig-Veda stands for all speech, the Sama-veda for all breadth of life, so that *Om* may be conceived again as the symbol of all speech and all life. 'As all leaves are held together by a stalk, so is all speech held together by *Om* ,verily Om is all this. Verily, *Om* is all this'. (Chandogya *Upanishad* II.23.3). *Om* thus becomes the name, not only of all our physical and mental powers, but also of the living principle, especially the *Prana*, or the spirit. This is explained by the parable in the second chapter of Chandogya, while in the third chapter, the spirit within us is identified with the spirit in the Sun. He who meditates on *Om*, meditates on the spirit in man as identical with the spirit in nature, or in the Sun; and thus the lesson that is meant to be taught in the beginning of the Chandogya-*Upanishad* is really this, that none of the *Vedas* with their sacrifices and ceremonies could ever secure the salvation of the worshiper. In other words, sacred works, performed according to the rules of the *Vedas*, are of no avail in the end. But that meditation on *Om* alone can procure true salvation, or true immortality. Thus the pupil is led on step by step to what is the highest object of the *Upanishads*, viz. the recognition of the self in man as identical with the Highest Self or Brahman. The lessons which are to lead up to that highest conception of the universe, both subjective and objective, are no doubt mixed up with much that is superstitious and absurd; still the sight of the main object is never lost. Thus, when we come to the 8th chapter of the Chandogya *Upanishad*, the discussion, though it begins with *Om* or the *Udgitha, and* ends with the question of the origin of the world; and though the final answer, that *Om* means *ether (akasa)*, and ether is the origin of all things, may still sound to us more physical than metaphysical, still the description given by it than the physical e ther, and that ether is in fact one of the earlier and less perfect names of the *Infinite,* of *Brahman,* the universal *Self.* The *Upanishad* itself says: 'The *Brahman* is the same as the *ether* which is around us; and the Ether which is around us is the same as the Ether which is within us. And the Ether which is within us is the ether within the heart. That ether in the heart is omnipresent and unchanging. He who knows this obtains omnipresence and unchangeable happiness' (Chandogya Upanishad III.12, 7-9).

Om is spirit. Everything is but *Om. Om* permits, *Om* gives the signal. *Om* begins the ceremony. All chants begin with *Om.* All hymns begin with *Om.* The priest begins with *Om.* His commands are in the name of *Om.* The sacrificer offers the oblation with *Om.* The teacher begins with *Om.* The pupil begins with Om. The pupil murmuring *Om* seeks for Spirit. In the end he finds Spirit.

There are three ways of experiencing *OM* ! One is to be constantly aware of ether; the other way is to be constantly aware of oneself, and the third, the easiest way is to be happy and peaceful in all conditions of life.

Our sages considered the *Om* as a *mantra* so important that it has formed the subject for elaboration in several scriptural texts, for example:

'Worship ye *OM*, the eternal Syllable, *OM* is Udgitha'.
'The essence of all beings is earth,
The essence of earth is water,
The essence of water are the plants,
The essence of the plants is man,
The essence of man is speech,
The essence of speech is the *Rig-Veda,*

The essence of *Rig-Veda* is the *Sama-veda*,
The essence of *sama-veda* is the Udgitha (*OM*),
That *OM* is the best of all essences,
The highest, Deserving the highest place.'

(Chandogya Upanishad I:1: 1-3)

Yama (the king of Death) speaks to Nachiketas: 'The goal that all the *Vedas* glorify and which austerities declare, for the desire of which men practices holy living, of that will I tell thee in brief compass. *OM* is that goal. For this syllable is Brahman, this syllable is the Most High; If one knows, this syllable, whatsoever one shall desire it is his. This support is the best, this support is the highest, knowing this support one grows great in the world of the Brahman' (Kathâ Upanishad I:2: 15-17).

Shaibya Satyakama asked Rishi Pippalada: 'Lord, he among men that meditate unto death on *OM* the syllable, which of the world does he conquer by its puissance?' Pippalada answered: 'This imperishable word, *Om*, is the Higher Brahman and also the Lower. Therefore the wise man by making his home in the word, wins to one of these. If he meditate on the one syllable *OM*, by that enlightenment, he attains swiftly in the material universe, and the hymns of the Rig-Veda escort him to the world of men. There endowed with askesis and faith and holiness he experiences majesty' (Prasna Upanishad V: 1-3).

'*OM* is this imperishable word, *OM* is the Universe, and this is the exposition of *OM*. The past, the present and the future, all that was, all that is, all that will be, is *OM*. Likewise, all else that may exist beyond the bounds of Time that too is *OM*' (Mundukya Upanishad I:1).

'*OM* is the bow and the soul is the arrow, and that, even the Brahman, is spoken of as the target. That must be pierced with an unfaltering aim; one must be absorbed into that as an arrow is lost in its target' (Mundaka Upanishad 2:II: 4).

'By making the body the lower piece of wood and *Om* the upper piece, and by the continuous practice of meditation as the process of rubbing, one should see the luminous Self hidden like the fire in the wood.' (Shvetashvatara *Upanishad* I: 14).

'Uttering the one syllable Brahman '*Om*' thinking of Me, he who thus leaves his body attains the Supreme State' (Bhagavad Gita VIII: 13).

Krishna said: 'I am the father of the Universe and its mother; I am its nourisher and its grandfather; I am the knowable and the pure; I am *OM*; I am the sacred scriptures' (Bhagavad Gita IX: 17).

'Soak the mind with the roar of *OM*; identify the mind with the sound of *OM*; *OM* is Brahman, the ever fearless. He who is always unified with *OM* shall know no fear whatever' (Mandukya Karika, I:25).

'*OM* is verily the beginning, the middle, and the end of all. Knowing *Om* as such, verily one attains immediately to that Supreme Reality' (Mandukya Karika, I:27).

'Know *OM* to be *Isvara*, the Lord, ever present in the minds of all. The man of discrimination realizing *OM* as all-pervading and does not ever grieve' (Mandukya Karika, I:28).

'One who has known *OM*, which is soundless and of infinite sounds and which is very peaceful because of negation of all duality in it, is the true sage; none other' (Mandukya Karika, I:29).

'Verily, when one learns the RK, one sounds out *OM*. It is the same with *Saman*, (it is) the same with *Yajus*. This sound is that syllable, the immortal, the fearless. Having entered this, the gods become immortal, fearless.' 'He, who knowing it thus, praises this syllable, takes refuge in this syllable, in the immortal, fearless sound, and having entered it, he becomes immortal, even as the gods become immortal' (Chandogya Upanishad I.4: 4-5).

'But when he (soul) thus depart from this body, then he goes upwards by these very rays or he goes up with the thought of OM. As his mind is failing, he goes to the sun. That, verily, is the gateway of the world, an entering in for the knowers a shutting out for the non-knowers' (Chandogyaopanisad VIII: 6. 5).

Bibliography

Brown, Kerry (ed), *The Essential Teaching of Hinduism*, Rider Book Publication, London. 1988.

Parthasarathy, A., *The Vedanta Treatise*, Vedanta Life Institute, Malabar Hill, Bombay, 1984.

Parthasarathy, A., *The Symbolism of Hindu Gods and Rituals*, Vedanta Life Institute, Bombay, 1983.

OM, Symbol of Truth, Mananam Publication Series, Vol. XI. Number 4, 1988.

Chapter 16

The Gayatri Mantra

Gâyatri is prayer and a *mantra* combined, and is therefore, very powerful. It is a prayer in which the worshiper prays for the light of *jnâna* or saving knowledge—not for himself alone but for all. And it is also a *mantra* which embodies the deity that is invoked. The deity in this case is *Savitri*, the Mystical Sun, the light of all lights, who symbolizes the highest *Brahman*. In the *Gitâ*, the Lord says, the light that pervades the Sun and the moon is all my light. A pure *mantra* depends for its effectiveness upon the *mantra sakti* or power inherent in the sound. *Gâyatri mantra* has also in it the tremendous power of prayer in it as indicated by the definition '*Gâyantam trâyate iti Gâyatri*', i.e. that which saves the chanter. When the power of a *mantra* is combined with the power of prayer we have a far more effective instrument for the unfolding of our spirituality.

Gâyatri mantrâ is the most sacred hymn of the Vedas. *Gâyatri mantra* occupies a place of paramount importance among psalms, hymns and devotional songs. From the ancient times, *Gâyatri mantra* has been recited in our prayers. It is one of the few *mantras* that is routinely chanted even today. In the Mahâbhârata, Bhisma Pitâmaha advised Yudhisthira that the *Gâyatri mantra* can be recited at any time and at any place, whether we are resting, walking or working. Peace of mind can be realized by anyone who chants this *mantra* with the utmost reverence. A true devotee suffers no anguish. Among all creatures of the world, man has been endowed with the highest intellect. It is with this intellect that man has gained supremacy over the lower animals and succeeded in bringing under control the forces of nature. Lord Krishna said: '(Five) senses are superior to the physical body; superior to the senses is mind; superior to the mind is the intellect (*Buddhi*); superior than intellect is He (God)' (*Bhagavad Gitâ* III. 42). So it is essential that this intellect should be pure and of high quality. Intellect (*buddhi*) is the instrument for the perception of all objects like a lamp placed in front amid darkness. It has been said, 'It is through the mind that one sees, and that one hears. Indeed, everything is perceived on being invested with the light of *Buddhi* like an object in the dark illuminated by a lamp placed in front. The other organs are but the channels of *Buddhi* (Shankara: Commentary on Brhadaranyaka

Upanishad IV: 3,7). In *Gâyatri mantra*, we pray for such an intellect. *Gâyatri mantra* is not a means to attain wealth, strength, power and supremacy, nor is it used as a weapon with which we hope to destroy our enemies or keep our sorrow away. *Gâyatri mantra* is a means to attain pure and refined intellect. We should always ask God to bestow us with such an intellect. Wisdom thus attained exhorts us to tread the path of righteousness and to perform noble deeds. Thus, we are assured of true happiness and godly bliss.

The word *gâyatri* is derived from the root *'gai'* which means 'to create sound'. It, therefore, became gradually associated with the goddess of speech, *vâk*. The author, Taimini argues as follows: 'The only true and effective way of knowing the Vedas is through *Gâyatri* which brings about a progressive unfoldment of our consciousness and eventually enables us to contact the Universal Mind, in which all knowledge of the *Vedass* are contained.'

Gâyatri mantra is a prosody consisting of three stanzas, namely: *Tat Savitur Varenyam*: Glorification of God; *Bhargo Devasya Dhimahi*: Communion with God; and *Dhiyo Yo Nah Prachodayat*: Entreaty to God. There are twenty-four syllables in the *Gâyatri Mantrâ*, and each one of them is in the form of power (*shakti*). Each syllable of the *mantrâ* of Gâyatri is a veritable treasure chest of endless knowledge.

Gâyatri mantra is known by the following three different names: (1) *Gâyatri mantra*, (2) *Guru mantra* and (3) *Sâvitri mantra*. The first two *Gâyatra mantra* by which boys are initiated during *Upanayan* (sacred thread ceremony) is called *Tripâda* (three legged) *Gâyatri*. *It has* essence of three *Vedas*, viz., Rig, Yajur and Sâma *Vedas*. The Athurva Veda has its own Gâyatri.

Guru mantrâ: Before the *guru* (teacher) gives to his pupils the knowledge of the *Vedas*, he makes them understand the significance of the *Gâyatri mantra*. *Sâvitri mantra*: In this *mantra* God is glorified by the use of the word *Savitâ* because He is the Creator and the life-spring of this universe. Hence, this *mantra* is also called *Sâvitri mantra*. The prayer is addressed to the Sun, the source of all light and energy in our universe. The *Savitri* is the aspect of the Sun before sunrise. He is golden all over. He establishes people in their respective places. He gives life and energy and guides people in the right path. The nourishing and life-supporting aspect of the Sun is personified and praised as *pusan*. He is exceedingly beautiful. He destroys the evil ones with the discus he wears. He looks upon all with an equal eye. He is extremely generous and ever ready to protect. *Gâyatri mantra* is dedicated to this *Sâvitri*. The *Sâvitri* stands not only for the sun of our solar system, but also for the spiritual Sun, the Supreme Brahman, the ultimate cause of this universe. Since the sun shines on all beings this prayer has a special and universal appeal as being the one upon which mediation reveals the cosmic consciousness. The *mantra* chanted invokes *Savitâ* or the spiritual Sun. It has got limitless power which is exhorted by *upâsanâ* and *Japa* or repetition. The divine Mother appears at dawn in the form of *Gâyatri* as a young girl red in colour, riding the swan. At midday, she appears white in colour, youthful and blossomed. She is *Sâvitâ* at this juncture. At twilight in the evening she appears as *Saraswati,* with all auspicious attributes, dark in colour, bedecked with all jewels. She is maiden at dawn, middle-aged at midday and natural in the evening. *Gâyatri, Sâvitri, Saraswati* correspond to the Sunrise, Noon and Sunset respectfully. Each gives the boon she is expected to give, but Gâyatri is the whole form or *samista* and gives the very *'Isvara'* to the worshipper. She is worshipped through the *mantra* and leads to totality of knowledge. Realization of the true nature of the self can be attained by identifying oneself with *Gâyatri, Savitâ and Saraswati.* This is the basis of the *Sandhayâ vandanams* which are done during the three *sandhyas,* i.e. dawn, noon, and sunset. When repeated 108 times during these *sandhyâs,* it confers brilliance and, if done with sincerity 1000 times for forty days, confers illumination upon the devotees. The aspirants who utter the *Gâyatri mantra* with devotion are sure to become seers by controlling their senses, and by steadying their minds and concentrating on *Prambrahman* or God, resident in the spiritual orb of the Sun, indistinct and inseparable from the Devi or power.

It is mentioned in the Mahanârâyana *Upanishad,* 'I invoke Thee as *Gâyatri* (Giver of Illumination); I invoke Thee as *Sâvitri* (Giver of Life); I invoke Thee as *Sarasvati* (Giver of Knowledge and Wisdom)' (Mahanârâyana Upanishad ;Sec. XXXV.I).

This is to be realized through the *Gâyatri Japa* that the *Japa* may culminate in *yoga,* the worshipper or *upâsaka* has to go through the following three stages: First, there should be repetition being conscious of the sounds that form the *mantra.* Second, the meaning of every word of the *mantra* must be understood very well. Third, the whole meaning of the *mantra* leaving behind the words in the background must be grasped firmly.

We all have the right to use the prayer that helps us obtain wisdom and thereby receive true happiness. This right to pray should not be limited to a few nor should it be the treasured property of a chosen few, but available to all who wish to experience God.

The Gâyatri mantra
OM BHÜR BHUVAH SVAH,
TAT SAVITUR VARENYAM,
BHARGO DEVASYA DHIMAHI,
DHIYO YO NAH PRACHODAYAT.
(Rig *Vedas* III. 62. 10)

'We meditate on the adorable glory of God, who is the primordial cause, who is the remover of ignorance, May He enlighten our intellect.'

The full Gâyatri mantra has got in fact a fourth line also, *'paro rajasac savad -
Om'-'* He who is transcending the effulgence in this.' The fourth line is
mentioned in Chandogya, Brihadaranyaka and Brahma Sutra. This line has
always been preserved as very sacred and secret, and it is only given out to full-
time seekers or to self-dedicated *sanyasins*. This line is not so much for chanting
as for experiencing in the highest moments of intense meditation in *samâdhi*.

Om is the Supreme name of God. The word *Om* or *AUM* has the power of
expressing various ideas and qualities (see Chapter of AUM).

The first three words, *Bhur, Bhuvah, Svah,* express the nature of God. The
word *Bhur* indicates the existence of the eternal God. *Bhur* is also indicative of life
(*Prâna*). God is the life-giver and He sustains our life. God is absolute
consciousness. The word *Bhuvah* means remover of pains and sufferings. Pain
and suffering are merely expressions of our mind. That is why we are often
mentally grieved. *Svah* is symbolic of God's bliss. Except for God, every-one-else
feels pain, trouble, calamity and obstacles in life. The controller and director of
this universe is *svah*. *Svah* also denotes that God pervades the universe and thus
keeps the world under His supervision. *Bhur* also means earth, *Svah* the heaven,
and *Bhuvah*, the intermediary region of the sky. They stand for the three principal
planes of existence, for example, the gross, the subtle and casual. Thus the whole
universe has to be brought into image while chanting *Bhur, Bhuvah and Svah*
(Brhadâranayaka *Upanishad* V. 14. 1). He who knows this line of *Gâyatri* to be
such wins as three worlds extend. *Bhur, Bhuvah and Svah* are indicative of the
following set of words as an explanation: *prâna, apâna,* and *vyâna*; earth, sky, and
heaven; and true existence, consciousness, and bliss, respectively. The goal of
every Being is to Becoming and aim of every Becoming is to achieve bliss. *Bhur,
Bhuvah* and *Svah* is also called Being, Becoming, and Bliss. Thus, the trio finally
mingle with *Om* (Chândogya Upanishad II. 23).

Tat means that, and also represents the power of thought. *Tat* is that whom
we have thought of and whom we know. That God whom I know and whom I
remember is *Tat*.

The word *Savitur* is used for God, who has power to create this universe. He
also bestow refinement to His creation, which is called *Savitâ*. That is why the
Gâyatri mantra is also called the *Sâvitri mantra*.

Varenyam means one who is worthy of acceptance and who is transcendent.
It also means One who is eligible. We have elected Him to be our leader. Our
happiness and our sorrows are in His hands. As a sincere devotee we accept His
will. In whatever condition God keeps us we will be contended. We dedicate all
our actions and thoughts to God because our God is *Verenyam*.

Bhargo means glorious light. The power with which God destroys sins and
afflictions is called *Bhrago*. *Bhargo* is God's pure, faultless and sin-destroying
glory. God is the light of all lights. Thousands of suns appearing at the same time
cannot match His light. We are moving in a world of darkness. Vices have taken

control of our senses. Therefore, the correct path is not visible to us. When we establish *Bhargo*, the Glorious light in our hearts illuminate the luster of our soul. The impurities and the veil of darkness will be destroyed for ever. All actions, words and thoughts of the devotees will be free from sin.

The word *Deva* has many meanings. God who is to found everywhere and within everything is the only *Deva*. We remember the same *Deva* or Eternal God in the *Gâyatri mantra*. That is the *Saviture*, i.e. the Creator, the *Varenyam*, the most excellent and the *Bhargo*, the light of all lights. We remember that *Deva*. He can endow us with the divine power and He is our guide.

Dhimahi means to meditate, and to contemplate upon the glorious form of God. Our mind must only have the thoughts of God within. If we have chosen Him as being worthy of acceptance and if we have understood His creative power, then it should not be difficult for us to concentrate on Him.

Dhiyo means intellect. We have realized the divine power of God and have seated Him in our heart.

Yo means that God to whom we pray for good intellect, to whom we have adored as being worthy of acceptance, and who is free of all defects.

Nah means ours. We pray not only for ourselves but for every one of us. We do not live only for ourselves but we belong to each other. Therefore, *Nah* here includes all our fellowmen, and we pray for all.

Prachodayât means enlighten or direct. We ask God to direct our energies in the right direction and to enlighten our intellect.

O! Lord Supreme that exists for all time to come; may we meditate on you so that we might obtain the great glory of Lord *Savitâ* that enlightens our intellect! That Supreme Being that has created all the worlds including *Bhu*, *Bhuvâh*, *Svah* is none other than He, who is symbolized by *OM*, that *Paramâtamân*, who enlightens our intellect with glory that can dispel the darkness—the spiritual Sun (*Savita*) who is adorable—on Him we meditate. *Tat saviturvarenyam* implies surrender to the will of the Supreme. It refers to all regions—*Bhu*, *Bhuvâh* and *Svah*. *Bhargo devasya dhimahi* refers to the establishment of the Supreme in the heart. *Dhiyoyonah prachodayât* leaves the intellect completely under the guidance of the Supreme and the attainment enlightenment through intuition. That light which shines beyond heaven, beyond universe, beyond everything in the highest world, i.e. the world beyond which there is no higher, is the same light as the light within man. There are various translation of the *Gâyatri*. One translation is: 'May we meditate on the effulgent light (power) of Him who is worshipful and who has given birth to all the worlds. May He direct the rays of our intelligence towards the path of the good'. Another translation is by Colebrook and that is: 'Aum (*OM*), earth, sky, heaven. Let us meditate on the most excellent light and power of that generous sportive resplendent sun (praying that) it may guide our intellects'.

From the three *mâtras* of *Om or Aum* come the three feet of *Gâyatri*. And from its three 'feet' came the three *Vedas* and the three Vyâhrtis *Bhur—Bhuvah -Suvah*, representing the three cosmic world planes. From **A**, came out *'Tat Savitur Varenyam'* (That Adorable Splendor of That Savitr, the Originator of the Universe), which expanded itself into the *Rig Veda* and the Cosmic plane *Bhuh*; from **U**, *'Bhargo Devasya Dhimahi'* (May we meditate upon That splendour of the Divinity), which expanded itself into Yajur Veda and the plane of *Bhuvah*; and from **M**, *'Dhiyo Yo Nah Prachodayât'* (And may He enlighten our intellect), which expanded itself into the Sâma Veda , and the plane of *Svah*. The first para is (*stuti-para*) devoted to devotion, the second para is (*Kriyâ-para*) devoted to work, and the third para is (*jnâna-para*) devoted to knowledge. So by the meditation upon the different *mâtras* different ends are attained according to the significance of the *mâtras*.

Eating, sleeping, mating, fear and life are common to man and animals. Man is different from the animals in the intellect only. Human beings are superior to other creatures by virtue of the fact that they possess intelligence. With *Gayatri mantra*, we ask God to enlighten our intellect, grant us the power of discrimination to distinguish right from wrong, truth from falsehood, and good from bad. Good intellect alone is sufficient for us to chart our destiny. In the *Upanishads*, the intellect has been called the charioteer of the soul, senses are horses and the body is chariot. Good intellect can control the senses and take the body to the right path. Without intellect, a man may develop blind faith and this will lead to conceit and egoism. Man is ignorant and his knowledge is limited. His bad intellect can deceive him. If our intellect is pure then we would entertain nobler thoughts to perform virtuous acts. The mind is the instrument of acquiring knowledge (*jnâna*), through the sense organs; intellect assimilates knowledge. Assimilation, understanding and discrimination are the properties of intellect.

Gâyatri mantra may be described as containing the essence of *Jnana-yoga*, *Bhakti-yoga*, and *Karma-yoga*. It is the essence of *Jnâna-yoga*, because we are no longer subject to the primal *ajnâna* of preferring our own transitory desires to the purpose of the Supreme spirit. It is the essence of *Bhakti-yoga* because we willingly surrender ourselves to the Sovereign Ruler of the universe. And it is the essence of *Karma-yoga* because we are able to be prompted in all our activities not by self-will, but by the will of God. *Gâyatri mantra* thus contains in a nutshell the highest religious philosophy of the Hindu.

This remarkable prayer first appeared in the (Rig Veda III. 62 - 10) and latter in the other *Vedas*, *Upanishads* and the Tantras. This can be considered as the epitome of the *Vedas*. Many Rishis have referred to the efficacy of this prayer in very high terms. The verse of the *Gâyatri*, with the words, *Bhur, Bhuvah* and *Svaha* occurs in the (Yajur Veda XXXVI. 3). The main *Mantrâ* appears in several other places, such as the (Sâma Veda S.N. 1462), and the (Yajur Veda III. 35; XXii. 9;

XXX.2). The *Gâyatri* had earlier been revealed to Vashistha, according to some authorities. The *rishi* responsible in all of the above cases, except the last one, is Vishwâmitra, while Nârâyana is the *rishi* of the Yajur veda *mantrâ*; to whom God reveals the vedic *mantras* are known as *rishis*. It was, however, Vishwâmitra, who popularized the *Gâyatri*. Its exaltation is discussed in the (Chândogyopanishad III. 12. 1-8; III. 16.1), and the ritualistic and meditational application of *Gâyatri* is mentioned in (Brihâdâranayaka Upanishad V. 14. 1-8; VI 3. 6).

The significance of *Gâyatri* has been given in the Brhadâranayaka *Upanishad* (Brhadâranayaka Upanishad V. 14. 1-6) as follows: 'There are four feet of *Gayatri*. Each of the three feet is composed of eight syllables. Thus, *Gâyatri* is composed of twenty four syllables. One foot is earth, sky and heaven; another foot is the three *Vedas*, Rig-Veda, Yajur-Veda, and Sâma-Veda; and the third foot is life-breath composed of *prâna* (the in-breath), *apâna* (the out-breath) and the *vyâna* (the diffused-breath). And the fourth foot is bright and shining high above the skies, the *turiya*, a stage where the individual self unites with the Universal Self. If some one thus knows the first foot of *Gâyatri*, he receives the three worlds of wealth; he who thus knows the second foot of it, receives as much as the three fold knowledge of the *Vedas*; he who thus knows the third foot of it, receives as much as there is breathing here; and he who thus knows the fourth foot of it, receives *turiya*, and thus shines himself also with happiness and glory.' The fourth foot cannot be compared to any material objects.

With the following words, the salutation was given to *Gâyatri* in the *Brhadâranayaka Upanishad* (V. 16. 7): 'O *Gâyatri*! the three worlds is your one foot, the three Vedic knowledge is your second foot, the three life-breath is your third foot, and the bright above the dark sky, *turiya*, is your fourth foot, or you are footless for you do not go about. We pronounce salutation to your fourth foot. Indeed my cherished wish is to attain your fourth foot, the '*turiya*.' Thus, the *Gâyatri* should be meditated upon in its entire form in order to receive the full benefit of its blessings.

Once King Janak asked Budil Asvatarâsvi: 'How is it that you who spoke of yourself as the knower of *Gâyatri*, have become an elephant that carries me? He answered: 'Because, Your Majesty, I did not know its mouth. Its mouth is compared to a fire which consumes a large quantity of fuel; in the same way *Gâyatri* also consumes all evil and makes a man pure, clean, and free from decay and death' (Brhadâranayaka Upanishad V. 16. 8).

The importance of the *Gâyatri mantra* has been stated in the *Chândogya Upanishad* (III. 12. 1-8) as follows: 'The *Gâyatri* is like the earth, for everything that exists here rests on the earth. This earth is; is which the body is in man, for on it these vital breaths are established. What the body is in man, is what the heart is within man, for on it these vital breaths are established. *Brahman*, the Supreme God, is under the disguise of the *Gâyatri*. Brahman is the same as the ether which is around us, within us, ether in the heart as *Brahman* is omnipresent and unchanging. He who thus knows the *Gâyatri* obtains omnipresent and unchanging happiness.'

The *Gâyatri* has two forms, one *Tripâda Gâyatri* of 24 letters. Every disciple is initiated into this *mantra* at the time of the *Upanâyana* ceremony. Its objectives are four *Purusâthâs, viz., dharma, artha, kâma* and *moksha*. The second form which is esoteric, and the more subtle of the two is to be initiated and practiced as the disciple becomes more advanced and competent in his discipline. The second form is the *Mantra Tripada Gâyatri* with the addition at the end of the letters '*Paro rajasi sâvadam*'. This is called the *Caturthapâda* or *Turiyapâda* of the *Gâyatri mantra*.

The full meaning of this *Gâyatri mantra* is as follows: 'Let us meditate or become one with that great effulgence, who has no attributes of any kind except of reality, consciousness and bliss (*satchitânanda*), who is radiating from the heart of the Sun, and is that power that goads our minds which are conditioned by various limitations, who is extolled by Vedâs and other sacred texts as being competent to free us from the sins and limitations and who is the cause of the triad, birth, preservation and destruction of the universe and is our blissful refuge. Let She, that mother who is beyond all the attributes, save us.

One will comprehend the loftiness of the concept contemplated by the *Gâyatri mantra* if one only looks into the meaning of the *slokâs* of the *Gâyatri Avâhana* in the Sandhyyâvandanâ. An English rendering of the same is given as follows: ' The single letter '*Om*' represents the ultimate reality. Its meter (*chandas*) is the *Gâyatri*. It is the personification of the ultimate itself. Its *sâdhanâ* is only for the union of the individual self with the ultimate. Let the *Gâyatri*, indestructible, the giver of blessings, come and reveal to me the ultimate. *Sâvitri* the power inherent in the Sun is the deity. Agni (fire) is her face, Vishnu the preserver is Her heart. Rudra the destroyer is Her coiffure. Prithvi, the earth is her medium of creation. She is alive with the five vital breaths, *viz., prânâ, apâna, vyâna, udâna* and *samâna*. She is white in colour, i.e. eternal *Tatvâs*, has three feet, viz., three *Vedas*, and having six faces, i.e. in the six cardinal sides. Her purpose is to take us to the ultimate.'

Bibliography

Mukhyânanda, Swami, *Om Gâyatri and Sandhyâ*, Sri Ramakrishna Math, Madras, 1989.

Chapter 17

Hinduism and Christianity

Christianity with its distinctive characteristics cannot be traced either to its Jewish source or to its Greeco-Roman contact, but there are striking resemblance between Buddhism and Chritianity. Hinduism is not a missionary religion like Islam, Buddhism, or Christianity, though its traveled over a great part of Europe and over all of Asia from ancient times. India has commercial relationship with nearly all of the civilized world. Great philosophers like Pythagorean, Plato, Philo and Plotinus were all strongly influenced by Hindu ideas (Sttfield, H.E. M., Mysticism and Catholicism, 1925). Christianity began to spread at the time when this contact was closest. We know that Indian ascetics occasionally visited the west, and that there was a colony of Indian merchants at Alexandria. The possibility of India influence on Neo-Platonism and early Christianity cannot be rules (Garratt, T., Ed: Legacy of India, Oxford, 1937). Radhakrishnan says: 'Jesus' religious environment was considerably helped by Indian influences. His teaching of the Kingdom of God, life eternal, ascetic emphasis, and future life He breaks away from the Jewish tradition and approximates Hindu and Buddhist thought' (Radhakrishnan, S., Eastern Relions and western thought, pp, 176. Oxford, 1940).

Similarities in the titles 'Krishna' and 'Christ' and in the tales of the miraculous birth and early life of Krishna and Christ led some analyzing mind to propose that they were indeed one and the same person. This idea can be wholly rejected, based on even scanty historical evidence in the countries of their origin. Nevertheless, some similiarities are there. Both were divinely conceived, and their births and God-ordained missions foretold. Christ was born in a lowly manger; Krishna, was born in a prison (where his parents, Vasudeva and Devaki, were held captive by Devaki's wicked brother, Kansa, who had usurped the throne of his father). Both Christ and Krishna were successfully spirited away to safety from a death decree to all male infants meant to seek out and destroy them at birth. Christ was referred to as the good shepherd; Krishna in his early years was a cowherd. Christ was tempted and threatened by Satan; the evil force pursued Krishna in demonic forms seeking unsuccessfully to slay him. Both Lord

Krishna and Jesus Christ were born in a very disturbed situation in the country at the time and both died with a sharp spear and arrow. Their teachings were the same-love and peace to the humanity.

'Christ' and 'Krishna' are having the same spiritual connotation: *Jesus* the Christ and *Yadav* the Krishna. These titles identify the state of consciousness manifested by these two illuminated beings, their incarnate oneness with the consciousness of God omnipresent in creation. The Universal Christ Consciousness or Universal Krishna Consciousness, is 'the only begotten son' or sole undistorted reflection of God permeating every atom and point of space in the manifested cosmos. The full measure of God's consciousness is manifested in those who have full realization of Christ or Krishna consciousness. As consciousness is universal, their light is shed on all the world. The complexion of Krishna was blue in colour. He is often shown as dark blue to connote divinity. Blue is also the colour of the Christ Consciousness when epitomized in the spiritual eye as circle of dark blue light surrounding the silvery white star of Cosmic Consciousness. *Brahmavaivarta Purana* states: '*Krishna*' means the Universal Spirit. *Krsi* denotes a generic term, while *na* conveys the idea of the self, thus bringing forth the meaning 'Omniscient Spirit' In this we find a parallel to the Christ Consciousness as the Intelligence of God omnipresent in creation. It is interesting to note that a colloquial Bengali language rendering of 'Krishna' is *Krista*, in Greek *Christos* and Spanish *Cristo*.

People consider the Bhagavad *Gitâ* as the Hindu Holy Bible. In a way there is a similarity in both the religions, Hinduism and Christinity. The teachings of Jesus Christ regarding devotion and oneness with God, we also see in the Bhagavad Gita. The *Gitâ* describes oneness with God in chapters 11, 12, 13, 14, 18 with lines such as *enters into Me, attains Me, abides in Me, realizes Me, attains Brahman, etc.*

(1) All through the Bhagavad *Gitâ*, Lord Krishna has said: *I am the way and come to Me.* In the Holy Bible, Jesus Christ has also said the same statement a number of times (St. John 14/16). Both Lord Krishna and Jesus Christ spoke similarly, because both are the *Infinite Power* came in *Finite Forms.*

(2) To understand the immortal words of Christ, one needs the *Bhagavad Gita* and other Hindu scriptures. Without the aid of Hinduism, one may even come to erroneous conclusions, when one tries to explain the saying of Christ. Christ said: '*And if thy right eye offend thee, pluck it out, and cast it from thee; for it is profitable for thee that one of thy members should perish, and not that thy whole body should be cast into hell.' 'And if thy right hand offend thee, cut it off, and cast it from thee. For it is profitable for Thee that one of thy members should perish, and not that the whole body should be cast into hell* (Methew 18:8, 5-29, 28; and also Mark 9-45). How will one explain this. If you read the Gita (II: 58-70) you will see very detailed explanations for

what Christ has said above. Lord Krishna said: *'All senses (indriyas) have love affairs with sense-objects. Just like a tortoise withdraws its limbs to its shell, when it perceives danger, so too wise man, withdraws his senses (indriyas) from sense objects, when he sees that the senses are losing themselves in the sense objects. Without the proper control of senses (Indriyas), nobody can realise the 'Absolute Truth* (Gita II:58). When Jesus urged, 'if thy hand offend thee' (prevent these from entering into God's kindom) 'cut it off,' he was not advising literal dismemberment, but rather the severance of the impulse that had actuated it to do evil. Removal of a man's eyes does not destroy his desire for sensuous beauty. Cutting off the hands does not affect one's power of desire to hurt or to steal. What is needed is to control the misery-making *desire* that guides man's instruments of perception and action. The senses are mere instruments of the mind; they cannot act by themselves. It is the mind and discrimination that must be freed from enslavement. A wise man keeps his wisdom free and steady, directing his life on the God-ward path.

(3) To condone defensive force in certain circustances is not to demean the superiority of spiritual power over brute force. Even a tiger in the company of a *yogi* filled with love of God becomes a pussycat. Patanjali says: 'In the presence of a man perfected in *ahimsa* (non-violence), enmity (in any creature) does not arise' (Yoga Sutra II:35). 'Love your enemies' is a central part of the teaching of Christ. *'Love your enemies, bless them that curse you, do good to them that hate you, and pray for them which despitefully use you, and persecute you.* (Matthew 5:44). This is not a sentimental dictum nor a gesture merely to ennoble the giver, but expresses an important divine law. When man tunes in with God's love and consciously directs its vibratory force against evil, it neutralizes the power of evil and reinforces the vibrations of good. Love smothers that fire by denying it fuel! Jesus could have borrowed twelve legions of divinely armed angels to destroy his enemies (Matthew 26:53)—but he chose the way of non-violence. He conquerred not only the Roman Empire, but mankind, by his love and by saying: *'Father, forgive them, for they know not what they do* (Luke 23:34). The non-violent Jesus, by allowing his blood to be shed and his body to be destroyed, immortalized himself in the eyes of God and man. Similarly, Mahatamâ Gândhi got the independence of India from the British Empire by non-violence and *satyagarh*. Gandhi explains *satyagraha* in a book (Satyagrahi in south Africa 1926,pp.178-179) as follows: '*satyagraha* expects the *satyagrahi* to love the opponent; at least hatred of the opponent has no place in *satayagraha*, but is a positive breach of its ruling principle. In *satyagraha*, there is not the remotest idea of injuring the opponent.' From time immemorial, non-violence had occupied the highest place among

the Hindu cardinal virtues for individual action. *'Ahimsa paramo dharmah'*, i.e. Non-violence is the highest virtue, is written in Hindu scriptures. If *ahimsa* disappears, Hindu religion disappears. We have Hinduism of the *Gitâ*, the *Upanishads*, and Patanjali's Yoga Sutra which is the acme of *ahimsa* and oneness of all creation. In first—three stanzas of the 16th chapter of *Gitâ*, Lord Krishna described 26 *sattvic* or ennobling qualities, and non-injury (*Ahimsa*) is one of them. Similarly, one of the ten commandments in the Bible is: *'Thou shalt not kill* (Exodua 20:13). Mahatamâ Gandhi once described *ahimsa* as 'the avoidance of harm to any living creatures in thought or deed.' A man of nonviolence neither willfully gives nor wishes harm to any. He is a paradigm of the golden rule: *'Do unto others as you would have them do unto you'* (Matthew 7:12).

Can Hinduism, following the doctrine of *ahimsa*, consistently teach people to defend their country's freedom by force? Can it teach, 'Meet force with force.' The answer is 'Yes'. The classical example in Hinduism is the example of Rama and Krishna who used once most reluctantly and, as a last resort, when all their attempts to bring about a just, amicable settlement had failed. In the larger interest of the society, it is our belief to maintain *Dharma* (Righteouness) we may have to kill men in battlefields in self-defense. There is a great difference between a righteous and unrighteous war. A coountry may be purposely aggressive and forment wars to satisfy its greed; a war so motivated is righteous action by the aggressors and no soldier should cooperate with it. To defend one's country against the aggression of another, however, protecting innocent, helpless people and preserving their noble ideals and freedom, is righteous duty.

(4) *Gitâ* says: *'To an enlightened Brahaman (spirit) all the Vedas are as useful as a tank when there is a flood everywhere* (Gita II:46). Real success does not perish with this earthly life. Your success is conditioned by the law of cause and effect and your environment. Jesus also said: *'Seek ye first the kingdom of God, and His righeousness; and all these things shall be added unto you'* (Mattew 6:33). When you seek success by the material way, you are governed by the law of cause and effect, but when you have communion with God first, then success is given to you innumerable ways, both subtle and material. Compare the lives of saints and others who lived with God to the lives of non-spiritual people. The saints have everything because they have God.

(5) Krishna advises the devotee to keep on working for the state of emancipation, even up to the moment before death. *'That man attains peace who lives devoid of longing, freed from all desires and without the feeling of ' I' and 'mine.' This, O Parth, is the Brahman state. Attaining this, none is bewildered. Being established in it even at the death-hour, a man gets into oneness with Brahman* (Gita II: 71-72). Jesus also assures man: *'Him that overcometh will I make a pillar in the temple of my God, and he shall go no more*

out (will reincarnate no more)' (Revelation 3:12). A soul must attain freedom from earthly desires and egoism before death in order to escape from the merry-go-round wheel of births and deaths. If this freedom is not attained before physical death one has to incarnate again on earth. Strive ceaselessly; never be impatient. Once the finality is achieved , incarnations of troubles will be over, just as when light is admitted within a closed room, the darkness vanishes instantly,

The culmination of the religion of devotion in both Hinduism and Christianity have a faith in the Incarnation of God. Hinduism and Christianity declare that God incarnates Himself in human form; that God of grace is worshipped by His devotees to get beyond the ocean of mortality. According to the Christian point of view, there is only one incarnation of God. Hinduism says that there have been many incarnations from time immemorial, and there will continue to be Incarnations as long as human beings live in this world and need the help of God. Lord Krishna said: 'Whenever, O Arjuna, righteousness declines, and unrighteousness prevails, I body myself, assume human form, and live as a human being' (Gita IV: 7). Further He said: 'In order to protect the righteous and also to punish the wicked, I incarnate Myself on this earth from time to time' (Gita IV: 8). Similarly, Jesus said: If God were your father, ye would love me; for I proceeded forth and came from God; neither came I of myself but he sent me' (St. John VIII: 42).

Krishna, Jesus, and many other saviours of mankind have returns to earth as *avatârs*. In the Hindu scripture, *avatâra* signifies the descent of Divinity into flesh. At a time when superstition and callousness prevailed among the Jews, Moses came. The Buddha came when great reform in Hinduism was particularly needed. And Sri Krishna and Jesus Christ also came at especially critical time in the lives of their peoples. When this human life requires readjustment on a large scale, the Divine Being incarnates Himself in human form—to teach human beings, and to guide the benighted world towards true light. There are differences in the manifestation of divine love, divine power and divine wisdom in these great spiritual personalities. The differences are due mostly to the needs of the age and the psychological conditions of the people who hear the message.

Again and again, the *Upnishads* have declared that the way a person goes beyond birth, growth, decay and death is by realizing the changeless Self. There is no other way. Anything you acquire in this world is temporal; God alone is eternal in the midst of the non-eternal. Whatever you gain, you will undergo reincarnation until you realize God. Jesus said, "That which is born of the flesh is flesh." As long as you identify yourself with the physical body, the "mass of skin, flesh, fat, bones, and filth", you will have no escape from the cycle of birth, death, and rebirth. And physical rebirth means you are subject once again to pain and pleasure, hope and fear, love and hatred, good and evil, and all the other dualities that make up this worldly existence. You cannot enter the Kingdom of God beyond dual experience unless you gain consciousnes of your spiritual self.

In Christianity, the idea of reincarnation is demonstrated in the following passage from the Gospel of St. John: 'And his disciples asked him, saying, Master who did sin, this man, or his parents, that he was born blind' (St. John IX: 2)? The question was: 'did this man commit sin?' which indicates the probability that man existed in a previous life; otherwise he himself could never have comitted a sin to cause his blindness at birth. The early Christian fathers also accepted the idea of reincarnation and were very much influenced by it. It is the doctrine of *karma* allied with reincarnation that explains the inequalities of life. Otherwise there is no satisfaction. Law of heredity of modern genetics assists in explaining the differences for the sufferings a child may have congenital defects. The new mutation or a normal parent may be a carrier of a defective gene or a chromosomal aberration which can cause defects in an offspring and not in other child. The selectivity of a defective gene by a new born is due to the result of his/ her prior life *karma*. There is a destiny of a person, it cannot be removed. It could be reduced, or increased, but not removed. Suppose you have a bud desting, you become a tree devotee of God, your bad destiny is reduced to a certain degree. If you have a bad destiny, and you do wrong things, then your bad destiny could become greater. Through becoming a devotee of God You can increase your good destiny, decrease your bad destiny. Reincarnation allied with the doctrine of *karma* has been accepted by many thinkers of the western world, among them, Plato, Voltaire and Nietzsche. The law of *karma* is one of the main pillar of Hinduism.

In keeping with the doctrine of *karma*, which guarantees future reactions for all present actions, the idea of non-resistance is very prominent in Christianity. Jesus Christ taught ethical precepts such as 'Resist not evil,' 'love your enemy,' and 'Bless them that persecute you.' Six hundred years before Christ, Buddha taught: 'Let a man overcome anger by love; let him overcome evil by good; let him overcome the greedy by generocity; and a liar by the truth. For hatred does not cease by hatred at any time; hatred ceases by love, this is an old rule' (Dhammpada, vs. 5). In Hinduism the teaching of non-resistance was proclaimed centuries before Buddha by Sri Krishna (Bhagavatam XI: 22, 57, 58).

(6) The idea of renuciation has been taught in Hinduism from very ancient times. In both Hinduism and Buddhism, we find this ideal of asceticism and renuciation prevelent. Renunication was another important teaching of Jesus Christ: "Take no thought for tomorrow," "You cannot serve God and mammon." In the Gospel of St. Luke (18:28-30) we find: "Then Peter said, Lo, we have left all, and followed Thee. And He said unto them: Verily I say unto you, there is no man that hath left house, or parents or bretheren, or wife, or children, for the kingdom of God's sake. Who shall receive manifold more in this present time, and in the world to come, life everlasting."

(7) Arjuna is confused at the advice of his *guru*, Krishna, who extols wisdom (*jñâna yoga*) as superior to action and at the same time advises him to act (*karma yoga*). Arjuan asks Krishna in the beginning of the third chapter of *Gitâ*: '*If it is held by you, O Janardana, that knowledge is superior to action, why then do you enjoin on me this terrible action? With these perplexing words, you are, as it were, confusing my comprehension. Tell me with certainty the path by pursuing which I may get at the Supreme* (Gita III:1-2). Spiritual advice is often paradoxial. Far from being contradictory, it rather reflects the inadequacy of corporal expression to convey that which is above the familiar 'this or that' duality of Nature. Among Christian saints, how given to paradoxes is Saint John of the cross in his *mystical* poesy: 'The music without sound.' 'With fire that can consume and yet do no harm,' 'Eternal life you render / And change my death to life, even while killing!' Jesus said: '*For whosoever will save his life shall lose it; but whosoever will lose his life for my sake, the same shall save it* (Luke 9:24). Similarly, whenever Krishna advises, in essence, '*Live in this world but do not live in it,*' He ment that man should live and fulfill his duties in this world since God put him here, but he should not live in attachment to its wiles and ways.

(8) There are thousands names of God. Why do *Vedas* emphasise the word *Om*? One thought is connected with a thousand words, although the idea of God is connected with hundreds of words, and each one stands as a symbol for God. The manifesting word of God is *Om. Om* is the supreme name of God. The word *Om* has the power of expressing various ideas and qualities. *Om* represents the *saguna* (anthropomorphic conception) as well as *nirguna* (formless or shapeless) reality. There is the *absolute reality,* which is nameless, formless, and attributeless, but that alone manifests itself as the cause of this entire world, which in Vedic language is called as *saguna Brahman.* The absolute reality is called *nirguna Brahman. Om* represents both these aspects and that is why it is called *pranava.* The word *pranava* comes from the root word *nu. Nu* means to salute, to praise. With the help of *Pranava* one can praise or meditate on the deity of one's own choice, either the manifested aspect of reality which is *saguna,* or on the absolute reality which is *nirguna. Aum* of the *Vedas* became the sacred word *hum* of the Tibetans, *amin* of the Moslems, and *amen* of the Egyptians, Greeks, Romans, Jews, and Christians. *Amen* in Hebrew means 'sure, faithful.' *Aum* is the all-pervading sound emanating from the Holy Ghost as it performs its work of creating and maintaining the universal structure. *Aum* is the voice of creation, testifying to the Divine Presence in every atom. '*These things saith the Amen, the faithful and true witness, the beginning of the creation of God*' (Revelation 3:14). '*In the beginning was the Word, and the Word was with*

God, and the Word was God ..... All things were made by him (the Word or Aum), and without him was not anything made that was made..... and the Word was made flesh and dwelt among us' (John 1:1,3,14). *'Faith cometh by hearing , and hearing by the Word of God'* (Romans 10"17). Kaivalyadarsna says: *'Parambrahma causes creation, inert Nature (Prakriti), to emerge. From Aum (Pranava, the Word, the manifestation of the Omnipotent Force), come kala, time, desa, space, and anu, the atom* (the vibrating structure of creation).'

(9) *'Thy human right is to perform your duty, never for the resultant fruit of actions. Do not consider thyself the producer of the fruits of thy actions; neither allow thyself lean towards inaction'* (Gita II:47). When the Lord says not to desire the fruits of action, it does not mean that one should work like an automation, without thought for the probable results of one's activities! The teaching of Lord is to work intelligently, ambitiously, keenly and trying to create the right fruits of actions, not for oneself, but for God and all His children. The devotee who performs all good actions just for God lives on earth with divine approval and great inner satisfaction, without being hurt by failures or overjoyed by successes. Jesus also spoke: *'This is My beloved son, in whom I am well pleased'* (Matthew 3:17). It is the burden duty of every soul as a child of God to win the approbation of Father. To work toward liberation is to please God; to please God is to become liberated.

(10) Lord Krishna tells the *yogi* to follow the art of scientific control of the senses. An adept *yogi* can withdraw his mind from all sensations of the material world and can unit his mind and energy with the intoxicating joy of inner ecstasy or *samâdhi*. *'When the yogi, like a tortoise withdrawing its limbs, can fully retire his senses from the objects of perception, his wisdom manifests steadiness'* (Gita II:58). Christ issued a similar commandment to his disciples: *'But thou, when thou prayest, enter into thy closet (the silence within), and when thou shut thy door (withdrawn the mind from the senses), pray to thy Father which is in secret (in the inner transcendent divine consciousness); and thy Father which seeth in secret shall reward thee openly (shall bless you with the ever new Bliss of His Being)'* (Matthew 6:6). St. Paul said: *'I die daily'* (I Connthians 15:31). By this he mean that he knew the process of controlling the internal organs and could voluntarily control the internal organs and free his spiritual self from the body and mind— an experience that ordinary untrained people only feel at final death, when the spiritual self is freed from the worn-out body. By the scientific method or *yoga*, the self can be felt as being separate from the body, without final death. *Kirya yoga* is an ancient spiritual science that includes certain *yogic* techniques of meditation.

There are basically two approaches to God-realization: the outer way and the inner or transcendental way. The outer way is by right activities, loving and serving mankind with the consciousness centered in God; the transcendental way is by deep esoteric meditation. By the transcendental way, you realize all the things you are not, and discover that which you are: 'I am not the breath, I am not the body, neither bones nor flesh. I am not the mind or feeling. I am that which is beyond the consciousness of this world, knowing that you are not the body, or the mind, and yet aware as never before that you exist—that divine consciousness is what you are. You are that in which is rooted everything in the universe.

(11) *'He is full with contentment who absorbs all desire within, as the brimful ocean remains unmoved (unchanged) by waters entering into it—not he who lusts after desires'* (Gita II:70). Thus the advice of the *Gitâ*: Do not drain dry your reservoir of peace by diverting its waters into channels of small but ever-growing desires. The true devotee desires less and less and finds more and more in his soul an idea of contentment. This counsel does not mean that one should abandon good aspirations, such as helping others to know God. By noble desire the devotee does not lose his peace, which gathers reinforcement by distribution! This paradox is similar to Jesus' words: *'For unto every one that hath not shall be given, and he shall have abundance, but from him that hath not shall be taken e away even that which he hath'* (Matthew 25:29). In spiritual life, giving is receiving. A desire gives joy to others and the outgoing activity of giving peace to others bring back to the devotee a great peace and joy. But the satisfaction of any selfish desire leaves the devotee a poorer man.

(12) The Bible says,*'Know ye not that ye are the temple of God, and that the spirit of God dwelleth in you'* (I Corinthians 3:16). All of us as individuals are so many reflected spiritual selves of the universal blissful spirit—God. Just as these appear many images of the one Sun when reflected in a number of vessels full of water; so is mankind apparently divided into many souls, occupying these bodily and mental vehicles, and thus outwardly separated from the one universal spirit. In reality, God and man are one, and the separation is only apparent. 'Kingdom of God is within you' (St. Luke 17:21). This passage can be explained by the Hindu doctrine that the self (*âtman*) of human being is ever united with the Supreme (*Pramâtman*)—birthless, decayless, deathless—you are really pure, free, illuminated, when you become aware of this truth, you are free.

"*He who serves Me with an undeviating devotion, he, going beyond the gunas, is fitted for becoming Brahman. For I am the basis of the infinite, the immortal, the indestrubctible; and of eternal dharma and absolute bliss*" (Gitâ XIV: 26, 27). In the above *slokas*, Krishna speaks as the *Pratyagatma*, the soul or true being of man that is identical with God: Spirit or the Absolute. Krishna's words: "*I am the basis of the Infinite,"* are akin in divine scope to those uttered by Jesus: *"Before Abraham was, I am"* (John 8: 58). Krishna and Christ spoke from the depths of self-realization, knowing that *"I and my Father are one"* (John 10:30).

Psalms (46: 10) says: *'Be still, and know that I am God.'* Saint Teresa of Avila said: *'You need not go to heaven to see God; nor need you speak loud, as if God is far away; nor need you cry for wings like a dove to fly to Him. Only be in silence, and you will come upon God within yourself.'* *'Tat Tvam Asi'* (Thou art That)—the human soul is coexistent with God Himself, not as an emanation from Him, not as a part or effect, but as an eternal verity, birthless, ageless, and undecaying. *'Tat Tvam Asi'* (Thou art That) and *'Sarvam khalu idam* Brahman' (Everything is Brahman) appear in many ancient memory songs sung well before the time. This *mantra* itself remains current in the later Vedic, past-Vedic and modern era. It was quoted in (Chândogya Upanishad IV:8.7). Besides, its many variants current in Hindu thought have also found a pride of place in other Vedic literature—for instance, in the *Brihadâryanaka Upanishad,* we have: *Aham Brahmâsmi*—I am Brahma, the infinite and *Ayam Atmâ Brahman*—this self (soul) is Brahman. This can be explained in the following way: Both the 'dead body' and 'living body' are identical, but the 'living body' has something that 'dead body' does not have. That which is missing in the 'dead body' is spirit—*Brahman,* and at the same time, when *Brahman* is present in the body, it creates the greatest illusion (*maya*) that 'I am the body.'

(13) Gita says: *'Presiding over the mind and the senses of hearing, sight, touch, taste, and smell, He enjoys the sensory world'* (Gita XV: 9). The Bible says: *'O Lord! Thou hast created all things, and for Thy pleasure they are and were created'* (Revelation 4: 11). The Hindu scriptures also tell us that the creation of man and the universe is only God's *lila,* play or creative sport. The Lord as the *jiva* experiences the delights of the world that He made.

(14) Lord Krishna says: *'The light of the sun that illumines the whole world, the light from the moón, and the light in fire—know this radiance to be Mine'* (Gita XV:12). The Bible contains the following passage: *'God said, let there be light: and there was light. And God saw the light, that it was good'* (Genesis 1: 3,4).

(15) Lord Krishna said: *'Abiding in the body of living beings as Vaisvanara, associated with Prana and apana, I digest the four kinds of food'* (Gita XV:14). Lord Jesus also said: *'Take no thought for your life, what ye shall eat'* (Matthew 6:25). That is, do not constantly fuss about the body's needs; eat to live just for service to the Lord—not for satisfying whims of the palate, which produces disease and suffering.

(16) The Blessed Lord Krishna said: *'Fearlessness, purity of heart, steadfastness in knowledge and yoga, alms giving, control of the senses, yjnâ, study of the scriptures, austerity and straight-forwardness. Non-injury, truth, absence of anger, renunciation, peacefulness, non-slanderousness, compassion for all*

creatures, absence of greed, gentleness, modesty, lack of restlessness. Vigour, forgiveness, fortitude, purity, absence of hatred, absense of pride, these beolongs to one born for a divine state, O Bharata' (Gita XVI:1-3). In stanza of *Gitâ*, 26 *sattvic* or good qualities are mentioned that lead devotees to self-realization. One of the qualities is purity of heart—the heart or *chitta* should not be influenced by the pairs of opposites; only thus may it enter the divine bliss of meditation. Jesus says: *'Blessed are the pure in heart: for they shall see God'* (Matthew 5:8). These 26 qualities are divine attributes of God; they constitute man's spiritual wealth. A God-seeker should strive to obtain all of them. The more he manifests these virtues, the more he reflects the true inner image of God in which he is made. The more he expresss these virtues, the more he expresses the image of God in which he is made. Christ said: *'Be ye therefore perfect, even as your Father which is in heaven is perfect'* (Matthew 5:48).

(17) Lord Krishna said: *'Whatever is sacrificed, given or performed and whatever austerity is practised without shraddha or faith* (devotion) *is called asat, O Partha. It is worthless here and in the hereafter'* (Gita XVII:28). Unconditional devotion or faith is necessary for success in the spiritual path. *'Without faith it is impossible to please Him: for he that cometh to God must believe that He is, and that He is a rewarder of them that diligently seek Him'* (Hebrews 11:6).

Lord Krishna told his devotee, Uddhava, about devotion: 'I', the dear Self of the pious, am obtainable by devotion alone, which is the outcome of faith; the devotion to Me purges even the low-born of their congenital impurites.' 'Piety joined to truthfulness and compassion, or learning coupled with austerity, never wholly purifies a mind which is devoid of devotion to Me.' ' As gold smelted by fire gives up its refuse and gets back its real state. So the mind by means of systematic devotion to Me win now off subtle impressions of past *karma* and attains Me.' 'O Uddhava, neither *yoga*, nor knowledge, nor piety, nor study, nor austerity, nor renunciation captivates Me so much as heightened devotion to Me' (Bhagavatam XI:14, 20, 22).

The Christian emphasis on devotion is well known. In the New Testament we find: 'Keep yourselves in the love of God, looking for the mercy of our Lord Jesus Christ unto eternal life' (Jude 21). 'He that loveth father or mother more than me is not worthy of me: and he that loveth son or daughter more than me is not worthy of me' (St.Matt. X: 37). 'Jesus said unto him, Thou shalt love the Lord thy God with all thy heart, and with all thy soul, and with all thy mind' (St. Matt. XXII: 37, 38). This is the first and great commandment.

(18) In God-consciousness you find the kingdom of God wherever you are. It has no special reference to space or time, for in any place, at any time, you can enter this kingdom of Heaven. Jesus used this expression in the sense of God-consciousness, of experiencing God in your heart. He says:

'The Kingdom of God cometh not with observation: Neither shall they say, Lo here! or, lo there, behold, the kingdom of God is within you' (St.Luke 17: 20, 21). Another passage which corroborates this idea is found in St. Luke: 'But I tell you of a truth, there be some standing here, which shall taste of death, till they see the kingdom of God' (St. Luke 9: 27). 'Know ye not that ye are the temple of God, that the Spirit of God dwelth within you?' (I Cor. 3: 16).

Vedanta declares that God is not far away from anything. He is not apart from anything. God is within you. Nothing exists outside Him, He includes everything. The finest of all existences. He underlies each and every form of existence. God is the one self-effulgent Supreme Reality, lying hidden everywhere, the very perfection of existence, self-luminous pure Consciousness. That Reality, the Supreme Being, God, is right here within you as your inmost self. This self-evident, conscious spirit which you cannot deny, is the immediate and direct manifestation of the Supreme Spirit. You can realize this Supreme Spirit by realizing your spiritual self. To reach the soul of the universe you first have to reach your own soul; you contact Supreme Spirit through spirit. There is no other way of direct communication with the Supreme Reality. Lord Krishna says in the *Bhagavad Gîtâ*, 'I am the Self dwelling in the heart of all beings.'

Kena Upanishad (1: 5) says: 'That which the organ of speech cannot apprehend, but which apprehends the organs of speech, that is Brahman, the Supreme Reality, shining in the heart.' During sleep when the light of Consciousness recedes from the organs, the eyes cannot see, the ears cannot hear, the hands cannot grasp, the mouth cannot speak. Just a little bit of consciousness is left so autonomous functions can continue. 'That which the mind cannot apprehend but which apprehend the mind' (Kena Upanishad 1: 6). Are you not observing the mind, can't you see it change? You are not the mind, for the observer and the observed can not be the same. Further it states: 'That which the eyes cannot see, but which perceives the eyes, because of which the eyes see; that which the ears cannot hear, but which perceives the ears, because of which the ears hear; that which the nose cannot smell, but because of which the nose has the power of smelling—know that to be the Supreme Reality, ever dwelling within you' (Kena Upanishad 1: 7-9).

Just as every ray of light coming from the sun belongs to the sun, similarly when you realize this individual spirit, you find it belongs to the Infinite Spirit. As it is said in the *Katha Upanishad (1:2:20):* 'Finer than the finest, greater than the greatest, that Supreme Self, soul of the universe, is hidden in the hearts of living creatures. Persons free from sense desire realize that Supreme Being through the purification of the body and the mind.' When men realize that, they find the source of all joy, of all light, of all life.

So Jesus Christ says: 'Blessed are the pure in heart: for they shall see God.' It is through the purification of the mind that you see God.

(19) There cannot be a greater expression of the principle of returning good for evil. Just as a sandalwood tree hewed by a woodcutter envelops the woodcutter in its fragrance, similarly even when a person is persecuted, his compassion and love must enevelop the wrong-doer. Many centuries before Jesus Christ, Lord Krishna taught the same ideal to Uddhava: 'Even though scolded by the wicked, or insulted, calumniated, beaten, bound, robbed of his living, or spat upon, or otherwise abominably treated by the ignorant—being thus variously shaken and placed in dire extremities, the man who desires his well-being should deliver himself by his own effort (through patience and non-resistance)' (Bhagavatma, XI: 22, 57, 58). This sublime ethical principle of returning good for evil is based on a very deep spiritual truth—the understanding of Oneness of all. Those who develop this spiritual vision of one Reality—one Supreme Self dwelling in the hearts of all as the innermost self—find their individual self expanding and enveloping all beings.

In His Sermon on the Mount, Jesus Christ said: 'Ye have heard that it hath been said, an eye for an eye, and a tooth for a tooth. But I say unto you, that ye resist not evil; but whosoever shall smite thee on thy right cheek, turn to him the other also. And if any man will sue thee at the law, and take away thy coat, let him have thy cloak also. And who soever shall compel thee to go a mile, go with him twain. Give to him that asketh thee, and from him that would borrow of thee turn not thou away.' 'Ye have heard that it hath been said, Thou shalt love thy neighbour, and hate thine enemy. But I say unto you, Love your enemies, bless them that curse you, do good to them that hate you, and pray for them which despitefully use you, and persecute you' (St. Matthews 5: 38 - 44). By the non-resistance of evil, Jesus Christ does not mean only the passive endurance of sufferings caused by others. He means doing positive good in return for wrong.

It sometimes seems that people are so ungrateful, but we should always be prepared to do good to others though they appear that way. 'Do not expect any kind of gratitude,' the sage said. 'Do your own part of serving human beings, seeing God in them, and never return evil for evil.' He illustrated this teaching with the folowing story.

One day a holy man was seated on the bank of the Ganges where he was practicing his daily meditation, worshiping the Lord. All of a sudden he noticed that a scorpian was drifting away in a current of the river. Taking pity on the scorpian, he took it in the palm of his hand and put it safely on the ground. But after a while, he found that the scorpian had again fallen into the water, and was again being carried away by the current. a second time he took it in his palm and put it back on the ground. Each time the scorpian stung him, and he felt sever pain. Before long, yet the third time the holy man found the scorpian in the water, being carried away. Though he was feeling much pain from the stinging he had twice received, he again took the scorpian and put it very far from the water.

Standing not far away, an observer had been watching the holy man take the scorpian each time from the water, being stung each time, and still trying to save the scorpian. So he asked, 'Sir, I noticed that you took the scorpian in the palm of your hand and were badly stung, and still you helped three times. What is the reason?' The holy man replied, 'You see, it is the nature of the scorpian to sting, but the nature of a holy man to always help everyone. So if the scorpian cannot give up its nature, why should I give up mine?'

(20) In Hinduism and Christianity, however, we find another element we do not find emphasized in Buddhism, and that is the idea of the grace of God. Lord Krishna very much stressed this idea in the (Gitâ X: 8): 'I am the origin of everything and everything arises out of Me; by knowing this men offer everything to Me and worship Me with loving devotion.' Further He said: 'It is very difficult to cross this ocean of mortality, this phenomenal world, to reach the Ultimate, the Real, where there is absolute peace and blessedness. But those who take refuge in Me alone cross this ocean' (Gitâ VII: 14). In this way a life of complete self-surrender, devotion to God, and dependence upon His grace has been emphasized in the above *sloka*. The concept of grace is Christianity is demonstrated in many passages in the New Testament. Jesus Crist says: 'I am the bread of life; he that cometh to me shall never hunger, and he that believeth on me shall never thirst' (St. John 6: 35). But seek ye first the kingdom of God and his righteousness; and all these things shall be added unto you' (St. Matthew 6: 33).

(21) Jesus said: "Be ye perfect, even as the Father which is in Heaven is perfect" The Hindu takes this literally. You are already perfect, your impurities have only to be removed for you to discover your essential unity with God.

Now there are numerous English translation of Bhagavad Gitâ written both by Indian and western writers.

If you follow the teachings of the Bhagavad Gitâ in a very logical and scientific manner, you will achieve salvation, since the Gitâ contains the unwritten laws of the universe. On the other hand, if you read it with devotion to Lord Krishna and if you follow the Gitâ on devotional basis, still you will achieve salvation. Both intellectual way and the devotional way will lead you to God.

Quotations

When Yudhishthira with his four brothers and wife were in exile, Yaksha wanted to test their abilities to become a ruler of the country. Yaksha asked them the following questions. These questions are short, simple and direct but not easy. Their relevance is, of course, timeless. They have the character of what Alder calls 'recurrent basic questions which men must face.'

Kimsvidgurutararam bhumeh
kimsviduccataram ca khât
kimsvidccheghrataram vâyoh
kimsvidbahutaram trnât

Mâtâ gurutaru bhumeh
khâtpitoccatarastathâ
manahshighrataram vâtâ
ccintâ bahutari trnât

What is weighter than earth?
What is taller than the sky?
What is faster than the wind?
What is more numerous than grass?

Mother
Father
Mind
Thoughts

Kim nu hitvâ priyo bhavati
kim nu hitvâ na shocati
kim nu hitvârthavânbhavati
kim nu hitvâ sukhi bhavet

Mânam hitvâ priyo bhavati
krodham hitvâ na shocati
kâmam hitvârthavânbhavati
lobham hitvâ sukhi bhavet

By renouncing what does one become loved?
By renouncing what is one free of sorrow?
By renouncing what does one become wealthy?
By renoùncing what does one become happy?

Pride
Anger
Desire
Greed

Dhanyânâmuttamam kimsvid
dhanânâm syâtkimuttamam
lâbhânâmuttamam kimsyât
sukhânâm syâtkimuttamam

Dhanyânâmuttamam dâkhyam
dhanânâmuttamam shrutam
lâbhânâm shreya ârogyam
sukhânâm tushtiruttamâ

What treasure is the best?	Skill
What wealth is the best?	Education
What is the greatest gain?	Health
What is the gretest happiness?	Contentment

Kim jnânam procyate rajan
kah shamashca prakirtitah
dayâ ca kâ parâ proktâ
kim carjavamudahrtam

Jnânam tatvarthasambodhah
shamashcitta prashântatâ
dayâ sarvasukhaishitvam
ârjavam samacittatâ

What is knowledge?	Experience
What is tranquility?	A serene mind
What is the supreme kindness?	The good of all
What is simplicity?	A quiet mind

Kah shatrurdurjayah pumsâm
kashca vyâdhiranantakah
kidrshashca smrtah sâdhur
asâdhuh kidrshah smrtah

Krodhah sudurjayah shatrur
lobho vyâdhiranantakah
sarvaabhutahitah sâdhur
asâdhurnirdayah smrtah

Which enemy is nearly impossible to conquer?	Anger
What is man's endless disease?	Greed
Who is good?	One who seeks the good of all
Who is not good?	One who lacks compassion

Ko modate

Pancameahani shashthevâ
shâkam pacati sve grhe
anrni câpravâsi ca
sa vâricara modate

Who is happy?

That person who is free of debt, not in constant travel and who eats a frugal, satisfying hot meal in his own home every evening.

Kimâscharyam

Ahanyahani bhutâni
gacchantiha yamâlayam
sheshâh sthâvaramicchanti
kimâshcaryamatah param

What is amazing?	Every day creatures die and yet everyone thinks he lives forever. What can be more amazing?

Rajan kulena vrttena *svâdhyâyena shrutena vâ* *brâhmanyam kenabhavati* *prabruhyetatsu nishcitam*	*Shrnu yaksha kulam tâta* *nasvâdhyâyo nacashrutam* *kâranam hi dvijatve ca* *vrttameva na samshayah*

King, how does one become a Brahmin: by birth? character? study of the *vedas*? education? Tell me precisely.	Listen, Yaksha, it is neither birth nor education nor even the study of the *Vedas*. Without doubt, it is character alone that marks a Brahmin.

Dharmashcârthasca kâmashca *paraspara virodhinah* *eshâm nitya viruddhânâm* *kathamekatra sangamah*	*Yadâ dharmasca bharyâca* *paraspara vashanugau* *tadâ dharamârtha* *kâmânâm* *trayânâmapi sangamah*

Dharma, artha and *kama* conflict with each other. How can these contraries be reconciled?	When *dharma* and one's wife are in harmony, *dharma*, *artha* and *kama* are reconciled.

In order to keep that balance, a man has to have a wife who is dharmic. It is that protection coming from the wife, that torchlight, that spirit of cooperation and sacrifice which gives a reasonable chance for a man to meet the challenge of these conflicting requirements. The special role of a wife described above is the basis for Hindus to refer to a wife as *dharmapatni*, i.e. *wife-in-dharma*.

_____ **** _____

Yama speaks: 'One thing is the good and quite another thing is the pleasant, and both seize upon a man with different meanings. Of these who so takes the good, it is well with him; he falls from the aim of life who chooses the pleasant.' (Katha *Upanishad* 2.1)

'The good and the pleasant come to a man and the thoughtful mind turns all around them and distinguishes. The wise chooses out the good from the pleasant, but the dull soul chooses the pleasant rather than the getting of his good and its having.' (Katha Up.2.2)

'Having taught the Veda, the teacher instructs the pupil: Speak the truth. Practice virtue. Neglect not the study of Veda. Having brought to the teacher the wealth that is pleasing, do not cut off the thread of thy race. Let there be no neglect of truth. Let there be no neglect of thy duty, thou shall not be negligent of welfare. Let there be no neglect of study and teaching of Veda. Let there be no neglect of prosperity. Thou shalt not negligent of thy works unto the Gods or thy works unto the Father.' (Taittirya *Upanishad* 1.11).

The Lord said: 'Non-injury, truthfulness, non-stealing, non-attachment, modesty, non-accumulation of wealth, faith in God, chastity, silence, patience, forgiveness, fearlessness.'

'Purity of mind and body, repetition of the Lord's name, austerity, offering of oblations in the sacred fire, faith in one's self, hospitality, worship of Me, visiting of holy places, working for the good of others, contentment and service unto the teacher.'

'These groups of twelve virtues enumerated in the above two verses constitute the *yamas* and *niyamas*. These, my friend, if rightly practised by men, surely produce results according to their desires.' (Srimad Bhagavatam, Skandha 11, Chapter 19, Verses 33-35)

'Calmness is a steady attachment of the mind to Me. Self control is control of the sense-organs. Fortitude is the bearing of grief. Patience is a perfect control over the palate and sex-impulse.' (Srimad Bhagavatam, Skandha 11, XIX:36)

'The highest charity is the relinquishing of the idea of violence towards beings. Penance is the giving up of desires. Valour is the conquest of one's nature. Honesty is looking upon everything with an equal eye.' (Srimad Bhagavatam, Skandha 11, XIX: 37)

'Truthfulness is true and agreeable speech which the sages praise. Purity is non-attachment to work, and renunciation is the giving up of work.' (Srimad Bhagavatam Skandha 11, XIX: 38)

'Religion is that wealth which men may covet. I, the Supreme Lord, am the sacrifice. The imparting of knowledge is religious remuneration. The highest strength is the control of *prana*.' (Srimad Bhagavatam, Skandha 11, XIX: 39)

'Fortune is my Divine State. The best profit is devotion to Me. Knowledge is the destruction of the idea of multiplicity in the self. Shyness is abhorrence of evil deeds.' Srimad Bhagavatam, Skandha 11, XIX: 40)

'Beauty consists in virtues such as spirit of independence. Happiness is the transcending of pleasure and pain. Misery is the hankering after sense-pleasures. A scholar is one who can distinguish between bondage and liberation.' (Srimad Bhagavatam, Skandha 11, XIX: 41)

'A fool is one who identifies himself with the body, etc. The right way is that which leads to Me. The wrong way is that which causes disturbance of the mind. Heaven is the rise of *sattva* in the mind.' (Srimad Bhagavatam, Skandha 11, XIX: 42)

'Hell is the rise of *tamas* in the mind. The teacher, who is no other than Myself, is the friend (O Uddhava). The human body is the home. He indeed is called rich, who is rich in virtues.' (Srimad Bhagavatam, Skandha 11, XIX: 43)

'One who is discontented is poor. He who is not a master of his senses is mean. One who is not attached to sense-objects is lordly. One who is ttached to sense-objects is the reverse of him.' (Srimad Bhagavatam, Skandha 11, XIX: 44)

'Here, O Uddhava, I have fully answered all your questions. Well, what is the use of dilating on the characteristics of merit and defect? Defect is distinguishing between merit and defect; and to be free from both is merit.' (Srimad Bhagavatam, Skandha 11, XIX:45)

_____ **** _____

'Satyam mâtâ pitâ jñânam dharmo bhratâ dayâ sakhâ
shânti patni kshamâ puta shadaytey mama bandhava'

A person learns truth from his/her mother, knowledge from his father, law or equality from his brothers and kindness from his friends. From his wife he learns patience and forgiveness from his son, and these six are my/our close relatives and the preachings are the gospel.

_____ **** _____

Introspection:

The secret of progress is self-analysis. Introspection is a mirror in which to see recesses of your mind that otherwise would remain hidden from you. Diagnose your failures and sort out your good and bad tendencies. Analyze what shortcomings are impeding you.—(Paramhansa Yogananda. 'The law of Success').

Many people excuse their own faults but judge others harshly. We should reverse this attitude by excusing others' shortcomings and by harshly examining our own. (Pramhansa Yogananda, 'The Law of Success').

By constantly following the inner voice of conscience, which is the voice of God, you will become a truly moral person, a highly spiritual being, a man of peace.—(Pramahansa Yogananda, Lecture).

Divine Love:

He is the nearest of the near, the dearest of the dear. Love Him as a miser loves money, as an ardent man loves his sweetheart, as a drowning person loves breath. When you yearn for God with intensity, He will come to you.— (Pramahansa Yogananda, ' Sayings of Yogananda').

God's love is so all-embracing that no matter what wrongs we have done, He forgives us. If we love Him with all our hearts He wipes out our *karma*. (Pramahansa Yogananda, 'Self-Realization Magazine').

Humility:

Humility comes from realizing that God is the Doer, not you. When you see that, how can you be proud of any accomplishment? Think constantly that whatever work you are performing is being done by the Lord through you. (Pramahansa Yogananda, 'Self-Realization Magazine').

The greatest man is he who considers himself to be the least, as Jesus taught. A real leader is one who first learns obedience to others, who feels himself to be the servant of all, and who never puts himself on a pedestal. Those who want flattery don't deserve our admiration, but he who serves us has a right to our love. Isn't God the servant of His children, and does He ask for praise? No, He is too great to be moved by it. (Pramahansa Yogananda, 'Sayings of Yogananda').

The rains of God's mercy cannot gather on mountain-tops of pride, but flow easily into valleys of humbleness. (Pramahanasa Yogananda, 'Sayings of Yogananda').

Will Power:

Mind is the creator of everything. You should therefore guide it to create only good. If you cling to a certain thought with dynamic will power, it finally assumes a tangible outward form. When you are able to employ your will always for constructive purposes, you become the controller of your destiny. (Pramahansa Yogananda, 'The Law of Success').

Whatever you make up your mind to do, you can do. God is the sum total of everything, and so can you, if you learn to identify yourself with His inexhaustible nature. (Pramahansa Yogananda, 'Self-Realization Magazine').

Habits:

Good and bad habits both take time to acquire force. Powerful bad habits can be displaced by opposite good habits if the latter are patiently cultured. (Pramahansa Yogananda, 'Scientific Healing Affirmations').

Do not continue to live in the same old way. Make up your mind to do something to improve your life, and then do it. Change your consciousness; that is all that is necessary. (Pramahansa Yogananda, 'Self-Realization Magazine').

Prayer:

Though God hears all our prayers He does not always respond. Our situation is like that of a child who calls for his mother, but the mother does not think it necessary to come. She sends him a plaything to keep him quiet. But when the child refuses to be comforted by anything except the mother's presence, she comes. If you want to know God, you must be like the naughty baby who cries till mother comes. (Pramahansa Yogananda, 'How You Can Talk With God').

The best course is to pray: 'Lord, make me happy with awareness of Thee. Give me freedom from all earthly desires, and above all give me Thy joy that outlast all the happy and sad experiences of life.' (Pramahansa Yogananda, 'Self-Realization Magazine').

Remember that finding God will mean funeral of all sorrows. (Swami Sri Yukteswar, in 'Autobiography of a Yogi').

Happyness:

Happyness depends to some extent upon external considtions, but chiefly upon mental attitudes. In order to be happy one should have good health, a well-balanced mind, a prosperous life, the right work, a thankful heart, and above all, wisdom or knowledge of God. (Pramahansa Yogananda, 'The Law of Success').

You have the power to hurt yourself or benefit yourself. If you do not choose to be happy no one can make you happy. Do not blame God for that! And if you choose to be happy, no one can make you unhappy... It is we who make of life what it is. (Pramahansa Yogananda, SRF Lesson').

Mother's Day:

In India we like to speak of God as Divine Mother because a mother is more tender than a father. The mother is a representative of the unconditional love of God. Mothers were created by God to show us that He loves us with or without cause. Every woman is to me a representative of the Mother. I see the Cosmic Mother in all. That which I find most admirable a woman is her mother love. (Pramahansa Yogananda, 'Self-Realization Magazine').

Peace:

Be honest with yourself. The world is not honest with you. The world loves hypocrisy. When you are honest with yourself you find the road to inner peace. (Pramahansa Yogananda, Lecture).

Each time a swarm of worries invades your mind, refuse to be affected; wait calmly, while seeking the remedy. Spray the worries with the powerful chemical of your peace. (Pramahanasa Yogananda, in a 'Par-a-gram').

Expansion:

Learn to see God in all persons, of whatever race or creed. You will know what divine love is when you begin to feel your oneness with every human being, not before. (Pramahanasa Yogananda, SRF Lessions).

We should train ourselves to think in grand terms: Eternity! Infinity! (Pramahanasa Yogananda, 'Sayings of Yogananda').

Freedom:

Freedom means the power to act by soul guidance, not by the compulsions of desires and habits. Obeying the ego leads to bondage; obeying the soul brings liberation. (Pramahanasa Yogananda, 'Sayings of Yogananda').

Before you act, you have freedom, but after you act, the effect of that action will follow you whether you want it to or not. That is the law of *karma*. You are a free agent, but when you perform a certain act, you will reap the results of that act. (Pramahanasa Yogananda, SRF Lessions).

Right Attitude:

Live only in the present, not in the future. Do your best today; don't look for tomorrow. (Pramahanasa Yogananda, 'Self—Realization Magazine').

Overcoming Temptation:

Doing something wrong from a moral or material standpoint is not the only meaning of temptation. Forgetting your soul by becoming engrossed in the body and its comforts is temptation too. (Pramahanasa Yogananda, SRF Lessons).

Temptation is a sugarcoated poison; it tastes good but always kills you eventually. The happiness that people look for in this world does nor endure. But divine joy is eternal.... tearn for that which is lasting, and be hardhearted about rejecting the (unwholesome) pleasures of this life. You have to be that way. Don't let this world rule you. Never forget that the only thing which is real is the Lord. Your true happiness lies in your experience of Him. (Pramahanasa Yogananda, 'Self-Realization Magazine').

Evil has its power. If you side with it, it will hold you. When you make a misstep, return immediately to the ways of righteousness. (Pramahanasa Yogananda, 'Sayings of Yogananda').

When you permit temptation to overcome you, your wisdom is a prisner. The quickest way to banish temptation is first to say 'no' and get out of that particular environment; then reason it out when calmness and wisdom return. (Pramahanasa Yogananda, SRF Lessons).

Desires are the most unrelenting enemies of man; he cannot appease them. Have only one desire: to know God. Satisfying the sensory desires cannot satisfy you, because you are not the senses. They are only your servants, not your Self. (Pramahanasa Yogananda, 'Sayings of Yogananda').

The old orthodox way is to deny temptation, to suppress it. But you must learn to control temptation. It is not a sin to be tempted. Even though you are boiling with temptation, you are not evil; but if you yield to that temptation you are caught temporarily by the power of evil. You must erect about yourself protecting parapets of wisdom. There is no stronger force that you can employ against temptation than wisdom. Complete understanding will bring you to the point where nothing can tempt you to actions that promise pleasure but in the end will only hurt you. (Pramahanasa Yogananda, SRF Lessons).

Simplicity:

It is not necessary to explain things to God, for He knoweth your need before you speak, and is more ready to give than you are to ask. (Sister Gyanamata, 'Self-Realization Magazine').

Everything has its place, but when you waste time at the cost of your true happiness, it is not good. I dropped every unnecessary activity so that I could meditate and try to know God, so that I could day and night be in His divine consciousness. (Pramahanasa Yogananda, 'Self-Realization Magazine').

Silence:

The true practice of religion is to sit still and talk to Him. But you don't get to that point of intensity, you don't concentrate enough, and that is the cause of your remaining in delusion. (Pramahanasa Yogananda, 'Self-Realization Magazine').

Patience :

Do not look for a spiritual flower every day. Sow the seed, water it with prayer and right endeavour. When it sprouts, take care of the plant, pulling out the weeds of doubt, indecision, and indifference that may spring up around it. Some morning you will suddenly behold your long-awaited spiritual flower of realization. (Pramahanasa Yogananda, in a 'Par-aagram').

_____ ******** _____

WHAT IS LIFE?
(Quoted from Bhagvad Gita)

Life is a challenge.	Meet it.
Life is a gift.	Accept it.
Life is an adventure.	Dare it.
Life is a sorrow.	Overcome it.
Life is a tragedy.	Face it.
Life is a duty.	Perform it.
Life is a game.	Play it.
LIfe is a mystery.	Unfold it.
Life is a song.	Sing it.
Life is an opportunity.	Take it.
Life is a journey.	Complete it.
Life is a promise.	Fulfill it.
Life is a love.	Enjoy it.
Life is a beauty.	Praise it.
Life is a spirit.	Realize it.
Life is a struggle.	Fight it.
Life is a puzzle.	Solve it.
Life is a goal.	Achieve it.

_____ ******** _____

THOUGHTS ON SUCCESS
GO FOR IT

1. The Door of opportunity won't open unless you do some pushing.
2. Whenever the going gets easy, be sure you are not going down hill
3. The seeds of failure are sown at the heights of prosperity.
4. The surest way not to make any money is just to sit around and wait for a break.
5. With all thy getting, get knowledge and wisdom.
6. Decide today to turn your life around.
7. The foundation of wealth is a decisiion well made.
8. Act as if it were impossible to fail.
9. The will is more important than the skill.
10. You won't win unless you begin.
11. As a man thinketh in his heart, so is he.
12. Nothing can resist a human will that will stake even its very existence on the extent of its purpose.

_____ **** _____

TIRUKKURAL
'VIRTUE'
****

Guard thou as wealth the power of self-control;
Than this no greater gain to living soul!

Make not thy poverty a plea for ill;
Thy evil deeds will make thee poorer still.

Speak not a word which false thy own heart knows,
Self-kindled fire within the false one's spirit glows.

Greater is he who speaks the truth with full consenting mind,
Than men whose lives have penitence and charity combined.

Outward purity the water will bestow;
Inward purity from truth alone will flow.

Of all good things we've scanned with studious care;
There's nought that can with truthfulness compare.

Whatever you may fail to guard, guard well your tongue;
For flawed speech unfailingly invokes anguish and affliction.

A small income is no cause for failure, provided expenditures do not exceed it.

———— **** ————

THOUGHTS TO PONDER

A soft answer turns away wrath, but grievous words stir up anger.

A pure heart penetrates heaven.

Happiness begins where wishes end; he who hankers after more, enjoys nothing.

If it is not right, do not do, if it is not true, do not say it.

Successful men are those who build their foundations out of the stones thrown at them.

Life is a journey, not a home.

There are three things that make life lovely: beauty of reverence, dignity of patience and joy of usefulness.

For the lips, truth; for the voice, prayer; for the eyes, pity; for the hands, charity; for the figure, uprightness; for the heart, love—this is the best spiritual cosmetic.

Injure not the feelings and reputation of others.

He who digs a pit for others, himself falls in it.

Knowledge is a blessing, but a curse if it creates a sense of pride.

A slip of foot you may recover; a slip of tongue you never get over.

Put not your trust in money, but put your money in trust.

Riches and rank do not make for happy life; happy lives are useful lives.

The great pleasure of life is to discharge your duty with pleasure.

Think no evil, speak no evil, see no evil.

Ego is the seed-pot of all vice and viciousness.

Jealousy arises out of lack of confidence in oneself.

A jealous person can never be a well-wisher of others.

There is nor substitute for conscience; either you have it or you don't.

Conscience is a watchdog that barks at sin.

There is no tranquil sleep without good concience, nor any virtue without God-concience.

Do everything in the name of God and for God.

_____ **** _____

Science without religion is lame;
Religion without science is blind.

- Albert Einstein

An aim in life is the only fortune worth finding.
in recent years, there's still a lot to be said for the smile.

- Franklin P. Jones

Your body is the baggage you must carry through life,
The more excess baggage, the shorter the trip.

- Arnold H. Glasow

He has the right to criticize who has the heart to help.

- Abraham Lincoln

You cannot do a kindness too soon,
for you never know how soon it will be too late.

- Ralph Waldo Emerson

We do no err because truth is difficult to see.
It is visible at a glance.
We err because this is more comfortable.

- Aleksander Solzhenitsyn

Nothing produces such odd results as trying to get even.

- Franklin P. Jones

There are two freedoms:
The false where a man is free to do what he likes;
The true where a man is free to do what he ought.

- Charles Kingsley

Even with a dull ax you can blaze a trail.

- Robert Powers

A barking dog is often more useful than a sleeping lion.

- Washington Irving

_____ **** _____

One possible explanation for difference in outcome involves differing genetic potential and venturability as implied in the old truism.

———— **** ————

The same fire that hardens steel melt butters.

———— **** ————

Life is like a grindstone, which either wears us down or polishes us up depending on the stuff we are made of. The 'stuff we are made of' depends on interaction between inherited potential (or vulnerability) and subsequent experiences that affect both body and behaviour.

———— **** ————

> Just think,
> you're here not by chance,
> but by God's choosing.
> His hand formed you
> and made you the person you are.
> He compares you to no one else-
> you are one of a kind.
> You lack nothing
> that His grace can't give you.
> He has allowed you to be here
> at this time in history
> to fulfill His special purpose
> for this generation.

(Roy Lessin)

———— **** ————

Let noble thoughts come from every side.

— Rig Veda, 1-89.1

Plough with truth.
Plant the seed of desire for knowledge.
Irrigate the mind with the water of patience.
Supervise your work by introspection and self-analysis.
And build the fence of right conduct and rules.
Nothing else is required to attain eternal bliss.

— Tirumurai

The eyes do not see Him,
Speech cannot utter Him,
the senses cannot reach Him,
He is to attained neither by austerity
nor by sacrificial rites.
Wen through discrimination the heart has become pure,
then, in meditation, the Self is revealed.

— Artharva Veda,
Mundaka *Upanishad*.

The rites of oblation, O lovers of truth,
which the sages divined from the sacred verses,
were variously expounded in the three-fold Veda.
Perform them with constant care.
This is your path to the world of holy action.

— Artharva Veda
Mundaka *Upanishad* 1.2.1

Let there be no neglect of the duties
to the Gods and the fathers.
Be one to whom the mother is a God.
Be one to whom the father is a God.
Be one to whom the teacher is a God.
Be one to whom the guest is a God.

— Krishna Yajur Veda,
Taittiriya *Upanishad* 1.11.1-2

The secret of health for both mind and body
is not to mourn for the past,
not to worry about the future,
or not to anticipate troubles,
but to live the present moment wisely and earnestly.

— Gautam Buddha

As oil in sesame seeds, as butter in cream,
as water in river beds, as fire in friction sticks,
so is the *âtman* grasped in one's own self
when one searches for Him with truthfulness and austerity.

— Krishna Yajur Veda
Svestasvatara *Upanishad* 1.15

Truth is the Supreme, the Supreme is truth.
Through Truth men never fall from the heavenly world,
because Truth belongs to the saints.
Therefore, they rejoice in Truth.

— Krishna Yajur Veda
Mahanarayana *Upanishad* 505.

Let the stronger man give to the man whose need is greater;
let him gaze upon the lengthening path of life.
For riches roll like the wheels of a chariot,
turning from one to another.

— Rig Veda

I love all religions, but I am in love with my own.

— Mother Theresa.

As one not knowing that a golden treasure lies burried
beneath his feet may walk over it again and again yet never find it,
so all being live every moment in the Supreme yet never find Him,
because of the veil of illusion by which He is concealed.

— Sâma Veda
Chandogya *Upanishad* VIII: 3.2.

The subtle self is known by thought in which
the senses in five different forms have centred.
The whole of men's thought is purvaded by the senses.
When thought is purified, the self shines forth.

— Atharva Veda
Mundaka *Upanishad* III.1.9

The man who rejects the words of the scriptures,
and follows the impulse of desire attains neither his perfection,
nor joy nor the path supreme.
Let the scriptures be, therefore, thy authority
and to what is right and what is not right.

— Bhagavad *Gitâ* XVI:23-24.

The sage does not talk;
The talented ones talk,
The stupid ones argue.

— Kung Tingam

We are to practice virtue, not posses it

— Eckhart

Sprituality is neither the previlege of the poor nor the luxury of the rich.
It is the choice of the wise man.

— Swami Chinmayananda.

References

Dehino 'smin yathâ dehe
    kaumâram yauvanam jarâ
tathâ dehântaraprâptir
    dhìras tatra na muhyati (Gita II.13)

Antavanta ime dehâ
    nityasyo 'ktâh sarìrinah
anâsino 'prameyasya
    tasmâd yudhyasva bhârata (Gita II.18)

Na jâyate mriyate vâ kadâcin
    nâ 'yam bhûtvâ bhavitâ vâ na bhûyah
ajo nityah sâsvato 'yam purâno
    na hanyate hanyamâne sarìre (Gita II.20)

Vâsâmsi jìrnâni yathâ vihâya
    navâni grhnâti naro 'parâni
tathâ sarìrâni vihâya jìrnâny
    anyâni samyâti navâni dehì (Gita II. 22)

Nai 'nam chindanti sastrâni
    nai 'nam dahati pâvakah
na cai 'nam kledayanty âpo
    na sosayati mârutah (Gita II. 23)

Acchedyao 'yam adâhyo 'yam
    akledyo 'sosya eva ca
nityah sarvagatah sthânur
    acalo 'yam sanâtanah (Gita II. 24)

Avyakto 'yam acintyo 'yam
    avikâryo 'yam ucyate
tasmâd evam viditvai 'nam
    nâ 'nusocitum arhasi (Gita II. 25)

Sukhadukhe same krtvâ
    lâbhâlâbhau jayâjayau
tato yuddhâya yujyasva
    nai 'vam pâpam avâpsyasi (Gita II. 38)

Niyatam kuru karma tvam
    karma jyâyo hy akarmanah
sarìrayâtrâ '-5 ca te
    na prasidhyed akarmanah (Gita III.8)

Karmanai 'va hi samsiddhim
    âshitâ janakâdayah
lokasamgraham evâ 'pi
    sampasyan kartum arhasi (Gita III. 20)

Na me pârthâ 'sti kartavyam
    trisu lokesu kimcana
nâ 'navâptam avâptavyam
    varta eva ca karmani (Gita III. 22)

Yadihy aham na varteyam
    jâtu karmany atandritah
mama vartmâ 'nuvartante
    manusyâh pârtha sarvasah (Gita III.23)

Utsìdeyur ime lokâ
    na kuryâm karma ced aham
samkarasya ca kartâ syâm
    upahanyâm imâh prajâh (Gita III. 24)

Saktâh karmany avidvâmso
    yathâ kurvanti bhârata
kuruyâd vidvâms tathâ 'saktas
    cikìrsur lokasamgraham (Gita III. 25)

Indriyasye 'ndriyasyâ 'rthe
    râgadvesau vyavasthitau
tayor na vasam âgacchet
    tau hy asya paripanthinau (Gita III. 34)

Kâma esa krodha esa
    rajogunasamudbhavah
mahâsano mahâpâpmâ
    viddhy enam iha vairinam (Gita III. 37)

Indriyâni parânya âhur
    indriyebhyah param manah
manasas tu parâ buddhir
    yo buddheh paratas tu sah (Gita III. 42)

Yadâ-yadâhi dharmasya
    glânir bhavati bhârata
abhyutthânam adharmasya
    tadâ 'tmânam srjâmy aham (Gita IV.7)

Paritrânâya sâdhûnam
    vinâsâya ca duskrtâm
dharmasmsthâpanârthâya
    sambhavâmi yuge-yuge (Gita IV. 8)

Janma karma ca me divyam
    evam yo vetti tattvatah
tyaktvâ deham punarjanma
    nai 'ti mâm eti so 'rjuna (Gita IV. 9)

Vîtarâgabhayakrodhâ
    manmayâ mâm upâsritâh
bahavo jñânatapasâ
    pûtâ madbhâvam âgatâh (Gita IV. 10)

Na mâm karnâni limpanti
    na me karmaphale sprhâ
iti mâm yo 'bhijânâti
    karmabhir na sa badhyate (Gita IV. 14)

Yasya sarve samârambhâh
    kâmasamkalpavarjitâh
jñânâgnidaagdhakarmânam
    tam âhuh panditam budhâh (Gita IV.19)

Tyaktvâ karmaphalâsangam
        nityatrpto nirâsrayah
karmanya abhipravrtto 'pi
        nai 'va kimcit karoti sah (Gita IV. 20)

Nirâsìr yatacittâtmâ
        tyaktasarvaparigrahah
sârìram kevalam karma
        kurvan nâ 'pnoti kilbisam (Gita IV. 21)

Yadrcchâlâbhasamtusto
        dvvandvâtìto vimatsarah
samah siddhâv asiddhau ca
        krtvâ 'pi na nibadhyate (Gita IV. 22)

Gatasangasya muktasya
        jñânâvasthitacetasah
yajñâyâ 'caratah karma
        samagram pravilîyate (Gita IV. 23)

Sreyân dravyamayâd yajñâj
        jñânayajñah paramtapa
sarvam karmâ 'khilam pârtha
        jñâne parisamâpyate (Gita IV.33)

Api ced asi pâpebhyah
        sarvebhyah pâpakrttamah
sarvam jñânaplavenai 'va
        vrjinam samtarisyasi (Gita IV.36)

Yathai 'dhâmsi samiddho 'gnir
        bhasmasât kurute 'rjuna
jñânâgnih sarvakarmâni
        bhasmasât kurute tathâ (Gita IV. 37)

Na hi jñânena sadrsam
        pavitram iha vidyate
tat svayam yogasamsiddhah
        kâlenâ 'tmani vindati (Gita IV. 38)

Ajñâ câ 'sraddadhânas ca
    samsayâtmâ vinasyati
nâ 'yam loko 'sti na paro
    na sukham samsayâtmanah (Gita IV. 40)

Y6gasamnyastakarmânam
    jñânasamchinnasamsayam
âtavantam na karmâni
    nibdhnanti dhanamjaya (Gita IV. 41)

Tasmâd ajñânasambhûtam
    hrtstham jñânâsinâ 'tmanah
chittvai 'nam samsayam yogam
    âtistho 'ttistha bhârata (Gita IV.42)

Samnyâsah karmayogas ca
    nihsreyasakarâv ubhau
tayos tu karmasamnyâsât
    karmayogo visisyate (Gita V. 2)

sâmkhyayogau prthag bâtâh
    pravadanti na panditâh
ekkam apy âsthitah samyag
    ubhayor vindate phalam (Gita V. 4)

Yat sâmkhyaih prâpyate sthânam
    tad yogair api gamyate
ekam sâmkhyam ca yogam ca
    yah pasyati sa pasyati (Gita V. 5)

Samnyâsas tu mahâbâho
    dukham âptum ayogatah
yogayukto munir brahma
    nacirenâ 'dhigacchati (Gita V. 6)

Nai 'va kimcit karoî 'ti
    yukto manyeta tattvavit
pasyañ srnvan sprsañ jighrann
    asnan gacchan svapañ svasan (Gita V. 8)

Pralapan visrjan grhnann
  unmisan nimisann api
indriyânî 'ndriyârthesu
  vartanta iti dhârayan (Gita V. 9)

Yuktah karmaphalam tyaktvâ
  sântim âpnoti naisthikîm
ayuktah kâmakârena
  phale sakto nibadhyate (Gita V. 12)

Sarvakarmâni manasâ
  samnyasyâ 'ste sukham vasî
navadvâre pure dehî
  nai 'va kurvan na kârayan (Gita V. 13)

Nâ 'datte kasyacit pâpam
  na cai 'va sukrtam vibhuh
ajñânenâ 'vrtam jñânam
  tena muhyanti jantavah (Gita V. 15)

jñânena tu tad ajñânam
  yesâm nâsitam âtmanah
tesâm âdityavaj jñânam
  prakâsayati tat param (Gita V. 16)

Tadbuddhayas tadâtmânas
  tannisthâs tatparâyanâh
gacchanty apunarâvrttim
  jñânanirdhûtakalmasâh (Gita V. 17)

Ihai 'va tair jitah sargo
  yesâm sâmye sthitam manah
nirdosam hi samam brahma
  tasmâd brahmani te sthitâh (Gita V. 19)

Na prahrsyet priyam prâpya
  no 'dvijet prâpya câ 'priyam
sthirabuddhir asammûdho
  brahmavid brahmani sthitah (Gita V. 20)

Bâhyasparsesv asaktâtmâ
     vindaty âtmani yat sukham
sa brahmayogayuktâtmâ
     sukham aksayam asnute (Gita V. 21)

Ye hi samsparsajâ bhogâ
     duhkhayonaya eva te
âdyantavantah kaunteya
     na tesu ramate dudhah (Gita V. 22)

Saknotî 'hai 'va yah sodhum
     prâk sarîravimoksanât
kâmakrodhodbhavam vegam
     sa yuktah sa sukhî narah (Gita V. 23)

Yo 'ntahsukho 'ntarârâmas
     tathâ 'ntarjyotir eva yah
sa yogî brahmanirvânam
     brahmabhûto 'dhigacchati (Gita V. 24)

Sparsân krtvâ bahir bâhyâmas
     caksus cai 'vâ 'ntare bhruvoh
prânâpânau samau krtvâ
     nâsâbhyantaracârinau (Gita V.27)

Yatendriyamanobuddhir
     munir moksaparâyanah
vigatecchâbhayakrodho
     yah sadâ mukta eva sah (Gita V. 28)

Yogî yuñjîta satatam
     âtmânam rahasi sthitah
ekâkî yatacittâtmâ
     nirâsîr aparigrahah (Gita VI. 10)

Sucau dese pratisthâpya
     sthiram âsanam âtmanah
nâ 'tyucchritam nâ 'tinîcam
     cailâjinakusottaram (Gita VI. 11)

Tatrai 'kâgram manah krtvâ
    yatacittendriyakriyah
upavisyâ 'sane yuñjyâd
    yogam âtmavisuddhaye (Gita VI. 12)

Samam kâyaasirogrîvam
    dhârayann acalam sthirah
sampreksya nâsikâgram svam
    disas câ 'navalokayan (Gita VI. 13)

Prasântâtmâ vigtabhir
    brahmacârivrate sthitah
manah samyamya maccitto
    yukta âsîta matparah (Gita VI. 14)

Nâ 'tyasnatas tu yogo 'sti
    na cai 'kântam anasnatah
na câ 'tisvapnasîlasya
    jâgrato nai 'va câ 'rjuna (Gita VI. 16)

Sarvabhûtasthitam yo mâm
    bhajaty ekatvam âsthitah
sarvathâ vartamâno 'pi
    sa yoî mayi vartate (Gita VI. 31)

Ayatih sraddayo 'peto
    yogâc calitamânasah
aprâpya yogasamsiddhim
    kâm gatim krsna gacchati (Gita VI. 37)

Kaccin no 'bhayavibhrastas
    chinnâbhram iva nasyati
apratistho mahâbâho
    vimûdho brahmanah pathi (Gita VI. 38)

Etan me samsayam krsna
    chettum arhasy asesatah
tvadanyah samsayasyâ 'sya
    chittâ na hy upapadyate (Gita VI. 39)

Pârtha nai 've 'ha nâ 'mutra
    vinâsas tasya vidyate
na hi kalyânakrt kascid
    durgamatim tâta gacchati (Gita VI. 40)

Prâpya punyakrtâm lokân
    usitvâ sasvatîh samâh
sucînâm srîmatâm gehe
    yogabhrasto 'bhinjâyate (Gita VI. 41)

Athavâ yoginâm eva
    kule bhavati dhîmatâm
etad dhi durlabhataram
    like janma yad îdrasam (Gita VI. 42)

Tatra tam buddhisamyogam
    labhate paurvadehikam
yatate ca tato bhûyah
    samsiddhau kurunandana (Gita VI. 43)

Pûrvâbhyâsena tenai 've
    hriyate hy avaso 'pi sah
jijñâs4r a-5 y6gasya
    sabdabrahmâ 'tvartate (Gita VI. 44)

Prayatnâd yatamânas tu
    yogî samsuddhakilbisah
anekajanmasamsiddhas
    tato yâti parâm gatim (Gita VI. 45)

Tapasvibhyo 'dhiko yogî
    jñânibhyo 'pi mato 'dhikah
karmibhyas câ 'dhiko yogî
    tasmâd yogî bhavâ 'rjuna (Gita VI. 46)

Manusyânâm sahasresu
    kascid yatati siddhaye
yatatâm api siddhânâm
    kascin mâm vetti tattvatah (Gita VII.3)

Etadyonîni bhûtâni
    sarvânî 'ty upadhâraya
aham krtsnasya jagatah
    prabhavah pralayas tathâ (Gita VII. 6)

Mattah parataram nâ 'nyat
    kimcid asti dhanamjaya
mayi sarvam idam protam
    sûtre maniganâ iva (Gita VII. 7)

Raso 'ham aspsu kaunteya
    prabhâ 'smi sasisûryayoh
pranavah sarvavedesu
    sabdah khe paurusam nrsu (Gita VII.8)

Punyo gandhah prthivyâm ca
    tejas ca 'smi vibhâvasau
jîvanam sarvabhûtesu
    tapas câ 'smi tapasvisu (GitaVII.9)

Bîjam mâm sarvabhûtânâm
    viddhi pârtha sanâtanam
buddhir buddhimatâm asmi
    tejas tejasvinâm aham (Gita VII. 10)

Bahûnâm janmanâm ante
    jñânavân mâm prapadyate
vâsudevah sarvam iti
    sa mahâtmâ sudurlabhah (Gita VII. 19)

Yo-yo yâm-yâm tanum bhaktah
    sraddhayâ 'rcitum icchati
tasya-tasyâ 'calâm sraddhâm
    tâm eva vidadhâmy aham (Gita VII. 21)

Sa tayâ sraddhayâ yuktas
    tasyâ 'râdhanam îhate
labhate ca tatah kâmân
    mayai 'va vihitân hi tân (Gita VII. 22)

Sâdhibhûtâdhidaivam mâm
    sâdhiyajñam ca ye viduh
prayânakâle 'pi ca mâm
    te vidur yuktacetasah (Gita VII. 30)

Antakâle ca mâm eva
    smaran muktvâ kalevaram
yah prayâti sa madbhâvam
    yâti nâ 'sty atra samsayah (Gita VIII. 5)

Tasmâ sarvesu kâlesu
    mâm anusmara yudhya ca
mayy arpitamanobuddhir
    mâm evai 'syasy asamsayah (Gita VIII. 7)

Prayânakâle manasâ 'calena
    baktyâ yukto yogabalena cai 'va
bhruvor madhye prânam âvesya samyak
    sa tam param purusam upaiti divyam (Gita VIII. 10)

Aum ity ekâksaram brahma
    vyâharan mâm anusmaran
yah prayâti tyajan deham
    sa yâti paramâm gatim (Gita VIII.13)

Ananyacetâh satatam
    yo mâm smarati nityasah
tasyâ 'ham sulabhah pârtha
    nityayuktasya yoginah (Gita VIII. 14)

Mâm upetya punarjanma
    dukhâlayam asasvatam
nâ 'pnuvanti mahâtmânah
    samsiddhim paramâm gatâh (Gita VIII. 15)

â brahmabhuvanâl lokâh
    punarâvartino 'rjuna
mâm upetya tu kaunteya
    punarjanma na vidyate (Gita VIII. 16)

Agnir jyoti ahah suklah
    sanmâsâ uttarâyanam
tatra prayâtâ gacchanti
    brahma brahmavido janâh (Gita VIII. 24)

Mayâ tatam idam sarvam
    jagad avyaktamûrtinâ
matsthâni sarvabhûtâni
    na câ 'ham tesv avasthitah (Gita IX.4)

Na ca mâm tâni karmâni
    nibadhnanti dhanamjaya
udâsînavad âsînam
    asaktam tesu karmasu (Gita IX. 9)

Tapâmy aham aham varsam
    nigrhnâmy utsrjâmi ca
amrtam cai 'va mrtyus ca
    sad asac câ 'ham arjuna (Gita IX. 19)

Ananyâs cintayanto mâm
    ye janâh paryupâsate
lesâm nityâbhiyuktânâm
    yogaksemam vahâmy aham (Gita IX.22)

Yânti devavratâ devân
    pitrn yânti pitrvratâh
bhûtâni yânti bhûtejyâ
    yânti madyâjino 'pi mâm (Gita IX. 25)

Pattram puspam phalam toyam
    yo me bhaktyâ prayacchati
tad aham bhaktyupahrtam
    asnâmi prayatâtmanah (Gita IX. 26)

Api cet sudurâcâro
    bhajate mâm ananyabhâk
sâdhur eva sa mantavyah
    samyag vyavasito hi sah (Gita IX. 30)

Ksipram bhavati dhamâtmâ
    sasvacchântim nigacchati
kaunteya pratijânîhi
    na me bhaktah pranasyati (Gita IX.31)

Manmanâ bhava madbhakto
    madyâjî mâm namaskuru
mâm evai 'syasi yuktvai 'vam
    âtmânam matparâyanah (Gita IX. 34)

Yo mâm ajam anâdim ca
    vetti lokamahesvaran
asammûdhah sa martyesu
    sarvapâpaih pramucyate (Gita X.3)

Aham âtmâ gudâkesa
    sarvabhûtâsayasthitah
aham âdis ca madhyam ca
    bhûtânâm anta eva ca (Gita X.20)

Sargânâm âdir ântas ca
    madhyaam cai 'vai 'ham arjuna
adhyâtmavidyâ vidyânâm
    vâdah pravadatâm aham (Gita X. 32)

Mrtyuh sarvaharas câ 'ham
    udbhavas ca bhavisyatâm
kîrtih srîr vâk ca nârînâm
    snrtir medhâ dhrtih ksamâ (Gita X. 34)

Yac câ 'pi sarvabhûtânâm
    bîjam tad aham arjuna
na tad asti vinâ yat syân
    mayâ bhûtam carâcaram (Gita X. 39)

Divi sûryasahasrasya
    bhaved yugapad utthitâ
yadi bhâh sadrsî sâ syâd
    bhâsas tasya mahâtmanah (Gita XI. 12)

Tatrai 'kastham jagat krtsnam
  pravibhaktam anekadhâ
apasyad devadevasya
  sarîre pândaavas tadâ (Gita XI. 13)

Matkarmakrn matparamo
  madbhaktah sangavarjitah
nirvairah sarvabhûtesu
  yah sa mâm eti pândava (Gita XI. 55)

Ye tv aksaram anirdesyam
  avyaktam paryupâsate
sarvatragam acintyam ca
  kûtastham acalam dhruvam (Gita XII. 3)

samniyamye 'ndriyagrâmam
  sarvatra samabuddhayah
te prâpnuvanti mâm eva
  sarvabhûtahite ratâh (Gita XII.4)

Ye tu sarvâni karmâni
  mayi samnyasya matparâh
ananyenai 'va yogena
  mâm dhyâyanta upâsate (Gita XII.6)

Tesâm aham samuddhartâ
  mrtyusamsârasâgarât
bhavâmi naacirât pârtha
  mayy âvesitacetasâm (Gita XII. 7)

Mayy eva man âdhatsva
  mayi buddhim nivesaya
nivasisyasi mayy eva
  ata ûrdhvam na samsayah (Gita XII.8)

Atha cittam samâdhâtum
  na saknosi mayi sthiram
abhyâsayogena tato
  mâm icchâ 'ptum dhanamjaya (Gita XII. 9)

Abhyâse 'py asamartho 'si
  matkarmaparamo bhava
madartham api karmâni
  kurvan siddhim avâpsyasi (Gita XII. 10)

Athai 'tad apy asakto 'si
  kartum madyogam âsritah
sarvakarmaphalatyâgam
  'atah kuru yatâtmavân (Gita XII. 11)

Idam sarîram kaunteya
  ksetram ity abhidhîyate
etad yo vetti tam prâhuh
  ksetrajñâa iti tadvidah (Gita XIII. 1)

Mahâbhûtâny ahamkâro
  buddhir avyaktam eva ca
indriyâni dasai 'kam ca
  pañca ce ndriyagocarâh (Gita XIII. 5)

Icchâ dvesah sukham duhkham
  saamghâtas cetanâ dhrtih
etat ksetram samâsena
  savikâram udâhrtam (Gita XIII. 6)

Ya evam vetti purusam
  prakritim ca gunaih saha
sarvathâ vartamâno 'pi
  na sa bhûyo ;bhijâyate (Gita XIII.23)

Dhyânenâ 'tmani pasyanti
  kecid âtmânam âtmanâ
anye sâmkhyena yogena
  karmayogena câ 'pare (Gita XIII.24)

Anye tv evam ajânantah
  srutvâ 'nyebhya upâsate
te 'pi câ 'titaranty eva
  mrtyum srutiparâyanâh (Gita XIII. 25)

Anâditvân nirgunatvât
  paramâtmâ 'yam evyayah
sarîrastho 'pi kaunteya
  na karoti na lipyate (Gita XIII.31)

Sattvam rajas tamaiti
  gunâh prakrtisambhavâh
nibadhnanti mahâbâho
  dehe dehinam evyayam (Gita XIV.5)

Tatra sattvam nirmalatvât
  prakâsakam anâmayam
sukhasangena badhnâti
  jñânasangena câ 'nagha (Gita XIV. 6)

Rajo râgâtmakam viddht
  trsnâsangasamudbhavam
tan nibadhnâti kaunteya
  karmasangena dehinam (Gita XIV. 7)

Tamas tv ajñânajam viddhi
  mohanam sarvadehinâm
pramâdâlasyanidrâbhis
  tan nibadhnâti bhârata (Gita XIV. 8)

Sattvam sukhe sañjayati
  rajah karmani bhârata
jñânam âvrtya tu tamah
  pramâde sañjayaty uta (Gita XIV. 9)

Rajas tamas câ 'bhibhûya
  sattvam bhavati bhârata
rajah sattvam tamas cai 'va
  tamas sattvam rajas tathâ (Gita XIV. 10)

Sarvadvâresu dehe 'smim
  prakâsa upajâyate
jñânam yadâ tadâ vidyâd
  vivrddham sattvam ity uta (Gita XIV. 11)

Lobhah pravrtir ârambhah
    karmanâm asamah sprhâ
rajasy etâni jâyante
    vivrddhe bhratarsabha (Gita XIV. 12)

Aprakâso 'pravrttis ca
    pramâdo moha eva ca
tamasy etâni jâyante
    vivrddhe kurunandana (Gita XIV.13)

Yadâ sattve pravrddhe tu
    pralayami yâti dehabhrt
tado 'ttamavidâm lokân
    amalân pratipadyate (Gita XIV. 14)

Rajasi pralayam gatvâ
    karmasangisu jâyate
tathâ pralînas tamasi
    mûdhayonisu jâyate (Gita XIV. 15)

Karmanah sukrtasyâ 'huh
    sâttvikam nirmalam phalam
rajasas tu phalam duhkham
    ajñânam tamasah phalam (Gita XIV.16)

Sattvât samjâyate jñânam
    rajaso lobha eva ca
pramâdamohau tamaso
    bhavato 'jñânam eva ca (Gita XIV. 17)

ûrdhvam gacchanti sattvasthâ
    madhye tisthanti râjasâh
jaghanyagunavrttisthâ
    adho gacchanti tâmasâh (Gita XIV. 18)

Gunân etân atîtya trîn
    dehî dehasamudbhavân
janmamrtyujarâduhkhair
    vimukto 'mrtam asnute (Gita XIV. 20)

Kair lingais trîn gunân etân
      atîto bhavati prabho
kimâcârah katham cai 'tâms
      trîn gunân ativartate (Gita XIV. 21)

Yad âdityagatam tejo
      jagad bhâsayate 'khilam
yac candramasi yac câ 'gnau
      tat tejo viddhi mâmakam (Gita XV. 12)

Gâm âvisya ca bhûtâni
      dhârayâmy aham ojasâ
pusnâmi cau 'sadhîh sarvâh
      somo bhûtva rasâtmakah (Gita XV. 13)

Aham vaisvânaro bhûtvâ
      prâninnâm deham âstritah
prânâpânasamâyuktah
      pacâmy annam caturvidham (Gita XV. 14)

Sarvasya câ 'ham hrdi samnivisto
      mattah smrtir jñânam apohanam ca
vdais ca sarvair aham eva vedyo
      vedântakrd vedavid eva câ 'ham (Gita XV. 15)

Dvâv imanu purusau loke
      ksaras câ 'ksara eva ca
ksarah sarvâni bhûtani
      kûtastho 'ksara ucyate (Gita XV. 16)

Uttamah purusas tv anyah
      paramâtme 'tv udâhrtah
yo lokatrayam âvisya
      bibharty avyaya îsvarah (Gita XV. 17)

Kâmyânâm karmanâm nyâsam
      samnyâsam kavayo viduh
sarvakarmaphalatyâgam
      prâhus tyâgam vicaksanâh (Gita XVIII. 2)

Tyâjyam dosavad ity eke
     karma prâhur manîsinah
yajñadânatapahkarma
     na tyâjyam iti câ 'pare (Gita XVIII. 3)

Na hi dehabhrtâ sakyam
     tyaktum karmâny asesatah
yas tu karmaphalatyâgî
     sa tyâgî 'ty abhidhîyate (Gita XVIII. 11)

. Yatah pravrttir bhûtânâm
     yena sarvam idam tatam
svakarmanâ tam abhyarcya
     siddhim vindati mânavah (Gita XVIII. 46)

Sreyân svadharmo vigunah
     paradharmât svanusthitât
svabhâvaniyatam karma
     kurvan nâ 'pnoti kilbisam (Gita XVIII. 47)

Bhaktyâ mâm abhijânati
     yâvân yâs câ 'smi tattvatah
tato mâm tattvato jñâtvâ
     visate tadanantaram (Gita XVIII. 55)

îsvarah sarvabhûtânâm
     hrddese 'rjuna tisthati
bhrâ0ayan sarvabhûtâni
     yantrârûdhâni mâyayâ (Gita XVIII. 61)

Sarvadharmân parityajya
     mâm ekam sarnam vraja
aham tvâ sarvapâpebhyo
     moksayisyâmi mâ sucah (Gita XVIII.66)

Index